THE JERSEY

Also by Peter Bills

Sportsviewers' Guide: Skiing

Sportsviewers' Guide: Darts

Sportsviewers' Guide: Wrestling

Sportsviewers' Guide: Snooker

Jean Pierre Rives: A Modern Corinthian

Allan Border: A Peep at the Poms

David Campese: On a Wing and a Prayer

Will Carling: A Man Apart

Dean Richards: Deano

Passion in Exile: The Official History of London Irish RFC

Gareth Edwards: The Autobiography

Gareth Edwards: Tackling Rugby –
The Changing World of Professional Rugby

Willie John McBride: The Story of My Life

Bill McLaren: My Autobiography

The Right Place at the Wrong Time:
The Autobiography of Corne Krige

Rucking & Rolling: Sixty Years of International Rugby

Ashwin Willemse: Rugby Changed My Life

400 at 5.30 with Nannies:
Inside the Lost World of Sports Journalism

Sporting Great Britain:
The 100 Most Famous Photos – Captions

PETER BILLS

THE JERSEY

THE SECRETS BEHIND THE WORLD'S
MOST SUCCESSFUL SPORTS TEAM

MACMILLAN

First published 2018 by Macmillan
an imprint of Pan Macmillan
20 New Wharf Road, London N1 9RR
Associated companies throughout the world
www.panmacmillan.com

ISBN 978-1-5098-5668-8 HB
ISBN 978-1-5098-5670-1 TPB

9 8 7 6 5 4 3

A CIP catalogue record for this book is available from the British Library.

Typeset in 11/14 pt Utopia Std by Jouve (UK), Milton Keynes
Printed and bound by CPI Group (UK) Ltd, Croydon, CR0 4YY

Visit **www.panmacmillan.com** to read more about all our books
and to buy them. You will also find features, author interviews and
news of any author events, and you can sign up for e-newsletters
so that you're always first to hear about our new releases.

For Hannah, Katie and James

With apologies for the long absences down the years

Contents

Author's Note

The author wishes to acknowledge the assistance of New Zealand Rugby in the compiling of material while writing this book. However, I also want to make it clear that the views expressed herein are solely mine and, unless directly attributable by means of quotes, are not necessarily shared by those employed by New Zealand Rugby. Likewise, any errors, whether factual, statistical or simply unintended, are not the responsibility of New Zealand Rugby, but mine alone.

One further point. This book was written for a worldwide audience, not just for readers in New Zealand. If at times some points may already be familiar to the latter, I would ask for patience. They have been included to help explain the whole story to readers across the globe.

Acknowledgements

I first went to New Zealand in 1975. It wasn't the sort of experience you forget.

It took about five years to get there and then I got half-drowned at the infamous New Zealand Test match against Scotland at Eden Park in Auckland. What's more, these were the days of the notorious 'six o'clock swill' and 'Loosehead Len', two icons of New Zealand social history.

I've been going backwards and forwards pretty much ever since.

Finally, in 2017, I spent almost five months in the country researching this very detailed book. In that time, the population of those delicious green-lipped mussels took a terrible battering, I can tell you. Not to mention supplies of New Zealand Sauvignon Blanc. The world's best.

A large number of people, not just all over New Zealand but right around the world, helped me immensely with the book. I want to thank them, warmly and genuinely.

The project has taken three years, from creation to completion. In all, I've interviewed more than ninety people worldwide.

Even so, it is doubtful whether the book would have got over the line without the great commitment of my agent in London, David Luxton, and also Ian Long, formerly of New Zealand Rugby. I am deeply grateful to them for their patience and efforts.

The same goes for New Zealand Rugby CEO Steve Tew and All Blacks coach Steve Hansen. Without Tew's backing for the project, first requested during the 2015 Rugby World Cup, it is unlikely to have seen the light of day. Likewise, Steve Hansen.

The long list of well-known rugby people who gave me whatever time I needed, follows below. To every one of them, thank you for your help, not to mention your hospitality. But friends in New Zealand and elsewhere contributed in myriad ways too, by reading some chapters, offering suggestions and advice or simply by means of providing meals and/or accommodation.

Of those who read chapters of the book and/or made many valuable suggestions, I would like to thank former All Black Conrad Smith, ex-South Africa coach Nick Mallett, Murray and Sharon Deaker, Jeremy Hapeta, Lecturer in Physical Education at Massey University, Tracey Kai at New Zealand Rugby, Peter Franklyn, David Mayhew, Roger Payne, Ian Malin, Serge Manificat, Tim Arlott, Brian Lawrence and Liz Griffiths. All were sage and thoughtful counsellors throughout.

In South Africa and then back in the UK, Mark Baldwin offered a hugely valuable oversight of the entire project for which I am extremely grateful.

Others in New Zealand who contributed in a multiplicity of ways included Roger and Diane Hall, Ross and Tricia McKay, Mary and Andrew Collow, Margaret Kennedy, Mike and Ben Dormer, Will Fairbairn and Gary Carter. Sarah McDonald at the excellent Southern Cross Hotel in Dunedin was another who provided immense help. Not least was the great assistance of Vic and his team at Ace Rentals throughout New Zealand, still by a distance the best and most helpful car-hire people in the land. Thank you to you all.

In terms of rugby personnel, I was grateful to Head Coach Steve Hansen and his fellow coaches Ian Foster, Wayne Smith and Gilbert Enoka (Manager – Leadership), all of whom welcomed me into their homes for lengthy interviews. Likewise, Sir Brian Lochore, Sir Graham Henry, Sir Bryan Williams, John Hart, Graham Mourie and Andy Haden.

All Blacks Manager Darren Shand gave me invaluable assistance, both in New Zealand and at Cape Town during the 2017 Rugby Championship. Grant Fox took me to Super Rugby matches to explain his role as All Blacks selector, as well as sitting down for a lengthy interview back in Auckland. Brad Johnstone was a warmly welcoming host at North Shore RFC, Frank Bunce similarly at Manukau.

Many others were equally generous with their time and thoughts. Of the present-era All Blacks, thank you to Ryan Crotty, Dane Coles, Waisake Naholo, Jerome Kaino, Aaron Smith, Beauden Barrett, Brodie

Retallick, Damian McKenzie, Kieran Read and Wyatt Crockett. Then there was Liam Messam, Digby Ioane, Richie McCaw, Andy Dalton, Chris Laidlaw, Reuben Thorne, Kees Meeuws, Wayne Shelford, Craig Dowd, Scott Robertson, Tony Brown, Brent Impey, Tony Johnson, Sir John Key, Hamish Riach, Richard Kinley, Jeremy Knowler, Dale Stanley, Merv Aoake, Andy Hunter, Judy Clement, Melissa Ruscoe, Anne Blackman, Grant Hansen, Steve Cole, David Galbraith, Ceri Evans and Dave Askew.

At the New Zealand Super Rugby franchises, I would like to thank media officials Juliet Cleaver at the Crusaders, Nikita Hall at the Chiefs, Amanda Gould at the Highlanders and Glenn McLean at the Hurricanes.

In Australia, Brad Burke, June Catchpole, John Connolly, Bob Dwyer, John Eales, Alan Jones, Nick Farr-Jones, Andrew Slack, Wayne Smith and Ed Jolly were immensely helpful. In South Africa, Victor Matfield, Gary Player, Joel Stransky, Brendan Venter, Ali Bacher, Ashwin Willemse and Steve Nell all contributed significantly.

Back in the UK, Dick Best also offered some sound thoughts.

In France, Dan Carter gave me his considered reflections in Paris, as did Sir Tony O'Reilly in Normandy. In the south-west, that great heartland of French rugby, Conrad Smith, Pierre Berbizier, Pascal Ondarts, Andre Boniface, Francois Moncla, Fabien Pelous and Thierry Dusautoir all gave their invaluable time and assistance.

Finally, in Ireland, another former All Black Doug Howlett offered many ideas at his Munster base, while Willie John McBride and Tony Ward also helped greatly. Rebecca Winfield, David Luxton's colleague at David Luxton Associates, also deserves my thanks. Thanks also to Robin Harvie, Laura Carr, Chloe May, Alex Young, Paul Martinovic and all the team at Macmillan. I hope the final product repays their faith.

Last but by no means least, I want to thank Averil who has given me great assistance throughout as well as many invaluable suggestions.

Sadly, two former All Blacks died during the writing process of this book. Sir Colin Meads and Ian Smith both gave me valued assistance at their homes. They passed away a few months later.

I cannot pretend this is *the* definitive book on New Zealand rugby. There have been too many previous excellent tomes to make that assertion. But what I believe this book offers are fresh perspectives, different angles and original ideas concerning rugby in this unique country, and a new look at the most successful period in New Zealand rugby history.

Quintessentially, this is an outsider's view of rugby football in New Zealand with the assistance of many All Blacks, past and present, plus senior figures inside New Zealand rugby. The opinion of the publishers is that this is a strength and not a weakness.

But I hope what the book does do is answer the question with which I began the project. How on earth did a country of just 4.8 million people conquer an entire world sport? The many answers to that question and the reasons why the All Blacks have become the world's most successful team, are scattered liberally throughout the book, like breadcrumbs left on the table. Digest them carefully. They merit much debate.

Peter Bills
Cape Town, April 2018

PROLOGUE

In the calm before the storm, for the briefest and most precious of moments, he retreated from his very public world. The clamour, adulation and physical confrontation all awaited him, like the bullfighter and his prey. But, within these four walls, it was different.

The captain of the New Zealand All Blacks is public property in his homeland. His life is theirs, not his own. His interests are dissected with microscopic scrutiny. But here, hidden away from the enquiring eyes of his audience and the media's prying lenses, he enacted his private ritual one last time.

Walking to his corner of the dressing room, he reached his peg and unzipped his kit bag. There on top lay the Valhalla for every New Zealand male, the coveted All Blacks jersey. It was and remains a prize so special that it stands alongside the most hallowed, legendary sporting objects the world has known. Like the Masters Green Jacket at Augusta National.

Except that this was black. Always had been, always will be. If symbolism becomes reality in the sporting arena, then this simple rugby jersey, idolized by New Zealanders around the world, takes on a different aura. Universally revered, the All Blacks are arguably the most dominant team in sporting history. At once, the famed jersey inspires a deep respect. Fear, too, in some cases.

It had been his life's ambition. In his youthful naivety, he had believed that to wear this fabled garment just once would calm the cravings of ambition that had fuelled his whole childhood. Now, in private reflection, he smiled at his own flawed judgement; he had found the experience so addictive that, far from retreating, the cravings for it had only increased over time.

Thus he stood deep in the bowels of England's Twickenham

Stadium, facing the wall; a man in his own space, his own time. The battle ahead was the 2015 Rugby World Cup Final against his nation's trans-Tasman foes, Australia, which the All Blacks would win 34–17, would make them the first ever team to retain the Webb Ellis Cup. It would be physically and mentally enervating. But that came with the territory. The two nations were like some lovers; unable to live together, unable to be apart for long.

But before he heard the explosion of sound that would greet the combatants on their field of battle, there was this one familiar ritual.

Taking the coveted jersey in both hands and lifting it from the bag with the delicacy of a father holding a newborn infant, he leaned his face forward and buried it in the jersey. Yet this was more than just a personal and indulgent emotional outpouring. No cathartic exercise, given the uniqueness of his circumstances.

For the hundred and forty-eighth and final time, Richie McCaw momentarily put aside the demands of his teammates. Briefly, he retreated into his own private domain.

In those moments, he saw again the child who had first trodden a rugby field. Not one of this importance, of course; rather, a simple pitch in the small community of Kurow, situated in the Waitaki Valley in New Zealand's beautiful South Island, between the Waitaki River and the St Mary's mountain range.

He turned back the years in his mind's eye, to that child's eager participation in any activity associated with a rugby ball. There he was, just seven years of age. Knees muddied as with all little boys, wearing a jersey and shorts that were a tad too big, and socks flapping at his ankles. The child was intently watching from the touchline a game played by the club's senior men. How that boy longed to be out there with them.

He smiled to himself as he recalled the boy chasing a wayward kick over the line, racing to be first to get hands on the sacred piece of leather and carry it back to the field of play. He thought of his impatience finally to get onto the field and play a proper match.

He recalled, too, the lessons of his first mentor, Barney McCone. He taught both his own son and one of his boy's closest friends, Richard McCaw junior, son of a farmer in a nearby valley, the basics of this game that had been a part of his nation's identity from its earliest inception in the 1870s.

Now, he pondered silently all that work, the prodigious physical exertion over so many years, the honest striving to master the basics of this game and acquire the skills that would help take him to the summit of world rugby. He saw again the long, hard road he had walked, its twists, turns and climbs. He remembered the sweat, blood and the often-crushing physical effort that the journey had demanded.

In those private moments, he saw, too, the boy become a man, the hopeful child protégé first to wear an All Blacks jersey and later earn the ultimate honour. Captaincy of New Zealand's rugby team.

As his face stayed hidden in the jersey, still secreted away from the outside world, he reminded himself that this was what he had always dreamt of doing. He sought these moments of reflection because he wanted to ward off, as if it were a strong, jolting hand, any element of familiarity. Even today, on the occasion of his hundred and forty-eighth and final cap.

'By doing this, it always put a bit of perspective around it. Because sometimes you get there, you just go and play. I took the time to think before every match, "This is where I want to be, so enjoy it."

'It filled my head. And the thought "Don't take it for granted" was strong in my mind. It was just my little thing. I never wanted to roll into a game, just play it and then think afterwards, "You know what, I didn't really give that the performance or the effort that was needed."

'So I did that before every match just to make sure. It was a wee reminder to me about how privileged I was to wear that jersey and never take it for granted.'

The importance of the ritual was not lost on his teammates. They understood his need for time and space.

Of course, it was his life's work. For sure, in retirement, life would be very different. But always, whatever the time or place, rugby would attempt to drag him back, like the enthusiastic youngster demanding just one more kickabout with his dad on the local field, as the light faded and the winter gloaming descended.

In the years ahead, he would come to ponder these times, marvel at their memory and give thanks for his pre-eminence at this game. But he would celebrate chiefly, not his own achievements on the rugby fields of the world, but the enduring legacy of the jersey he had worn with such distinction and pride. To him, the greater glory was to his nation. New Zealand.

His considered opinion was that he was the fortunate one, not the country's rugby team that had embraced him so warmly for so long.

Like coach Steve Hansen, the man who masterminded New Zealand's triumph at that 2015 Rugby World Cup and who will lead their bid to achieve sporting immortality when they attempt to win the 2019 tournament in Japan, McCaw used a single word to describe his association with the fabled jersey. Privilege.

It is a word as familiar among New Zealand rugby men as a muddy field on a winter's day in Dunedin. It is the jersey, not the man that has earned pre-eminence. It is revered at every turn in New Zealand society, and indeed worldwide. From Canterbury farmer to Bluff oyster fisherman; from Wellington bureaucrat to Auckland entrepreneur, men and women all over the country figuratively doff their caps in respect to this jersey.

Heads are bowed with an almost religious zeal at sighting the icon. Those who wear it are respected and categorized as special beings for their brush with the sacred garment.

There are myriad reasons for this. To understand them, you must travel deep into the soul of New Zealand, a country that, in the words of one citizen, is 'a small country no one has ever heard of, down at the bottom of the world'. In 2017 I spent almost five months travelling around the country, talking not just to men and women who play or follow their nation's No. 1 sport, but also to people from all corners of Kiwi society. Were there particular reasons for New Zealand's supremacy in the game? Indeed, how had a nation of just 4.8 million people conquered an entire world sport? What were the critical factors that enabled the Kiwis to achieve a mastery of the game that has resisted all but the occasional setback?

With the help of rugby people both in New Zealand and around the world, this story offers a uniquely revealing insight into what has gone into making New Zealand the rugby world champions.

We know this much. Stats and facts litter the rugby fields of New Zealand, like old paper blown across a ground. But one statement is incontestable. When you play New Zealand at rugby, you play a nation, not a team.

1

THE PIONEERS' DNA

*Contributions from
Sir Wilson Whineray, Sir Brian Lochore,
Richie McCaw, Waisake Naholo.*

'The pain which is felt when we are first transplanted from our native soil, when the living branch is cut from the parent tree, is one of the most poignant which we have to endure through life.'

A nineteenth-century traveller, bound for New Zealand

They called it 'a Colonial Life'. Like some modern-day cruise company offering 'a Mediterranean Odyssey'. Beguiling. But beware. This was no pampered existence, no canapés at sunset.

From the busy ports, large and small, that dotted the British and Irish coastlines of the mid-1800s, they sailed with few possessions. Hearts pounded, as heavy as anchors, as the creaking, groaning wooden ships made for sea. The promised longevity of the journey, anything up to fifteen or sixteen weeks depending on the winds, was as intimidating as the heaving, threatening seas.

They were bound together by one horrible truth. Just about all those who had made the agonizing decision to sail to the other end of the world in search of a new life, concealed an awful reality. By their decision, they were admitting failure in their old lives.

The passages offered a new life for those weary of the unending struggle at home. And they came shuffling forward, names listed for the passage, luggage stowed. They arrived from all corners of a Britain and Ireland in the nineteenth century that was grossly unequal. The arrival of mechanization and the subsequent loss of jobs in so many industries, the potato famine in Ireland and the ongoing cruelty of many landowners and landlords, men without pity for their plight, had forced their decision.

Most knew only lives of misery at home. It could hardly be worse on the other side of the world, they reasoned. But be careful what you wish for.

Their destination had long been known by men of the sea. Abel Tasman, the great Dutch seafarer, had first charted the west coast of this land in 1642, leading an exploratory expedition of the Dutch East

India Company. He named the country he found 'Nieuw-Zeeland', after the province in his native Holland.

Yet even Tasman had to defer to the sailors of Polynesia in the discovery of this so-called 'new' land. Much, much earlier, explorers from the Polynesian islands had climbed into their outrigger canoes, known as *waka hourua*, and followed birds flying south to escape the cyclone season. Their chief navigational aids were the sun, stars and ocean currents.

'The compass can mislead, but the sun and stars, never', wrote one early Tongan sailor.

But of course, there was nothing 'new' whatever about it. For centuries, the Maori forefathers had made the perilous journey across the volatile waters from the islands of Polynesia, in tiny crafts. The *Pakeha*, or white people, who began to arrive in the first half of the nineteenth century, might have been figures of intrigue. But they were certainly not trendsetters. Not when set against the history of the Maori.

Tradition has it that Kupe was the first Pacific voyager to arrive on this new land, perhaps eight hundred or even a thousand years ago. His wife is said to have exclaimed when she saw the shore: 'A cloud, a white cloud, a long white cloud.'

The Maori word for a long white cloud is 'Aotearoa'.

To a far-flung destination with a Maori name, the steady trickle of human beings mired in penury began. The first Pakeha woman is said to have settled in the South Island in 1832, eight years before the Treaty of Waitangi was signed by Maori chiefs and representatives of the British Crown, allowing the British hegemony over this 'new' land.

Many of these new settlers' lives had been defined by misery. Scottish weavers earning a mere subsistence wage could only stand and grieve as their young children fell sick and died. Multiple illnesses plagued the poorer areas of so many British cities such as Glasgow, Edinburgh, London, Birmingham, Leeds and Manchester.

They had little money. The extent of their labours in no way effected an upturn in their fortunes. Starvation, poverty and struggle were a trinity of relentless foes, like the muggers who lurked in dark alleys.

Some came from as far north as the Shetland Islands in the icy waters of the North Atlantic off the north-east coast of Scotland. There, a landowner would sometimes clear out fifteen crofts, dispossessing the inhabitants in the process. Many Shetlanders went to New

Zealand and found life there remarkably compatible with their previous existence, albeit without the constant threat of dispossession.

The potato famine in Ireland in the second half of the 1840s hastened a mass departure. Linen weavers, farmers and domestic workers found their lives imperilled by the famine, but also by the quickening march of technology which led to mass unemployment.

Irish farm workers, Scottish weavers and Cornish tin-mine workers – this desperate collection of humanity arrived at the same conclusion. Only by enduring a journey to the far side of the world could they ever hope to improve their lives. But as to what they could expect when they got there, none had a scintilla of an idea.

Yet first, there were matters of more pressing concern to assail their minds and senses. England was traditionally a seafaring nation. But only professional sailors really knew the sea and truly understood its forbidding threat. Women and children from the poorhouse in Plymouth or a Manchester slum had little inkling of the hidden fears lurking on these rough, twisting, rolling, bucking ships.

The first settlers' ship, the *Aurora*, left Gravesend, on the Thames Estuary in Kent, on 18 September 1839 and arrived in New Zealand on 22 January 1840, a journey of eighteen weeks. Two babies, first a boy and then a girl, were born at sea. Soon after, four more ships, the *Oriental*, the *Duke of Roxburgh*, the *Bengal Merchant* and the *Adelaide* similarly made land. Around the same time, French settlers began landing at Akaroa, on the coast east of Christchurch. The great migration had begun. Just fifty-two years after the First Fleet had sailed into Botany Bay on Australia's eastern seaboard, the ships crammed full of convicts, New Zealand was experiencing the arrival of its own first European migrants.

'Pots, kettles, casks, boxes, doors slamming and knocking about ... the sea roaring, the wind whistling, creaking, children crying ...'

These were the words of a traveller on an 1850s emigration barque, the *Charlotte Jane*. In New Zealand, on Saturday 18 January 1851, the *Lyttelton Times* reported the arrival of four ships from the UK, among them the *Charlotte Jane*. Captained by one Alexander Lawrence, she weighed just 720 tons and carried 154 passengers: 104 of them had travelled in steerage class, where few frills were to be found. A lucky twenty-six had private cabins.

Peering through murk and mist, melancholy choking their

emotions, the *Charlotte Jane's* passengers had taken their final glimpse of the British shore at Plymouth Sound, on the Devon coast; ninety-nine days later they disembarked at Lyttelton, a port close to Christchurch on New Zealand's South Island.

When they arrived, on 16 December 1850, it is said that the governor of the colony, Sir George Gray, sailed down the South Island's east coast in HMS *Fly*, a sloop-of-war, to greet them.

One traveller who made the long journey wrote:

'I felt a very strange and watery sensation as we found ourselves slowly moving away from our own shores. We stood on deck waving, waving, till we could see no more responsive handkerchiefs. Some of my favourite lines recurred to my mind at this moment . . .

> *'As slow our ship her foamy track*
> *Against the wind was cleaving,*
> *Her trembling pennant still looked back*
> *To that dear Isle 'twas leaving.*
> *So loth we part from all we love,*
> *From all the ties that bind us,*
> *So turn our hearts as on we rove*
> *To those we left behind us.'*

There was fear, for sure, from the tearing winds and alarming contortions of the boat. Three entries from a journal penned by one of the female passengers sketches images of the challenge that every day brought.

'Friday 24 July: One of the coldest days we have had; very rough night, followed by a very rough day, sea mountains high and very strong gale. None of us ventured on deck, we had only the saloon trot to turn to, for warmth. This has been a dull, miserable, comfortless sort of day.

'Saturday 25 July: A fine day, but cold and blustering, we made a good run. Twelve weeks on board today! How I long for shore, and yet rather dread the unseen, the unknown future.

'Monday 27 July: A very, very cold, stormy, blustering day; sea higher than ever; deck very slippery; several of the sailors had falls; none of us ventured on deck; great waves came even over the poop . . . We had just moved away from the table preparatory to our evening's trot round to get warm, when a monstrous wave came over the poop and poured through the canvas of the skylight right onto tables and benches and all. I, as usual, was frightened. The ship rocked and pitched about in a mighty unpleasant manner.'

Isolation. Fright. Fear. The journey had catapulted them into a world for which their lives hitherto could never have prepared them. They were like gamblers, staking their lives on a last throw of the dice. How would they look when the dice stopped rolling? Would they even survive the journey, never mind live to see this new land to which they had committed their and their families' entire futures? Medical facilities aboard barques such as the *Charlotte Jane* were primitive at best. Seasickness was an inevitability. But it was more serious conditions that alarmed them. Burial at sea brought its own unique sorrow upon those witnessing such a sad sight.

They had come from myriad places in their own lands – cities, towns, villages and the countryside. In 1842, sixty people sailed from the town of Helston, on the River Cober in Cornwall, bound for New Plymouth on the west coast of New Zealand's North Island. They might as well have booked passages to the moon, such was the enormity of the trip at that time.

What they found when they got there was next to nothing. Yet conversely, their epic travails now became their sustenance, invaluable experiences that prepared them for the immense task of making a life in a new land. Used to walking miles each day to work, and then labouring for hours in grim conditions, they rolled up their sleeves to tackle the job. They were to prove themselves phlegmatic, dogged, good decision makers and dedicated to whatever task they attempted. Stoicism was akin to a soothing balm on aching shoulders.

The steady trickle of arrivals up and down the coasts of both islands seemed to bear no logic or clear order. As early as 1839, shortly before the Treaty of Waitangi was concluded with the Maori in the far north of New Zealand's North Island, a strange event occurred.

The Maori called the area we know today as Wellington Harbour '*Te Whanganui a Tara*', meaning 'the great harbour of Tara'. It is said to have been named Port Nicholson by Captain James Herd, who arrived there in 1826. Before he left, Herd named it after the Sydney harbourmaster of the time, Captain John Nicholson. It kept the name until 1984, when it became Wellington Harbour.

Just thirteen years after Herd's departure, other white men arrived. Lieutenant William Wakefield, principal agent for the New Zealand Company, sailed into the harbour to negotiate land purchases. He and his entourage, wearing ruffled collars, smart jackets and hats, were astonished to find a lone white man living there, a former sailor named Joe Robinson. How he had got there, no one knew and Joe wasn't telling. Was he perhaps a deserter or escaped convict from Australia? No one knew. But Robinson had put down roots as best he could, settled to the life, married and established himself as a boat builder.

The discovery of this solitary white man mystified Wakefield and his party. But their presence, and the subsequent arrival of other ship-loads of migrants, threatened Robinson's life of seclusion. His story ended in sadness. Drinking too much at a celebration, he got into a fight, was badly hurt and then slung into leg irons and handcuffs by policemen who had come from Australia and were used to dealing with convicts. Robinson was put roughly into a boat headed for a nearby jail. No more was ever heard of him.

Meanwhile, back in Lyttelton, the intrepid travellers were taking a first look at their new country. To call them 'underwhelmed' would be an understatement. The cold, raw, foggy weather dampened their spirits still further.

'The Port is a small town but oh!, the sorry show in this case, all round the same black, forbidding-looking upheavals met the eye and enclosed the Port; the appearance was very strange to English eyes. I think what struck me more than all was the poverty-stricken look of the place.

'The harbour is certainly a very fine one . . . but there seemed a silence and dullness over all.'

Nor was it much better in this traveller's eyes when she ventured inland to Christchurch itself.

'It is generally called "The City of the Plains" and is named after Christ Church, Oxford – and well indeed it deserves its former title. It is as flat as a kitchen table just turned and planed from a carpenter's hand. This great plain extends for miles and miles, indeed every street is a mile long, and look this way, that way, north, south, east, west, whichever way you will, but you will not find one curve, one bend, one undulation, mound or hillock – the effect is dismal in the extreme and most depressing to the spirits, whether viewed in summer or winter . . . It is about as dull a spot as anyone would wish to pass their days in – there is very little amusement; everything is horribly local.'

They carried this sense of depression as heavily as their baggage from the ship. Yet miraculously, they would discover a mythical well. From it, they would draw liberally the qualities that would come to hallmark the nation. From these depths of dejection rose an inner-most zeal. In time, a sense of doughty durability would rise inexorably to the surface.

This desire to make something of their lot in life was unbreakable. It would become a characteristic of these people. It brought together quite different types of people who found themselves clustered together in adversity, in an ill-prepared colony at the extreme margin of the known world.

Inevitably, the earliest settlers had it toughest. Every hand was precious in carving out a human imprint upon this land. Men, women, boys and girls were put to work in whatever way was profit-able; every one of them was labouring to establish a life for them and their family. In the 1850s and 1860s, there was a wide range of occu-pations in Akaroa – farmers, shopkeepers, carpenters, sawyers, bush-men, schoolteachers, postmen, boatmen, hotel keepers, brick makers, coopers, lawyers, doctors and customs officers.

How tough was it? Between 1851 and 1860 in Akaroa, of a total of twenty-four people who were buried, only four had lived beyond the age of forty. The average lifespan was just below twenty-seven years. These premature deaths were, said a document, 'due mainly to the struggle against nature, as the records so poignantly show'. The gap between Maori and Pakeha life expectancies expanded, as the Pakeha brought new diseases to New Zealand. By the late 1870s, Pakeha could expect to live into their fifties, one of the highest life expectan-cies in the world. But Maori were far behind. By the start of the 1890s, the estimated life expectancy of Maori men was twenty-five and that of women just twenty-three. Consequently, the Maori population declined steeply, from about 100,000 in 1769 to around 42,000 in 1896. European-introduced diseases such as measles, mumps, whooping cough, bronchitis and tuberculosis were responsible for the deaths of large numbers of Maori.

The stoicism demonstrated by the new arrivals would form a core characteristic of the white people of this 'new' land that would be passed down through the generations. They would make this faraway, at that time inhospitable, land a unique place among the nations of the world. To an overwhelming degree, wherever you look today, these qualities still define the people of New Zealand: teamwork, resilience, an ability to think and operate in adversity, to solve difficulties without recourse to others. To take a risk. Here are the first clues of what has made New Zealanders supreme in the game of rugby union.

As Sir Brian Lochore, the esteemed All Black would say, 'I think we are quite a physical nation, and that started from way back. That still goes through people in modern times. The people that play rugby are physical people. They want contact, they like being physical, and that is a tradition.'

Most pioneers started to make the best of it the moment they stepped off the boat. Land was cleared, trees cut down, simple shacks erected to provide some shelter from the elements. It is worth remembering, this was barely fifty years before the start of the twentieth century.

Fish and fowl were plentiful as a food supply. Then, as the second half of the nineteenth century gathered pace, sheep farming became a staple industry. The first sheep were introduced to New Zealand by Captain James Cook on his voyages in the 1770s. Others later imported the animals in the early 1800s, mainly from Australia. A migrant from Lithuania would write: 'We saw those hills full of stones . . . from the ship. Everyone thought what a stony country. But when we came closer, the stones started moving. The hills were full of sheep.'

It quickly became clear that the South Island offered better grazing than the North Island. There were areas of the North Island used for rearing the animals, such as the Wairarapa, north of Port Nicholson (now Wellington). But expansion of these sheep farms was limited by the need to clear vast areas of bush cover and the heavy rains which did not suit Merino sheep, which were originally from Spain but had arrived in New Zealand via Australia. Much of the land in the South Island had been acquired from the Maori by the late 1850s. The rest, both on the South and the North Island, was rented from the Crown. It was a different story in the drier regions of the Canterbury Plains and Otago. Here, they prospered and extending the areas for roaming was straightforward, so vast was the landscape.

The Deans brothers, William and John, arrived in New Zealand in the early 1840s. They took control of around four hundred acres of land at Riccarton in Canterbury. They were 'pre-Adamite' settlers, having arrived before the official settlement of Canterbury in 1850, when the first ships from England sailed into the harbour. They initially farmed cattle, but gradually changed to sheep. Their land is still in the original owner's family. Robbie Deans, who would later play for the All Blacks and coach the Canterbury Crusaders with huge success in a glorious era, is part of that family tree. His father farmed near Cheviot, in North Canterbury. Before becoming a professional rugby coach, Robbie Deans described his occupation as 'shepherd'.

Much of the hill country and plains of the east coast of the South Island had large areas of tussock land, which was suitable for grazing the fine-wool Merino sheep. The British Crown controlled development through land-settlement companies who sold or rented land to the pioneers. But problems arose especially around the New Zealand Government and their unlawful actions, which they are still paying for today via Treaty Settlement claims. The New Zealand Wars between the government and the Maori were all about land being wrongfully and unlawfully taken off Maori by the Crown.

What gave impetus to the sheep-farming industry was the growing demand for fine wool from the textile industries of Britain, the United States and Europe in the 1800s. Indeed, sheep farming would become synonymous with New Zealand. The benefit of farming sheep was clear; a single animal offered profits in two markets – meat and wool.

Farming prosperity inevitably ebbed and flowed in the intervening years. But not until the closing years of the twentieth century did this situation radically change. Then, with worldwide demand for wool declining, New Zealand found itself attached to a declining industry. There was only one solution. Mass slaughter. It is estimated the sheep population was reduced in a few years from around sixty to twenty million, as dairy farming took off. Yet, lamb prices seldom dropped much, even for such a locally sourced product.

In the mid-nineteenth century, both rearing and shearing sheep were essential practices. If any of the early settlers had imagined an easier life for their wives and children, they were to be sadly disillusioned. Men and women worked endlessly to clear the bush and begin farming. Gender was no ticket to an easier ride.

One woman is said to have given birth to sixteen children – many future hands to assist with the task of nation-building. It was said a girl could shear a hundred sheep in a day. Her father could probably double that number. Women found that, in extreme circumstances, they possessed skills such as boat building. Everyone did their bit to help, like an army swelling its ranks.

But if industrial amounts of physical labour and sheer hard work were mandatory in this 'new' land, one element was of even greater importance. Mental resilience. Without it, the new country could hardly have been forged. Here, too, were key qualities that would underpin the men who would later wear the All Blacks jersey.

Thus, a newly arrived migrant in the 1880s, initially depressed at the sight confronting her at the port town of Lyttelton, took a brighter, more positive approach to her new surroundings around Christchurch. 'There are other public buildings . . . There is the hospital which is a nice building, pleasantly situated, with a good garden and grounds, and the river Avon which is a pretty stream, is close by; then not very far from here is the museum, considered the best in New Zealand, then follows the public library, free from ten to ten, and also open on Sunday evening from seven till nine, and fairly well attended . . . For a small community, the library is very good. The school is a fine building . . . They have lately built a very fine hotel called the Hereford in the centre of the town [Cathedral Square] which would be a credit to any town of Christchurch's size . . . There are some good shops. There is a very good working men's club in Christchurch. I must say, I passed two or three most agreeable evenings at these entertainments.'

Yet at other times the writer lapses back towards melancholy, her default position:

'The general aspect of the town, taken as a whole, with the exception of just the centre near the cathedral, is squalid and very poor looking, with no architectural beauty, and nothing to please the fancy or imagination.'

But reality conquered melancholy. The settlers had to make something of this land, of their lives. As the writer also reflected in a letter to her brother: 'Though so far, things are most distasteful to me, I must try and keep my "pecker" up.' Hard work was an antidote to most complaints; that and sharing experiences with others. Together, with all manner of new migrants, they would somehow make this enormous challenge work in their favour. Bleeding hands and bleeding hearts, yes. But steadfastness prevailed. And in time, in an amalgam of all the peoples, this mental fortitude was a quality that would serve nobly a succession of rugby teams representing New Zealand.

*

Right across both islands, the first seedlings of small communities were seen to be springing up, watered with the sweat of their own brows. Part of Dunedin, the main city of the Otago settlement, was known as 'Little Paisley', and the city came close to being christened 'New Edinburgh'. In 1843, the Scottish writer and publisher William Chambers wrote a letter to the New Zealand Company, engaged in drawing up a prospectus for the settlement, imploring them to reject 'New Edinburgh'. His letter read:

> *Sir,—If not finally resolved upon, I should strongly recommend a reconsideration of the name, New Edinburgh, and the adoption of another, infinitely superior and yet equally allied to old Edinburgh. I mean the assumption of the name Dunedin, which is the ancient Celtic appellation of Edinburgh, and is now occasionally applied in poetic compositions and otherwise to the northern metropolis. I would at all events hope that names of places with the prefix 'new' should be sparingly had recourse to. The 'news' in North America are an utter abomination, which it has been lately proposed to sweep out of the country. It will be a matter for regret if the New Zealand Company help to carry the nuisance to the territories with which it is concerned.*
> *—W. Chambers.*

The settlement became officially known as Dunedin in 1846, its links to the Scottish city strengthened thereafter by its soubriquet 'the Edinburgh of the South'. It was therefore entirely appropriate that it was the son of a Scotsman, from Edinburgh, who gave this new country of New Zealand its defining sporting activity. The game of rugby union.

Charles John Monro was a louche figure and a sporting maverick. He was born near Nelson, on the northern tip of the South Island, and educated at Nelson College. He lived off his inheritance, enjoying life and himself in equal measure, in the style of fortunate young men of the era. He participated in the first ever game of polo played in New Zealand. He helped found the Manawatu Golf Club. In between times, he played croquet at Craiglockhart, the large home he had built near Palmerston North, and he was a regular visitor to the Manawatu Club to play billiards and snooker.

Some said it was sheer chance that rugby union became so popular in the country. But it wasn't, for one compelling reason. The rough and tumble that the game offered ideally suited its young, energetic citizens, both Maori and Pakeha. Small rural communities or local towns could raise teams of fit young men, physically hardened by their lives working the land or controlling animals. They were the perfect fit for a game that required the physical ability to rip the ball off an opponent, run hard with it and tackle. Courage and bravery were all in this game. New Zealand at that time was awash with both qualities.

In 1867 when he was sixteen, Monro left for England, ostensibly to be educated for a career in the army. Except that he had no interest in such a future. He went to Christ's College at Finchley, North London, a school that played 'football', as it was known under the rules of Rugby School. Monro himself played in the school's 2nd XV, before completing his studies and returning to New Zealand.

History relates that the handling game was invented by William Webb Ellis, who had picked up a football during a game at Rugby School in 1823 and run with it. It would take nearly half a century before the first game of rugby union was played on the other side of the world in New Zealand, at the Botanical Reserve in Nelson. Monro was fortunate in his crusade. Having already persuaded the Nelson Club to try the new game, the next man he had to convince was Nelson College Headmaster, the Reverend Frank Simmons, who had himself attended Rugby School. This was elementary. Simmons agreed immediately, and the date was set for the first game.

They gathered at the beautiful tree-lined Botanical Reserve for a two o'clock kick-off on Saturday 14 May 1870. Tall, mature, majestic trees peered down upon this strange spectacle. By happy coincidence, the location was in the sunniest region of all New Zealand.

The match was between Nelson Club and Nelson College. But it wasn't quite the game of rugby union we know today. For a start, each side fielded eighteen players, and goals kicked were conversions from a 'try', which was achieved when one team got the ball over the line. The Club team won 2–0, with two goals kicked from such 'conversions'.

It is recorded that around 200 spectators witnessed this new game. Whether they had even the slightest idea of what was going on, was a moot point. But New Zealand had staged its first game of rugby union. A mighty strut of this great future nation had been driven into the turf of an oval ground at Nelson. A report at the time in a Nelson newspaper called it 'a noisy, rushing, shouting game'. Another publication, *The Colonist*, commented, 'Rugby appears to be threatening to assume extensive proportions.'

Quickly, word spread of the new game. On 9 September 1871, a match was played between the students of Otago University and the pupils and ex-pupils of the Boys High School. The idea for the match is said to have come from a teacher, Mr G.M. Thomson, who had played the game for Blackheath, the oldest rugby club in the world, which had been founded in London in 1858. Thomson was said to be 'looking for some way to amuse boys on Saturday afternoon'. Better than sending them up chimneys, in the Victorian way.

The game, featuring teams of twenty-two players, sounded chaotic. A report said, 'With forty-four players, plus two umpires, on a small ground, no player could go far before bumping into someone.' Sounds rather like the modern game. Except today, there are thirty players. But still no space.

One of the sport's virtues was that it was so easy to play. All you needed was a reasonably flat paddock and a pig's bladder for the ball. (Christchurch schoolboys were said to have used a bullock's.) Anyone up for a physical challenge qualified for this game. Just about anything was permissible on the rugby field. Workers, labourers, sheep shearers, builders, carpenters – all indulged.

On Stewart Island, off the southern tip of the South Island, sawmills were plentiful, which meant recruits abounded for a team of tough, muscular young men. In time, an annual fixture, Stewart Island versus Bluff, the southernmost town of the South Island, would be staged.

Young men from any sector of society or working background anxious to burn off the frustrations or excess energy of everyday life, gravitated naturally to the game. Its popularity spread rapidly. In late 1870, as Europe was consumed by the Franco-Prussian War, the first ever international fixture was played, a game between Wellington and British sailors. The concept of physical confrontation was a major attraction to all. As one twenty-first-century exponent of the sport, the Fijian-born All Blacks wing Waisake Naholo explains, it is the intense physicality that is the essence of the game. Naholo is a man who knows what he is talking about. He is well equipped for a bit of physicality. Not only does he stand 1.86m (6ft 1.2ins) tall and weigh 96 kg (15st. 1lb), but he exudes power in his running.

'Every Pacific Island player has that flair – it is different from local players. We have an explosive power. Growing up in the islands and coming from a family there, Islanders pride themselves on what used to happen in wars. People never wanted to be the weak ones. With all the big hits and big running, everyone wants to be dominant. It is different to many local New Zealand players. I like the physical contact part of rugby, it is challenging. It is interesting to me to see how tough, how manly you are. In rugby, you have got to dominate or you get dominated. You don't want to be the weak one.'

Yet the need for speed and skills was not to be ignored. Rudimentary it might have been in those early times, but the foundations were being laid for a game of skill. It soon became clear that players would also require some cerebral matter to master it completely. New Zealanders would prove themselves most adept in that category, too.

It certainly fulfilled the expectations of a male-dominated society. In 1864, the *Southern Monthly Magazine*, discussing whether New Zealanders would inherit the British liking for what was termed 'manly sport', wrote that so far, the bar and billiard room appeared the 'chief resorts of our youth'. They needn't have worried. By the turn of the century, the game had taken off like a bush fire.

Alas, rugby had one problem. In the minds of governments, prime ministers and the military, the game couldn't hold a candle in terms of appeal compared to another exercise in physical confrontation. War. Alarmingly, the two were seen by some as perfect partners. In 1902, a Maori lawyer named Tom Ellison called rugby 'a soldier-making game'. If some New Zealanders, whatever their heritage, thought that distance alone meant complete isolation from the rest of the world, they were to be proven sadly mistaken in the closing years of the nineteenth and first half of the twentieth centuries.

Even within New Zealand, the nineteenth century's rapacious desire for wars had been prevalent. The inter-tribal fighting between the Maori that started in the 1820s and became known as the Musket Wars, took a terrible toll. Michael King, in his *History of New Zealand*, wrote, 'If any chapter in New Zealand history has earned the label "Holocaust" it is this one. In some actions . . . many hundreds of men, women and children were killed, and many more enslaved. Some small tribes were all but wiped out, with only one or two families surviving the fighting and its aftermath of executions.

'Some of these actions involved considerable cruelty. In the wake of battles, for example, the captured killers of warriors might be turned over to the widows of the men they had slain. The resulting deaths were prolonged and painful. At Waitangi Beach on Chatham Island, the Ngātiwai hapu of Ngāti Mutunga staked Moriori women to the ground alongside one another and left them to die slowly.'

King says that over a period of thirty years, the fighting led to the deaths of at least 20,000 Maori, and possibly many more. He adds, 'Even this figure would make these wars the costliest of any in which New Zealanders previously or subsequently took part.'

From 1845 to 1872, a series of battles known as the 'New Zealand Wars' or, by some, as the 'Maori Wars' were fought between the Maori and the New Zealand Government. It is important to emphasize that the New Zealand Government, put in place by the British Crown, are still paying today for the wrongs committed in the past against Maori.

Disputes over the purchase of land, and indeed over the actual details of the 1840 Treaty of Waitangi, were at the heart of the fighting. No fewer than 18,000 British soldiers, together with cavalry, artillery and local militia, were engaged in these wars in the 1860s. The Maori could not match such firepower but their guerrilla tactics of fighting from 'pa' (fortified villages) before tactical retreats, caused significant losses among their enemy.

Inevitably, the Maori fought with immense bravery. As their tradition dictated. Sadly, many paid with their lives. Eventually, more than 500 chiefs signed 'Te Tiriti o Waitangi' (the Te Reo Maori version). Yet only thirty-five chiefs signed 'The Treaty of Waitangi' in English, simply because they could not understand it.

The link with the British Crown on the other side of the world might have seemed tenuous, yet it was close enough to cost thousands of young New Zealanders their lives in wars fought in the final quarter of the nineteenth century. The so-called 'South African War' or 'Second Anglo-Boer War', fought from 1899 to 1902, was the first overseas war to involve New Zealand troops.

The New Zealand Government was as keen to sign up to the adventures of the British Empire as a fox to membership of a hen house. It was an era where wars stained the history of nations. No one, perhaps least of all New Zealanders and Australians, sat down to ponder the wisdom of sending 'the flower of a nation's youth' to a ghastly death in a faraway land. They saw the sacrifice as essential in the building of their nations.

Perhaps the worst illustration of this policy came at a sheer cliff face looming out of the waters of the Dardanelles Peninsula, in north-western Turkey, on the boundary between Europe and Asia. This was a madcap overseas adventure dreamed up by Winston Churchill, then head of the British Navy, under the inspirational message 'Storm the Dardanelles'. Families across the world soon had cause to curse those words that sacrificed the youth of nations including Australia, New Zealand, Great Britain, France and Ireland. The French alone lost 10,000 of the 79,000 soldiers; Great Britain and Ireland more than 21,000.

Gallipoli was a disaster. Eager young recruits from Australia and New Zealand sailed to Egypt, received only a modicum of training and were then sent into a fighting arena so hot that the only appropriate phrase for what ensued was 'pitiless slaughter'. The beachhead on which they landed was barely eight paces wide in some parts. Unsurprisingly, it became a killing ground as the Turks poured sustained fire on the hapless men below from a commanding height. Whenever the invading soldiers broke cover they were subjected to murderous fire.

Yet the Maori still distinguished themselves in battle. At Chunuk Bair, according to one report, the Maori unit more than played its part, advancing in silence with fixed bayonets and empty rifles, towards a position known as No. 3 Post. Six times that night they uttered a tremendous haka to terrify Turkish defenders as they charged. They thought this would alarm even the Turks, and it did. When they reached the first Turkish trench, there was no one in it. Indeed, these attacks on the foothills on 6 August were the only successful aspects of the assault on Chunuk Bair. It was said that a large part of that was due to the Maori unit. New Zealand's Maori Battalion may only have been 500 strong. But they were lauded as the 'fiercest fighters on the Gallipoli Peninsular'.

It is now believed that around 14,000 New Zealand soldiers served at Gallipoli, as opposed to the 8,556 listed in documents published in 1919, the result of a miscalculation by a British general. New Zealand lost 2,779 men, two of whom, Albert Downing and Henry Dewar, were

All Blacks at the time. One New Zealand soldier, Corporal Robert Heaton Livingstone, of the Canterbury Battalion, wrote an account on 23 July 1915 that was awful in its simplicity: 'If ever there was a hell on earth, Saturday 8 May was it. The ground was honestly dusty with bullets, we had to double forward 500 yards with machine guns and rifle fire sweeping the line continuously. Three bullets wiped the toes of my boots and passed on. The 1st Canterbury lost 64 out of its 160 that day, waiting for action – rather heavy casualties for two hours work. The strain throughout was severe.'

Then there was the Western Front. There, the Allied generals' moustaches generally made more progress over the course of a few days than their men could manage in weeks from their miserable locations out in the trenches. Within the course of just six months during 1917, members of the New Zealand Expeditionary Force were sucked into the major Somme battles at Arras, Messines and Passchendaele. At the latter, New Zealand rugby lost legendary All Blacks captain Dave Gallaher, leader of the renowned 1905–6 'Originals', the first touring party to the British Isles, France and America. Gallaher was seriously wounded in action, and died a few hours later.

In all, thirteen former All Blacks perished in the First World War, four of them within a fortnight in June 1917, during the assault on Messines Ridge. Typically for many young men of the time, Gallaher, enthused by a desire to do his duty, had given a false age to ensure he was accepted for service in the South African War, in 1901.

In 1915, Otago University reported it was 'without the services of fourteen of the previous year's A team, and fifty-six in all were at the front.' They came from almost every city, town and rugby club, large and small, throughout New Zealand. Later, when the war was over, the Otago University RFC would report, 'Football was back to its usual organisation in 1919, but the war had claimed a terrible number of the adventurous players from the immediate pre-war period.

'Twelve of the fifteen regular members of one Southern team had been killed, and all other clubs had suffered crushing losses.'

Passchendaele, Messines, Gallipoli, Chunuk Bair in World War One; El Alamein, Tobruk and other corners of Libya, Crete and other areas targeted by the many Kiwis flying for the RAF against enemy forces in World War Two. These were place names that came to define the proud record of service by all New Zealanders in the first half of the twentieth century. Everyone is remembered, very movingly, each ANZAC Day.

From these two small islands far away at the bottom of the world, heroes kept coming. In Auckland one day in 1941, a six-year-old schoolboy in his short trousers was hurried by his mother to get ready for the big day. Little shoes were polished until gleaming, school jacket thoroughly brushed down, clean shirt ironed and tie knotted impeccably. All to see the troops.

'We all went and stood in Queen's Street to see them as they marched down to the docks to board the ships that would take them away,' remembered the burly former All Blacks captain Sir Wilson Whineray, years later. 'We would do the same, go out to see them when they were coming home. Except that it didn't take long to realize that many more had gone than were coming back.' Whineray, by then just a retired citizen of the nation that knew him so well, silently wiped away a tear.

Perhaps one single piece of writing epitomizes best the courage and commitment of New Zealand troops. Alan Moorehead, writing in his renowned *Desert Trilogy*, witnessed at first hand men from New Zealand engaged in North African desert fighting in World War Two:

'At last we cut through a field of cactus and joined the main road north of Sousse. With the main road we hit the New Zealand division coming head-on towards us – in the way the enemy would see it coming.

'They rolled by with their tanks and their guns and armoured cars, the finest troops of their kind in the world, the outflanking experts, the men who had fought the Germans in the desert for two years, the victors of half a dozen pitched battles.

'They were too gaunt and lean to be handsome, too hard and sinewy to be graceful, too youthful and physical to be complete. But if ever you wished to see the most resilient and practised fighter of the Anglo-Saxon armies, this was he.'

This was the New Zealander in battles right across the world, across the ages. Gaunt and lean, hard and sinewy . . . The warrior soldier. The man refusing to contemplate defeat, the man able to dig deep at times of crisis. The man capable of handling danger, remaining calm and making decisions. This, surely, was also many a New Zealand rugby player of the future. The warrior rugby man, giving all for his cause, accepting physical pain and suffering for the benefit of those around him as much as himself.

There is a direct link between the New Zealand founding culture and the ethos that has shaped the All Blacks. The hardships that confronted the earliest settlers, today define the characteristics of all New Zealanders. One soldier who survived Gallipoli was asked later what drove them towards the enemy guns and almost certain death. He is said to have responded, without a moment's hesitation: 'Your mates were going out there into the fire. You couldn't leave them alone. You went together. You wouldn't let down your mates.'

When at last the guns had fallen silent, leaving only the sound of weeping from those left behind and that of the spade digging endless graves, these qualities would come to underpin another cause. Rugby football. The pursuit of the game.

Whatever the era, these factors are omnipresent. Unwillingness to accept defeat, able to dig deep and stay calm in adversity, able to continue making coherent decisions while all around is chaos. The sacrificing of personal concerns or causes to the mantra of helping your mates. A philosophy of sticking together, sustaining morale among one another.

It is easy to imagine a boy of farming stock like Richie McCaw in a New Zealand Expeditionary Force uniform at Gallipoli in 1915 or at Passchendaele two years later. Brave, courageous, committed to the cause, willing to lay down his life. Utterly committed to those around him.

Would *he* have gone to serve?

'I remember as a team, we were talking about those things and it rather put into context what you do. People talk about being brave in rugby, but this was a different sort of bravery. No one was trying to shoot you on the rugby fields. But you would hope if we were in that same period we would do the same thing. That is what I always ask myself. Would you go? I hope I would, absolutely.'

Government officials spying spare seats on a hugely popular bandwagon as they pursued their own feel-good factor following New Zealand's triumph at the 2011 Rugby World Cup, put out feelers to McCaw regarding how he'd feel about a knighthood. 'Not just for me, I was only part of the team,' he is said to have replied. What of his mates? The tradition endures.

Many of those who had perished in the various wars had

been rugby players, too, not necessarily All Blacks. But still keen participants. In their youth they had run and passed, kicked and tackled. Celebrated and commiserated. Then they were gone. But not forgotten.

So what did the sacrifices of All Blacks like Dave Gallaher mean to McCaw?

'Put aside the All Blacks stuff, my grandfather fought during World War Two. I had a lot to do with him when I was growing up so I guess I had a little understanding about what they did. But it wasn't really until we started talking about it, probably around 2005, the centenary anniversary of the "Originals" of which Gallaher was captain, that I understood more.

'We did quite a few talks to the team about what these guys did. I suppose being over in that part of the world and seeing where my grandfather had been and all the stories he told me when I was growing up, made sense having been there.

'You realize how lucky we are just from a nation's point of view what those guys did. Then you put it in a rugby context . . . Those guys went over there in 1905 to pave the way. It was a massive thing to go away for six months to the British Isles, France and America to play those games and then going off again, to war, a few years later . . . and some not coming home.'

A warrior people, a tougher people.

McCaw confesses he only reflected on the link recently when someone pointed out the almost uncanny resemblance of soldiers and rugby players in their shared characteristics.

Now he sees it through a different prism. 'It does probably have a bit of truth in it. We talk about the old New Zealanders being pretty good at figuring things out and making them work. But you think about the ancestors that came here. Imagine in the 1800s, getting on a boat not knowing where you are going, coming out here to an underdeveloped country and making your way. That's going to make you pretty tough and I guess, if you have got that sort of outlook that has been passed down through the generations, I think we are all probably benefitting . . . from that sort of attitude. That does make a bit of sense.'

A hard life, emotionally as much as physically.

'If you were here in the 1800s and you needed something done, you couldn't just ring someone up and get help, you had to do it yourself. That kind of self-sufficiency remains. Maybe it's not as strong as it was but it still runs through us as a people. Look at the Maori people and how they used to survive in a tough environment. You put all that together and you have a bunch of people throughout the place that have that resilience and tough attitude.'

These are a people undemonstrative in their manner, shorn of frills. They eschew false glories, fake idols. They are resilient, dedicated and determined, qualities they still require to this day. These characteristics, these defining traits, have been with them since their nation's creation or, in terms of our story, since rugby union was first played in this land. One thing is certain. If you were building the perfect identikit rugby man, he would be rich in such qualities.

2

WAR YEARS: THE ULTIMATE SACRIFICE

Contributions from, among others,
Wayne Smith, Willie Apiata, Tony Johnson.

'Out there in France they did their part, there in France they lie.
Carved upon a national heart, their fame shall never die.
Then sleep in fields where poppies grow,
Sleep 'neath the summer sun.
Sleep when the fields are white with snow,
Soldier, your work is done.'

Extract from a poem written in 1916 by Elinor Lamont, sister-in-law of
Nisbet Shirreffs Lamont, Private 11178, 2nd Battalion Otago Regiment
(born 2 February 1896, Brooklands, Southland, New Zealand:
died 1 October 1916 at the Battle of the Somme, aged twenty)

He had sailed without a care in the world. A sense of fun in his mind, happiness in his soul. He was with his mates, fellow rugby men. A new era was dawning for several of them.

Robert Stanley 'Bobby' Black was the son of Harry and Emily Black of Grant Street, Dunedin, and a native of Arrowtown, Invercargill. He was, like all New Zealanders called to the elite All Blacks, eager and proud to wear the famous jersey. Others around him were also new to the colours. Their sporting life's ambition realized.

There were pats on the back, jokes cracked to celebrate making the trip. Laughter, not seriousness. Except when it came to one topic. Winning. They were no different to today's generation in that respect.

As the boat ploughed its steady, measured course across the Tasman Sea, bound for Australia, Bobby Black's mind must have raced. Here was his chance, that long dreamed-of opportunity to become an All Black in an international match.

They reached Sydney, and some weeks later played the first Test against Australia. It was the eighteenth day of July. The year was 1914. And they triumphed, just, with a 5-0 win at the Sydney Sports Ground. Black had made his Test debut aged twenty-one. A long career as an All Black beckoned.

Alas, King George V made his fateful announcement that Britain and her Empire was at war with the Central Powers just seventeen days later. The Great War had begun. Despite the war, New Zealand played two more Test matches in Australia that August before returning home. They won the second Test 17-0 in Brisbane and the third, back in Sydney, 22-7. The European war seemed remote.

But all too soon, Black was sailing again, and this time to war.

Now, there were few smiles and those were only to mask grave concerns. There was no rugby kit in their bags.

Quite soon, Black, now of the 2nd Battalion Canterbury Regiment, would be in action. And on 21 September 1916, aged just twenty-three, he was killed. He was the youngest All Black to die in the First World War. Jim McNeece, from New Zealand's Southland region, who had scored the only try in that 1914 first Test against Australia, would also perish.

If ever a single conflict defined a people, as the cold winter winds of the Russian steppes hallmark a harsh landscape, the 1914–18 War will forever resonate in New Zealand's history. Gallipoli, Chunuk Bair, the Somme, Messines Ridge, Passchendaele . . . these are places indelibly stained by New Zealand blood.

Manifestly, that war helped make the nation we see today; determined, filled with national pride, conditioned to accept adversity in all its guises, gutsy, rich in spirit, self-sufficient. Men from all backgrounds willing to embrace risk and dedicated to a cause. These same characteristics also define the nation's finest rugby men.

It is clear, with hindsight, that New Zealand paid largely in the blood of its troops for nationhood. The First World War touched almost every person, every paddock back home.

The people left behind in New Zealand would not know of the wounded man, bravely attempting to stumble back to his own lines in the Passchendaele mud but losing his footing and disappearing into the liquid waste of a shell hole ten-feet deep. Nor would they comprehend the concept of men being used as cannon fodder.

In the graveyards of northern France and Belgium, Rudyard Kipling's immortal phrase, 'Known unto God', is seared into the visitor's memory, as a hot poker marks a steer. Kipling well knew the agony of surviving parents. His own son John died at the Battle of Loos in 1915. He was eighteen years old.

New Zealand paid a hideous price for its involvement in the Great War. In percentage terms of those nations that sent troops to fight, New Zealand topped the list of those killed and wounded. According to one report, from a population of little more than one million, New Zealand contributed 110,000 men. Of this number, 18,000 were killed and 55,000 wounded, totalling 73,000 casualties or 66 per cent of its men.

They came not just from North and South Islands. Indeed, men from Polynesia were recruited by New Zealand to fight in both world wars. In the First World War, 500 men from the Cook Islands comprised the 1st Rarotongan Contingent, and 150 men from Niue also joined up. Others came from Fiji, Samoa, Tonga and Tahiti, as well as the Gilbert and Ellice Islands. In World War Two, a Maori Battalion included Polynesian men.

The loss of so many men severely affected the nation. Two thirds of those who died (estimated at almost 12,500) fell on the Western Front. The war will forever be defined as one of New Zealand's most costly in human terms. An entire generation was scarred by the suffering. It was a war where men pushed themselves into the line of fire, against every inclination of human preservation.

Bobby Black's body was never found, one of a multitude whose names are listed on the New Zealand Memorial to the Missing at the Caterpillar Valley Cemetery in Longueval, on the Somme. The cemetery records the names of 5,570 servicemen, of whom nearly 3,800 remain unidentified.

One report of the campaign in which Black lost his life, stated:

'The attack started on Friday 15 September at 06:20, supported by huge artillery fire. They walked into battle shrouded in smoke and mist. By the end of the day, they had seized a wedge of land from the German Army, to the east of the village of Flers, and formed a defensive line.'

But the New Zealanders, many of them who had fought at Gallipoli, had advanced well beyond neighbouring British divisions and found themselves defending an awkward salient where they were exposed to murderous fire by German artillery batteries that rained down shells on their positions.

It was another five days before the Division had shored up the salient – during that time it launched four more attacks, suffering many casualties. The New Zealand Infantry were in the line for twenty-three consecutive days. Rain swept over them, creating cloying mud. The shell holes that littered the battlefield were soon full of water. Corpses lay strewn all over no man's land. The stench of death was everywhere.

This was the infamous 1916 Battle of the Somme which lasted from 1 July to 18 November. Somewhere out there, even now, lie Bobby Black's remains.

Today, when you stand on the spot from which the New

Zealanders launched their attack, a single word invades your mind. Not 'agony', not 'hatred' nor 'death'. But 'peace'.

Gentle breezes blow across from High Wood, one of the worst of the killing fields of the Somme. High above, a swallow swoops on the air currents; in the distance, a farmer's harvester works its way across a golden field, cutting corn. The calm, silence and peace all hit you as a wave. The beauty of the landscape is a bitter irony.

By brutal contrast, the noise of the attack that September morning was shattering. The explosions of shells from the British artillery barrage, the whistles to advance and shouts of encouragement from the advancing soldiers, the chatter-chatter of the responding German machine guns, and then the cries of men hit, their bodies broken amid the detritus of war.

On the first day of this Somme offensive, a conflict in which tanks were deployed for the first time, 58,000 men were killed or wounded. Total British and French losses on the Somme would be in excess of 600,000 alone. More than 2,000 New Zealanders lost their lives there, and 6,000 more were wounded. Most of the dead, like Bobby Black, have no known grave. It was said that, for every hundred metres of ground the Allies gained, more than a thousand Allied lives were lost.

Dave Gallaher was wounded by shrapnel that penetrated his helmet during the attack on Gravenstafel Spur, on 4 October 1917. He died later that day at an Australian casualty clearing station and was buried in Nine Elms British Cemetery at Poperinge in West Flanders, Belgium, one of 117 New Zealanders laid to rest there. He was forty-three years old and was there by choice – his age exempted him from military service, but he had volunteered. Three of the four Gallaher brothers died in service during the war. Douglas and Henry also perished. Only Charles survived, though he was badly wounded at Gallipoli.

The great All Black lies in a truly ANZAC line. On one side of his gravestone in Plot III, Row D, No. 3 lies a man from the Australian Machine Gun Corps; on the other, one from the 44th Battalion Australian Infantry. Further along the row, there are fellow Kiwis from the Auckland and Wellington regiments.

The flowers of ANZAC youth mercilessly cut down, like the corn still harvested there today.

At the foot of Gallaher's tombstone lies a rugby ball with a heartfelt inscription:

'We will never forget but will always respect. You started the greatest rugby team in the history of the game.'

For the 1905 All Blacks, the so-called 'Originals', rugby football was a manly pursuit, at a time when New Zealand was an ambitious young nation. Tony Johnson, Sky TV commentator in Auckland, has studied this period extensively:

'There was this desire to go to help the mother country. Maori, too, wanted to do their bit. There was this wish to say afterwards, "Look at what we have done, are you proud of us?" That was the motivation initially.

'The Prime Minister Richard Johnston underwrote that Originals tour [in 1905]. He saw we needed more people in the country so he regarded the tour as a fantastic chance to show Britain that these people, these young, fit, strong rugby men were the product of a country with a healthy outdoor lifestyle. In effect, they were saying to the people of the UK, "Come and live in our country."

'So we were starting to look for our own identity, too. As a nation, that fuelled it. New Zealanders felt this was a way we could make our name on the world stage. It installed the feeling that sport was a way for this small, remote country to gain a sense of achievement, to be noticed.'

More than a hundred years later, that remains true. It is yet another reason for the sustained supremacy of New Zealand rugby teams. The phrase, 'When you play New Zealand, you don't play a team, but a nation,' has a stirring resonance.

Dave Gallaher's parents, said Johnson, went out to New Zealand on a hare-brained scheme. 'People were sold this idea of lifestyle blocks, but the land still needed to be tamed. His father was old when he came here and had no chance of doing serious hard work. His mother became the breadwinner, but she got cancer and that killed her.

'She must have been an incredibly strong woman. Clearly, Gallaher got his strength of character from his mother. She was a true pioneer; she was determined but endured a lot of hardship, pain and suffering.

'He had to look after younger siblings and became a natural leader. He was a sergeant in the army, a natural leader of men. It was a sense of duty that sent them there. To them, in those days, it was a great adventure.'

In another part of northern France, in another of the beautifully preserved cemeteries, lie more New Zealand victims of the slaughter. The detonation of nineteen mines under the German lines at Messines in June 1917 caused an artificial earthquake. These explosions were the climax of two weeks of intense shelling and heralded an Allied infantry attack on 31 July 1917. Yet many of the German machine guns had survived the barrage and unleashed their cruel intent on unknowing soldiers.

At Messines Ridge lie more lines of Kiwi dead. Their task had been to ascend the gently rising ground to the ridge at the top. It was a walk to death; open and exposed, they had no cover from the hail of bullets that mowed them down.

Had he been born at another time, Ben Mason could have been one of them. The young Aucklander had always wanted to visit the New Zealand Memorial at Messines – and now, here he was. 'I grew up in the Harry Potter era, but wasn't interested in that, only in history and war books,' he told me. So, together with his girlfriend, he had journeyed to this part of northern France and cycled to the Memorial. He put up a New Zealand flag, a personal memorial to the three members of his own family who had served in World War One. Astonishingly, one of them survived the entire war, including Passchendaele.

Today, a sculpture of a lone New Zealand soldier stands proudly on a plinth beside the town square in Messines. In 2017, one hundred years after the battle, a simple exhibition at a local cafe commemorated the New Zealanders' sacrifice.

George Sellars, who had played fifteen matches for the All Blacks, including two Tests in 1913, and had been in the first New Zealand Maori team to go overseas, lost his life at the Battle of Messines. He was killed while carrying a wounded colleague to safety on his back, and is commemorated by name on the New Zealand Memorial at Messines Ridge.

Sellars died on 7 June 1917, the same day as James Baird, another All Black, and two more, Reginald Taylor and Jim McNeece, died that month. Taylor had been in the Taranaki team that beat Auckland in the Ranfurly Shield in 1913, and played two Tests for the All Blacks in the same year. A formidable forward, he was twenty-eight when he died.

McNeece, an Invercargill man, played five Test matches for the All

Blacks in 1913 and 1914. Baird represented his country in a single Test, against Australia at his native Dunedin, in 1913.

Close to Messines there is a wood. I climb a fence and stand alone in it; the haunting silence broken only by the occasional crowing of a cockerel on a nearby farm. Just occasionally, a farmer's tractor rumbles by. Otherwise, as the light finally begins to fail at the end of one seemingly endless summer evening, the eerie silence is broken only by the sound of birdsong. Yet a hundred years earlier, such calm and serene silence were but a fantasy of the soldiers' imagination.

'I died in hell – they called it Passchendaele', wrote the poet and soldier Siegfried Sassoon. These eight words told millions of the horror. One old ANZAC veteran gave a vivid account of his experiences at Passchendaele. This is what he remembered:

12 October, Battle of Passchendaele. We had to go up this blasted track. It was all mud and water. The ground had about an inch and a half of water on it, brown colour. All in among it were shell holes, about eight to ten feet deep. If you didn't see the difference in the colour of the water and you stepped in it, that was the end of it, you wouldn't come up again.

We went down to an old broken-down farmhouse. There were a couple of Germans in there; one was dead, the other was wounded, so we knocked him off. I was trying to send messages back to headquarters, about 500 yards behind us, on an electric signalling lamp, a Lucas lamp. I was sighting when a bullet went right into the wall behind me. My nose was touching the wall right beside where I was standing. That was how close it was. That could only have been a sniper who'd taken a shot at me.

So I said to young Rogers, one of our runners who was there, I said, 'I'm going to get down in that trench and see if I can find this fellow.' He said, 'I'll come with you.' He didn't know hardly one end of a rifle to the other. But we jumped down in there and were both looking for this sniper. Rogers found him and pointed him out to me. He was about 300 yards away so I topped him off pretty smart.

And then, all of a sudden, from up here near Passchendaele, a machine gun opened on us from this hill. Not on the top but two parts of the way up it. The bullets were hitting the brick wall just behind us and ricocheting all around us. They couldn't have been missing us by much. We kept our heads down until the bursts stopped. Then I put my eye just above this brick wall and they opened up again, another burst. I saw a flash from the end of the machine gun – that was all I could see. I couldn't see any-body, but as soon as they stopped again, I had marked down where the flash was, and I popped up and sent a couple of bullets up there, then ducked down again.

That went on for about an hour and a half. Anyhow, they stopped all of a sudden when I was letting go at them, so we didn't have any more trouble with that. But I put another three bullets in there for good measure.

I said to Rogers, 'Well, that's the end of them,' and he said, 'Yeah.' Then suddenly, BANG, another one opened up, about a hundred yards to the left of us. They nearly got us, as a matter of fact. But I saw a flash from them, too, so I put a few bullets into them now and again. So after about an hour or more, they ceased, too.

And I was damned if another one didn't open straight oppos-ite us. There were three machine guns there. Well, we had a terrible battle with that one because he was firing straight at us and they [the bullets] were coming down . . . right at us so we had to keep up against this brick wall. It hit you on the back as they passed over.

However, we got onto them and they quietened down. That's what I got my Military Medal for – or should have. Do you know what the citation said? That I organized communications and that kind of thing. There were no communications whatever until near twelve o'clock. If we'd sent a runner out, he'd have been cut to pieces by one of those machine guns.

Yet, in the New Zealand section of the museum at Passchendaele under the title of 'Relaxation – What Soldiers Did', hangs a curious item: a pair of old, brown leather rugby boots, with khaki-coloured laces. Somebody went to war carrying a pair of rugby boots. Can we ever doubt the New Zealanders were here? Their DNA is writ large upon this land.

The sacrifice given by the men of New Zealand continues to inspire respect and awe, even to this day. Which is why some All Blacks teams have travelled here to pay their respects. Wayne Smith,

All Blacks assistant coach until his retirement in late 2017, remembered his own emotions when he came this way.

'The first thing I thought was, why didn't we learn about all this at school? How come I didn't know about this? I had tears in my eyes when I saw that imperceptible hill they were fighting over. And the fact that they were dying in the craters, drowning in them. Imagine how ice cold it would have been. I thought it was an absolute tragedy.

'There is a huge monument dedicated to the ANZACs . . . men who came from New Zealand and Australia, fighting a war they probably didn't even understand. They were put in that situation. I couldn't even put myself there as to what it was like.

'It makes you angry just reading the books about it. The stupidity . . . leaders who wouldn't have had the first idea of leadership, sending these valiant young men to their deaths. They were truly lions led by donkeys.'

He also recalled meeting Willie Apiata, New Zealand's most recent recipient of the Victoria Cross, soon after he had visited Gallipoli. Apiata is, by nature, a man of few words, but Smith told me, 'He could hardly talk afterwards. I saw him and said, "You look jet-lagged." But he said, "I am not jet-lagged, I am devastated at what I actually saw."

'Those men, as soon as they got out of the trenches, they knew they were going to die. You start thinking, "Why did they go out of the trench?" The answer is, for their mates. They wouldn't let their mates die alone.

'You just look back through history. Conflict is a thing we do as humans. That disappoints me because of our children, the next generation. That's what we're raising our children in the world for. This is the world they're going to live in.'

A warrior people? Smith does not see himself like that. But he concedes, 'New Zealand is definitely full of pioneering spirit. We have all got a bit of that in our DNA. Vibrant, brave soldiers.'

I walk slowly and silently down a row of graves at the massive Tyne Cot Cemetery, where there are 11,961 white headstones marking the Commonwealth soldiers killed during the Battle of Passchendaele. Lost in thought. Yet the irony is that, amid such brutality, there is beauty. Ahead of me a delicate butterfly flutters carefree, dancing delightfully in and around the tombstones. Red rose bushes and other shrubs entice softly humming bees. In another section, a dragonfly rests momentarily on a white tombstone, like a kindly stranger offering a hand on a fallen soldier's shoulder. The citation reads, 'A Soldier of the Great War, a New Zealand Regiment.'

The annihilation of a people from the other side of the globe had serious consequences back in New Zealand. The war claimed 58 per cent of the country's available labour, which led to falling production and increased prices. Only by introducing women into the labour market and continuing to export produce to Britain was a collapse in the New Zealand economy prevented.

Of course, many women were already involved in the war. More than 550 New Zealand nurses served at military hospitals at the front. Ten, most of whom were from the South Island, were among thirty-one New Zealanders who were drowned when the hospital ship *Marquette* was torpedoed by a U-boat in the Aegean Sea on 23 October 1915, killing 167. Five hundred more nurses from New Zealand worked as volunteers at hospitals in France, Belgium and England. Several were honoured with the Queen Elizabeth Medal for their work.

One French village has gained a place in New Zealand folklore for different reasons. Le Quesnoy (pronounced 'Le Ken-Wah') is a typical small French town, a short drive south of the city of Valenciennes. It is an oddity, as many of the street names are of New Zealand origin. 'Rue Helen Clark' is close by 'Rue Adrian Macey' (a recent New Zealand ambassador in France). There are signposts for 'Rue Nouvelle Zelande' and 'Rue Aotearoa' on the same street. Not far away is 'Rue Graeme Allwright' (a New Zealand author and composer). You turn a corner and come to 'Avenue des Neo-Zelandais', which is just metres from 'Place Des All Blacks'. Then a plaque in the wall, reading '1914–1918: Avenue D'Honneur Des Neo-Zelandais'.

What happened here, in the final days of the war, was another illustration of New Zealand resourcefulness. The kind of 'can-do' mentality that has been at the heart of the nation, not to mention its rugby teams. On 4 November 1918, just seven days before the Armistice, New Zealand troops were ordered to attack and take the northern French town, held under German occupation since 1914. But the attackers ran into a problem. When they reached the inner walls, they found them too high for their ladder. The entire operation was imperilled.

But the Kiwis' resourcefulness soon emerged. Some feet above a sluice gate they spied a small brick ledge, which was just big enough to take the ladder. One at a time, the New Zealand troops scaled the ladder, and a German sentry was shot. Hearing gunshots close by and realizing the inner walls of the town had been breached, the main German garrison panicked. They laid down their arms and surrendered; the occupation was over.

Almost a hundred years later, Le Quesnoy remains forever a foreign corner of New Zealand, a town in northern France where the country has roots deep in the soil. And the exploits of those soldiers all that time ago are now told proudly to the new generation of New Zealand youngsters in their schools.

3

SCHOOLS: WHERE IT ALL BEGINS

Contributions from, among others,
Jerome Kaino, Beauden Barrett, Liam Messam,
Wayne Smith, Reuben Thorne, Steve Cole,
Alan Jones, Grant Hansen, Doug Howlett,
Sir Graham Henry.

'I think the school system in New Zealand is the secret, the key to the All Blacks' success. It is about the quality of the young players produced at school level. The heart of our game is at the grassroots, but I think it's even earlier where the crucial work is done. For me, the success of our All Blacks sides starts a lot earlier than at a school's 1st XV. I think even earlier than Under 12s.'

All Blacks forward Jerome Kaino

Ask a New Zealand youngster to name six great New Zealand rugby players and six great New Zealand prime ministers. Chances are he or she would rattle off twelve names in the first category and probably struggle to remember a couple of the latter.

In rugby-mad New Zealand, it has always been this way. Loving the game is a virtual birth right.

Stories of the nation's great rugby ancestors are handed down to younger generations like family heirlooms. Legendary names from decades past trip easily off the tongue of the modern generation: Dave Gallaher, George Nepia, Cyril Brownlie, Bob Scott, Billy Wallace, Bob Deans, Colin Meads and Richie McCaw. These, and others, illustrate the pages of history and of New Zealand's rugby history – the two are intertwined.

It goes further back than living memory. Indeed all the way to 1888 and the astonishing tour of the 'New Zealand Natives', the first side to wear the now-famous black jersey. They were the first representative rugby team to tour Britain; twenty-one of their twenty-six players were Maori, reflecting the strong Maori association with the early game. By the start of the 1880s, there were already several all-Maori club teams.

The touring team of 1888 did not believe in doing things by halves. They played a remarkable 107 matches during the tour, winning seventy-eight of them. They played seventy-four matches in the British Isles alone, winning forty-nine, losing twenty and drawing five. The rest of the tour consisted of sixteen matches in Australia and seventeen in New Zealand. It must have been an extraordinary experience.

Then there were the 1905 'Originals', a team captained by Irish-born Dave Gallaher, of whom E.H.D. Sewell, a writer for the London

Evening Standard, would say, 'He was a hard bitten colonial, as tough as a bit of leather.' It was said that Gallaher trained for rugby by running through the New Zealand backcountry in heavy boots, followed by a vigorous bout of two-man pit sawing.

The New Zealand journalist Christopher Tobin wrote of Gallaher in his 2005 book, *The Original All Blacks: 1905-06,* 'He worked as a foreman in the rugged environment of a freezing works, which by modern standards were quite primitive blood-and-guts places. He was tough-minded and when on the rugby field, ruthless. His 1905 teammate Ernie Booth would describe him as a remorseless foe. As an opponent in play, he was simply merciless.' Decades later, the Welsh outside-half Cliff Morgan would describe his Wales and 1955 British Lions teammate Clem Thomas, a butcher by trade, in similar terms: 'Clem was the only man I ever knew,' said Morgan in his mellifluous Welsh lilt, 'who took his profession onto the rugby field.'

Enduring arduous sea journeys, those 1905 pioneers toured the British Isles, France and the United States of America. Their memory lives on, not least for one major reason. After beating Scotland (12-7), Ireland (15-0) and England (also 15-0), they lost 3-0 to Wales. Men have gone to their graves insisting the All Black R.G. Deans scored a try that would have levelled the scores. But the referee, bizarrely dressed in street clothes and with no studs on his boots, was some way from the action when Deans claimed he grounded the ball over the line. When he eventually arrived at the scene, he refused to award the try. Thus, New Zealand lost to a single Welsh try, and a century of argument, claims and denials followed. They persist to this day, together with the nation's obsession for the game.

Those first All Blacks of 1905 proved their value in more ways than one. Such was the interest in their tour that vast crowds flocked to see them, and the funds of the fledgling New Zealand Rugby Football Union were transformed. They had initially travelled third class in the UK, and stayed in hotels of a similarly modest grade, but by the time they went home, they had bolstered the NZRFU coffers by £8,000 (around £915,000 at today's values), a vast sum in those times.

Soon, a hundred years will have passed since the so-called 'Invincibles' made their historic tour of the British Isles, Ireland, France and Canada in 1924. That team achieved sporting immortality by winning every one of their thirty-two tour matches. And they introduced future sporting legends to the world, men like the great Maori full-back

George Nepia, and Maurice Brownlie, both of whom made their Test debuts on that tour. Amazingly, Nepia played in every match.

During their trip, captain Cliff Porter visited Dave Gallaher's grave at Passchendaele with some of his teammates. Such acts established the link between past and present. They ensured that the greats of the past would be revered in perpetuity.

As that 1924 tour garnered increasing winning momentum, so public interest grew. For their final international match, against France in Toulouse, it was reported that an astonishing 115 journalists were in attendance: fifteen from the British Isles, twenty from Paris and eighty from the rest of France. Interest in the tour had turned into mania. The New Zealanders duly won, by thirty points to six, before heading for home via Canada.

Two years later, in July 1926, another team from New Zealand, the first official New Zealand Maori team, set off on a tour of Australia, France, Great Britain and Canada. They played forty games, winning thirty-one, drawing two and losing seven, one of which was a 6–5 defeat against the Welsh club Pontypool, on New Year's Day in 1927.

The 1924 All Blacks had clearly been exceptional. Yet, perhaps unknowingly, we sepia-tint our memories and dire contests of the time assume the status of glittering entertainment during the passing years. Nostalgia marches across all fields of sport.

What these early rugby players did was entice a nation to their sport. Fathers would tell sons of their glorious deeds, most often in faraway lands. Later, as grandparents, they would settle the next generation on their knees and recount tales of those times and their heroes. And so it has carried on in New Zealand, ensuring that the great game remains in the nation's heart.

Yet New Zealand teams did not win every game they played – far from it. A close study of the New Zealand All Blacks in the inter-war years reveals uncertain progress. True, this era included the triumphs of the celebrated 'Invincibles'. But in this period, New Zealand played thirty-six Test matches and lost thirteen. Two were drawn, with twenty-one wins.

Compare this with the era that is the real focus of this book, the thirteen years from 2004 to 2017, when the All Blacks played 145 Test matches, winning an extraordinary 123 and losing just nineteen. There can be no comparison with the exploits of those men in black from earlier times. Yet those star men from so long ago are eulogized, their names recalled in hushed, reverential tones. The passing years have bestowed immortality on them. So what will time do to the supremely successful men of the modern era who have worn the famous jersey?

Undeniably, the game has always represented a grand obsession in the minds of these people. Nowadays, you can wake up in the morning to rugby in New Zealand. Go to sleep at night with it still on TV. If you can't sleep, you can get up in the middle of the night and watch old matches on repeat. It's like a twenty-four-hour drug store on the street corner: always available and offering something familiar. It's close by. Comforting. If you're a rugby junkie and you need your fix, you know where to go.

Kids are born and raised in this rugby cocoon. The human umbilical cord is severed at birth, but this is different. The cord between a child and this sport in New Zealand is secured at birth, rarely to be loosened.

Keen parents spend small fortunes sending their sons to so-called 'rugby schools'. They invest endless hours trying to generate a passion for the game, hoping that one day, their child might miraculously wear the famous All Black jersey.

You could try to persuade otherwise sensible parents to save their hard-earned money. And the words of former All Blacks assistant coach Wayne Smith might offer the best lesson in sobriety. Smith has always believed that kids and their parents should have a proper life. Rugby can happen after that.

Smith was talking at a schools' camp, at St Paul's Collegiate School in Hamilton. Eight out of the ten top schools in the country were there, and a lot of parents had turned up. It wasn't just about the rugby. Respect and responsibility featured heavily, too. It emphasized that if your boy was in the game just to be a professional player, he was in it for the wrong reasons. Rugby is about life skills, grit and being part of a team. All those things were pushed. The egocentrics were sidelined.

There were about 150 kids there and Smith asked the parents a simple question. How many did they reckon would become professional players? One said one, another said five. The answer was 3 per cent. That's the good news. The bad news is, they would on average have only three years as a professional, because of injury and not being good enough.

'The point is,' said Smith, 'you need to make sure you are developing a career and developing as a person because professional rugby union is a short-term prospect.'

Yet kids throughout the land go on fantasizing they will be the next Beauden Barrett, the new Sonny Bill Williams. Or even, dare we mention it, the new Richie McCaw. Most parents, drowning in nationalistic sentiment, encourage them. The solution is a proper sense of balance. Not just in the minds of youngsters, but in their parents', too.

Maddeningly, it's usually the offspring of parents who hardly know one end of a rugby ball to the other who reach the highest echelons of the game. Take Reuben Thorne, good enough to lead the Canterbury Crusaders to the Super 12 title in 2002 and captain the All Blacks at the 2003 Rugby World Cup. Was Thorne given a rugby ball to nurse the moment he'd cast off his nappies? Was he hustled straight off to the country's finest school as a five-year-old to be groomed and prepared for life as an All Blacks captain?

'I didn't grow up in a rugby family at all, my parents weren't into sport. But, whatever I learned as a youngster, perseverance was one of the chief things.'

Thorne says his connection with rugby football as a kid was about as tenuous as the rudimentary signal of the Thorne family television set. The aerial was connected to a rough piece of wire on a fence post on the family farm in the Taranaki region of the North Island. The wire ran up to the top of the hill behind the house, but the quality of the picture depended on the weather. It was always hit and miss whether you'd be able to see it on the day of a Test match. And, even on a good day, the television picture was still black and white. The first Test he wanted to watch was the 1991 Rugby World Cup Final. But the weather was poor. 'I could hardly see any pictures, just a few ghostlike images appearing now and again on the screen. The sound came and went, too, because reception was so bad.

'We lived in a valley with a steep hill behind us where sheep grazed. If the weather was bad on Mount Taranaki, you had no chance of a picture. You might just hear the words if you were lucky.'

A different era. But the transformation of New Zealand society has driven major changes at every level in most fields. Perhaps schools are the best example. Picture this. A young man from humble surroundings in South Auckland walks into the grounds of Saint Kentigern College for the first time. It is one of Auckland's most-renowned educational establishments. The kid is awestruck. His name is Jerome

Kaino and he's only sixteen. He's not used to anything like the facilities he sees here. It wasn't like this back in American Samoa when he was a five-year-old. Today, eighteen years later as a thirty-four-year-old, Kaino looks back and smiles at his own naivety.

'I went there for the last two years of my school life. I've since come to understand it wasn't that flash when I was there. The gym was about to be put up.'

Today Saint Kent's, as the school is universally known, inhabits another planet. One day I drove out of the city. I wanted to find this school in the Auckland suburb of Pakuranga. I thought I'd found it and drove in. But no, this couldn't be it. On my right lay a vast construction, shrouded in scaffolding and screens. It looked more like an aircraft hangar under construction. What I didn't know was that I was looking at the future of rugby union at Saint Kentigern College. This vast building being erected at that time was the independent Presbyterian school's new sports centre. Without a word of exaggeration, most rugby-playing *nations* of the world would have drooled at such facilities.

My guide was Steve Cole, who was at the time the school's headmaster and a keen rugby man. He explained that part of the building would be an indoor training field, with another part given over to nutrition. Then there was the physiotherapy section, plus one or two lavishly stocked gymnasiums and an area for coaches and their equipment. Showers, dressing rooms and other such facilities would be on site, too.

'How much is all this actually costing?' I asked, incredulous.

'About NZ$12.5 million,' was Cole's matter-of-fact response.

So how could a school charging parents no more than NZ$20,000 a year in fees afford NZ$12.5 million for a gigantic sports facility such as this? The answer lies in faraway Hawick, on the borders between Scotland and England. In 1806, one William Goodfellow was born in Hawick, the sixth of eight children to Hugh and Elspeth Goodfellow. William became a baker, taking over the family business in 1839. But he decided to create a new life in Australia and set sail from Greenock, Scotland, in a ship named the *Palmyra*.

The vessel docked in the Clyde for repairs. There, quite by chance, Goodfellow saw a prospectus for the New Zealand Company. On a whim, he decided to go instead to New Zealand. He sailed first to

Sydney and then crossed the Tasman on a whaling ship, landing at Port Nicholson, now Wellington Harbour.

Goodfellow set up business as a baker in a town named Britannia. We know it today as Petone. In time, his wife and children joined him at the other end of the world. Alas, he soon discovered the land was prone to flooding and he decided to make a new life in faraway Auckland. But his journey there was surreal. He walked from Port Nicholson to Auckland, a journey that is 650 km today (400 miles), but would have certainly felt much further in those primitive times. He went via the scenic west coast, guided by Maori. He forded rivers, swam lakes and was put across rivers and harbours in canoes. The Maori liked him and called him 'A, te Korewhero' ('the good fellow').

When he finally got to Auckland, he set up business and a new home, buying land and growing wheat for his bakery. A devout Presbyterian, he and his wife had ten children, four of whom became farmers. He died in 1890, a valediction of the time recording that, 'He was a man of sound judgement on all matters affecting his district. By industry and integrity and shrewd business capacity in making investments in land in the early days, he had acquired considerable wealth.'

These traits were to become hallmarks of the Goodfellows. The family's business interests grew, incorporating the Waikato Dairy Company (founded in 1909) and carried on with an equally shrewd guiding hand. Douglas, one of five sons and a daughter, led the business wisely, in time becoming the father of two sons, Bruce and Peter.

In the fields of dairy, refrigeration, fishing and clothing, the family fortune ballooned. In 1959, Douglas sent his two sons to Saint Kentigern College, a new school in the Auckland suburbs that had been founded in 1953. He himself played an active role, firstly as a member of the school board between 1959 and 1996, and also as a respected Chairman of the Trust Board from 1965 to 2000.

His son Bruce once said, somewhat presciently, that his father was 'capable of an instant decision and action and usually gets his way.'

In 1994, Douglas Goodfellow was revealed by the *National Business Review* Rich List to be the richest person in New Zealand; in 2014, the same newspaper judged that the Goodfellows were worth at least NZ$500 million. The truth became clear when Douglas Goodfellow died in 2014, at the age of 97. It is alleged that in his will, he left his sons Bruce and Peter NZ$1 million each. But Saint Kentigern College did rather better. They were alleged to have been left a bequest of NZ$250 million.

This bequest was an extraordinary testimony to the family's links with the school. Inevitably, it created all kinds of opportunities for the school to deepen and develop its reputation, building a state-of-the-art sports centre as well as strengthening a recruitment link with the rugby-playing islands of Polynesia. Under this arrangement, rugby officials from Saint Kentigern College could fly to an island to talk with local officials and choose the stand-out young rugby stars as candidates for a scholarship to the Auckland school.

A Fijian-born boy named Joe Rokocoko was one. So was the American Samoa-born Jerome Kaino. Then there was John Afoa, another boy destined to become an All Black. Other future All Blacks who attended the school, albeit not arriving directly from the islands, were Steven Surridge and Seta Tamanivalu, the latter a winner of the Super Rugby Trophy in 2017 with the Canterbury Crusaders.

Kaino had arrived from a public school and found the experience eye-opening. Papakura High School, he said, was more relaxed; Saint Kent's, by contrast, far more driven. You had to turn up to class on time and make sure your books were ready. Education was the focus but everything with sport was just as meticulous. It took him a while to get used to that. They made sure they pushed their pupils, whatever they did, whether sport, music or the arts.

'I was there with Joe Rokocoko and John Afoa,' he said. 'It was great to have some of my mates from South Auckland with me. I was offered a scholarship to go there, probably because of my rugby reputation. A friend's dad was coaching the 1st XV and asked if I was keen to change schools. I got offered a scholarship and I am very glad that happened. Who knows where I would have been in life if I hadn't made that change? My time there was awesome, I loved it.'

Do the schools express any regret for their policy of selecting boys from the islands? Steve Cole, then with Saint Kentigern College, admitted he often lay awake at night, pondering the merits of the scheme and wondering if it was too professional.

'But we tried to do the same when it came to the school choir and the netball programme. The fact is, there is a path for these young kids to follow for their futures, whether it is professional rugby, professional netball or the performing arts. I thought it suited the philosophy of the school, and a number of our kids have gone on to lucrative careers in such fields. Several are very good rugby players and some will become All Blacks. Jerome Kaino was here for two years and we have six or seven in the Auckland Blues squad, but they are still quite young. I think there were fifteen kids of ours from recent years in professional rugby set-ups in 2017.

'We have strength and conditioning people, two of them full-time but not just for rugby. They teach to years nine and ten. We have one full-time coach on our payroll but every other coach is a teacher from the school.

'We recruit some promising youngsters from other South Auckland schools, maybe three a year. If we are short of a prop or someone like that, we go and find one. We brought two kids from Fiji. We actively go and look in the Polynesian islands, but then most schools do it.' Albeit without Saint Kent's enormous resources.

'These kids always have a choice. They could stay in the islands and play for Fiji, Samoa or Tonga. They might still make it at the highest level, but it's a different world there, so different.'

Cole asks why these boys should not go overseas to ply their trade. Just as he went to the UK to be a schoolmaster. People in business go overseas, he argues. He doesn't see why promising young rugby players from the islands shouldn't be allowed the same chance. If you were a good cricketer, he says, would you not go to a top school in Australia if they offered you a place?

Such youngsters from Polynesia, or from the poorer areas of South Auckland, are usually fifteen or sixteen when they go to a school like Saint Kent's. How do they adapt? 'It can be a struggle,' Cole admitted frankly, 'but they do make friends. I can only think of one who left after his first year. He went back for personal reasons. Others have stayed two or three years and have gone on to be very successful. Many have done seriously well.

'I have heard these arguments about New Zealand Rugby pillaging the islands for talent since 1985 but I don't get it. Besides, most guys who play for the All Blacks now from that background are second- or third-generation.'

Yet Cole does not see a glittering of gold settling on everything he surveys. The numbers playing the game are quite worrying, he says. At Saint Kent's, they have ten or eleven teams playing rugby, but thirty soccer teams. Yet those playing football still go and watch rugby because it's in their DNA, he says.

'The game suited us as a people right from the start because of our colonial nature. We have a class system in New Zealand but we were quite egalitarian. Rugby bound us together. It is something we are good at. The secondary schools have had a lot to do with that in terms of the tribal nature. These kids' desire is to play for the 1st XV, and whenever the game is played it is always seriously competitive. It evolves from the 1st XV competition in Auckland at school level and beyond. Plus, the best sporting brains have evolved into rugby coaches.'

This issue, of opportunity and privilege for the few, goes to the heart of New Zealand education today. But it has far wider importance to the story of New Zealand rugby. For this seemingly endless stream of young local rugby playing talent has been nurtured and developed at no more than ten or fifteen schools in the country. It has created an elite, coveted not just by ambitious, pushy parents but also by those who run the brand known as 'All Blacks rugby'.

Two eminent rugby names agree on this topic. Sir Graham Henry says, emphatically, 'To me, the reason New Zealand is producing top rugby players is because of the key competitions throughout the country and the coaching. Both are so good. School 1st XVs are so good because the competitions they play in are very competitive. There is a huge amount of pride. They all have their own haka. Up to 3,000 people watch those school matches every week, and sometimes you might get up to 10,000 people there. Those competitions, with such good coaching, are producing quality young footballers.

'Our kids start at five to six years old with reduced numbers, so they get more touches of the ball. They play seven- to nine-a-side, which means all the kids handle the ball often. Also, kids of all ages watch the All Blacks and try to emulate what they do. So if the All Blacks are kicking the leather off the ball, they do that. But if they run with the ball in hand, which is their gameplan most of the time, the kids follow that. It means they're learning good habits from a young age.'

Jerome Kaino goes even further. 'I think the school system in New Zealand is the secret, *the* key to the All Blacks' success. It is about the quality of the young players produced at school level. The heart of our game is at the grassroots, but I think it's even earlier where the crucial work is done. For me, the success of our All Blacks side starts a lot earlier than at a school's 1st XV. I think even earlier than Under 12s.'

This trend has been so successful it is underpinning New Zealand's supremacy of the sport worldwide. Of course, other factors are important. After all, even the finest diamonds dug out of the ground require some polishing.

Yet we should dismiss completely the notion that New Zealand's supremacy in the world game has been forged solely on a bunch of eager young men, rough at the edges and with only a modicum of real talent, knocking on a door marked 'All Blacks' and once inside being magically transformed into geniuses.

Instead, it is in a handful of schools in this country where these rugby gems of the future are being discovered, developed and honed. But consider their schedule. As Chiefs and All Blacks back-rower Liam Messam says, a school like Hamilton Boys' High School runs training every morning in preseason before lessons begin. Their players also train three or four other times a week. When he was at school, it was Tuesday and Thursday after school and turn up on Saturday to play. 'It was almost an afterthought,' he said, comparing the two different schedules.

Is this fair? Is being so selective, and especially picking boys from Polynesia, really in the spirit of rugby? Offering a potential life of social progress and financial riches to a hand-picked few and not much else to the rest, is hardly within the spirit of the game. But on the other hand, is such sensitivity warranted? After all, the game today and of the future, the one young people are confronting, is not rugby union as the older generation knew it. The latter must accept it is gone. However, young people seeking a career in this harsh new sporting world should implicitly understand its pitfalls.

What of values, principles, sensitivities and traditions: the characteristics of the old amateur game? In most countries, time has rendered them irrelevant. As Sir Tony O'Reilly, former businessman and a British & Irish Lion in 1955 and 1959, memorably remarked, 'The world is increasingly a vulgar place and rugby football is not about to buck that trend.'

In this new rugby world, the best flourish, while the lesser creatures are spat out by the system. Pieces of eight and pieces of meat . . .

*

According to legend, the Greek philosopher Diogenes was a man of many talents. Indeed, the words of the old sage, born in 404 BC, could have been crafted solely for New Zealand rugby and its devotees. 'The foundation of every State is the education of its youth,' he declared. These words are a perfect fit for rugby in New Zealand. Rather like Wellington and a good storm. What is clear from observing the school system across New Zealand is that at the foundation of every All Blacks side is the education of its young players. From the earliest age right up to senior level, every cog in the educational system is geared towards helping the All Blacks win and retain their dominance over the sport. Whatever the level, the All Blacks are at the front of most people's minds when it comes to educating young rugby players.

Mount Albert Grammar School, alma mater of Sir Bryan Williams, the great former All Blacks wing of the 1970s, is another school in the Auckland suburbs. In 2017, the school named its 1st XV ground the 'B.G. Williams Field'. It was a big occasion. Dignitaries were invited and lunch was prepared. Alas, showers blew across the ground at regular intervals. It was cold and miserable. Still, the great man, with his familiar, slightly loping gait, received the honour in his usual modest and endearing manner. A slightly sheepish grin played on his lips. There was a handshake for everyone. 'Bee Gee', as he is universally known, is a national treasure. If ever you want to know the true meaning of humility, just spend five minutes in his company.

He led the Mount Albert team onto the field, resplendent in their light blue and yellow rugby caps like proud, prancing peacocks. But theirs was not the most striking appearance of the day.

Auckland Grammar, their opponents, had a player called Tua Herman. A tight-head prop, he stood 1.92m (6ft 3ins) tall and had boots about the size of the Jolly Green Giant's. He weighed around 130 kg (20st. 6lbs), and he was only seventeen years old.

One of his teammates, second five-eighth Matt Timoko, also caught the eye. His immense physicality troubled every opponent. Why run around people when you can run through and over them, seemed to be his philosophy.

Timoko, it emerged, was already in the clutches of the New Zealand Warriors, the Auckland-based rugby league club. He still had much to learn, admitted Dave Askew, the school's coach. But his physicality had already attracted the agents. This would be a talent likely lost to union, at least in the early years of his career.

These supremely prepared, powerful athletes had too much fire-power for the Mount Albert team, who fell like slender stalks of corn before the harvester. It was a vivid reminder of the standards that are expected at New Zealand's top rugby schools.

The school system, however, doesn't only produce leviathans. The ball skills on display in the top school teams can be to die for. From kindergarten days, young boys have the importance of perfect ball skills drilled into them. And always, it goes without saying, under constant pressure. These are then practised and honed religiously over all their years of rugby education. It is a relentless process, a mantra, and almost a mania. What is more, it continues even at the level of the All Blacks.

Yet sheer pleasure from playing the game and practising it also remains at the core of the sporting educational process.

As All Blacks hooker Dane Coles says, 'We had fun at school and enjoyed the game. That is a huge factor when you are young. Teachers at school taught us the basics of rugby, from five years old to college years. But I never felt any pressure involved in learning the game. It was natural, something you just wanted to do, being a New Zealander.'

Of all the reasons for New Zealand's rugby supremacy, this is critical, for it is fundamental to the game. If you cannot perform the basics, then your contribution is flawed. It is a creed inculcated by rugby teachers at schools throughout the land. Do the basics, consistently and well.

I saw one example in Christchurch's beautiful Hagley Park one autumn morning. Out for an early-morning run, I watched a group of youngsters practising on one of the playing fields. A whistle blew and their coach brought them together to talk. What followed was revelatory. As the coach began talking, I counted about fifteen rugby balls whizzing backwards and forwards between pairs of boys. They were spinning passes to their mates, first off the left hand, then off the right. Still the coach went on talking, still they spun passes to each other. There was hardly a player in the group not giving and taking a pass as the coach spoke.

I could imagine the reaction of some rugby coaches in other countries. 'Put those bloody balls down and listen,' would be the gist of it. But not here. These kids were listening. But they were also practising and practising their ball skills. The search for technical proficiency, of truly mastering the basics, is ingrained within the young players, and is viewed as fundamental to their performance.

Jerome Kaino reveals the demands that are made. 'At a young age, the basics of this game are pushed a lot harder than how to score a try or anything like that. If you are catching a ball, put your hands up so you can catch it easier, and when passing, make sure you are pointing to where you pass. This big focus on the basics when young is so that it becomes second nature when you grow older.

'You just keep doing it. It's like speaking a language – use it or lose it. Even at our level [All Blacks and a professional franchise], we are drilled in the basics at every session. Just to make sure that when the pressure comes on, the basics are still there, they are ingrained.

'Making the right decision is heavily linked to these ball skills. That is why the basics are driven really hard, whatever we are doing. But every individual is different in how they react and do things under pressure. For us, those basics are the reason why we perform well under pressure.

'It's easy to do all the flash things when you are playing against a lesser team and there is no pressure. The real judgement comes when you are under the hurt locker and everything is on you and you execute what you have practised day in, day out. That is where you get judged and how you determine what has worked, what hasn't.'

A stone's throw from Auckland Grammar, Grant Hansen is these days deputy head of the adjacent St Peter's College.

Hansen – no relation to Steve – spent twenty-seven years with the prestigious Auckland Grammar, fifteen of them as coach of the 1st XV. He also coached New Zealand Secondary Schools for four years. Furthermore, he coached the Black Ferns, the women's national team, at two World Cups. Hansen masterminded one of the great rugby breeding grounds in all New Zealand during his time at Auckland Grammar. But, like all breeding grounds, it attracted the sharks. He regards the threat from agents loitering within a school complex as a dangerous trend.

'Rieko Ioane [a member of the All Blacks' squad for the 2017 Test series against the British & Irish Lions and scorer of eleven tries in his first thirteen Test appearances] will go on to huge things in the game. He went straight from school into the NZ Sevens squad as a seventeen-year-old. These kids are well connected. But it's something that has to be watched. The whole thing is about making them aware of what they could come across. At Auckland Grammar, we didn't allow agents to talk to boys who were still at school. Otherwise we would have had agents going everywhere talking to the kids, and that's scary.'

Even so, last year a couple of seventeen-year-olds at the school told Hansen they had been approached by agents. 'This is the social-media world and it's difficult to contain. I felt we were quite successful at Auckland Grammar. But the danger is the kids listen to these people, commit themselves and sign things they are not ready for. My feeling is, "Leave them alone, they are schoolboys." '

Which is precisely the point outlined by Wayne Smith – that all students need first an education and a potential career path, before focusing on rugby and its possible riches. Smith's reality check that few will ever make it in the professional ranks cuts ever deeper. In those brutal circumstances, everyone looks after himself.

The Auckland Rugby Union, under CEO and ex-All Blacks captain Andy Dalton, talked to young players all the time about the realities of the professional game, including the topic of pushy parents. Dalton confesses he has been 'staggered' by the behaviour of some parents, to what he calls 'the detriment of their poor kids'. Out-of-control children is one thing, but parents losing the plot seems a twenty-first-century problem, whether on the rugby touchline, at the wheel of a car or in a queue for petrol.

'We have had quite a drive here at the Auckland Union about sideline behaviour. There has been some pretty horrendous stuff from that point of view.'

Dane Coles is another who weighs in on the topic, with some insight: 'All those that the parents work so hard on, hardly any of them make it through to the top. Because that is the last thing kids want, that pressure from their parents . . . grown-up people screaming at them. It is embarrassing when your parents are yelling, telling you off because you dropped the ball. That is not encouragement, that's not showing your kids the right way.'

The 'pushy parents' syndrome rears its ugly head in manifest ways. 'Some Polynesian kids go through rugby academies and they don't even know who Michael Jones [the legendary former All Black] was,' says Dalton. 'Now, in the professional era, rugby is seen by some more as a vehicle to get on in life.

'That is a brittle philosophy because of the risk of injuries, especially in the modern game. But there is a really strong drive from some Polynesian people to push their own lads through for the family's benefit. In some cases, unhealthily so. It is a feature of the professional era.'

Life was tough in South Auckland, where Jerome Kaino's family settled when they arrived from American Samoa. It still is, and maybe even more so. Money is limited, crime has endless adherents. Drugs are an insidious danger to dejected minds, shorn of hope and ambition. The downward paths here are as slippery as the ski slopes of Queenstown, in the South Island.

'Who knows where I might have ended up,' Kaino said to me. I thought I detected a trace of despair on his handsome face. 'When I look at my life now and all I have been able to see and experience, I am deeply grateful that I was given that chance by the school. It changed my life.'

You knew he meant it.

So who is to make the counterargument? That it is too selective to single out just the exceptional young rugby players like Jerome Kaino for life-enhancing opportunities when still in their teens? Of course, he is one of many. But it is not just New Zealand teams that have been the beneficiaries of these outstanding young rugby men from the South Pacific. The list of suitors has spread across the world and now invaded the northern hemisphere, too. For example, the French club ASM Clermont Auvergne has established a Nadroga Academy in Fiji, intended to produce future young players for its use.

Hypocrisy being a common condition, we had what might be termed 'the bleating of the blazers', in the northern hemisphere for some years. The rugby establishment raised a hue and cry about what they indelicately called 'the rape and pillage' of Polynesia's finest rugby talent. But the ledger needs to be balanced. Firstly, a diaspora of people southwards from Polynesia to New Zealand has existed for centuries. Traditionally, they have come to a land they see offering greater opportunities than they can glimpse in the islands. That might have been a hanging offence in the eyes of those in charge at Lansdowne Road or Murrayfield. But it only reflected historical trends.

But of late, those voices have been a little muted. Might that possibly be linked to the discovery of certain South African-born rugby players nestling amid the heather of the Scottish glens? Might the protests from Wales have been diluted, even dissipated, by the example of a certain Shane Howarth, Auckland-born and educated at St Peter's College? He was as Kiwi as the Coromandel, and proved it by winning four caps for the All Blacks in 1994. But, post-professionalism in rugby union, after a brief spell in rugby league, Howarth made his way to the northern hemisphere. There, a strenuous tug of war erupted for his services. After all, this was a time when anyone who'd so much as changed planes in New Zealand was regarded as a rugby maestro. In the end, Wales triumphed, the Kiwi qualifying, or so we were assured, on the basis that his grandfather had been born in Wales. Howarth went on to play nineteen times for the Welsh national team between 1998 and 2000. But they were feeding us jungle juice.

Alas, a problematic detail emerged, as Howarth was embroiled in his own version of 'Grandpa-gate' – it turned out that his grandfather had not actually been born in Wales but in New Zealand, and he was disqualified from representing the Welsh. Howarth was about as Welsh as a Bluff oyster.

The chorus of disapproval from the northern hemisphere at New Zealand's acquisition of Polynesian talent quietened somewhat after the Howarth case. Today, of course, all is fair in love and war, not to mention in the world of professional rugby union. Thus, France now selects a succession of Polynesian players on its wings, every one of them, I'm quite certain, fluent in the words of 'La Marseillaise'. Meanwhile, England can find a slot for Nathan Hughes, a Fijian-born player who told the nation of his birth where they could go when they invited him to join their 2015 Rugby World Cup squad. He was too far down the road of qualifying for England through three years of residency to bother with little Fiji's World Cup campaign.

Thank goodness, we should therefore say, for a once gutsy, nuggety little rugby-playing half-back from Argentina named Agustin Pichot. Elected the vice-chairman of the IRB (now World Rugby) in 2015, Pichot pursued such anomalies with the dedication of a bloodhound chasing its prey. Today, his diligence has paid off. Players wishing to abandon the land of their birth for more propitious opportunities with leading rugby-playing nations will have to serve a five-year qualification period from the end of 2020, rather than the current three. Pichot has served the game he loves nobly by driving through such a change and his vision should be applauded. It blows away the sinuous fog of uncertainty that has swirled freely in and around this part of the game for too long. But in New Zealand it is unlikely to make much difference. Second- and third-generation Polynesians are now born in the country and grow up regarding themselves as little Kiwis. Future All Blacks, too, if they're lucky.

These school proving grounds, located in almost all the main centres of the nation, offer an endless stream of young playing talent, ready to be nurtured and developed at a higher level. Forget analogies with factories in terms of production. Machines can break down. This production line never falters. And it produces seriously talented, seriously big teenagers. In his first year at Saint Kent's, Jerome Kaino was part of a pack of school 1st XV forwards whose front row weighed more than the All Blacks' front row at the time, even though the boys were only seventeen. Undeniably, this has been a factor in the enhanced popularity of soccer, a sport increasingly taken up by boys physically intimidated by the size of some opponents in rugby and encouraged by their mothers to steer clear of such physical dangers. After all, few mums like to see their sons' faces rearranged before they reach eighteen. Even the best All Blacks understand this syndrome.

But a word of caution. It is perhaps too easy to become stereo-typical and suggest it is only little white boys who cower in fear at the size of Maori or Pasifika players. Sometimes the opposite is true: compare the size of young men like Scott Barrett to Aaron Smith.

'The island kids are natural athletes,' says Beauden Barrett, present incumbent of the coveted number ten All Blacks' jersey. 'They develop a little bit earlier, too, so they come through school as bigger boys. They are very comfortable putting in those big hits, which is quite challenging when you are facing them, especially for guys like me when I was growing up. There were times when I wondered whether I would be able to cope with that level of physicality. But we were always told we would develop a bit later on. So as long as we were fitter it would be OK.

'That was one reason my mum made me and my brothers run home from school. Five kilometres, barefoot. I was about ten years old and it certainly gave us tough feet. We usually had to do it when we didn't want to. Especially when we didn't want to. But we had to develop other areas where we could compete with these island boys. I think our fitness and skills got us through in the end.

'It also instilled that work ethic, realizing it doesn't come easy and the importance of that level of fitness. You enjoy sport and especially rugby when you are fit, so I guess that was just a base. I was a first five-eighth and I had to be fit.'

The debate over the influence of those mothers who allegedly abhor the physical brutality of modern-day rugby rumbles on in New Zealand society, like a persistent thunderstorm. How many youngsters of school age have actually given up rugby in favour of soccer? Precise numbers do not exist. But to suggest that New Zealand is in danger of running short of suitable candidates for a future All Blacks squad, is to believe the moon is made of blue cheese. As the former Australia national coach Alan Jones says, 'They [the New Zealanders] have been very careful to quarantine any challenge to the game. Now rugby league has got a significant foothold, but they can manage that. Rugby in the schools is very strong.

'By contrast, in Australia, they are now putting up AFL [Australian Football League] goalposts at the GPS [Great Public Schools Association of Queensland], and at the King's School in Sydney they have got more soccer teams than rugby teams.'

Jones is right to underline the continuing strength of the New Zealand school system – it is better than any other in the world. New Zealand's youngsters are not about to fall out of love with rugby union, because their pursuit of the All Blacks jersey is eternal. And so much of that devotion is inculcated in the schools, if not at birth.

As Grant Hansen says, 'There are fifty different sports played at Auckland Grammar School, but the key one is rugby. Especially 1st XV rugby. The kids all want to be a 1st XV player, it's that tradition and culture.

'When New Zealand's All Whites soccer team did well in the early 1980s, reaching the FIFA World Cup Finals in 1982, there was a challenge to rugby's dominance. But at heart, the best athletes are born with a rugby ball.'

Hansen was born in Canterbury, studied Physical Education at the University of Otago and did a year at Teacher Training College. He applied for the job in Auckland aged twenty-one, his first teaching role. He was just an assistant teacher of PE but he found the difference between rugby in Canterbury and Auckland very significant.

'In Canterbury, I hadn't been exposed to the dominance of Polynesian rugby. Here in Auckland, it was weight-restricted. I wasn't aware of the size and skill of these Polynesian boys – they were unbelievable.' But again, we should be careful. The 'narrative' isn't necessarily the reality.

Weight-restricted rugby is now common practice in modern-day Auckland rugby. Under-12 weight restrictions are 49 kg and, for capped players only, 74 kg. At Under-13 level, it is below 55 kg while for capped players, it is extended to 100 kg. Under-9 and Under-10 grades have four weight divisions: Under 35 kg, Under 40 kg, Under 50 kg and Under 60 kg.

Weight restrictions for club rugby are Under 85 kg, or Open. The latter is, of course, the most prestigious competition at club and provincial level.

This was done, says Hansen, to get guys to stay in the game and it has worked. 'Rugby at those levels is a different challenge, it's not based just on size. It kept everyone in the game. We always had about twenty rugby teams at Auckland Grammar. It's still the same, and that's fantastic.'

These days, even someone like Grant Hansen admits many of the boys are massive. His word, not mine. A hundred kilograms is now minimal, he reports.

'I don't know whether it will be enough in the future simply to divide kids at an earlier age by weight-restriction rules. Overall it is just getting a massive game, these boys are big athletes. Their size, strength and power is enormous. When Jonah Lomu emerged, people thought he was a freak. But now there are quite a few almost as big. Nutrition is contributing a lot to this. For me, I want kids to play the game and enjoy it. If they just want to play, then I've done my job. But it is always important with schoolkids to find that balance.

'I think the way we develop all-round young men and the way they present themselves off the field is a credit to this game. It's a pretty good product to look at.'

Nevertheless, size has become a prerequisite of the modern game, whether in international rugby or any level down, as far as schools. It is close to an essential ingredient for playing the game anywhere, and in the Auckland region and also in Wellington, the numbers playing the game who boast immense physicality, given their island background, are very significant. Yet sometimes, one other quality unrelated to size can be like gold dust on the rugby field. Pure speed remains an asset revered in the sport. The man who is a flier on the ground represents lucrative currency.

Take Doug Howlett, one of Auckland Grammar School's most distinguished alumni. Everything Howlett did, according to Grant Hansen, he did 100 per cent. He was so lethal a runner and so committed a player, that he first made the Auckland Grammar School 1st XV in the fourth form, an almost unheard-of achievement. It meant that he played in the school's premier side for four years.

'His intuition to be at the right place at the right time was uncanny,' said Hansen. 'But I would say the two reasons he was successful were that firstly he was well grounded and secondly his family were very supportive.'

Howlett did a whole lot more than dazzle on the rugby field. During the summer, he was a champion runner in athletics. He also studied assiduously to get his grades. Today, Howlett will freely concede that the mentality instilled in him at Auckland Grammar was a critical factor in his eventual success with the All Blacks.

'I learned values there that have helped me throughout my whole life.'

Howlett is referring to aspects both on and off the rugby field. This relates to Wayne Smith's maxim for young men. Carve out a balanced life, look to embrace as many activities as possible and achieve as much as you can in your education to lay down a platform for a future life. Those who have succeeded so spectacularly on New Zealand's rugby fields are in a tiny minority. Many thousands, indeed hundreds of thousands over the years, have ultimately come up short in their quest to reach the top of the rugby pile. We remember just the few, the great names. What of the untold numbers who never even reached their school's 1st XV?

Hansen says Doug Howlett was always a down-to-earth character. Yet he rose to be Head of School and played for the Auckland 1st XV in provincial rugby while still at school. He often returns to Auckland from his base in Limerick, Ireland, where he works for Munster Rugby as Head of Commercial and Marketing, to see old friends and meet up with Hansen. Amusingly, he still calls him 'Mr Hansen'.

'I've just about given up asking him to call me Grant. He just says, "Yes, Mr Hansen."'

They always had to manage Howlett a little. At times, they felt he was giving too much. They reminded him his number-one priority should be his studies. You must get your time management right, they counselled. But he found the balance in the end.

Yet he concedes today that outside factors influenced him and the subtle unspoken pressures became a factor. Such as? 'Well, passing the school's honours board every day and looking up to see the names of about fifty guys who went on to play for the All Blacks. Not a word was spoken but that was an inspiration to be one of them, one day. The history and success they have had as a school is very enticing. I like that history. It was a huge part of Auckland Grammar School. You want to be part of that legacy even before you make the team. You think to yourself, "If I just got a chance." '

He was sixteen or seventeen years old when he began to take rugby really seriously. But he reckons he was probably practising those skills for eight years or more before that.

'It gets serious at school from Under-16 level. For the first time you allow yourself to wonder what you need to do to put on a New Zealand jersey. Until then, I was playing every sport, track and field athletics especially.

'I admire schools' rugby, it is very intense. You are still coming to terms with your emotions, because you are a young lad. You feel nervous and you think to yourself, "Don't mess up here." '

Hansen says that the culture of Auckland Grammar was deep in integrity; the values all those guys learned there helped them in life, he believes. It is the same at almost all the elite educational establishments in New Zealand: schools like Hastings Boys High School, Otago Boys High School, New Plymouth Boys High School, Hamilton Boys High School, and Christ's College and Christchurch Boys High School, the two great Christchurch schools.

No wonder they are able to mine from so rich a seam for future All Blacks.

Yet some concede a sense of uneasiness at a structure so weighted in favour of the elite. Down in the South Island at Christchurch, Reuben Thorne coaches the game at Christ's College. While he enjoys his work, he accepts the argument concerning privilege for a few and poverty for the majority.

'The stronger schools have become stronger. There is more separation between top and bottom than there used to be. Those days, you had traditionally strong schools like Christchurch Boys High School. But kids are getting recognized earlier now because it's all more professional.

'I would have loved the opportunity kids have today through the training, coaching and facilities they enjoy. Who knows what it will produce in the long run?

'It seems we are ending up with a small number of very good schools at the top. But I would like to believe you could still make it from anywhere. I look at guys like Richie McCaw and Dan Carter. Richie came from a tiny country area – he grew up on a farm like me. But both he and Dan had the same amazing work ethic. They ended up at very good schools. But I know others who haven't been to elite schools and they haven't had the same opportunities.'

Thorne, an impressive, quietly spoken man, uses an arresting analogy. 'Now, the modern facilities are more like American Football with its amazing college system. When I played for New Plymouth Boys High School, you didn't get touched by Taranaki – they wouldn't interfere with your development until you had played senior rugby. Now all these provincial unions and academies are really watching high-school kids.

'I am not a huge fan of that. At Christ's College, we have a sponsorship programme and this year we have two kids. The most we'd have would be two per year. They usually come at year ten or eleven, when they're fourteen or fifteen. I don't believe in bringing someone in for their last year, as some schools do. And we don't usually go to the islands to get them. Although we have one Fijian boy who came on a scholarship. He's now in his last year, he's seventeen.'

Does Thorne think his school, in small part, is helping to denude future Fiji teams by their actions?

'It's tricky. This Fijian kid is getting everything paid for. It probably costs Christ's College NZ$50,000 a year. He has been given the opportunity of education at one of the best secondary schools in New Zealand. It must benefit him and his future life. There is definitely an upside for students who come across from the islands. There is no obligation for him to stay in New Zealand when he has finished school.

'He is certainly a very good rugby player at the level he's at now. If he wanted, he could perhaps play Super Rugby. He's a good athlete. But because we are quite a small school, the whole scholarship thing is not a big focus for us. We would prefer to develop kids from here.'

Back in the poorer suburbs of South Auckland, the area Jerome Kaino left behind, you can find struggling schools aplenty. There are few super-equipped school gymnasiums around here, no specialist nutritionists on site to advise on the best foods to eat. Or those to avoid. Here, life is without the frills of the elite. Misbehaviour, in-discipline and educational failure are more common. Fighting your way out of this world takes some doing.

The contrast with mainly Pakeha youngsters being driven to their private, privileged schools by Mummy in the family's 4 × 4, and receiv-ing expert coaching in the sport of their choice, could not be greater. It's also disturbing. It should remind the nation that, like so many other countries, so significant a gap between rich and poor is unacceptable. Devotion to the task of closing it, if not eliminating it altogether, will need to come from all corners of society, rugby included.

A FORTUNATE LIFESTYLE

*Contributions from, among others,
Steve Hansen, Richard Kinley, Gilbert Enoka,
Richie McCaw, Dan Carter, Liam Messam,
Damian McKenzie, Beauden Barrett,
Andy Haden, Grant Hansen.*

'One of my bugbears is that high schools start making kids play one particular sport too young. They say, "You have got to pick a sport." My view is, let them play as many sports as possible because it will enhance them. You should change only when you are ready.'

All Blacks Head Coach Steve Hansen

It is a picture that defines a nation. Rugby boots, a mud-splattered jersey, an old leather ball. Somehow, it is New Zealand personified.

The image seems to speak of an entire country. Yet not every player in this land is under the watchful eye of the national selectors. Not everyone is destined to wear 'the jersey'. Most have not a hope of ever joining that most exclusive of clubs, the All Blacks elite. And yet, in their own small way, vast numbers of people in this land continue to contribute to the image. By the generations' unending passion and support for this game, the people of New Zealand ensure the country's love for a single sport knows no bounds.

Take one club in one tiny community. No one beyond its confines has heard of Mount Somers. Yet it is a club that is the epitome of those who support this game, from cradle to grave . . .

A great cloud of dust filters the shafts of strong, midwinter afternoon sunlight.

Mike Carter is helping corral around 10,000 sheep, massing in the sheep yards outside the shearing shed at Mount Possession Station. Behind the yards stands a scene worthy of an artist's canvas; deep blue winter skies, majestic mountain peaks carpeted in snow.

Tall, lean and tanned, Carter wears his drover's coat with a style that suggests he's just stepped off the set of the movie *Australia*. But then, I don't suppose Nicole Kidman, the film's co-star, has spent much time in sheep-shearing sheds. Especially out here.

Ten shearers on the shearing board, their backs bent double as they try to grip the wriggling animals, apply the cutters to take off excess rear-end wool. Down the years, millions of sheep have waited their turn for shearing in these pens.

These are images that go to the heart of rural life in New Zealand.

But it is a lifestyle in decline. The steady exodus towards the cities began long ago. For a farming life is a tough existence, particularly out in these rugged mountains. Beautiful in summer. Cold and cruel in midwinter.

Unlike club coach Carter, team captain Dale Stanley doesn't work at Mount Possession. But he's just as familiar with the animals. He's a shepherd on another local farm. You can't get a lot more local, in rugby club terms, than Mount Somers. Close to the beautiful Ashburton Gorge in mid-Canterbury farming land, about an hour and a half or so from Christchurch, this small rural club, founded in 1953, is the axis of the local community. Around 90 per cent of their players are local guys. And 100 per cent of the men and women who provide the vital services to keep a small rural club such as this one alive live and work locally.

Most of the players are, like Stanley, shepherds on local farms. They're a throwback to past times in New Zealand rugby circles. Like when Colin Meads and his brother Stan carried a sheep under each arm for the photographers. Or when another ex-All Black farmer Brian Lochore did likewise up in the Wairarapa, in the North Island. They managed the land and dug in fence posts – tough, physically demanding exercise that few enjoyed. But it prepared them for the great game. For these fields, these rolling acres, wherever they were in New Zealand, were the rugby men's gymnasia of their day.

If you want to find the heartbeat of a small community like Mount Somers, then head to the rugby club. Out on the 1st XV pitch on Saturday afternoons, they'll clobber rivals and clamber over foes in that timeless pursuit of victory. Come Saturday evenings, laughter will fill the clubhouse from the voices of up to eighty people, on a good night.

They have one Senior B team, plus Under-6 and Under-7 teams. They're the future. Until 2016, they only had the Seniors, plus the Under 6s. And that was the first time they'd had a junior team for sixteen years. It was always really a one-team club.

So they're pleased to have re-established the Under 6s, and even more so to have added an Under 7s. But then, more than a hundred kids attend the local school, including several from the surrounding farm areas. Which means that a lot of the youngsters are keen to play rugby.

The kids get at least ten games each per season, plus training; the seniors a minimum fourteen games. In 2016, the club was in the local headlines, filling the radio airwaves of the region. Mount Somers' senior team reached the final of their competition and excitement gripped the community. The underdogs up for the cup. The stuff of romantic sporting legend. They played the final on the Ashburton Showgrounds, in the nearest large town to Mount Somers. Stanley remembers, 'We took a special coach with forty supporters over there. It was a great day for our little club, even though we lost to Southern in the final. A day to remember.'

Mount Somers has a healthy squad of around thirty from which to choose a senior squad for a match. They have lots of players but not many front row guys, props or hookers. They can offer work to people, on the farms. But Dale Stanley smiles. 'Really, we are in the middle of nowhere. The closest town is Ashburton, and that is half an hour away.'

But they survive on generous helpings of goodwill. Not least from their sponsors, almost all of whom are inevitably local businesses. Then there are the ladies who make the post-match teas and dinners. Plus the club officials who mow the field, paint the markings for a game and then go out and play, too. At thirty-seven, Dale Stanley is no youngster. But he's got the club at heart. He's played for them as man and boy.

Anyone on a farm in the area looking to employ workers is given strict instructions. Check that they play rugby when you interview them! Since they don't have too many big, heavy forwards (because working on a farm mainly produces lean, fit young men), they try to play a running game. They're one of the smallest teams in the competition but the idea is that they can use their fitness to wear out opponents.

They have their problems of course, and their fears. But they focus more on hope, built around the youngsters currently in the junior teams. 'Their parents have farms and hopefully one day they will take over them,' says Stanley. 'We have to keep the kids interested in the game and in the area.'

You may believe this has absolutely nothing whatsoever to do with the future of professional rugby in New Zealand. It might be a quaint quirk, a relic of a bygone era. That it has no relevance at all to the modern game. Especially not to professional rugby and the All Blacks. But while these farmers and players may be off the grid, they have not escaped the notice of Steve Hansen. For the All Blacks coach has a theory. Hidden away as a six- or seven-year-old in a tiny New Zealand rural community like Mount Somers might well be the next Dan Carter or Richie McCaw. The facts overwhelmingly support his case. New Zealand has produced a stream of outstanding All Blacks with rural roots. Richie McCaw's roots are in Kurow, a small town with a population of just 350 in the Waitaki district of the South Island. McCaw was a farm boy but not a farmer. After school at Otago Boys' High, he was urbanized in Christchurch and became a professional at the Canterbury Crusaders. Dan Carter joined his local club in Southbridge, a small town of just 720 people on the Canterbury Plains, 45 km south-west of Christchurch. Then he, too, joined the Crusaders' franchise. The McKenzie brothers, Damian and Marty, are also among those who have come from a rural background; Seaward Downs, east of Invercargill, in their case. There are many more examples. Indeed, many of the greatest players came from rural communities. From small roots grow great oaks.

Colin Meads was a farm boy then a farmer, before being chosen for the All Blacks from his rural team, King Country. In Meads' era, some All Blacks were selected from rural provincial teams such as South Canterbury and North Otago. Now they are selected from Super Rugby teams in urban areas: Auckland, Hamilton, Wellington, Christchurch and Dunedin. But there is a long history of All Blacks coming from rural parts of the country, something that Steve Hansen is intent on fostering well into the future.

This rural factor explains the preponderance of brothers in the All Blacks ranks throughout history. Many players grew up in isolated rural communities, which meant family rivalry flourished – often, a younger or older brother was the only source of opposition in the backyard. It meant that seven- or eight-year-olds learned the hard way how to compete with tougher older siblings. It bred a resourcefulness and ability to handle extra physicality.

In the 1920s, the Brownlie brothers Cyril (the first player to be sent off in a Test match), Maurice and Laurie all represented the All Blacks, as did the Nicholls brothers Harold, Mark and Ginger in the same era. In more recent times, Colin and Stan Meads played for New Zealand in three decades, the fifties, sixties and seventies. Also in the fifties and sixties the brothers Adrian and Phil Clarke both won caps for the

All Blacks. Don Clarke and his brother Ian both represented New Zealand, and three of their other brothers also played for Waikato.

The Goings, Sid and Ken, and the Brookes, Zinzan and Robin, are others. Father Frank Oliver and his son Anton were both All Blacks captains, and both Ray Dalton and his son Andy were capped. More recently, the Franks brothers, Owen and Ben, have both worn the All Blacks jersey as front row warriors.

In contemporary times, too, the Barrett brothers, Beauden, Scott and Jordie, all became All Blacks after growing up on a farm in Taranaki. The Whitelock brothers, George, Sam and Luke, also became All Blacks after early lives in the rural areas.

This strong, persistent link between the game and the rural community fascinates Steve Hansen. The importance of that rural link is, in his words, 'massive.'

He explained, 'It is proven that kids that come from rural areas develop a far greater range of skills than the kids that play in the cities. There is a major reason for that. In the country, everyone plays in all the teams, whether it is soccer, rugby, basketball or hockey. So as a young child, you are learning and picking up different skills from each sport which you can then bring to one sport later on when you specialize.

'In the cities, what tends to happen because there are so many kids, is that you don't need to go and play soccer as well as rugby. In that case, you are only developing the skills down one channel if you only ever play one sport. Therefore, unless you are exceptional, you don't have the ability to cross-pollinate.

'One of my bugbears is that high schools start making kids play one particular sport too young. They say, "You have got to pick a sport." My view is, let them play as many sports as possible, because it will enhance them. You should change only when you are ready. Some guys have played cricket for New Zealand and rugby for the All Blacks. Jeff Wilson was the last one, and he played basketball as well.

'Look at Andy Leslie back in the 1970s. He played softball, basketball, water polo . . . and when he came on the rugby scene he was seen to be a little different, because he was a very, very skilled player. I think it has been there for the ages. It's not by design in the country – it's by necessity that they need everyone to play everything sport-wise.

'I came from a rural background myself and at school, particularly primary school, we played everything and loved it.

'It would be a big loss to New Zealand rugby if that link with the rural areas were ever broken. If you go through our really great players, a high percentage of them come from a rural background at some point. Because of that, they have been exposed to multiple sports. And a work ethic. If you have got talent and a work ethic, you are going to be hard to stop. Talent alone is not enough.'

Hansen cites the example of soccer players and marvels at their skills in finding space. 'You don't see it, but their heads and eyes are moving all the time. They understand space and their balance is beautiful to run at speed with the ball at their feet.'

Some might believe we are talking of skill sets at complete variance: rugby and soccer. It might seem that the two cannot have a relevance together. But Hansen quashes the suggestion.

'If you pick that guy up and give him a rugby ball and he has got the attributes of a soccer player, but he is playing rugby now; well, he is going to bring that balance with him to play rugby. To me, it is a no-brainer. Some people say a rugby guy is beautifully balanced on his feet. Some of that may be natural but some may be because he was used to playing another game as a youngster.'

Hansen's theory finds an echo with the words of Richard Kinley, General Manager of Otago Rugby in Dunedin. One of Kinley's own children, his sixteen-year-old son, plays five different sports. Badminton has been his latest, but he's also played rugby, basketball, volleyball and cricket, besides other sports with his mates.

Kinley says, 'It's not true that all young kids in New Zealand are constantly playing rugby. It's not like that. Quite often, the players that have been successful who have children themselves find that their kids have a more holistic approach to sport because their parents have tended to encourage them to do other sports.'

And with that multiplicity of sports, youngsters build an overall fitness, not just a one-sided physical power to the detriment of their skills. To get fit for all these sports activities, New Zealand youngsters don't spend every waking moment in a gym unlike some young rugby players in other countries. Richie McCaw regards this as a critical element in the equation. 'It's pretty important in the future that All Blacks are not prepared for Test rugby just in gymnasiums. One of the strengths of New Zealand rugby is that we don't have athletes who are just gym bunnies. To be a good rugby player these days you need to get that balance right. We are in danger sometimes of getting it wrong.

It has been a bit of an Achilles' heel for some of the England players for a while. They have spent a lot of time attempting to be good athletes whereas they aren't good rugby players.

'You want a good rugby player to be a good athlete. But just because you are a good athlete doesn't mean you are a good rugby player. That is one of the great things about New Zealand, where kids grow up throwing the ball around and are able to catch and pass. A guy that is able to do that when it counts, even if he is not the best athlete, is probably more valuable to you than the guy that does alright by the book but can't see what he needs to do. It is being able to get both.'

The Otago Union has thirty-three clubs; twelve are metropolitan and the rest are country clubs. No other sport in the region has that kind of reach. So the rugby club is often the hub of the community. Furthermore, says Kinley, you can transfer skills, if you are a young person.

'We tend to give children a really good platform to build from. Our top sports people are not just good at rugby, they do a bit of everything. That is the foundation a lot of our sports are built on in New Zealand. Kids will have the skills and it's up to the sports to provide a pathway. Rugby has always had the best pathway.'

Kinley says that soccer tried a different approach a few years ago. They brought in a coach from Holland to run a soccer programme in Otago on a European model. They tried to immerse the kids in soccer, winter and summer. But it didn't work, because the youngsters wanted to play other sports.

All Blacks mental-skills coach Gilbert Enoka is another who signs up to this theory. 'If you look at most of our greatest All Blacks, they have come from a small town in New Zealand. Clearly, there is something happening in that sphere. It's whether the local community centres everything around the rugby club. Whether they are spared the distractions of this "instant, everything available culture" that we currently have, where everything is open to them.

'It is many things but that is one of them. Our physical environment shapes you and our social environment conditions you. That is where we have a heck of an advantage.'

However, Hansen's cause célèbre may at least be under pressure since, in many areas, small rural schools have recently closed, in favour of larger centralized schools. Once a rural school closes, the community declines. The school in the community of Orari, near the town of Geraldine in the South Island, is a good example; it was once a three-teacher primary school. Now it is closed.

If small rural schools had an advantage for the production of All Blacks, that scenario is being eroded. Indeed, the modern trend is that parents of boys in provincial towns who show rugby skills are transferring them to big city schools where there is a Super Rugby team close by. Yet Hansen's belief that kids in rural areas learn a greater variety of sports as youngsters, thereby enhancing their ball skills, remains intact.

But there is another element in this equation. Kids growing up in the country tend to demonstrate greater resilience. Like animals in the wild, they are accustomed to the hardships wrought by nature; they understand better the basic aspects of everyday life. It is a simpler, more pragmatic life. But it has different challenges to an urban existence, and many of them are character-forming. Kids growing up on farms also learn early the need for a strong work ethic. There are always more jobs to be done, and you're seldom finished for the day.

They think for themselves more; there is a greater element of self-entertainment. Youngsters in cities have a far broader range of ready-made entertainments available at their doorstep. Few make their own. Life in the cities is softer and the people are more insular.

Making your own entertainment not only makes people tougher and more resilient. Perhaps more social interaction such as learning how to fix things, make things and grow things, produces not just a more rounded person but also someone capable of leading and inspiring others. Then there is the element of adversity, omnipresent in some form in rural life, and the need to come together, stay calm and focused but to work with others to confront it. This creates the element of gathering others around to confront challenges which is the kernel of a sports unit, a team. What is more, these lessons, inculcated at an early stage, remain in the subconscious for life – they are highly prized attributes to take onto the field of sporting contest.

Few men have demonstrated these attributes more vividly than All Blacks captain Richie McCaw in the 2011 Rugby World Cup Final. Expected to stroll to victory against the erratic French, New Zealand were struggling on two counts that night in Auckland: firstly, to find their best form and secondly, to subdue the nerves and doubts that came with the fact that they had not won a World Cup for twenty-four years. McCaw led by example, steering them home to an 8–7 win, the narrowest of victories. His physical performance was brave and determined; his hand, on the pulse of the team, was strong and never wavered. It was the quintessential illustration of inspirational captaincy.

*

In the late summer of 2017, New Zealand seemed almost like a country at war. Not on some foreign battlefield, but against its oldest foe. Nature. In Christchurch, scene of the devastating 2011 earthquake in which 185 people lost their lives, ruined buildings still half stood among the wreckage. Driving on the uneven roads, filled-in fissures from the earthquake that lifted tarmac all over the city proliferated. It was like riding in a rodeo.

Up the South Island's east coast, workers battled to repair the extensive damage from the Kaikoura earthquake of 2016 in which two people died. In that region, the earth had shifted by up to ten metres on some fault lines, terrifying residents and killing animals.

Travellers heading north out of Christchurch for Picton, gateway to the North Island by ferry, had to undertake a tortuous diversion through the mountains of the Lewis Pass. A straightforward four-hour journey up the east coast became a long and tiring seven-hour trek along narrow, twisting mountain and valley roads.

At frequent intervals on that road in all weather conditions, men and women of the New Zealand Transport Agency laboured to repair roads, arrest landslips and improve conditions ahead of winter's onslaught. When the great battle of Man versus Nature would commence all over again . . .

For the human combatants, it is a wearying, character-defining process, yet it defines the people of this nation. In adversity, whether it be on or off the rugby field, they come together to confront a multitude of problems. And they do it with a unique Kiwi resolve.

In Christchurch in 2017, the scars from a series of major fires in the Port Hills on the fringe of the city once known as the Oxford of the southern hemisphere, remained visible as autumn slipped into winter. There was freshly disturbed, scorched earth where helicopter pilot Steve Askin had crashed while fighting the blazes.

One of his fellow airmen, Richie McCaw, had stood impassive at his funeral. In New Zealand they are used to heartbreak and tragedy, so often the consequence of nature's rage. It is this kind of stoicism that is a reminder of the stories of the first settlers and how adversity shaped their character and that of the nation in its earliest years.

'During the Christchurch earthquake in 2011, you might have lost a bit of faith watching TV about what people are like these days,' said McCaw. 'Actually, you saw a good side of the human spirit. People just getting on, not complaining. From what I saw during and after the earthquakes, it restored your faith in what humans do for each other.

'We [he and his mates at Christchurch Helicopters Company] had a lot to do with Kaikoura [and the 2016 earthquake there], helping people. Being able to do that, you see people shrug their shoulders, think to themselves, "This is life, just get on with it."

'When you take a step back and see some of the things like that . . . people losing their houses in the floods in Edgecumbe, in the Bay of Plenty [in 2017] . . . it was a dreadful mess, yet most people just said, "Well, where do I start cleaning up?" By and large, people accept what it is and get on with it.'

Meanwhile in the capital Wellington, now thought to be the most vulnerable of New Zealand's cities owing to its precarious position between the Australian and Pacific fault lines, planners were assiduously preparing as best they could for a scenario they feared might split the capital into seven islands. They estimated it would take an earthquake smaller than the one that hit Kaikoura (which damaged some buildings in Wellington itself) to cut off suburbs of the city and wreck water, sewage, roads and other services.

As the British & Irish Lions squad prepared for their ten-match tour of the country in June and July 2017, plans had been drawn up by New Zealand Rugby for implementing a disaster action programme in the event of an earthquake in any of the major venues on the Lions' schedule.

Long hours had been spent toiling over deciding alternative venues, planning how thousands of supporters could be moved quickly and safely to the new location and whether accommodation demands could be met. Whatever challenges other rugby nations face day-to-day, they are hard to compare with this continual struggle with the forces of nature.

To the visitor to New Zealand, it becomes increasingly clear that within this ongoing geographical challenge lies one of the seeds of the nation's enduring prowess on a rugby field. The ability to withstand adversity, to fight it and conquer it. New Zealanders are long versed in this quality; they have been toughened, both mentally and physically, by the process, which can be traced back to the earliest settlers, a people forced to confront adversity at its harshest. The DNA strain may now be over 150 years old. Yet it resonates continually in these people through their endurance, determination and commitment to a cause. Fortitude is a consistent feature in the history of the country and their national rugby team. It underpins them and all they seek to do, just as it bolstered those first settlers.

Furthermore, they understand and remember the lessons that New Zealand's short history has taught them. Nothing worthwhile can be achieved without toil and there is no substitute for effort. If they didn't grasp it early in their youth, those who helped mastermind their respective paths to the top quickly reminded them of it. Remember, too, that many coaches in New Zealand rugby are former school-teachers, used to inculcating values such as discipline, dedication and organization within their charges.

*

Early in the New Year of 2017, somewhere out in the bitingly cold suburbs of Paris, an electronic entrance gate whirrs into action. It allows me access to the state-of-the-art training headquarters of the Racing 92 rugby club, French club champions the previous season. Amid the Samoans, Fijians, Tongans, Georgians and Argentinians, is arguably the rugby world's most-celebrated incumbent of a number ten jersey, Dan Carter. I have essentially come here to ask him one simple question. It is the core issue which this book addresses – how a country of 4.8 million people conquered an entire world sport?

Carter smiles broadly at the question.

'It is funny, because people go all over the world looking in every way at every angle to see if they can find the secret of New Zealand's success.'

Carter's belief is anathema to those who love a good fairy tale. Everyone, he suggests, has been chasing the end of a brilliantly illuminated rainbow. But when they finally got there, they found there was no single pot of gold. The All Blacks have not enjoyed such sustained supremacy on the world stage over such a long period for only one reason. However, the reality is, the All Blacks do have secrets.

There are critical factors why they dominate their sport and remain a benchmark for every other nation that plays the game.

What you can discover are the many explanations for this unrivalled supremacy. One sporting foe of the All Blacks, former Australia coach Bob Dwyer, has said of their dominance, 'They are the most insular and secretive rugby nation in the world. They are, also, unbelievably good; maybe the most successful sporting team ever.'

Sports coaches such as Dwyer are pragmatic men. They do not throw superlatives around like confetti. Carter calls it 'a combination of elements'. He talks, too, of love and passion for the sport.

'They say it's in our DNA as a New Zealander, that rugby drive and that desire. You might be born with it but if not, you'll soon get involved in it because all your friends are. It's what they're doing at lunchtime and after school; they're playing or watching rugby, or they're with a rugby ball in some way or another.

'If you go out to the rural parts of New Zealand where I grew up, it's still as strong as ever. You see kids running around, but when I was at school and even beforehand, there were probably even more. Those people are still involved and they'll be doing what they can to make sure children of today get outside, get involved, have a rugby ball.

'It's a possibility this will be lost one day with technology. But I think that the history the All Blacks has created is something so unique and it's been going on for so long, that it won't be lost in the short-term. There is something so powerful about it, I hope it will continue for generations.'

Steve Hansen concurs with the view that the character of the original New Zealanders still shows in the young rugby men of the present day. 'Yes, I think so because of who we are as a nation and we are well moulded. We are stoic as a people.

'The DNA strand definitely still exists. It's like any DNA, it gets modified. But it is still in there and what we don't want to do is lose that part of it that says, "I can fix this myself, I will do this." This factor translates into rugby teams and the decision-making process on the field.

'If you add on a bit that says, "I could do with a hand here," it won't be a bad DNA. Asking for help is not a sign of weakness, it's actually a sign of strength. It's better to say, "I can do this, but I am struggling and could do with some help."'

Thus, New Zealand's rugby men enter any sporting field armed with certain natural advantages. Young New Zealand players bring a different perspective to the game. They have realities in their lives unknown by their counterparts in most other nations. Many of these aspects have been shrewdly inserted by those who coach them. Tall poppies are liable to be scythed down at the first showing. Young men arriving for training wearing expensive watches or designer clothing will be quickly cut down to size. It is not the New Zealand way to flaunt wealth and success. It is not just rugby that comes down on such opulence like a ton of bricks in this country. The people in general have an inbuilt distaste for such acts of extravagance.

And then, after all this, there are the other ingredients. Take perhaps the simplest of all. The air. Hansen is convinced that simple fresh air is one of the elements in the production of so many healthy, talented young sportsmen and women in his nation.

'We are unbelievably lucky in the corner of the world where we grow up. Young people live a largely outdoor lifestyle, whatever sport they may happen to pursue. They breathe air that is clear, fresh and healthy. You can't say that in a lot of places in the world.

'I don't think there is any doubt that this contributes to the long-term health and vitality of our young people. Spending so much time outdoors in this quality air is a great advantage. Some people might dismiss this as a factor, but they shouldn't.'

As Abraham Lincoln said, 'In the end, it's not the years in your life that count. It's the life in your years.'

Damian McKenzie is a will-o'-the-wisp young rugby player. With impish good looks and shock of tousled hair, he'd be an absolute natural for the part of the Artful Dodger in *Oliver Twist*. Lean to the point of being skinny, McKenzie stands at just 5ft 9ins (1.73m) tall and weighs 81 kg (12st. 10lbs), even when covered in mud. At times on the field, when surrounded by enormous opponents, his prospects look as bright as a mackerel's in a shark-filled sea. Yet McKenzie was one of the standout players of the 2017 Super Rugby season. Playing at full-back for the Chiefs, he exploded like a firework; spinning off in one direction, soaring in another and dazzling audiences. He was described as one of the most exciting rugby players in the southern hemisphere. Even allowing for the hyperbole of such a sweeping generalization, there was no doubting McKenzie's talent. His lightning pace was perfectly suited to Super Rugby.

His then Chiefs teammate Liam Messam said of him, 'He is a

phenomenon, he's like a rubber ball. He is a brave kid, and he has no fear. I love his mindset on attack. He is willing to give it a crack from anywhere and it looks like he is enjoying his football. That is the main thing. Most young guys don't want to make mistakes. But he is willing to do that, to have a go and give it a real crack. Nine times out of ten, he comes out on top, too.'

So where did McKenzie learn those philosophies?

'Growing up, my dad always played rugby. He played full-back for the New Zealand Emerging Players. He played for the Woodlands Rugby Club in the Southland region, about twenty minutes north of Invercargill. Mum played hockey. Dad wasn't lightning quick, but he was quick enough. I guess that's where I get a little of my speed from.

'We lived on my parents' dairy farm in a small community called Seaward Downs. As a kid it was great being brought up in a rural life. You have got a lot of space whatever you want to do. My brother Marty and I loved playing rugby. We had friends and cousins to play with, too. We played in the backyard and it was a healthy lifestyle. Out in the country, you did a lot of country things, like fishing, shooting. There is a lot of freedom out there.

'It wasn't an enormous yard but it had quite a big lawn. Dad put up some wooden rugby posts out in the paddock. Rugby in that paddock was pretty competitive. My brother is three years older than me and, with your brother, you're trying to bring the best out of each other. You don't hold much back. I'd started playing when I was five in primary school, but we were playing in the backyard even before that.

'In runarounds like that, you learn to take chances. I think taking a risk is part of the New Zealand mentality. Players with skill sets like to make something from nothing. One thing is certain. You don't want to come off the field saying, "I could have done this or that." So it's about backing yourself.'

Alas, it wasn't always so positive from McKenzie's father's point of view. 'The grass started to grow quite long in our paddock and one day, my brother and I mowed a few strips to cut it down and play on. But unknown to us, the dairy farmers were short of grass at that time and when Dad saw us mowing the paddock, he was very unhappy! We were cutting valuable grass for the animals.'

Whether it's amid a rural landscape or in a bigger city, youngsters in this country get out there with a ball. It is endemic to the whole nation. But sometimes these rugby-mad youngsters just go too far. Former All Blacks captain Andy Dalton remembers a time as a seven-year-old when he found a nice leather ball somewhere at home, took it outside and started kicking it around the garden.

What Andy didn't realize was that the ball had been personally signed for his dad Ray by several members of the 1949 Springboks. Ray had been All Blacks vice-captain on that tour.

'I was in real trouble that day,' he remembered. 'I didn't notice it was a signed ball. As I kicked it all around the lawn, those precious signatures were gradually being rubbed off.' But every cloud has a silver lining as far as rugby-mad kids go. Andy Haden, who played forty-one Tests out of 117 matches for the All Blacks between 1972 and 1985, pinpoints another factor in the development of these youngsters. He talks of the momentum kids get out of the environment in which they have grown up. 'They are reminded constantly, every moment of the day, of the importance of playing well and winning. It is not just public pressure but words written in newspapers, it's the bloke at the gas station that says, "Play well on Saturday and win."

'That is right through the whole of society, that's the public. They are all so knowledgeable and they all apply that pressure in their own way. Kids growing up are living with it constantly and that keeps them focused, it drives them.

'This happens here far more than in any other country in the world. The players overseas don't get that momentum out of the public. But it's a good pressure. It's subtle, genuine and very knowledgeable.'

If we are sifting evidence to present a case for New Zealand rugby's dominance, this element would be a key exhibit.

On a dairy farm in Pungarehu in the coastal Taranaki region in the mid- to late 1990s, five eager youngsters, Kane, Beauden, Scott, Blake and Jordie Barrett, would be found out in their backyard, scrapping and competing for the ball the moment they were big enough to hold it. They had a stern taskmaster in their dad Kevin, a lock forward in his day who played 167 games for Taranaki. His reputation preceded him in New Zealand rugby. Even the toughest of the tough, the legendary late All Blacks lock Colin Meads, allegedly called Barrett Senior 'one of the dirtiest blokes who ever played rugby'. Some praise that from the famous 'Pinetree'!

What an extraordinary contribution the Barrett family makes to rugby in New Zealand. Beauden pinpoints the system for the reasons:

'It's amazing the pathways for a young rugby player growing up in New Zealand. It's all in front of you if you really work hard, put your mind to it and believe in yourself. Whether it is provincial rep sides, franchise reps or national reps, it's all in front of you if you make those teams and you work hard.

'We acquire the basic skills at a very young age. It starts with your dad passing you a ball when you are five years old, or even less. You are also watching your heroes play on TV, watching them and seeing how they do it. Then you take those lessons out into the backyard and do it with your mates.

'I had my brothers around, so it was pretty competitive. We used to pack down scrums, we used to be in a scrum, I would feed the scrum . . . we did everything. We got used to doing those skills because you never really know what position you are going to end up in or how your body may develop. We loved it and I guess that's what most Kiwi boys do growing up.

'In the country, there isn't a whole lot more to do except play sport. When you do it over a period of several years you are really going to develop your balls skills.'

Grant Hansen, deputy head at St Peter's College in Auckland, links the work ethic Beauden Barrett identifies with his namesake's belief that playing many different sports is a huge advantage to young New Zealanders. He preaches other values, too.

'When I coach a team, the first thing I talk about is the culture and pride of wearing that jersey. When I took the New Zealand Secondary Schools, for most of them it was their first national jersey and they would do anything to wear it.

'But in too many cases today, expectation is paramount. A lot of kids put their hands out rather than put their hands up. That is youth today. They ask, "What are you going to give me? What am I going to get out of it?" Too many of them don't understand the commitment required to be successful. A former player like Grant Fox would spend all day kicking goals. But nowadays some kids just expect to rock up on Saturdays.'

Or at least, those destined never to scale the highest peaks of the game sometimes do. To have such an outlook at a young age is a serious impediment to future progress in the sport, particularly in New

Zealand. As Grant Hansen says, 'It is never a coincidence that the kids who did go on to succeed worked incredibly hard. They would be the first ones at training and the last ones to leave. They would automatically adopt the fitness tests. What we try to do is bring back these role models that boys can relate to.'

Grant Hansen underlines Wayne Smith's point about the slim margins for those seeking a future in the professional sport:

'Modern-day school-kids with ambitions in sport need to be very well educated about the numbers that make it in a professional game. It is minimal. But if they are to be successful, the chances are they need the ability to be an all-rounder and play other sports. For example, most successful New Zealand Olympians played other sports. They did everything, summer and winter sports. Then they were successful.'

Nevertheless, New Zealand is a land like no other when it comes to devotion to rugby football. On a drizzly autumn night in 2017, I sat at a rugby stadium in the suburbs of Christchurch and engaged in conversation with a young mother as she attempted to keep two highly inquisitive small children in check.

One of them, a little girl named Alecia, was just thirteen months old and still a touch unsteady on her feet. The proud mum smiled at her tiny daughter. 'We're going to get her going with the junior girls as soon as we can. She already loves holding a little rugby ball.'

You could certainly say young Alecia had plenty of time on her side to master the arts of this game. As to whether she adopts the game permanently in the future, who knows? But one thing is certain about rugby in New Zealand. They start them young there.

5

THE HAKA: AN EXPRESSION OF IDENTITY

*Contributions from, among others,
Aaron Smith, Kieran Read, Kees Meeuws,
Sir Colin Meads, John Eales, Craig Dowd,
Gilbert Enoka, Sir John Key,
Nick Farr-Jones, Wayne Smith.*

'It has lost its *mana*. It has become a showpiece. They should do it at certain Test matches but not all. It was good a few years ago when they had a choice. But now they play fourteen Test matches a year and that's too much, as far as the haka is concerned. We should either have it at home or just away from home, like it used to be. Not both.'

Former All Blacks prop Kees Meeuws

There is something else that young people start watching and understanding at a very early age in New Zealand. The haka.

As an expression of national identity, the haka supersedes all else. It defines the nation and is a solid plank in New Zealand's ancestry. Some said it was first seen on an international rugby ground in 1888 when performed by the 'New Zealand Natives' touring party. But it is almost certain that it had by that point already been performed on New Zealand fields, in matches involving Maori teams.

Of course, it goes back deep into the mists and legends of early Maori history. It is an ancient posture dance, intrinsically a challenge from a tribe of one area to another. In earliest times, the local tribe would perform their haka, followed by the visiting tribe. Afterwards came speeches, followed by the pressing of noses.

'Ka Mate' is the most famous haka, with its story about the power of female sexuality. Haka were traditionally used to prepare a war party for battle. In one New Zealand household, there was a time when everything went silent. Breathing slowed and then all but stopped. A frisson of excitement crackled around the room, like an electric current. Anticipation matched the heights of emotion. The All Blacks were about to perform the haka.

He was only three or four years old when he first saw it. The memory is dim, hazy. But it's still there. Aaron Smith never forgot the first time he witnessed it. He was at home in Feilding, near Palmerston North. His parents liked to have a party when the All Blacks played in a home Test match.

'If you are a rugby family,' said the All Blacks half-back, 'it's one of those special moments. It's the time the TV gets turned right up and everyone goes quiet, it stops the party. More people might watch the haka than the actual game. All the men will watch the rugby but not all the women. But both will watch the haka.'

It is an electrifying spectacle. Eyes bulge, biceps are bashed. Tongues dart and tease; lips pout, faces contort. Neck muscles throb. Legs driven by bulging thighs stamp on the turf, as if to denote the team's defence of its territory. Hands quiver, fingers point or are drawn across throats. It is one of the great defining images of this land, a visual expression of nationhood.

By the time he was six, Aaron Smith was part of it. It was part of him, too. He knew how to do it by the time of the 1995 Rugby World Cup in South Africa. There he was, in front of the television at home. Whooping and hollering. Facial expressions to match.

'I remember doing it before that famous semi-final [against England] in the small hours of the morning. We were allowed up to see it, it was so important. A couple of friends were doing it with me. I don't know whether we were doing it right but we were up there doing all the actions! It was pretty crazy. As a kid, it fires your imagination. It is a bit of an out-of-body experience.'

It was also the match where Jonah Lomu marched all over England.

When he was a little older, Smith used to spend time in the Hawke's Bay region. There, he remembers seeing haka done at Tangi (funerals). He thinks carefully when I ask him to put into words exactly what it means to someone of his background.

'It is our one identity thing that only we have as a rugby nation that nobody else has, outside the Pacific. I think you can see the passion of what the haka means to us. It's a war dance and it's setting a challenge to the other team. We are saying, "We are here to win." It says, "This is what it means to us." We have been doing it for a hundred-and-something years. So we want to be a member of that culture and that is why we are very lucky we are still allowed to do it.

'The haka is not for Maori alone. It's for everyone in our country. It's a part of who we are. Our forefathers did it at the start, and then the Pakeha and Pasifika came into it later. They all live here, they're all part of it. The way we play rugby expresses ourselves and the haka is a very expressive thing. We show how we love the game by the way we play it from being young kids. All those different cultures add different things.'

He brings two of those cultures into play, for his dad is Pakeha, his mum Maori. Aaron Smith is proud and comfortable with the different qualities both have handed down.

The 'Ka Mate' haka is almost 140 years old, first composed by Te Rauparaha, Ngāti Toa Rangatira. The other haka are even older than 'Ka Mate', but it's doubtful it has ever been so widely talked about or debated. Is it fair? Shouldn't the opposition get to perform their own dance after the haka? It excites opinions almost like nothing else in New Zealand and world rugby circles. Former All Blacks first five-eighth Andrew Mehrtens has called it 'too commercialized'. Ex-England half-back Matt Dawson reckons it has lost its mystique.

Another former All Black, prop forward Kees Meeuws, says, 'It has lost its *mana*. It has become a showpiece. They should do it at certain Test matches but not all. It was good a few years ago when they had a choice. But now they play fourteen Test matches a year and that's too much as far as the haka is concerned. We should either have it at home or just away from home, like it used to be. Not both.'

A strange phenomenon, this. It affects all sorts of people in a variety of ways. Some are enraged, some supportive, some intrigued, some ambivalent. Australian David Campese used to take himself off to a corner of the field, chip a ball into the air and catch it while the All Blacks were performing it. Former Wallaby captain John Eales turned his back on it once and has regretted doing so ever since. Former South African wing Ashwin Willemse sensed he'd cracked it as far as staring down his opponent during a haka: 'I'd been very excited about the game because in my mind, a match against the New Zealand All Blacks was my first "official" Test match. I would not have felt complete, a true Springbok, if I hadn't played the All Blacks. It was the ultimate thing to do; face the haka and play them in a Test.

'During the haka, I had watched my opposite number Doug Howlett intently. Then he did something that made me think he was scared. Just before the end of the haka, he put his head down and looked away. I told myself that it meant I'd won and that he was either afraid or not prepared to face the challenge, as I was. I drew strength from that.'

Afterwards, it's probably true to say Howlett drew strength from the final score. He scored two tries and New Zealand won, 52–16.

'It was clear I was completely deluded for having held such a belief,' grinned the ex-Springbok.

Whatever its form and whatever the occasion, there is no doubt the haka raises hackles. Take Willie Anderson, bastion of Northern Ireland men, proud Ireland international rugby man, possessor of a bone-crushing handshake and focus of a few memorable moments in Irish rugby history. At Lansdowne Road, Dublin in 1989 against New Zealand, Ireland captain Anderson lined up his men on the halfway line to face the haka. They linked arms and were dragged ever closer to the dancing, gesticulating New Zealanders by Anderson, until they were almost in the All Blacks' faces. But it didn't come close to unsettling the All Blacks when the game started. They won 23–6.

In 2008, the Welsh let the haka pass and then mucked about for a few minutes, refusing to line up for the kick-off. They presumably wanted to let the New Zealanders' adrenaline drain away. It must have worked . . . to a degree. Wales had lost their two previous encounters with the All Blacks 3–41 and 10–45. So their 9–29 defeat this time was an improvement. Perhaps . . .

Former Wallaby coach John Connolly says that, in the old days, it was like 'who cares' when the haka was performed. 'They waved their arms around a bit but it was all pretty insipid. But now they have turned it around to mean something. It has become a real symbol of discipline and determination in the team. They have put values around the haka which they transfer to their rugby. They have been very clever in that respect.'

Even so, Connolly doubts they gain an intrinsic advantage from it. 'It's just part of the theatre. In fact, a few of them down the years have clearly psyched themselves up so much that they've let the adrenaline get out of control and it has ruined their start to the game. You have to control yourself to play Test footy. But some Australians down the years didn't understand that the haka was a challenge. It was a mistake not to stand to it and accept the challenge.'

Nick Farr-Jones was one who had to face them down. For the 1991 Australia World Cup winning captain, New Zealand was always the team to beat. But for much of his time as a Wallaby, Farr-Jones says Australian teams didn't face the haka. They would stand maybe sixty metres away, he remembers. It was only when the combative David Codey was chosen as Australia captain, for the only time, that the Wallabies accepted their new captain's demand that they face the haka and eyeball the All Blacks.

Farr-Jones said, 'Personally, I loved standing up to the haka. Why? Because it's such a great nation of 4.8 million people and respect is a really important thing. So rather than be sixty metres away and turn your back, to get up there and eyeball them sent a sign of respect to their nation.

'Hopefully, you are sending a second message. Like, guys we respect you, but you are going to have to play bloody well to beat us today. We are not going to roll over. You want to send back that second challenge.'

We started the conversation in the great ex-Wallaby's office, forty-two floors up in a tower block overlooking Circular Quay and Sydney Harbour. But, as you do with Aussies, we soon adjourned. To a bar on the street outside.

Farr-Jones went on, 'I enjoyed the arrowhead which the French did when they faced the haka [in 2011]. They got fined for it, stupidly, by the International Rugby Board, but they were sending back their own message. They were confronting it. I think it is a wonderful, great sporting tradition and I think people love it. I love watching the faces of the opposition because you know if they are up for the challenge or not. You get a sense of whether the guys are saying, "Bring this on," or whether they are thinking, "Shit, get me out of here."'

There is no doubt that the haka is a bold, vibrant symbol of national identity like no other. But there have been, and continue to be, those in New Zealand who question it.

A few months before he died in 2017, Sir Colin Meads said of it, 'We never did the haka in New Zealand, only overseas. But they put so much emphasis on the haka nowadays. They have two or three different versions. They even practise it. Our hakas were pretty rough. Mind you, you would be fined at the players' court session if you jumped out of sync with the others. But it has now become too big.

'They haka everything now. Some dignitary or sports person turns up or a film star at the airport and they haka them. It is ridiculous. I think it has become a celebrity thing. All the schools practise it. It should be done before games but as a form of respect to the Maori. We were haka-ed out there for a while and still are.'

John Eales is as respected a former player as any exists in world rugby. However, there was a time when most of New Zealand would cheerfully have strung him up from the nearest lamp post for dishonouring the haka. Eales understands he got it wrong. 'It was my first Test as captain and we didn't face the haka. I'd think that was disgraceful now. But I didn't understand it then. I suppose we were trying to detract from its power. But we ended up dissipating our own skills. We lost that match in Wellington 43–6. That is still the biggest losing margin ever by a Wallaby team against anyone. I always felt bad about what happened before that Test.'

But does it give the All Blacks an advantage? Eales believes it gives them a way to connect as a team. 'And any team that connects is a dangerous outfit. But physically I don't think it gives them an advantage.'

Eales felt so mortified by that experience, that it festered. Years later, in 2017, he flew to Auckland with a film crew to make a television programme about his experience. He wanted to explore the ways and means of the haka. It was something of a cathartic exercise. He did it, he now says, because he was looking for an insight into it. But as he began to do interviews and make the film, he came to realize that the real power of it lay not so much in the dance but in the way it connects with individuals and with the team. Perhaps also with the broader population of rugby for it is about their land.

'That really deep connection is what I took out of it. The "Ka Mate" haka talks of a warrior hiding from his enemies: "I am going to die, I am going to live." I reckon that is so powerful because there is this guy having a battle with himself about life. He is going through this internal conflict. He is hiding.

'He is saying, "I take one step and then another." It is a tale of survival against the odds. So when they do this they are connecting with their people, it is the battle that is coming. But this is an internal battle.'

Eales denies that New Zealand are more passionate than other nations. But he does concede one point. 'Someone playing for the All Blacks would know that losing has greater consequences for them.' More so than anyone else in the world, is the message.

Aaron Smith listens to the counter arguments, expressed by people like Meads. Outside people, he says, only see one haka but in New Zealand every town has one. 'Every tribe has a haka, every city has one. But the purity of the main two that the All Blacks do is pure in the sense that the way we do it we try to make sure we get the actions and words right and know the meaning of each action. All the actions were written for a meaning and purpose.

'I guess it can be seen a bit like that [Meads' criticism], but everyone is different. A lot of people love haka and I am a fan of them, but I don't think they should be done for any old thing. I don't agree with that.'

Smith remembers some school 1st XV haka that would go on for five or six minutes. There were big stand-offs; people wouldn't agree to be the first to break the spell. Then, one day, when he had become a regular in the national set-up, the All Blacks made him an offer he couldn't refuse. He was invited to lead the haka. Except that he could, and he did. 'I was first asked in 2013. There were a few injuries, and guys like Mealamu and Messam weren't there. But at the time I said no. I felt like I hadn't played enough games and I didn't yet have the respect to do it. I didn't want to do it without that respect. I didn't regret turning it down. Although I remember being at that game and thinking, "I could have led this."

'But I was glad that, when I had played some games, got more *mana* in the time that I became a leader, so that when I led the haka and spoke, it was with more *mana*. When I spoke, they moved and reacted well, which is important in the haka. There wasn't any feeling by then like, "This young guy has no idea."'

Mana is the key to a haka, according to Smith. Whoever leads it has usually been chief or head man. Richie McCaw led it on several occasions, but not all. *Mana* is an intrinsic part of the Maori culture and is hard-earned.

When they asked him again, Smith says he jumped at the chance. But he did a lot of homework on it behind the scenes. 'I practised in the shower, stuff like that. You have got to really nail it. I did research by watching people leading it who had inspired me, like Tana Umaga. I also looked at others who had led it, like Liam Messam. He is a great one to watch.'

Smith, who was described as 'the best rugby player in the world' by the British & Irish Lions coach Warren Gatland before the start of their 2017 tour, concedes that he gets a huge adrenaline rush from participating in the haka. His nerves are always right on edge anyway. 'But when you do the haka you get those butterflies coming, it is special. Before you do it, your hands are really going, the hairs on the back of your neck are standing up. That is your body telling you, this is a big thing.'

But with the role of haka leader comes responsibility. *Mana* is all. Aaron Smith's was damaged by an incident he got himself into with a young lady at Christchurch Airport in 2016. It disappointed his coaches, his teammates and himself.

Subsequent to his indiscretion, his role as haka leader was raised. 'I was one of the first to say, I should not be doing it, and that is what happened. It's a part of the *mana*, isn't it? You lose *mana* when you do things like that. T.J. Perenara took over and I was happy for him to do that because of the *mana* I had lost from what I had done.'

Even the best can stumble and fall. And even Aaron Smith admits he damaged his aura. So how does All Blacks coach Steve Hansen, a man who constantly drums into his players the need to be humble and respect culture and convention, handle those who slip from a lofty height?

'You have got to have character. You don't have to be perfect but a player has got to have a character that has got the ability to stand up to scrutiny and the pressure that comes from being an All Black. If his character defaults don't allow him to do that, then he is only going to take us somewhere where we don't honour, respect or enhance the legacy of this great team.

'They are young men, so some of them are going to make mistakes. That's not a problem. The problem is how quickly they learn from it, and the choices they make after that are most important. The responsibility of a coach is to create an environment where those guys can grow and become better people and better rugby players.'

Gilbert Enoka's philosophy on the matter is devoid of emotion. The All Blacks Leadership Manager said the team embrace accountability and personal responsibility. If someone does something that is not right for the team or for rugby, as Aaron Smith did, then they have to face the consequences:

'What Aaron did was so severe for himself personally that it shattered him hugely. But in the end, we see them as human beings, so our first priority is to keep them intact and make sure that extends to the family.

'Steve Hansen quite often uses the phrase, "Why do you have to lose to learn?" Because we have so much success you have got to have a different form of introspection and it is the same for guys like Aaron. He needs to think why he screwed up. It was like a tide that crept up. You think you are indestructible and above different things. But suddenly you come crashing down in a huge way.'

By October 2017, in the Cape Town Test against South Africa

Smith had reclaimed his beloved place as leader of the haka. Yet even so, Smith knew better than others that he'd paid a price for his slip.

'The haka is everything put together. It is a good little symbol of New Zealand culture, just the way we are. It's a bit strange that some people can't see some guys losing it. It's a war dance: that is the answer. Before they went to war they were warning them, "We are coming now, get ready, this is it." Of course, in those times, it was to the death.'

The former All Black prop Craig Dowd participated in the film John Eales made, together with Wayne Shelford and Frank Bunce. In a general discussion on the pitch at Eden Park, Auckland, he revealed that one opposition team had messed about after the haka had been done, the challenge set. The All Blacks had found themselves on edge, said Dowd. They were ready for war, but the opposition weren't. They were slow in removing their tracksuits; the All Blacks were ready and in their playing outfit. First, a trainer had to come onto the pitch to collect all their opponents' tracksuits. Then the opposition gathered in a huddle for last minute messages, which seemed to go on and on. Then, very slowly, they made their way to their starting positions.

'By this time,' said Dowd, 'we'd lost the momentum. We knocked on the kick-off, dropped a couple of passes and were all over the place for a while.'

The antidote to the passion? Perhaps. Irishman Tony Ward, for one, is convinced the haka is a valuable psychological weapon. 'There is no doubt it gives them an advantage. By a million per cent. Their anthem alone gives them an advantage first. But the haka stirs them up, gives them motivation at the expense of the opposition.

'The All Blacks have an advantage because they are physically active while they are doing it. In effect, they are warming up by doing it.'

Maybe two or three minutes should be allowed for the opposition to warm up similarly, once the haka is completed, Ward suggests. 'Bring the teams out eight to ten minutes before kick-off, let's have a lovely [level] playing field and both teams equally warmed up. I would hate to see the haka go from the game, there is something about the drama of it. But it's got to be an equal opportunity.'

But what is its role in the context of the modern game? Professionalism has altered rugby inexorably. The old ways have slipped quietly beneath the waves. Like England's Leicester rugby club wearing letters, not numbers on the backs of the players' jerseys, for instance. Professionalism swept it away. But not the haka.

Essentially, you feel that two questions arise. Should World Rugby continue to smile and tolerate it as a quirk of the old game? Particularly if, as some suggest, it is a clear advantage, an obvious motivational tool for the New Zealanders. That is a matter of opinion. But one team's view is as worthy as the other's. Secondly, and this is perhaps in a far broader sense, does New Zealand need to continue doing it on every single occasion? Is it not a special, unique part of New Zealand culture? Shouldn't it be respected as such, reserved perhaps for visiting Heads of State, royalty or a major rugby occasion, such as a World Cup final? But just any old rugby match? With all due respect, is that not downgrading the whole thing? And does it not risk diminishing its exclusivity?

The French faced and confronted the haka before the 2011 Rugby World Cup Final. Captain Thierry Dusautoir's men advanced, a couple of them over the chalk line designated by the IRB as the no-go area. It was fair, it was thrilling, it was challenging. Sadly, the IRB, predictably using a sledgehammer to crack a nut, dumbly fined them $5,000 for what they termed a 'breach of cultural ritual protocol'.

Even All Blacks manager Darren Shand said the incident should have gone unpunished.

'They [the French] came to play and that was great. The culture challenge is that. It should be done and then we get on with the real stuff. I hope it's not overstated.'

But does New Zealand need to do it any longer? Is the haka now a brand as well as an identity? And besides, is an expression of identity something this country still needs in 2018? An argument may once have been made for it, along the lines of it representing a little country fighting above its weight against world opponents. Some may have seen it as the personification of a country that still needed the emotional and cultural crutch it brought. But surely that is not the case nowadays? Former Prime Minister Sir John Key would doubtless sense the dangers of stumbling into a haka haranguing. Any politician's antennae are highly tuned for such pitfalls. As Key told me in Auckland in 2017, 'I wouldn't reduce it. This comes up all the time, but the fact remains the Maori culture is a unique culture to New Zealand. It is part of who we are. And its significance is growing.

'How many people make sure they are ready before a game to see the haka performed? I would say most and that's because they like it. It is part of the event. This is showbiz, this is entertainment.'

But is that what the haka has now descended to? Showbiz? A bit of cheap entertainment? I can't think many Maori chiefs would swallow that thought too comfortably. In 2009, the New Zealand Government assigned intellectual-property rights in the traditional Maori haka, the 'Ka Mate', to Ngāti Toa, a North Island tribal group. The new agreement was mainly symbolic but it was considered hugely important by Maori leaders to prevent, as the official settlement letter said, 'the misappropriation and culturally inappropriate use of the "Ka Mate" haka'.

Gilbert Enoka admits New Zealand rugby men themselves had reached something of a crossroads over the haka. 'There were a lot of guys saying they felt we were haka-ed out. They said, "We do the haka all the time, we have TV cameras in our faces." They hated it. 'They said, "All I want to do is get the damn thing done and over with." They said, "It's not for us anyway. It's just for the Maori people." So we had a real crisis of identity where we had to sit down and say, "Who are we as New Zealanders, who are we as All Blacks?" That was really where "Kapa O Pango" was born.'

'Kapa O Pango', a new haka created by Derek Lardelli of Ngāti Porou, took a year to choreograph. It modified the first verse of 'Ko Niu Tirini', the haka used by the 1924 All Blacks. Many experts in Maori culture were asked for their views. It is regarded as complementing 'Ka Mate' and is used for special occasions. First performed before a 2005 Tri-Nations international against South Africa in Dunedin, the words used were considered more specific to the rugby team than 'Ka Mate'. They refer to the warriors in black and the silver fern. For most of the New Zealand players, it was a more appropriate haka than 'Ka Mate'.

Enoka went on, 'That was certainly the moment we had to do a right angle turn because more of the same would not cut the mustard. That process we went through laid the foundations for what many people regard as a great run of consistent success. And I think the nation had a catharsis.'

Undeniably, the haka is a wonderful sporting tradition. But it is also a valuable motivational tool that gives New Zealand an advantage, whatever the percentage. And then there is the issue of overkill, a danger to which the late Sir Colin Meads referred. A World Cup final? Clearly. But in all three Test matches of one nation's tour to New

Zealand? Surely, before the first Test of the series would be enough. Then the challenge is set.

The 2017 Lions coach Warren Gatland, a native of Waikato, addressed this issue before that tour began. By the start of the Test series, Gatland admitted, the Lions would be 'familiar' with the haka, given that the Maori All Blacks and the Super Rugby franchises were, at that time, also preparing to perform it. Ten matches on the tour, and thus ten haka? That was clearly too much, in Gatland's opinion. He suggested that would dent the mystique of the famous challenge. In the end, the Hurricanes and the Highlanders did not perform haka. The Chiefs, the Blues and the Maori All Blacks did. The franchises did their own unique haka.

Gatland said, 'For me, the experience, the more times you face up to it, you don't mind it. It's a motivational thing, it's not intimidating. You become familiar with it. It becomes part of regular preparation for a game.' And with the delicate balance of the commercialization of the sport to contend with, if the haka loses its mystique then it loses touch with its heritage and its very purpose. Alarm bells ought to be going off in the heads of Maori at Gatland's statement, 'You don't mind it . . . It's not intimidating . . . It's part of regular preparation for a game.'

Is that what the real meaning of the haka has become? Surely, the challenge, a statement of intent, was its key element. If that has been lost, then it must weaken it. Or is the truth more sinister? Given that the new professional game is now utterly dependent on television money, is it not the case that, in effect, television is the real rights holder of the haka?

In the professional era, the haka has become part of the All Blacks' brand. And in the business world, what the consumer wants is king. Everything becomes a brand. If the television executives take a similar view to Sir John Key, that this is now showbiz, a bit of entertainment, is it likely they would allow New Zealand Rugby and the All Blacks to scale back the ritual? Who pays the piper, calls the tune . . .

Television executives will be more than aware of the truth of Aaron Smith's words. Women might not watch the whole game, but they watch the haka. TV moguls lick their lips at the prospect of men *and* women watching their show – their advertising market expands exponentially under such circumstances.

So would television accept it if the All Blacks decided to reduce the number of occasions on which haka was performed? It seems unlikely. Which brings us back to the depressing reality, that TV largely runs and controls the game. If it didn't, would every major New Zealand home Test match kick off at 7.35pm in midwinter, when many young fans are in bed? Not a chance. It means that many are missing out on sharing the experience of attending a live Test match.

But is it just rugby traditionalists who ought to be aware of this? Would allowing the haka to become an essential ingredient in the widespread commercialization of the game be in the interests of New Zealand culture? Would Maori elders smile benignly upon their successors who allowed this scenario to come to pass? The critical point is surely that the haka should be nurtured, protected, kept truly special, and in fact unique. Which it is. Do it at every turn, every opportunity before every game on every occasion and it will, in time, lose its allure. Even worse, it will become just a bit of showbiz.

Does anyone want that?

IMPORTANCE OF THE POLYNESIANS

Contributions from, among others,
Waisake Naholo, Jerome Kaino, Malakai Fekitoa,
Alan Jones, Sir Brian Lochore, Alan Sutherland,
Sir Bryan Williams, Conrad Smith, Wayne Smith,
Steve Hansen, Beauden Barrett, Dan Carter,
John Eales, Frank Bunce, Wayne Shelford,
Gilbert Enoka, Sir Colin Meads.

'I come to New Zealand and see kids, and man . . . they get it so easy. I don't want to be sad or mean. But they don't come through what I came through. You see many kids here being ungrateful. They want mobile phones, cars, everything . . .'

Waisake Naholo, All Blacks wing

He remembered the good times. When kids were carefree, running in the sand. The sea, fresh and inviting. Azure mixed with deep blue. A cappuccino froth of white on the far-out reef. And the wind. He always remembered the wind.

They lacked nothing in friendship and fun. The extended family, once cousins had been counted, was more than enough. Then his mum invited kids from far away to stay. It made sense. The school was close by. But it meant sleeping fifteen people in a two-bedroom home. Feeding them, too. A job for a magician. Or a saint. Especially when money was tight. Which it always was. Their simple clothes, handed down through the generations like family heirlooms, bore witness to that. There was Waisake, his sister and two brothers, his grandma and his grandad. And, at one time, ten kids from other families.

Today he's a man. Some man: 1.86m (6ft 1.2ins) tall, and weighing in at 96 kg (15st. 1lb). In those days, he was just a scrap of a lad. He comes to meet me on a foul day. Dunedin, one of the most southerly cities in the world, is renowned for it. Cold, steady rain. He pulls off a mitten to shake hands. The bone structure is massive. The neck under his top bulges. Biceps and thighs likewise. Yet when he speaks, his deep voice can be as soft as a kitten's.

Different man, Waisake Naholo. Different story. No kid from a wealthy New Zealand suburb, silver spoon in his mouth from birth. No 4 × 4 to take him to training. Not a chance. Just a kid from Fiji. But unexceptional? Far from it. He takes me on a journey. Back to the island. To those times . . . He's living with an uncle close to the family home at Sigatoka on Fiji's Coral Coast. It's forty-five minutes from Nadi. Waisake doesn't like Suva, the capital. Rains too much there.

He's nearly fifteen now. Has more space at his uncle's house. But he doesn't see his papa as much. He always seems to be up so early and back home late. He hasn't a clue that his father is struggling. To do two jobs, never mind one. But then, Waisake didn't understand the effect the letter had had on his family. It had arrived one day, amid great excitement. It was from a school in New Zealand. They knew about his reputation as a rugby player, and wanted to offer Waisake a place. They had someone fly to the island to watch him. The letter came soon after.

Alas, another problem emerged. The school could only offer a half-fee scholarship. Waisake shrugged. He saw no future in that. How could his poor family put up half the fees? An impossible dream. Like the fantasy that he would one day walk the other side of the wire fence. It divided the five-star hotel from his family and friends' modest homes. Its opulence mocked their poverty. He remembered that well.

'You get paid shit money on the island. My father had a job, but it didn't pay much. It made things hard for us. It is like two lives there, two countries in one. In the first, local people are struggling to find enough money to buy food. In the second, wealthy tourists are staying in these luxury hotels. I have seen how hard it is to make a living. I've seen how hard my parents had to work just to put food on our plates.'

But he didn't see something else. Not at the time. Happened right under his nose, it turned out. His papa would do his day job, then slip away to do the second job he'd taken on. Building *bures*, the Fijian-style thatched round houses. Nor did he know his uncle was working with him. Long into the evenings. Or that some of Waisake's cousins were also helping out, too.

He was already becoming a big lad. Polynesian boys grow up quickly. Yet he almost cried the day his papa told him the family could pay half the scholarship. He could go to school in New Zealand. It had been a beautiful sacrifice, a collective generosity of endless proportions.

He took the chance of his life and did well at school. Then he signed to play rugby for Taranaki, Graham Mourie's old province. After that, the Auckland Blues recruited him. Now he is with the Highlanders. He plays for the All Blacks, too. He combines raw power and aggression with the delicate touch of an artist. His offloading of the ball for New Zealand against the Barbarians at Twickenham in

November 2017, which earned his team important tries, was an aesthetic delight. But most vitally, he is earning more money from professional rugby in New Zealand than his mum or dad could ever have imagined.

A story of triumph. But why then does Waisake look sad?

'I come to New Zealand and see kids, and man . . . they get it so easy. I don't want to be sad or mean. But they don't come through what I came through. You see many kids here being ungrateful. They want mobile phones, cars, everything.'

His voice tails off. He remembers his friends back in Fiji. Some he went to the local school with. Some were cleverer, more talented than him. But their ticket to ride never came. Their parents couldn't afford the fees. Or even a proper lunch for them each day at school. So the youngsters quit. They went to work on the land. But it's hard to get money there, Waisake says. Now, years later, it's payback time. Each month, he puts aside a healthy percentage of his salary. And faithfully wires money home to the island. It's the last he will see of it, still less know what happens to it.

'I don't find anything wrong with that,' he tells me, his voice soft, reflective. 'What they do with the money, I don't have a say. But they need it. I know that. I am always going to do it and I am happy to. It's the experience of being brought up.'

He has a lot of cousins and tries to help them, too. But what happens when he stops playing rugby and the money tap is turned off?

'I have got investments. I bought a house here and I'm hoping to get a couple more. Part of my investments are to help bring my brothers through school in New Zealand. I have helped pay for that.'

Inside the cocoon, like in the northern-hemisphere countries such as England and France, where other young men play professional sport, most wouldn't understand his sense of responsibility.

But Naholo's background guarantees something. You learn fast the tougher lessons of life. It conditions you, burns into your soul. Assuming you have one.

'I cannot turn my back on my family. I see some people fighting with their parents and falling out. But I can't see myself doing that. When you are an Islander, you come from very big families. There are a lot of people to help out. My family means everything to me.'

Former All Black Malakai Fekitoa understands such sentiments. Fekitoa came from Tonga, lured to New Zealand by the offer of a scholarship at Wesley College in Paerata. He shared two traits with Naholo. Both were terrific rugby prospects, and both came from basic backgrounds. In Fekitoa's case, he was the eighth of fifteen children.

In mid-2017, he announced that he was leaving the Highlanders and accepting a two-year contract from French club Toulon. From Tonga to Toulon. It's a fair estimate to say he was probably tripling his money. He wasn't the first to go. Charles Piutau and Steven Luatua had already accepted lucrative offers. The deal for Luatua was so good that he even joined an English second-tier club, Bristol, from Auckland Blues. Super Rugby to super-ordinary. How could he? Someone in the know told me, 'You cannot imagine such an offer. Steven wasn't even in a position to think about it, it was that good. He had to take it.'

When Bristol subsequently signed Piutau, too, for £1 million a season, the Luatua deal became easier to comprehend. But Fekitoa's honesty shone through the affair.

'When we talk about family . . . for a lot of us in this team, that is all we play for,' he said. 'I would have loved to have grown up in a different scenario with a different life. But this is what we have to face. To look after all the siblings and stuff like that. All of us island boys are doing that. Even when my sister is married and has kids, I'm still doing that. That's what we play for. It's always "family comes first".'

Such stories reveal the eagerness and desperation of young rugby players in the Polynesian islands to get to New Zealand. To try to carve out a career in professional rugby. They know it offers their whole family a potential route out of poverty. It's easy to sneer, as many have done, when top New Zealand rugby players catch the plane to a land of milk, honey and money. But, as Naholo says, 'You have to weigh up what you want. Steven has got kids and also has a family back in the islands. So he has got to provide for them. Like me. I wouldn't criticize anyone for going. You have to look after yourself in this game.'

Selfish? What, in a sport where young men's bodies are used as pieces of meat? In a game so brutally physical that your next match could be your last. Ever. And concussion, with its unknown long-term consequences, is a ticking time bomb. You'd need a soul of steel to condemn such young men.

Fact is, playing top rugby, being successful, keeping up your form and thinking all the while about the needs of family members back in the islands, is a conundrum. There are a significant number of young rugby men in New Zealand juggling these enormous pressures and emotions. Consider this story of another island player. He was contracted to the Auckland Blues during John Kirwan's era as coach from 2013 to 2015. The player was exciting and dynamic, but he developed a problem. He turned up one morning late for training. Got a warning from the coach, was apologetic. But it happened again. Two days later. Kirwan did what any coach would do. Dropped him from the team. An hour or so later, as he walked to his car, the coach saw a sad sight. There was the player, sitting propped up against a wheel of his vehicle in the car park. Crying his eyes out.

'You just don't understand, coach,' he said. 'Before I came here this morning, I found out I'd had NZ$20,000 taken from my account.'

He knew who it was. His parents. Why? A sense of entitlement exists within the island community. It becomes incumbent upon the successful member of the family to help those back home. The responsibility on those providing money is immense. It is, says Sir Graham Henry, a cultural expectation. There is a far bigger picture here, in his view. The nuances of it have largely escaped those on the other side of the world. Some claim that denuding the islands of such talent has constantly undermined the chances of Samoa, Tonga or Fiji emerging as a leading rugby nation in their own right. True, to an extent. But those chiefly to blame are the people who administer the sport worldwide. World Rugby or, in its previous incarnation, the IRB. As ex-Australia coach Alan Jones says, 'You cannot put a lid on people's ambitions. Why should you stop sportsmen attempting to better themselves in what has become the world's number-one rugby nation?'

Instead, Jones points the finger of blame for the comparative weakness of the Polynesian islands at the game's rulers. Post-professionalism in 1995, he says, it was within their power to put in place a system of compensation for young men turning their backs on the islands of their birth. In a professional sport, most things come down to money. It would have been perfectly possible to assemble a system that gave the islands' rugby unions some compensation for lost stars of the present or future. That money could and should have been invested in growing the game in those islands. But there has been no major initiative from the sport's governing body to correct this imbalance. Jones is just one of those who has looked in vain to the game's rulers for meaningful action.

'The only criticism I have of New Zealand is they should not have been doing what they have done in the Polynesian islands. I object to the overuse of Pacific-origin players in these teams. It has weakened the islands' strength.

'People of talent are targeted to become an All Black. You can't blame them for that and equally you can't blame New Zealand for picking them. But I don't think it ought to be without some kind of recompense. You have now got many of these people playing for New Zealand and Australia. I have always argued if they wanted to do that and the players wanted to migrate to these countries, that is fine. But there should be a capitalization fee on those players and that money should go back to growing the game in the Pacific islands.

'But we don't do that. We just clean them out, then we say, "Well, you have already played for the All Blacks or Wallabies. So you can't go back and play for Samoa, Tonga or Fiji." '

This is no one-sided criticism. Jones is equally withering regarding his own country's rugby powers.

'Australia and New Zealand have weakened the game by their failure to develop their own players. They have relied on very big, powerful and skilful people from the Pacific islands. Australia are probably worse than New Zealand in this respect. In 2017, Queensland had twelve players in their team from the Pacific islands. Appalling. That is wrong.'

People from the Pacific islands have been migrating south to New Zealand to find work and a better life for centuries. This was no modern-day invention by a few rapacious rugby coaches. And you can't stop people chasing a sporting and financial nirvana. Even so, controlling it was surely possible. Especially once professionalism dawned. But this vacuum of visionary leadership has undermined the sport in too many ways.

One of the supreme ironies of this absence of decisive leadership in the game is that it now threatens to come back and haunt New Zealand. In the light of the failing challenges by Australia and South Africa, senior figures within the New Zealand game increasingly bemoan the fact that there is no major challenger to the All Blacks among the Pacific islands. But it is a consequence of the failure by the game's authorities to take tough decisions with regard to financial restitution. Had they done so years ago, in order to prevent the constant loss of the best Pasifika players to New Zealand and, more recently, to Australia, a strong Fiji, Samoa or Tonga might have emerged, or perhaps even a collective South Pacific team. But without assistance, that possibility vanished.

Not that every player who has ever originated from the Polynesian islands has been an instant success. Jerome Kaino readily accepts the point. He wasn't. Certainly not to begin with. Kaino was only five when his parents uprooted their family in American Samoa and re-located to South Auckland. But, like Naholo, Kaino quickly grew in the kind of physical way that made him a natural fit for rugby. Trouble was, although he had the physique – he was a big guy and super-fit – Kaino lacked the attitude. He didn't appreciate rugby's requirements. Wasn't prepared to make the necessary sacrifices. Alcohol and party-ing featured too prominently in his life. Instead of black caps, there were black marks against his name.

But then, two men stepped up to the task. Graham Henry and Steve Hansen. 'They gave me a lifeline, and not just by selecting me through those tough times,' he said. 'They also gave me a lot of good advice. Instead of jumping down my throat, they just said, "OK, it's human nature. But you are letting yourself down and letting your family down, too."

'They made me view it as if it was all up to me. The ball was in my court. They said, "We can help you. But you're going to have to make some of these tough choices yourself." That helped me a lot.'

There were those who reckoned the lads of island origin wouldn't, or couldn't, knuckle down to the New Zealand way. Discipline was big, responsibility assumed. Especially when you got to the Holy Grail. The All Blacks.

Some even thought the growing introduction of the island players could cost New Zealand rugby its pre-eminence. Alan Sutherland, an All Black in sixty-four matches and ten Tests from 1968 to 1976, remembers it well:

'Some people used to believe that New Zealand rugby would become a shocker under the influence of the island players. They thought it would weaken New Zealand. There were just the occasional ones years ago – B.G. Williams, Sid Going, etc. It was mainly thought that if there were too many of them, then New Zealand rugby would suffer. To be honest, I always thought they lacked a bit of heart. Traditionally, the New Zealand rugby player would dig deep. But the island players seemed to get downhearted quicker than anyone.'

The word was, they lacked discipline. Concentration. They wouldn't live up to the high demands. Good in short bursts for their explosive power, so the argument went. But over eighty minutes? They wouldn't sustain it and would weaken the core spine of New Zealand rugby. Namely, a team forged on physically strong, no-nonsense farmers. Rich in the DNA of their ancestors. Plus a back line of university students to add some craft and subtlety. It was formulaic. But it has been adapted, it has evolved. Evolution, not revolution. Even Sir Brian Lochore alluded to something of the sort: 'They're great impact players. As long as they have somebody next to them they love and can trust. Then they are fine.'

Colin Meads was forthright on the topic. 'It was common talk that the influence of the island players would somehow reduce the All Blacks. People said, "They will chuck it in if you get on top of them." But I don't see that now. They are really good players. They have been brought up with our education system. They have got education and they are disciplined. If they are not disciplined, they don't quite get to the All Blacks.'

So what happened? All the doubts and fears were blown away, like opponents in the tackle. The amalgamation was, and still is, a triumph. As Sir Bryan Williams says, the exact opposite has applied. The clever and gradual integration of these players into the New Zealand rugby fold, at all levels, has transformed the game throughout the land. Explosive power. Great physicality. Immense speed. Unreachable depths of courage, not to say commitment. A cheerful willingness to take a risk. The complete sacrifice of bodies. These are the qualities that have helped take New Zealand teams to another level. It is the rest of the world that has suffered, blown away by these immense physical specimens.

'New Zealand rugby has changed them,' reckons Sutherland. Maybe. But they've changed New Zealand rugby. Manifestly for the better, too. However, Colin Meads shook his head at one aspect. Is the game now obsessed with big hits, I asked him?

'Yes, it is getting that way. They are big players. You wouldn't want to get hit by a guy like Jerome Kaino. These boys are the ones with the big hits, and they practise them. That's part of their training. I don't agree with that. We never missed tackles, but big hits never came into our game. It has become a little like gladiators now. A lot of players are looking for contact now rather than space.' And taking guys out

Canterbury settlement in Akaroa Bay. Life was brutal in these early settlements. Between 1851 and 1860 in Akaroa, of a total of twenty-four people buried only four had lived beyond the age of forty. The average lifespan was just below twenty-seven years.

The 'New Zealand Natives' were captained by Joe Warbrick (Ngāti Rangitihi) and played an astonishing 107 matches. They were the first tourists to wear a black outfit with a silver fern. They played a running, free-flowing style of rugby. 130 years later, their 2018 descendants were doing the same.

The 1905 tourists were the first fully representative New Zealand team to visit the northern hemisphere. They won thirty-four of their thirty-five games, losing only by a disputed try to Wales (3–0). It is said they popularized both the haka and the name 'the All Blacks'.

The Original All Blacks 1905 magazine spread on the first New Zealand rugby tour of the British Isles.

Above, left. One of several graves of Maori soldiers at Ypres, Belgium, on the First World War battlefields. They are tended to, as if by family members, by the Commonwealth War Graves Commission.

Above, right. The legacy of a job well done. New Zealand street names in the northern French town of Le Quesnoy, erected in tribute to the New Zealand soldiers who liberated the town from the Germans in late 1918. Forever a corner of New Zealand far overseas.

Below. All Blacks captain Reuben Thorne (far right) and his teammates pay their respects to fallen compatriots at an Armistice Day remembrance service during their northern hemisphere tour.

The famous statue of 1905 'Originals' captain Dave Gallaher outside Eden Park, Auckland. Irish-born, Gallaher played for Ponsonby and Auckland but represented New Zealand in only six Test matches. Killed at Passchendaele in 1917, his legend surmounts so brief an international career.

Born in 1905, Nepia became famous on the All Blacks' 1924 northern hemisphere tour. Uniquely, he played in all thirty-two tour games in which they were unbeaten, earning the title 'the Invincibles'. Nepia became a giant of the game, perhaps not only the finest Maori player in All Blacks history, but the greatest fullback in their annals. Yet to some, he became an outcast when he turned professional with a London-based rugby league club in 1935. He signed for £500.

From left: Mike Cron, Ian Foster, Gilbert Enoka, Steve Hansen and Wayne Smith. Collectively, together with Sir Graham Henry, they have been by far the greatest rugby coaching brains anywhere in the world in the past decade.

Gilbert Enoka, the man who was key to unravelling the mystery of New Zealand's failure to win a World Cup from 1991 up to 2007.

Grant Fox (selector), Steve Hansen and Ian Foster. Their down-to-earth approach, common sense, rugby acumen and constant demand for the highest standards have laid a template for achieving success on the world stage.

Steve Tew, New Zealand Rugby CEO, with former coach Wayne Smith. Both have been hugely instrumental in steering New Zealand to the top of world rugby and keeping them there. Sir Graham Henry called Smith, 'the best coach I have ever seen with the All Blacks.'

Good enough to represent New Zealand at both soccer and rugby, Melissa Ruscoe won the Women's Rugby World Cup in both 2006 and 2010, the latter as captain. Now a teacher, she often expresses concerns about health, even in an outdoorsy nation like New Zealand. 'Playing sport and especially rugby is important. Obesity is definitely a problem in New Zealand, like the rest of the world,' she said.

All Black great Sir Bryan Williams shakes hands with Auckland Grammar boys.

A rough, rusting pair of rugby posts, but the home of Mount Somers rugby club, close to the beautiful Ashburton Gorge in mid-Canterbury.

New Zealand club rugby in its autumn glory: a typical Saturday afternoon scene at the North Shore club in Auckland.

Rugby at the Harbour Hawks ground, beside the waters of Dunedin harbour.
Up to twelve balls a season can be lost when booted into touch and into the harbour.

around the ruck or maul? 'In our day, if you ever tackled a guy without the ball, you got a bloody hiding, and rightly so. It's dangerous, because that's when people can get hurt.'

Yet Beauden Barrett believes there is a greater element than just physique that represents the enduring value of the island players to New Zealand rugby. 'Pasifika players do bring that raw physical power. But it's more than that. I think it's the ability just to pick up a ball and know how to play footy. It is even more instinctive to them than anyone else.'

Kaino uses a small word to describe the big influence of the Pasifika players on New Zealand rugby. 'Huge,' he says. 'It is growing, it's immense. We have contributed a lot to New Zealand rugby history. I think the way New Zealanders do things and the system, complements what the island players have already; their physical make-up and how they like to play the game. A bit of that discipline which it takes to become a New Zealand rugby player or to survive in the New Zealand system, helps us a lot. Sometimes that discipline doesn't come so naturally with the Polynesian players. What they learn, and the system, is invaluable.'

He says he always felt Samoan, even growing up as a young boy in New Zealand. Still feels a sense of being Samoan, and he's proud to be that. But, 'I'm also proud to be a Kiwi and I think you can amalgamate the two easily. With how you live in New Zealand, it allows you to keep that Samoan culture alive.'

Dan Carter makes the point that both sides have benefitted from this relationship. 'Pasifika players are a big influence. Their size, skill level and power are amazing. You know if you look at some of the best All Blacks, a lot of them have some kind of Pasifika background. We're extremely lucky to have so many living in New Zealand and representing the All Blacks. They're a pretty unique people and their beliefs and culture are special.

'But I think New Zealand rugby has improved them, too. So while New Zealand rugby has clearly benefitted from having them involved, I believe it is a two-way street.'

John Eales pinpoints precisely where the island lads have benefitted. 'The teaching has been a huge advantage to them. The New Zealand school system is superb at producing young rugby players. It isn't a guarantee New Zealand will win just because they have some

Pasifika origin players. But this population is so inclined to rugby. They have the physical build and natural strength.'

Sir Brian Lochore's maxim that the island players produce their best when they feel comfortable in their surroundings and with those they trust around them, is true in many cases. But it isn't only the island players who benefit from exposure to the supremely professional All Blacks environment. Long ago it became clear that trust was endemic in the relationship between the players and coaches in the All Blacks environment.

Conrad Smith was Ma'a Nonu's midfield partner for the Hurricanes and the All Blacks. The perceptive Smith says that Nonu was not the only one who benefitted from these relationships.

'As for Ma'a,' said Smith, 'he had a special relationship with all the All Blacks management, including Graham [Henry]. From 2008, I think Ma'a always performed well for the All Blacks, and the coaches knew they could get the best out of him just by being in the All Blacks environment. But then, I think there were many players like that, not just Ma'a. It was because the All Blacks environment is unique. It is a group of the best coaches, players, trainers in the country and the standards and expectations are set very, very high. Some players react very well to that environment and when they do, and perform well, they earn a lot of trust from the coaching staff.

'When they are out of that environment, some players let standards slip, which isn't ideal. But provided they still deliver when part of the All Blacks, they will always have the confidence of the staff. I think all players are like that to some extent, some more so than others. I don't think it was any one thing for Ma'a. Rather, just being in the environment, working with great coaches, playing alongside great players, getting the best assistance in terms of fitness training, medical care and mental toughness. When it all comes together, it can be very powerful.'

It is Bryan Williams' belief that playing rugby union is more natural to the island players than those of European heritage. Because, he says, they have this 'inbred explosive element'. Add to the equation aspects of the modern era, like discipline, a work ethic and planning, and you have a towering, intimidating creation. But they have brought more than just this, Williams argues.

'They have played a big part in terms of the adventurous nature of the game in this country. Back in the 1960s and 1970s when we didn't have many Pasifika players, the All Blacks lacked adventure. But over time, it has become what you see today. An adventurous, highly skilled team. Once, you had teams with big, powerful athletes with discipline. If you didn't adapt, you came second. But it was clear, players had to become faster with more skill and adventure in their play.'

Williams says the process of integration mainly took place in the 1980s and 1990s. He admits that, what started out as a trickle, ended up as a flood. His own club, Ponsonby in Auckland, was a good example of this process. He also accepts that this influx gave New Zealand a considerable advantage, especially in the earlier years. But people still had to harness the physical advantages, bring young players into line with other requirements of the game. Such as hard work, discipline and an understanding of tactics.

Key qualities are necessary to integrate peoples. Tolerance and patience are good starting points. Understanding would be another. But there have been the occasional lapses. Frank Bunce and Eric Rush could tell you about those. Called up for his New Zealand debut in 1992, Rush dumped his kitbag in the All Blacks dressing room and went out onto the field before the start. When he got back, his bag was missing. 'Look in the shower,' a voice said. It was there, alright. Under a running shower. Apparently just because he'd left it in the wrong spot of the dressing room.

Bunce, despite having played international rugby before, also encountered that kind of behaviour after making his All Blacks debut in 1992. 'That was how they treated their teammates at that time,' he says. 'They were arrogant. They thought that because of all the success they'd had, they were bigger than rugby.' 'They,' according to Bunce, were chiefly the Auckland and All Blacks stars.

Nor was it a whole lot different when Samoan-born Bryan Williams made his debut for the All Blacks in 1970. He was a trendsetter, the first Polynesian picked for New Zealand. 'Bee Gee,' as he would come to be known, developed into one of the great All Blacks, yet even he didn't feel welcome at the start. He was summoned to the back of the bus by some of the All Blacks senior players and given a verbal grilling. 'What have you got to offer?' was the line of questioning – it was standard form for the era.

'There was a time when I did feel uncomfortable there,' Williams told me. 'I was breaking new ground as a young Polynesian. My first tour was to apartheid South Africa and it was doubly scary, not knowing how I was going to be treated. I was partly responsible for the difficulty I experienced because I was so shy. I think I roomed with Chris Laidlaw but he didn't want to talk to me and I was too shy to talk with him.'

But Williams was lucky. His first All Blacks captain was Brian Lochore, an outstanding leader of men and someone who understood the importance of drawing together every player of a touring party. Lochore had made his All Blacks Test debut on the 1963–4 tour of the British Isles, Ireland and France. Like Williams in 1970, he had felt alone at times. He, too, had been in that situation, a new, young hopeful. Yet he ended up playing in two Tests on the tour, a sign of how good he was, even as a youngster. But for a lot of the period, he suffered like the young guys. In those days, there was a Saturday team and a Wednesday team. He could understand a lot of the younger guys were struggling.

The lack of empathy and communication with the ambitious young players didn't seem to bother the captain Wilson Whineray on that 1963–4 tour. He led a cabal of senior men who enjoyed each other's company and left the rest largely to fend for themselves. It was neither inviting nor instructive.

Sir Brian Lochore regrets to this day that he never confronted Whineray about it. He saw it, witnessed its effects but said nothing. Today, the venerable All Black confesses, 'I should have gone and had a yarn with him. But I didn't have the courage. In fact, quite a few times I didn't have the courage when it came to speaking to people. Not now, but when I was young. I was a very shy country boy.'

Steve Hansen typically gets straight to the heart of the issue. It is his way. 'It would be a travesty if we did not acknowledge that the Polynesian players have played a major part in what we have done . . . as a rugby nation.'

But to view this as a success story for just one particular people would be grossly misleading. Successfully as Polynesian-origin players clearly have adapted to and benefitted from the traditions of New Zealand rugby, there is a far bigger picture to paint here. To get a true perspective, I boarded an aircraft bound for Australia.

*

He comes to meet me in downtown Brisbane. It is a public holiday and the city is quiet. We sit in a luxury hotel beside the Brisbane River.

Impressive private yachts glide past on the water; joggers chew up the mileage on the towpath beside the park.

The progress Australia has made in the last 230 years is impressive. Except that one segment of the population got left behind: the indigenous people of Aboriginal descent. They represent Australia's dark secret, and comparisons in this field between these two trans-Tasman rugby neighbours are instructive.

Andrew Slack shakes his head at the thought, an image of sadness upon his face. But it is replaced with a gleam of hope when he compares Australia's example with that of their oldest sporting foes. The Wallabies' 1984 Grand Slam captain offers unconditional praise to New Zealand for one element of the modern-day All Blacks that represents the triumph of a nation. Fact is, few countries ever achieve the harmony enjoyed within the All Blacks by peoples of vastly differing backgrounds. Yet, due to considerable efforts by a variety of people – administrators, coaches, players and unknown numbers of ordinary rugby fans – New Zealand has successfully integrated three peoples – Maori, Pakeha and Pasifika – into a single nation and sports team.

'This amalgamation has been admirable,' says Slack. 'We in Australia are still working at it, we haven't worked it out. But they have had a bit more practice at it. There were a lot of Maori when we were playing [in the mid- to late 1980s]. I have always seen the New Zealand attitude to it as one country, one people. I have seen them only treated as part of a team. Perhaps the secret of successful integration of people is not to think about it. But, whatever the trick, it has completely enhanced them as a rugby nation and as a people. Because of the skills of Maori and island players, they have lifted the standard because they are such great athletes.' Slack's words are generous. But then, by anyone's yardstick, this successful human integration has been a very significant achievement.

Winning trophies is a triumph in sporting terms. But what New Zealand rugby has done in successfully bringing together quite different people and teaching them the values of harmony, and the power of the collective as opposed to the individual, is admirable. It has offered its society a vivid illustration of the possibilities from successful integration. Of course, it would be absurd to pretend that peace and harmony exist between different peoples in every walk of New Zealand life. That might be the idyll, but it is seldom achieved. Yet, if you want a vibrant example of how this almost seamless coming together was managed, then look no further than New Zealand rugby. At all levels, from the schools to humble clubs; from Mitre 10 sides to the Super Rugby franchises, there is clear evidence of the success of the process.

Steve Hansen is eloquent on the topic. 'There are a whole lot of ingredients for our success. But one part of those ingredients is the diversity of people that we have who are living in this country. It's true, this is a triumph of New Zealand. We are proud, first and foremost, of being New Zealanders. We are not too worried about where we come from and our past. We have an understanding of that but we are here as one nation.

'Rugby has been good at building those relationships because people have seen us all working together. You see a Keven Mealamu and an Andrew Hore, both born-and-bred New Zealanders, coming from totally different backgrounds and cultures, yet they are best mates. That is a beautiful thing, people coming together and working for one cause.'

But the key is the fact that New Zealand is no longer one people's soul, but three: Maori, Pakeha and Pasifika. The nation has evolved, and the All Blacks with it. In the fifty years between 1967 and 2017, it has changed out of all recognition. Just like the game played by today's All Blacks: more dynamic, faster, more powerful, infinitely more varied and altogether more exciting.

2017 Springboks defence coach Brendan Venter says the New Zealand Maori and Pasifika influence was huge in what they achieved.

'The Polynesians were made physically to play rugby and they had that influence. But somewhere, the tactical and skill levels rose and took over in New Zealand.

'That is why this new group of coaches are special. It is not just Steve Hansen. I think it started with Graham Henry. They set out their stall. They said to the players, "To be an All Black, you need to be better disciplined than others, work harder than others and you need to respect other people." Physically, they out-worked everybody. Yes, they have great skills and a great blend, but off the ball it is mind-boggling how hard they work. As a people, New Zealanders are, in my opinion, almost the nicest I have ever met, in rugby terms. But then, most people that win a lot are nice. What would they be like if they lost three or four matches in a row? They say your true character comes out when you struggle. They are proper human beings, humble people. They are not arrogant.'

Wayne Smith is insistent that there is no logical reason why New Zealand should stand at the top of world rugby. It is, he argues, a small country with limited finances and without the resources of several rivals. But that is to overlook the influence of the Polynesian-origin youngsters that he calls a critical factor in New Zealand's success.

What's more, he makes an intriguing comparison between youngsters from an island-origin family, whatever the generation, and the Pakeha youngsters. If you drive around New Zealand today, he says, the majority of kids you see playing with a rugby ball are Polynesian. Just as, thirty or forty years ago, the majority would have been Pakeha. The social waves ebb and flow, just like the seas that brought so many to this land.

'Some Pakeha kids are inside now, probably playing with a computer,' Smith says. 'Tongan, Samoan and Fiji-origin kids now have what the rural kids had years and years ago. They are hugely committed to playing the game, to getting out in the backyard and playing. New Zealand has been fortunate to have those strains coming through the population. They have been massive things in us maintaining our position in the world of rugby. Because we shouldn't have been able to, given our population size and isolation.

'We should not be at the top of the pile. But we are always striving to be there. Striving for excellence and it becomes self-fulfilling. Every time a new player comes into the All Blacks there is an expectation. Every time a new coach arrives there is also an expectation. They commit their whole lives to keeping up that excellence.'

That expectation applies to every member invited into this select fold: Maori, Pasifika or Pakeha.

Sir Tony O'Reilly shares Wayne Smith's view: 'There is nothing inherently, intrinsically in favour of New Zealand. It's not a climatic care issue, it's not bigger, bigger men. It's not the dazzling skills of four or five players every six years. I am undazzled by New Zealand's skills. But they're good players. New Zealand are unduly blessed with good, classy players. They automatically do the right thing.

'New Zealand is almost unique. It is the only country that is a unilateral place. The land, for 4.8 million people, is inherently the most economic landscape in the world for the normal farming of cattle;

beef, milk products, etc. It is hugely fertile. And the people offer innovative qualities that build on all that.'

Few feel more innovative than the talented Maori, Pasifika and Pakeha players at New Zealand's disposal. It has always been the case. Wayne Smith offered it as an illustration of the species: 'Even back in 1905, even in that age, on the boat to England, Dave Gallaher looked at the law book and saw that there was nothing to stop you having a player who played both in the forwards and the backs. And that was the development of the wing forward. So even in that age they were innovating. They were innovative thinkers. It has been a tradition in New Zealand rugby to be like that, to think of different ways to do things and come up with solutions.'

Smith and his family ought to know about innovation, durability and dedication to a task. His grandfather went out to New Zealand from Peterhead in Scotland in the 1920s, to help build the Arthur's Pass tunnel in the Southern Alps that would link Canterbury with the West Coast region. He stayed for two years. When, many years later, Wayne and his family were in Greymouth, looking at the little museum there, he asked the curator about those times. The response: 'If they stayed two weeks they were tough. So, two years?'

Not content with that, Smith's grandfather then went to Arapuni to work as a carpenter on the hydroelectric power station and dam. Then the depression hit. His wife was stuck in Peterhead with their two children, unable to travel to New Zealand. Her battling husband had to resort to planting forests around the South Waikato and Taupo areas, just to get food coupons. By the time his wife got out to New Zealand, their two children were seven and eight years old.

Steve Hansen concedes that New Zealand has its issues. Every nation does. But in his mind, there is a seismic difference: 'Because we are so far away, we have had to get on and work together. We haven't hung on to all the stuff that maybe other countries have clung to. We just get on with it. Isolation creates that attitude. That is a factor still in young men today in this country. And it has an important relevance to sports such as rugby.'

The role of the Maori is fundamental to this tale. Down among the seemingly endless farms of the Waikato, where the land feels as vast as the sky, Liam Messam has been the living heartbeat of rugby for the Chiefs. He enjoys respect as a proud Maori far from his own region. Messam's dedication, to his people and his sport, offers a model of selflessness for others to follow. Yet interestingly, he suspects rugby itself came second in the process of successful amalgamation of the different peoples in New Zealand society.

Why has there been this harmony, I asked him: 'You can say it is rugby that has done it. But I think it is Kiwis in general, although rugby does play a part. Kiwis as a people are very caring – we have massive hearts. We get in behind all our sports teams. It's in everyone's DNA; being a Kiwi, you want to get along with everyone.

'We acknowledge that the Maori are the natives. So it's not us and them, which you can get in other countries. The Maori invite everyone here and we unite as one. The Maori welcome all peoples. But people seem to bond, to mix. It's the Kiwi thing. If someone needs help on the side of the street you can guarantee there will be a Kiwi there to help.'

He smiles. It's a warm, deep smile, genuine and not disingenuous. As befits the man. 'Of course, once you cross that line of chalk and walk onto a rugby field, all that friendliness and welcome is over.'

Messam contends that Maori have played a massive part in New Zealand rugby. He sees it as a necessary and therapeutic exercise to satiate their style and characteristics as a people. 'It has been an opportunity for them to express the way they play, because Maori rugby is a lot different to any other rugby. There is a lot more flair, anything can happen from anywhere. Unpredictability is the word. There have been some awesome Maori rugby players that have come through, not only to represent their people but the country.

'The thing that is different is that the Maori team is all bound by one thing and that is blood. You all have the same blood, which is a little different to the All Blacks. We are not all connected by DNA. Somewhere along the line among the Maori people, you will find a second or third cousin.'

I like Messam. He doesn't bullshit, doesn't deal in platitudes. Just tells it as it is. He's the sort of rugby guy who ought to be a regular choice as captain of any Barbarians XV. He understands real values, yet grasps a sense of fun. He has his priorities right, too. He says what he loves most about the Maori is that rugby is second in importance. Their culture is far and away the priority.

'It is all about identity; who you are as a person and where you come from. That is one of the big differences compared to any other team I have been in.'

Intrinsically, Maori links to rugby are so strong for one predominant reason. The game suits them as a people. It is physically challenging but allows the opportunity for a rich streak of creativity, both qualities that are writ large in their creed. Maori love getting into the tough stuff. But they also love the opportunity to let their hair down. To throw the ball around, and just have fun. Which is why you never quite know what you are going to get from a Maori team.

But, in this successful process of integration, who moved the furthest? Which people became the most accommodating in the cause of social and racial harmony? Wayne Shelford says there is clear evidence to answer those questions.

'The New Zealand Pakeha have changed a lot their outlook and views regarding Polynesians and Maori. The European-origin white New Zealander has learned more in recent years about the culture of Maori and Polynesians. Their education in that respect has improved and they are learning all the time. The hakas have helped this process.'

Gilbert Enoka agrees. 'The white people had to be the most flexible to adapt, until we taught them about what it meant to be a New Zealander. That is different to being an All Black. They used to think the haka was just for the Maori people. But once we all understood that the Treaty of Waitangi made us a bicultural nation, we connected explicably.

'With the Polynesians, it was one of the biggest challenges we had. I said to them, you are a double-edged sword. There are two things you contribute to this culture. One is really positive, one really negative.

'The positive is that your sense of "*fano*", the connection to family, is so much more than what the Pakeha brings to it. Because the Polynesians are so giving, so warm and so inclusive to the point where they give a lot of their money straight to their family.'

But Enoka saw at once there was a downside to the Polynesian psyche: 'They are too submissive. They will accept what someone says, irrespective of whether he is right or wrong, just because he is older or in a position of authority.'

That has dangled a delicious task in front of him. 'It is one of my biggest challenges that someone has got to be the one that breaks that mould. You don't have to be disrespectful to the elders or these people to get points across that are going to enable the team to be more successful. We are chipping away at that. But there are still generations of conditioning in that sort of environment that are going to take a heck of a lot to change.'

A bit like trying to get Doug Howlett to stop calling his former school master 'Mr Hansen'.

Bryan Williams adds, 'We have been able to marry up the best attributes of Maori, Pasifika and European peoples down the years. I believe this blending of the races has been a considerable achievement, plus a great example to the rest of the world of how you can bring people of diverse backgrounds together and achieve a great deal. We live down at the far end of the world and basically, we have had to get on with one another. It seemed more natural to get on than not. We didn't have prejudices that might have existed elsewhere.'

Merv Aoake, one-time playing opponent of Steve Hansen and a proud Maori, concurs: 'It is the blend of the different cultures that I think gives the All Blacks their strength. What has been achieved is a great triumph, a wonderful story. It has always been one of the big reasons for the All Blacks being successful. They all bring different styles, different qualities.'

Different expectations, too. But despite all that, these often wildly varying ingredients have all gone into one pot and emerged with a shared sense of purpose. The significance of this for world rugby has been profound.

Yet there is one element of the Pasifika story that is a failure. Who says so? Steve Hansen.

I asked Hansen a simple question. Give me an approximate percentage of guys in the All Blacks squad that are super-talented. I had a figure in mind. Maybe 60 to 65 per cent. But Hansen demurred.

'Well,' he said, 'I think they are all talented. You wouldn't get there if you didn't have talent. But the ones with super, super talent? To be honest, I would say it is pretty low. Probably a third of your group. No more. That is where I think we have failed these super-talented athletes . . . the Polynesians . . . by not giving them a work ethic. They actually fail because they get up to that international standard and it gets tough. If you don't have a work ethic, you don't cope with how tough it is. It's about getting them to understand that what you put in is what you get out. It's not the ingredients, it's what you do with the ingredients that matters.

'But the hardest people to teach a work ethic to are those that are naturally talented. Because they don't have to have a work ethic to be successful at a young age. They can get rewards for doing just what they are good at without having to work hard at it. It just happens naturally.'

Where does Hansen think the biggest failure is? Auckland. 'It is our biggest centre and it has a massive amount of talent up there that gets wasted. Because we are not teaching them how to have a work ethic. It's not just rugby, it's all sports.'

And so it goes on. New Zealand rugby's endless quest for self-improvement.

7

WINNING!

Contributions from, among others,
Sir Colin Meads, Richie McCaw, Chris Laidlaw,
Steve Tew, Kieran Read, Joel Stransky,
Pierre Berbizier, Brad Burke,
Scott Robertson, Tony Brown.

'You have got to be prepared to come last to get first. That is my philosophy.'

Tony Brown, 2017 Highlanders coach, now Japan assistant coach

There is a reason for this 'endless quest for self-improvement'. In a single word, it is this. Winning.

It represents the entire *raison d'être* of New Zealand rugby. It drives them as a sporting people, day and night. The nation is consumed by a single ambition. Victory. No matter the opponent, occasion or competition. Theirs is a ruthlessness, an intensity of focus beyond the comprehension of almost all other nations. It is a desire that unites the entire country.

Nothing is allowed to come between New Zealand and winning. Even insensitivity to outsiders and their views. A 'them against us' culture has been fostered over the years to enhance this process. The sense of geographical isolation has helped, too. It sustains much of what New Zealand rugby does and how it thinks.

The 'winning mentality' was always there in New Zealand rugby circles. Perhaps unspoken, but relevant all the same. But of late, it has reached a stage where the demands of winning have now entered a new arena. It is known as an obligation. Even prime ministers genuflect to its importance.

'Winning' is a word that rolls off the tongue like fine wine. Sporting icons are just some of those attracted by its allure. Mourad Boudjellal (owner of French rugby club Toulon) bought the players he needed to achieve it. Plenty have cheated to taste its elixir, like Americans Lance Armstrong and Justin Gatlin. It has enticed mankind down the ages. It is the most potent of drugs.

Perhaps Muhammad Ali came closest to defining it: 'Only a man who knows what it is like to be defeated can reach down to the bottom of his soul and come up with that extra ounce of power it takes to win when the match is even,' he said.

Richie McCaw puts it another way. 'I have seen guys that have come to Super Rugby. They have been the star at school in the Super Rugby side. Always winning. But it is always going to get harder sometime and they have got absolutely no understanding of how to persevere or find the way. They think, "It shouldn't be like this, it should be easy." But it is not. Winning never is.

'The ones that have had a few ups and downs . . . they are the guys that when it gets tough they figure out a way. The question is, how do you build that resilience without knocking him back?'

It is a defining characteristic of the great All Blacks, like McCaw and Dan Carter. Both freely concede they remember the defeats more than the victories, even after their greatest triumphs. The mental anguish that they confronted in defeat and the desire to put it right next time never left them. For winning is a bug you can't cure; if it's in your body, if it's embedded in your mind, it is a lifetime condition.

It is why Steve Hansen still winces when he talks about the All Blacks' failure at the 2007 Rugby World Cup. It explains his confession of the mental pain that defeat induced. 'With New Zealand it is different. Not only have we got to win, we have got to win by a lot of points and play a game of rugby everyone wants to see. But in reality, that doesn't always happen. That is what you are striving for, and I think that is the difference between the two teams that line up for the anthems. Although both groups of men are there for the same reasons, the expectations of winning are not the same . . .'

In the case of New Zealand, it comes not least from the knowledge that an entire nation is behind you. Urging, willing, cajoling you to win. It's not like that in other nations. More than half of Australia couldn't care less whether the Wallabies win or lose. Some Australians hardly know who the Wallabies are.

England might play a rugby international on a Saturday at Twickenham. But the legions of fans at Manchester City, Liverpool, Tottenham and Manchester United couldn't give a fig about the outcome. By contrast, New Zealanders have a depth of allegiance to their national rugby team that other nations cannot know. Only one other major nation is united behind a national sporting team in a similar way – India and its cricket team. In New Zealand, everyone is concerned about just one thing. Will the All Blacks win?

Contained within this intensely focused nation and its obsession for the sport, lies yet another reason for New Zealand's pre-eminence.

There is, as one former All Black told me, not just an expectation of victory but an obligation. Critical phrase, critical difference. The doctrine enshrined within this philosophy revolves around commitment. The players are required to show utter commitment until the final hooter sounds. And then, as against Ireland in their famous last-gasp win in November 2013, even more commitment in those final moments when, irrespective of aching limbs and lungs drained of breath like oil from a car, impending defeat can be turned into glorious victory. Nothing and no one is allowed to challenge this doctrine of constant effort and total self-belief. Physical exhaustion is no excuse. All Blacks are built and trained to go to the last second.

Yet some disavow the notion that all demands, obligations and criticisms are fair. As Ryan Crotty says, 'We seem to be, as New Zealanders, a little more reserved. We just go about our work. If you are a tall poppy, you get cut down quickly.'

But Beauden Barrett is one of those who doesn't necessarily swallow all this comfortably. 'It's the Kiwi way,' he says. 'But there is a bit of tall-poppy syndrome in New Zealand I don't agree with. I don't think that's healthy – I think you should be encouraged and applauded when you do great things. But there is a fine line between doing great things and being cocky or arrogant about it. I think generally we are pretty good at living on that fine line. But it just does annoy me when the general public bring people down to earth when really, we should be applauding great achievements.

'I don't think the All Blacks are revered enough in their own country. That's what I mean by the Kiwi way. It could be the reason why we have been so successful because, no matter how good a win you get, you are always told by everyone it's on to the next job. However, there are times when you have to acknowledge the great things that have been done. But I guess that's just the general sense we get from the public and the fans. Whereas overseas, you do really appreciate the support you get over there for what the All Blacks achieve.'

The sheer desire for victory is the factor which has decided so many close contests. It is endemic among New Zealand rugby players. Put simply, it is a deeply entrenched demand that somehow, someone must produce that moment of magic to win the match. Yet the key is that fourteen players on the field are not sitting back waiting for someone else to come up with the decisive play. All fifteen are searching for it.

What every player has to offer is professionalism and a shrewd, deep knowledge of how to play the game to their team's advantage. In adversity, they understand intrinsically how to survive, while in more optimal moments, they know how to prosper. They can slow down or speed up a game to suit their own purposes. This streetwise ability is a critical weapon in their arsenal. It enables them to snatch vital victories or escape from parlous positions. And it applies not just at international level but also in Super Rugby. The New Zealand teams' supremacy over all southern-hemisphere opponents in the last few years (New Zealand Super Rugby teams' collective record over Australian opponents stretched to thirty-nine consecutive wins by mid-May 2018) has been forged on this trait, in addition to their relentless attitude, whether it be in defence or attack.

But what is the long-term effect of all this? A depressing message for most rugby nations, according to Pat Lam, now coaching English club Bristol but head coach of Auckland from 2004 to 2008 and then the Blues between 2009 and 2012.

'There is nothing to threaten New Zealand's dominance. You have got to have the right vision driving the culture of the place. The All Blacks' number-one goal is to keep winning rugby matches and by and large, that's pretty much what they do. Ultimately, all decisions made in New Zealand rugby are made to ensure the All Blacks are number one. New Zealand Rugby knows that funds the game. The All Blacks bring in 80 per cent of the revenue of New Zealand Rugby and that grows the game.

'You can talk about Super Rugby, but the fact is that South Islanders don't care whether the [Auckland] Blues win Super Rugby and North Islanders don't care if the Crusaders win it. But what unites them, what they all care about, is that the All Blacks win. That captures the whole country.'

However, some observers believe the levels of expectation concerning these young sportsmen have reached absurd proportions. After all, they can't win all the time. The 1960s All Blacks half-back Chris Laidlaw insists, 'The demands are too excessive. For example, there has been a rolling debate for years about these guys being role models, and people thinking they ought to act like role models. My reply? Don't be silly in expecting people to be role models for everyone else because they are role models for rugby only. It is unfair to say you are a role model for modern youth, that's quite wrong. Firstly, they can't live up to that and, secondly, they are professional rugby players. It's completely unrealistic to expect them to be role models for the rest of society. It says more about a society that puts these young men on a pedestal. Anybody who is a star is going to be scrutinized, watched, followed. Every action will be reported somewhere. That never used to be the case. So they are going to fail. Whenever I see any of these failures, I think well, that's fine, they just reflect the general population. Leave off the hand-wringing and accusations of failing to live up to something or someone else's expectations. That's not fair.'

Tales of New Zealand rugby players plumbing the depths of personal behaviour and not living up to expectations have excited much interest because they are comparatively few. Names like Keith Murdoch, Ali Williams, Aaron Smith and Zac Guildford seem to have entered a grim Hall of Infamy. But they represent the tiny minority who have transgressed.

As Otago and Oxford University-educated Chris Laidlaw says, teasingly, 'Ali Williams is a bit of a dope. He is a very immature guy but he is a perfect case of . . . for God's sake, don't put this guy on a pedestal. In fact, don't put any of these players on a pedestal, it's going to end in tears. He [Williams] is a party boy, a very good player who managed to combine the two when he was playing.'

Perhaps New Zealand Rugby CEO Steve Tew's line about Williams is the best. 'We couldn't control Ali when he played here in New Zealand. So what chance would we have when he's with a French club in Paris?'

What the best young rugby men of New Zealand are asked to handle is twofold: the obligation to win and keep winning, plus the demand that they demonstrate the social skills and behaviour of role models. Yet many do seem to manage such demands with something approaching equanimity. As Kieran Read says, 'Yes, it is an obsession. Almost everyone is deeply passionate about rugby in this country and we are privileged to be in the position we're in. Plenty of players would love to be doing what we do. New Zealand's nationality and pride affect how people feel about themselves and us as a nation. Life is not always easy in New Zealand for all manner of people. If we can lift the spirits of the community and the country by winning, that really transcends sport itself.

'It is hard to say we will continue to keep going in terms of the sustained success we have enjoyed. We will lose the occasional game; that is inevitable. That's sport and that's life. But because the foundations have been set so strongly in this environment, if we prepare as well as we have in the past and we remain modest with our feet on the ground, we have got the talent to stay at the top of the tree.

'Overall consistency is the thing that has set us apart from others throughout history. We have to keep that momentum by continuing to keep winning. But another challenge for all of us is to create a legacy even stronger than the one before. It is made very clear to you, and therefore you understand very early on, that getting into the All Blacks side is not the finishing point, it's the start. You are expected to leave it better than you found it.'

The South African Joel Stransky, whose drop goal against the All Blacks won the 1995 Rugby World Cup Final, calls the game 'a religion' in New Zealand. Stransky says, 'That breeds a culture of excellence and a desire to succeed. That is intrinsically much the way the Kiwis live. They have real talent but also incredible self-belief. It is not a general expectation but a real deep-seated belief that they will always be there at the end. They have a superb attitude to the game; that is the most important thing. There are a number of factors that make some teams and some environments great. The most important is in the mind.'

Kieran Read himself was handed the virtually impossible task of trying to follow Richie McCaw's supreme record as All Blacks leader. And, according to Laidlaw, Read's cares and concerns might be about to deepen. Even before the British & Irish Lions held New Zealand to a tied 1–1 Test series in 2017, Laidlaw was warning, 'Is there any reason why New Zealand's supremacy *wouldn't* change? I think we might be hitting the high water mark. The other countries are better prepared, equally physical. They might not be quite as dextrous and athletic. But that gap is closing and you can breed that into a team over time. England are doing it. They have some brilliant players. So where is our point of difference? Expectations, probably. We expect to win and that makes a little difference. There is a whole bunch of psychological techniques to get people to think in terms of winning. That, to me, is the only point of difference we have, apart from this odd little margin in terms of athleticism.'

Just occasionally it goes awry. In 1994 for example, out of nowhere, France sent a team to New Zealand which managed to win both Test matches against the All Blacks. It was the first time they had won a series against them in New Zealand. No one could quite work out how they did it. The mastermind of those French victories, 22–8 in Christchurch and 23–20 in Auckland, was Pierre Berbizier. The former French half-back and national coach pays his respects to what he calls 'a lot of good work' by New Zealand Rugby. Berbizier told me, 'They maybe only have about 150–200 [fully professional] players whereas other countries have many more. But they play a universal style of rugby and they work on continuity and stability.

'In France, we felt it would be impossible for New Zealand to replace McCaw, yet they did it because of this continuity. The main target of New Zealand rugby is not the players but the All Blacks. For me, if I were asked to define an All Black, I would say, "Spirit, inspiration." If you want to be an All Black, you have to work to have a mind like an All Black. It's not the same in France. To New Zealanders, it's more important generally and it's their character. That's the difference. The crucial factor is, to be an All Black and play for New Zealand is just more important than for a Frenchman playing for France.'

This exalted level of expectation once you reach the hallowed ranks of the All Blacks manifests itself in a plethora of ways. Expectation of victory, which rapidly morphs into an obligation, has been inculcated down the ages. Read talks of an overall consistency of success and what he means by that is this.

New Zealand first started playing Test match rugby against Australia in 1903, yet the Aussies did not win a series in New Zealand until 1949. Even then, most of New Zealand's best players were away on a tour of South Africa at the same time.

New Zealand rugby teams do consistent success like the Queen does decorum. From 1884 to 1914, in all matches, the New Zealanders played 114, won 107, drew two and lost five. This equates to a win ratio of 93.85 per cent, an extraordinary figure.

By contrast, between the 1920s and the 1940s, they had a win ratio of only 54 per cent. But things then started to improve. In the 1950s and 60s, it reached 80 per cent, with fifty-seven wins from seventy-one Tests. Things are never allowed to decline for long in the world of New Zealand rugby. The nation demands that the All Blacks win.

The most relevant statistic relates to the period between the advent of professionalism in 1995 and the end of 2017. In that time, New Zealand played 274 Test matches. They won 229, drew five and lost forty. Their winning ratio was 83.58 per cent. As for coaches, Steve Hansen's winning ratio as All Blacks coach between 2012 and the start of 2018 stood at 89 per cent.

Australia half-back Brad Burke, former captain of the Randwick club in Sydney, remembers playing the All Blacks an astonishing three times in seven days back in 1988. And in every game, says Burke, their philosophy was the same. You could see it. They had to win. It was a demand.

Burke first faced the All Blacks at Coogee Oval in Sydney, as a member of a highly talented Randwick side that included luminaries such as Lloyd Walker, David Campese, David Knox, Simon Poidevin, Eddie Jones, Ewen McKenzie and Gary Ella. The All Blacks had a large number of their 1987 World Cup winning side playing. They won 25–9, having trailed 9–3 at one stage.

Four days later, Burke captained Australia A against them at Ballymore in Brisbane. And three days after that, he played for New South Wales B against them at Gosford. How did he feel after that little work out? Sore.

'The most exciting thing for me was playing for Randwick. It was a club team versus the world champions, an incredible thrill. At the same time, it was terrifying. They were so strong, virtually untouchable. I remember the two hookers, Eddie Jones and Sean Fitzpatrick, never shut up for a minute. They just kept going at each other the whole match.

'Buck Shelford tried to take Simon Poidevin's head off . . . it was a pretty hard battle. But it was a lot of fun. Pure amateur football. They had this aura about them. It was a great experience and gave me a better understanding of what made them tick. They were very reserved as people but expressed themselves on the field. They are testing material; if you want to play anyone to test yourself as a footballer, you should play the All Blacks. It is a privilege to play against them.'

These are great memories. It was a Wednesday afternoon and Coogee Oval was bursting, with a crowd of around 6,000. All the flats overlooking the ground were packed on their terraces. People were everywhere, it was standing room only.

'There is a lot of that Scottish Lutheran influence in them, so they are very strong and reserved in their beliefs,' said Burke. 'Then, bring in the Maori culture and together they come up with a character that is very suitable for a strong sporting nation. Belief in that All Blacks ethos is something they all buy into. It's a great way to develop a super team.'

This never-ending desire to win, whoever the opponent and whatever the match, is the core element of New Zealand's supremacy in world rugby. The demand for victory is based on unique circumstances in New Zealand, where literally everything is done to help make the team at the peak of the pyramid, the All Blacks, consistently successful. But this mania to succeed can have a downside, something highlighted by Nick Farr-Jones, who captained Australia to a World Cup win in 1991: 'It's true, New Zealand kids grow up learning the basics really well. But the other thing is, they understand the laws better than anyone else. Because of that, they probably can just get on the wrong side . . .'

Only 'just', Nick? I could introduce you to people all around the rugby-playing world who would swear blind that Richie McCaw was actually born offside! Farr-Jones's 1991 World Cup coach Bob Dwyer is one of them. 'Their rugby philosophy means that they have an attitude of, "If the referee doesn't call it, it's not against the law",' says Dwyer.

'Some of the top All Blacks have been renowned for these things: Kieran Read, Owen Franks, Conrad Smith did whatever they liked. But, in fairness to Richie McCaw, his biggest fault wasn't offside, it was obstruction – playing players without the ball.'

Harsh criticism? No, says Dwyer, because the evidence supports his view. Won't New Zealand do just about anything to get over the line, to secure a victory, whether legal or illegal?

Take Kieran Read's knock-down of the ball from Scottish forward Jonny Gray's grasp as he headed for the New Zealand try-line during the tight Test match in November 2017. No arguments, it was an illegal act that should have brought a yellow card. It could well have prevented a try. But the referee, his two assistants and the television match official (TMO) all missed it. All Scotland seethed at their 22–17 defeat.

The Scottish assistant coach Dan McFarland said, 'That was just cynical, wasn't it? It should have been a yellow card, quite possibly a try, and quite possibly a penalty try. I can see that would be something for discussion, but that's not up for discussion now, is it?' The referee did see other incidents in a dramatic final quarter of that game that merited, in his view, yellow cards for All Blacks flanker Sam Cane and replacement prop Wyatt Crockett. McFarland says the repeat offending summed up the All Blacks' mentality: 'New Zealand are an extremely competitive side and everybody in world rugby knows that when you get the ball into their twenty-two the very last thing they want to do is concede a try. That's how they play. They're very streetwise, they're very clever.'

Was Read's act one befitting an All Blacks captain? In New Zealand eyes, that's not the point. You just do what you have to do to win the game.

Yet Farr-Jones has a more sanguine approach to such things. 'I don't have a problem with that. You have got to be smart and, as a captain, you are constantly communicating with the referee. So that you have that opportunity and the advantage of that communication stream to understand where you can gain an advantage. When you are a very good team and you have good people of significant presence, you have an automatic advantage. Why not use that? Because you are respected by the world but also by the international referees. They know you know the game. They know you are the best at the game. You understand the laws. So it is more difficult to blow them up, to penalize them, particularly when it is the captain talking to the official. So you question decisions.'

No other country in world rugby focuses so intently on ensuring that the cream always rises to the top. From school level, as far down as the Under 10s and 12s, through provincial, Mitre 10 and then Super Rugby, every New Zealander involved to a significant degree in the sport works with one ultimate aim: to ensure the All Blacks keep on winning.

This country-wide devotion to the project is a strength that is hard to define in precise terms, yet it is critical to the national team's achievements. Most of this unseen army of assistants are rarely identified, save those already in the public limelight for their high-profile roles, such as Super Rugby franchise coaches. Yet the work they do is of incontestable value, like worker ants.

Such a system appears to be anathema to the rugby men of nations like England or France. The owners of the top clubs in those countries pursue very different agendas to that of their national teams, which are unable to accommodate a New Zealand-style arrangement. The outcome is inevitable. At international level, in terms of sustained success, it seems inevitable that these nations fail as often as they succeed. It is far from a coincidence that since the New Zealander Joe Schmidt took over as Ireland coach in 2013 and began to implement a structure reasonably similar to that of New Zealand rugby, their results have been more consistent. Ireland's 2018 Grand Slam triumph was further evidence of their progress.

How does the New Zealand model work? Scott Robertson knows better than most. He masterminded the Crusaders' journey to the 2017 Super Rugby title in his first season as senior coach with the franchise. Robertson brought with him a reputation for not mincing words – tiptoeing around exchanging pleasantries is not exactly his preferred *modus operandi*. So how does Robertson, an All Black himself who played in twenty-three Test matches between 1998 and 2002, handle the requirements of the national coaches? Is there intrusion, and if there is, does he resent it? Isn't he tempted to tell outsiders where to go if they start interfering? Such a system is simply beyond imagination in France or England, because neither country will ever achieve such unity of purpose. Likewise, the concept that everyone is working so that one team, the All Blacks, succeeds above all others; it is demanded of every Super Rugby coach that he buys into this philosophy from day one. Just as there are expectations upon the best players, the same goes for the top coaches.

But who has the final word when it comes to debating whether an All Black with the Crusaders should be rested, and what if Robertson disagrees with a proposal handed down from above? The great thing about Robertson, and it is something that his players clearly buy into, is his honesty. He tells it like it is. 'They [the All Blacks coaches] are very good at making suggestions. But never any expectations go with it. That is one of Steve Hansen's strengths. Ian Foster and [before he stepped down] Wayne Smith are most hands-on with the Super Rugby teams. They ask good, challenging questions. I don't feel under pressure from this process but the players would. As for the outcome, there is no obligation but it normally works itself out.'

Contrary to a widely held belief that suggests uniformity in playing style is rigidly enforced among all the Super Rugby teams, Robertson denies there is any expectation on the style employed. But one thing is non-negotiable: skill set. 'They try every single skill set so that when they go back to the All Blacks, their basic skill set is world-class. They have to work on those skills all the time. We don't have a policy of automatic selection for All Blacks. If they are playing well, they get selected. It doesn't matter if you are an All Black – you have a chance of selection as long as you are playing well. You have to give them every opportunity to succeed, whatever their age.'

There is one definite stipulation. A New Zealand franchise is allowed no more than two overseas players, plus any Polynesian internationals, in its squad. And it can include only those two in its match squad. The contrast with France is not coincidental. Late in his playing career, Robertson went to France and played for Perpignan. What he discovered was an object lesson in how *not* to treat young players:

'When I was at Perpignan we used to play an "Espoirs" ['prospects' or 'hopes'] team on a midweek night sometimes. Some of those junior teams had magnificent players, some of them better than the guys in our starting XV. But they didn't pick them. There is this conservatism around the world. Four or five of that "Espoirs" team eventually went on to play for France. But they didn't stay at Perpignan. They didn't have the right people running the club.'

What is relevant here, in terms of New Zealand rugby, is the contrast between a nation that expects young players to achieve and empowers them in pursuit of that ambition, and one that is unwilling to advance talent at a younger age. This is a crucial difference between rugby nations like New Zealand and France. If you don't offer total support to young players, don't convince them that you have implicit faith in their abilities then you cannot expect them to have the confidence to perform on the ultimate stage. This is a straightforward equation: expectation = belief = winning. One thing is certain – you cannot short-change this process. The three elements are firmly linked.

Robertson went on, 'What I saw in France made me realize the coaches there had to win every week. So they weren't planning on the long-term and development. But to me, it's not just about winning every week. No one can do that. But bringing on young players and giving them their chance is something we do very well as Kiwis. We give guys opportunities at any age. Age is not seen as a barrier in New Zealand rugby. These kids are more tactically and technically aware than they used to be. So players are ready earlier and that is one of the reasons why the All Blacks continue to be successful. Our coaching from schools to clubs to academies to professional rugby is better than anywhere. And the skill level is strong enough to apply these tactics.'

Robertson coached New Zealand Under 20s for three years before he took charge at the Crusaders. He was struck by the discipline of the environment and how quickly players could step up. The All Blacks coaches have a handle on every level of the game. Even Robertson admits, 'They are looking over your shoulder. But mainly to make sure you are OK. I don't feel threatened or intimidated by that process. There is no fear. Steve Hansen coached me for six years and we have a good relationship.'

The winning mentality? 'We know who we are and how we like to play, because we are such a multi-cultured nation. We embrace who we are, we like to show our identity by expressing ourselves. Yes, the public have expectations for us to score tries. It helps the style of the competition. For me, the most important thing is that kids have got to see there is still enjoyment from the game. Give away the expectations of being a professional player and just play the game with your mates. We must continue to give young people the competitions and structures to do that.'

It is axiomatic that, if a country largely employs the same playing patterns at most levels, and if the national selectors are ready to step in and offer guidance, the nation must be stronger in a playing sense. A national coach who is forced to combine different playing styles from a mixture of club or provincial teams will need double, perhaps triple the time to get all his players operating in the same way. Even so, it is unlikely that he will ever achieve total transformation to a single style of play. Some have embraced a different playing philosophy for most of their careers. It is impossible to coach them into new beliefs in the course of a season or two.

This is a key factor in the building of New Zealand rugby and another reason for their supremacy. Players encouraged for years to play in a specific style, and forced to operate under pressure, will inevitably make better, smarter decisions on the field. Quick hands, quick feet, quick brains. Again, it's no coincidence the decision-making under pressure of New Zealand players is light years ahead of most of their counterparts in other countries. We're talking the difference between a Mazda and a Maserati. Furthermore, being brought through and offered opportunities in a system without age constraints provides early and invaluable exposure to the game at high levels. It is crucial to the learning process.

Tony Brown was an All Black between 1999 and 2001. Seventeen of his eighteen international matches were Tests. But of more relevance to this story is Brown's coaching experience, both as assistant coach to Jamie Joseph at the Highlanders, and as senior coach in 2017, before he departed to Japan to link up again with Joseph for the 2019 Rugby World Cup. He is also assistant coach at Japanese Super Rugby outfit the Sunwolves. Brown, like all his fellow New Zealand franchise coaches, was asked in 2017 to attend a meeting with the All Blacks coaches before the Super Rugby season began. Summoned to the headmaster's study? Brown didn't see it that way.

'The national selectors might say they see a certain player as a number twelve or number thirteen. If they don't have a preference, that helps us. But I didn't feel under special pressure because of this. Anyway, I wanted to keep the communication with the All Blacks selectors. Because we are all engaged in the ultimate goal of keeping the All Blacks winning. We, as a franchise, want to win games, too, of course, but at the top of the tree is the All Blacks. So our interaction with the All Blacks coaches is ongoing and vibrant. You feel you are helping them to be successful. It is performances that get your players into contention for the All Blacks.

'We might make a couple of selections that could affect the All Blacks selectors. But everything in the country is geared to that peak. Every player, whatever his level, wants to be an All Black and every coach wants to coach their players to become All Blacks. If you are a coach or player and you lose that feeling, you are losing what is great about rugby.'

It is just not like this at French or English clubs like Toulon or Bath. No one goes out each day there, thinking, 'Now what can we do to improve England's prospects?' There, winning for the club is the only item on the agenda. The national team comes second. In New Zealand, the opposite is the case and the nation is defined by their all-conquering rugby team. Hence, the national level is revered and deeply respected. In France and England it is, at best, tolerated.

The central theme of New Zealand teams' rugby revolves at all levels around two philosophies: do the basics consistently well, and attack. Winning should ensue. The pace is usually high, ball skills commensurate. They prove that it is perfectly possible to play the modern game with an attacking instinct and be successful, no matter how great the focus may be on defence by some opponents. If you are good enough.

Intrinsically, it is about playing the game in much the way it was always intended. And never underestimate the importance of that factor in unravelling the story of why a small country of less than five million people have come to dominate a whole world sport.

As Salvador Dali once put it, 'Intelligence without ambition is a bird without wings.'

8

AT ALL COSTS

*Contributions from, among others,
Graham Mourie, Willie John McBride,
Alan Sutherland, Ian Smith, Tony Ward,
Pascal Ondarts, Richie McCaw, Sir Colin Meads,
Chris Laidlaw, Andrew Slack, John Connolly,
Andy Haden, John Hart, Reuben Thorne, Jerome Kaino,
Victor Matfield, Gilbert Enoka, Tony Johnson,
Wyatt Crockett, Brodie Retallick.*

'When I look back, yes, there were one or two things I regretted, felt I went too far.'

The late Sir Colin Meads

There is one damaging consequence of New Zealand's obsession with winning at rugby.

At times, some of their leading players have gone too far in pursuit of their Holy Grail. Victory.

They have crossed the line that divides industry and effort from wanton violence on the field. The reputation of certain players and also of the national team has been damaged by such acts. If we accept the premise that, in terms of the pursuit of excellence, New Zealand stands alone at the summit of world rugby, then it is surely beholden upon them to play in a manner that upholds the highest standards and traditions of the game. But alas, these occasional acts of violence and cheap tricks have, at times, demeaned both the national team and the game at large.

How best to define that desire to win and the fear of losing? A couple of Yanks nailed it in specifying the fine lines between the two. 'I hate to lose more than I love to win,' said US tennis star Jimmy Connors. And from Vince Lombardi? 'Winning isn't everything, but wanting to win is.'

Or as Richie McCaw said, 'The big thing that really drove me was not having those off days. I didn't consciously think of that at the start. But when I did think about it, I didn't want to let that slip. The bad days hurt. Always. You remember them more than the days that were good. That is why we do what we do. Kiwis and All Blacks. We remember the worst days more than the good days. But that is what keeps you grounded. Keeps you going.'

No need for any psychologists. You won't do better than that in trying to understand the motives of the wannabe winner. It helps us understand why some sportsmen will do anything to clamber onto that winner's podium. It's the craving for the drug of ambition. Swallow carefully. It is a potent poison . . .

The date is 15 June 1968. View through this prism the events unfolding at the famous Sydney Cricket Ground (SCG) in Australia. A New Zealand rugby team containing some legendary names, the likes of Tremain, Gray, Lochore, Laidlaw and Kirton, is confronting an Australian side captained by Ken Catchpole, then regarded as the finest half-back in the world. There is another New Zealander, tough, physical, unsmiling, who offers a silent threat. He is Colin Meads. Renowned as the hard man of the All Blacks pack. The hammer in the builder's bag. The game is eight minutes into the second half and New Zealand are decisively ahead, 19–3. Then Catchpole is caught and quickly becomes trapped in a pile of bodies, all attempting to seize the ball, but the diminutive Australian's legs can be seen hanging out of the ruck.

According to the legendary book, *Men in Black: 75 Years of New Zealand International Rugby* by R.H. Chester and N.A.C. McMillan, 'Catchpole was roughly dragged from a ruck by Meads causing a severe groin injury which necessitated his retiring on a stretcher. This injury was to end the brilliant half-back's international career.'

This bold statement is palpably short on two things. Compassion and indictment. This single act, by a man worshipped universally throughout New Zealand in both life and death as one of the greatest ever (if not *the* greatest) All Blacks, represents one of the worst, most brutal assaults ever perpetrated by a New Zealand rugby player. At the time, Meads said, 'That's the game. You do what you have to do.'

Catchpole embraced a rather different philosophy. He always said he played for the enjoyment of the game. Colin Meads' philosophy was that you played to win. What Meads thought he 'had to do' was examined afterwards by Dick Tooth, the ex-Wallaby orthopaedic specialist. He diagnosed Catchpole's hamstring muscle had been completely torn from the pelvic bone. There were ripped and stretched groin muscles and a damaged sciatic nerve; he said it was the worst injury of its type he had ever seen. Three months after the incident, Catchpole still could not touch his toes. He told friends the pain was terrible. It was an agonizing recovery and, thereafter, he was always troubled by a weak thigh. The instant acceleration, once the hallmark of his play, never returned.

Sadly, we can no longer ask Catchpole for his thoughts on the injury that finished his glittering international career. Now aged seventy-eight, he is still in bed asleep when I knock on the door of his home, mid-morning in a leafy North Shore suburb of Sydney. His charming wife June greets me, makes me coffee, shows me the family scrapbooks and mementoes from her husband's career and offers to wake him for my benefit. But there is no point. Ken Catchpole has severe dementia. He now has, in the words of his wife, the mind of a child. Sometimes they argue like mother and child. He knows little or nothing of his past fame. His loving wife has put her sad emotions down in the form of a poem. She wrote this of the great old Wallaby:

> How extraordinary.
> He is there but I cannot find him
> The man I once knew has disappeared
> Gone as in death.
> Lost somewhere in the maze of his mind
> Bewildered.
> Confused without understanding
> Not knowing what to do.
> The whereabouts of things
> What is happening.
> I grieve the loss, feel the sorrow.
> Yet for him, he has no concerns
> For today or tomorrow
> Irrepressible in denial his charm and enigmatic smile.

Little more than six months after my visit, Catchpole died. 'Ken would never say a bad word against anyone,' June Catchpole told me. 'At the time, he called it "a silly accident, a silly thing to do. How could anyone be that vicious?" He was twenty-eight when it happened and he did play club rugby again. But never Test rugby.' Others in Australia were less forgiving. 'A heinous act of barbarism' someone called it.

On one occasion, Catchpole expanded on the injury and his feelings about the incident. 'The injury was extremely severe. I tore two muscles, one from where it was attached. I tore the hamstring but also tore the adductor muscle. It reduced my speed. Colin Meads had become, I believe, a little frustrated. He decided that I should release the ball and he would do something about it. So he actually grabbed hold of my leg which I believe was not a vicious action but a very stupid action, very foolish because it really served no purpose.'

It may be appropriate to note that seven months earlier, in December 1967, Meads had been sent off in New Zealand's tour match against Scotland in Edinburgh. He had been warned in the first half by Irish referee Kevin Kelleher for dangerous play at a collapsed maul. Late in the match, as Scottish fly-half David Chisholm went to pick up a loose ball, Meads aimed a kick at it and was promptly dismissed. He was only the second man ever to be sent off in Test rugby history, after another New Zealander, Cyril Brownlie, in 1924.

Unfortunately, Meads' story is far from the only one involving violence in the chronicles of New Zealand rugby history. Too many deeply unsavoury incidents have occurred over the years for them all to be merely coincidental. What it reveals is a mentality, an utterly ruthless focus on winning. At all costs, if need be.

In 1969, when Wales toured New Zealand, Welsh hooker Jeff Young had his jaw broken by a punch. In some quarters, Meads was blamed. But in this case, critics were off-target – All Blacks prop Ken Gray did it. Years later, in 2014, *New Zealand Herald* rugby writer Wynne Gray wrote of his namesake, 'He tarnished his reputation with too many acts of thuggery.'

Lock forward Alan Sutherland, who played for the All Blacks between 1970 and 1973, including Tests against the 1971 Lions, confirmed that, 'Meads was always tough, an intimidating player. But I certainly wouldn't say he was the dirtiest player. Alister Hopkinson was much harder. But Meads was fearless.'

Similar testimony about Meads comes from the 1960s wing Ian 'Spooky' Smith, who played twenty-four matches for the All Blacks between 1963 and 1966. How tough was Meads, I asked him a few months before his passing, at his beautiful home at Rose Bay, high on a hill looking out over the sea to Nelson, at the top of the South Island.

'Colin Meads probably had a couple of guys going for him every time he played. But I don't think he was particularly dirty, although of course he used to push a few people around. But we have had a few players in New Zealand who were dirtier than him. He had lots of things that made him special. For a big guy, he had exceptionally good hands. He was reasonably quick around the field and he never shirked anything. He was a pretty good footballer all round. He was a tough bastard. You were far better off with him in your side than playing against him.'

Nevertheless, the litany of acts of violence by New Zealand players is disturbingly lengthy. Prop Richard Loe smashed Australian wing Paul Carozza's nose with his elbow after the Australian had scored a try in a trans-Tasman Test in 1992 in Australia. The Australian Rugby Union made a formal complaint to their New Zealand counterparts. But astonishingly, Loe was exonerated.

In fact, Loe, who grew up in the tough North Canterbury rugby area, committed some appalling acts during a career dotted with controversy. In the final of the 1992 New Zealand National Provincial Championship, Loe was caught grabbing Otago full-back and fellow All Black Greg Cooper by the head, with his fingers hooked into Cooper's eye sockets. The incident was missed during the game but was subsequently noticed by a vigilant Television New Zealand tape editor the following day. A New Zealand judicial committee discussed the incident for nine hours before handing Loe a nine-month suspension from the game. When he returned, there was immense vocal public opposition in New Zealand to him being selected for the All Blacks again. But coach Laurie Mains insisted on picking him and Loe was a substitute in the 1995 World Cup Final. However, the following year when John Hart took over, he made it clear that Loe had no part to play in his plans.

Another All Blacks prop from Canterbury, John Ashworth, stamped on the face of Welsh full-back J.P.R. Williams as he lay trapped at the bottom of a ruck in 1978 at Bridgend. Williams left the field with blood pouring from his face, and the wound required thirty stitches. Years later, the Welshman said, 'I remember being nowhere near the ball and being stamped on twice. Luckily, I had previously broken my cheekbone and bones always grow back stronger. If I hadn't, then my cheekbone would have gone. My father stitched me up and I went back on to finish the game, which certainly wouldn't be allowed these days. There was no apology from anyone after the game and I have never spoken to Ashworth since.'

The egregious assault on England half-back Kyran Bracken by All Black flanker Jamie Joseph in 1993 at Twickenham was another completely needless act. Joseph stamped on the Englishman's ankle, two minutes into Bracken's Test debut, damaging the ligaments. The assault was so severe that, although he managed to complete the match, Bracken's ankle was seriously damaged. He did not play rugby again for three months and suffered a permanent weakness.

As *New Zealand Herald* rugby writer Gregor Paul wrote in July

2017, 'In the fifty years since Colin Meads was sent off at Murrayfield, the All Blacks winning narrative has been punctuated with a litany of incidents that would, in all objectivity, have reached the red card threshold.' Paul noted the example of Wayne 'Buck' Shelford punching Welshman Huw Richards unconscious in the 1987 World Cup semi-final. Richards, who had started the fracas, was ordered off when he eventually came round. In 2012, All Blacks hooker Andrew Hore knocked out Welsh lock Bradley Davies. No action was taken at the time but when Hore was later cited, a disciplinary panel banned him for five weeks. As Paul wrote, 'No red cards, though, and the All Blacks, if they are honest, will agree that they have ridden their luck to some extent in the last thirty years.'

But one of the worst assaults by New Zealand players on an opponent came in 2005, after only ninety seconds of the first Test match against the touring British & Irish Lions. The Lions captain Brian O'Driscoll was upended in a spear tackle, arguably the most dangerous in the game, by All Blacks captain Tana Umaga and hooker Keven Mealamu. He dislocated his shoulder and his tour was over – the Irishman didn't play rugby for five months. The fact that it took the then International Rugby Board *four months* to condemn the assault – I won't use the word 'tackle' – says everything about the vacuum in leadership of the game in those times.

By being driven head first into the ground, O'Driscoll could easily have broken his neck and been paralysed for life. It was a wilful, highly dangerous act. Ludicrously, neither player was even warned or carded, still less convicted of dangerous play. It took Mealamu twelve years to offer anything even approaching a mumbling apology. Umaga has never gone that far. Yet former Ireland coach Eddie O'Sullivan believes some good did eventually come out of a very distasteful business. 'The consequences of that O'Driscoll incident were that we are now ultra-cautious about anything like a spear tackle. That changed the whole interpretation of the tip tackle.'

In 2017, when the Lions were next in New Zealand, the referee of that 2005 Test, Frenchman Joel Jutge, admitted, 'It should have at least been one red card. Maybe Mealamu. Maybe Umaga. Maybe both. We didn't see it and so we didn't sanction it. I was really upset with myself.' The world of rugby ought to lament the fact that the Lions failed to make this a line in the sand, a never-again moment in the sport. Had they made such a stand, so much could have been different. Their management should have told New Zealand Rugby, 'We will not play against these players [Umaga and Mealamu] again on the tour. Unless you agree, we are going home.'

There could never have been a more worthy stand against violence on the field. O'Driscoll did not have the ball when he was spear-tackled. But the Lions shot themselves in the foot. British Prime Minister Tony Blair's PR official, Alastair Campbell, the wrong man in the wrong place as Communications Officer for the Lions' tour, became the story. His presence detracted from what should have been a strong stand and simple message against violence in rugby. 'We will take no more of this. The reputation of the entire game is more important than any single tour.'

What the dangerous play demonstrated, once again, was that New Zealand rugby players are willing to go to any lengths to win a match, particularly when you consider the roll call of names of those who have been targeted. Virtually nothing is off-limits. They will allow no one to come between them and victory. It is a trend that can be seen throughout their history. And very often, the victim happens to be a key opponent: Catchpole, O'Driscoll, J.P.R. Williams. A coincidence? There are plenty of New Zealanders who still see no harm and suspect no skulduggery in the spear tackle on O'Driscoll. Either way, 1980 Lions outside-half Tony Ward has few doubts. Ward, now a media analyst, says, 'Are New Zealanders ruthless? Yes. That comes with winning at any sport and more so in the professional era. You do anything that gives you an edge.' As for Brian O'Driscoll? 'He was taken out at the start of the 2005 Lions tour,' alleges Ward. 'Maybe it was a line in the sand, I don't know. What team doesn't take the physicality at times too far? Do they live on the edge of the offside law? Yes, but Ireland did that, and the Scottish teams of the 1970s and 1980s were the same. You just play the referee; that is all you do. The trouble is that most referees try to be overfamiliar and that sends out the wrong message. Nigel Owens is far and away the best referee in the world but even he drifts into that occasionally.'

Many further examples of dire deeds by New Zealanders can be listed. In 1971, the Lions Scottish prop Sandy Carmichael had both cheekbones shattered by punches during a scrum against Canterbury, shortly before the first Test. Carmichael, like O'Driscoll thirty-six years later, played no further part in the tour.

On the 1989 eight-match French tour of New Zealand, wing Peyo

Hontas from Biarritz had the lobe of one ear torn off by a kick to his head in a match against Wellington. Even Basque prop Pascal Ondarts, one of the toughest men ever to play the game, was taken aback by the incident. Ondarts told me at the hotel he owns in Bayonne, south-west France, 'That game in Wellington was tough. Not an easy game for us. Those midweek games were always the ones where the provinces, everywhere in the world but particularly in New Zealand, try to glorify themselves. I did not see exactly what happened with Peyo but at that moment, I saw him lying on the ground, his face bleeding. When I got closer to him with my teammates, we suddenly realized that the lobe of his ear had been torn off. We were all horrified. The lobe was on the ground. Peyo told us a flanker had kicked him in the face.

'Of course, at that time, there was no video, no slow motion. I don't even know if that game was live on TV. And of course, the Kiwi referee of the game had not seen anything. No yellow card, nothing! No punishment. The only guy punished in fact was Peyo himself who, beyond the injury itself, missed his first cap against the All Blacks and later never had any other opportunity to play them again. But fortunately for him, a local plastic surgeon sewed it on perfectly at the Wellington hospital and, since, Peyo has no scar at all.

'What is the most disturbing is that no New Zealand journalist covering the game mentioned the deliberate act of the offending player. When you think of what they all wrote after Nantes [France v New Zealand Test match] in 1986 . . . Almost everyone saw the guy that did it in Wellington. But no one said anything or wrote a word about it. It was part of the game.'

It was, and always has been, part of the New Zealand game. It is the stain on the family name, the element that has shortened some people's admiration for New Zealand rugby. Sonny Bill Williams' reckless and dangerous shoulder charge into the face of Lions wing Anthony Watson in the 2017 Lions second Test against the All Blacks, an act that brought him a red card, was another example. It's worth pointing out that, twelve years on from the O'Driscoll incident, rugby had finally acquired the stomach and the means for punishing the perpetrator. Had Williams' challenge happened in 2005, he might never have been sent off.

Yet New Zealand rugby has never been short of apologists. For all these acts. Even Richie McCaw claimed that those who accused

Umaga and Mealamu of deliberately hurting O'Driscoll were wrong, and didn't know the character of the two men. 'Early on we thought it would go away,' said McCaw. 'We knew Tana and Kevvie didn't do it on purpose – I know that for a fact. They never intended for it to happen.'

But we enter an area here known as responsibility. One that, incidentally, the game has at long last now embraced. The defence 'I never *intended* [my italics] it to happen' is rarely a defence in law, and doesn't both an irresponsible and a dangerous action lead to the same outcome? Someone has been injured. The people involved are the ones responsible. Can they duck out of their responsibility as simply as that?

Catchpole, Carmichael, O'Driscoll, Carozza, Young, Richards, Bracken, J.P.R. Williams, Davies and Hontas. How many more 'victims' of New Zealand rugby violence will there be? And how many more defences under the heading 'They never intended for it to happen'?

One man who didn't deny such charges may surprise you. Sir Colin Meads. On a soft, warm summer's afternoon in 2017, I made the long drive from Auckland to Te Kuiti to see him. I was expecting a grim scenario. 'Pinetree' had been diagnosed with pancreatic cancer six months earlier, with the dire prognosis that accompanies that awful disease. Yet old friends had rushed to help. Chris Laidlaw and Earle Kirton had contacted someone they knew in America, one of the world's experts on the disease. He had spoken with Meads' specialist in New Zealand to hear what treatment they were offering. Pancreatic cancer is normally a death sentence – the average life expectancy is four to eight months following diagnosis. Meads was to survive for another year. When he died, at Te Kuiti Hospital in August 2017, All Blacks coach Steve Hansen said movingly, 'It's always sad when one of the big Kauri trees falls.'

Meads' stature as a man in New Zealand society was underlined by coverage of his death in the *New Zealand Herald*. The newspaper on Monday 21 August devoted nine pages of stories and tributes to him, plus a four-page wrap-around picture special on the front of the newspaper. It was similar to when Kel Tremain, one of New Zealand's greatest ever flankers, passed away in Napier, in May 1992. Police officers standing guard at road junctions are said to have saluted the coffin as it went by. This was the passing of true New Zealand royalty.

On that summer afternoon when I visited Meads, I drove up the hill behind the town of Te Kuiti to his home. The old rugby fields where he and his brother Stan first appeared, carving out their names with a physicality matched perhaps only by the blacksmith at his anvil, lay in sight below. A gentle breeze whispered across the immaculately kept garden. 'Who does all the work here?' I asked him.

'Oh I do it all. Love it, actually,' he said. I was astonished. He was energetic enough for an eighty-one-year-old fighting cancer. There was the familiar strong neck, forearms like fence posts. And he was eating for New Zealand, this Knight of the Realm. His delightful wife, Verna made us scones for tea. The result was a rout. New Zealand 6, England 2. The cancer? 'I'll beat the bastard,' he said, gruffly. You didn't feel inclined to start an argument.

But Meads was in conciliatory mood on other matters. Did he go too far at times on the field in terms of brutality, I asked him? 'When I look back, yes, there were one or two things I regretted, felt I went too far. But you get misled.'

Meads told the story of a match against the French in November 1967 when he went around the back of a line-out, got caught and had his head opened up on the ground by a French boot. Meads knew instantly the culprit. 'Benoit Dauga was a big fellow for France at that time. He wasn't necessarily a hard, physical man. But he was a big, bloody ugly guy. Fred Allen [New Zealand coach] used to say to me, "Can you handle this guy?" By this stage I was having nightmares about him. So when I got my head cut open, all I could think was, "I'll get back at Dauga." '

They would later put eighteen stitches in Meads' head. Which, to you and me, is like an elastoplast on a tiny scratch. But, with the game continuing, Meads was just bandaged up and sent back on. It didn't take long for the winds of revenge to whistle through the stark Stade Colombes ground, outside Paris. Meads admitted, 'I took it out on Dauga. I hit him so hard he had a big black eye and lost a tooth, although I didn't knock him out. You didn't wear mouthguards in those days.'

At the after-match dinner, customary in those times, Meads' head was still weeping blood. He saw Dauga sitting on the French table but refused to acknowledge him. But at the end of the dinner, the Frenchman took the onus. He walked over to Meads, pointed to his beaten-up face and asked, 'Why you do this?'

'I said, "Look what you did to me, you dirty bastard." My hand was cut, my head was cut. But Dauga said to me, 'Non, it was not me. It was Alain Plantefol' [the Agen lock]. I told Fred Allen later that it was his fault, because he drove me on.'

That wasn't Meads' sole confession on that summer's day. 'In the odd club game here in New Zealand, I also regret silly little things that happened. There was a centre who left our club, Te Kuiti, and went to another club. When we played them next, I got him in a ruck and belted him. Not kicked him, mind; I never kicked a man.'

Meads protested his innocence over his 1967 sending-off at Murrayfield. 'The referee got his decision wrong. He still thinks I kicked the Scottish player [Chisholm], but I never kicked him. I kicked the ball. But I was on a formal caution for over-vigorous rucking. The Scottish hooker [Frank Laidlaw] got me sent off. I didn't think the referee saw it, but the hooker made sure he heard about it. I think he influenced the referee, going on about "that dirty bastard". When I was sent off, I went numb. I thought I had probably ended my All Blacks career. I felt ashamed. It was terribly upsetting and frustrating for me.'

But it would be a poor, one-sided argument if we were to pretend it was only ever New Zealand players who were involved in such acts. Violence was endemic in most countries in the old amateur game. The assault by Perpignan's Samoan wing Henry Tuilagi, on an opponent in one French Championship game against La Rochelle, was appalling. It was a desperate act of mindless violence. But at least Tuilagi received an immediate red card.

Similarly, some of the acts in the 1990 French Championship Final between Racing Club and Agen revealed a game of such wilful violence that you felt bruised just watching it from the stand. South African forward Garry Pagel stamped on Frenchman Jeff Tordo's head during a Western Province match against France in the early 1990s. Then there was the biting: by New Zealand-born Ross Cullen, playing for Australia against Oxford University on their 1966–7 tour; South African Johan Le Roux bit Sean Fitzpatrick in the second Test of the 1994 Springbok series; Englishman Kevin Yates received a six-month ban for biting the ear of London Scottish flanker Simon Fenn in 1998 whilst playing for Bath. Carnivore capers, you might call them.

The England second row forwards, Danny Grewcock and Simon Shaw, were sent off in 1998 and 2004 respectively. Grewcock kicked the All Blacks hooker Anton Oliver and Shaw kneed All Black lock Keith Robinson. But from neither was there the excuse of 'I never intended it to happen'. Rather, they took their medicine and accepted responsibility.

Graham Mourie, All Blacks captain from 1977 to 1982, was as physically committed as anyone else in his playing days. With Taranaki and the All Blacks, Mourie devoured the loose ball, caring nothing for the boots, bruises and cuts that were as much a part of his trade as finger cuts are for the local butcher. So does Mourie, respected around the world for his immense contributions to the game, consider New Zealand players brutal?

'Let's be realistic. The 1974 Lions in South Africa thought up the "ninety-nine" call [a signal devised by the Lions to attack every South African player in sight if someone was assaulted – a case of getting your retaliation in first, in their minds]. As for the French, they were absolutely brutal. I played two years for Paris University Club and you would not go down on the ground there, nor would I tell anyone to do so.

'I don't think New Zealanders were more ruthless than others. But I think they were more focused on winning. At school, I played senior-grade rugby at sixteen. Dad always said, "Don't worry about that stuff [the physical side of the game]. It's the result that counts." '

But Mourie does admit he lost respect for Meads at an early stage of his career. 'I saw him kick a guy on the ground, for no reason. It was Murray Kidd, a schoolboy playing for Taranaki. Meads was playing for King Country. I wasn't playing, but I saw and heard the injury. Meads kicked him in the head. That was never part of what I thought the game was about.

'I was pretty embarrassed when John Ashworth cut open J.P.R. Williams in New Zealand's match at Bridgend in 1978. [Mourie was All Blacks captain at the time.] When we played, punching was considered part of the game, but you never used your boots. It was an unwritten law. The game is about the sport, it's not about the battle. But you are there to win. The total focus was, how do you win and this goes back to growing up with the game as kids. The whole system in New Zealand is very competitive.'

The 1986 'Battle of Nantes' between France and New Zealand was probably the most brutal Test I ever saw. France had been beaten the week before, in the first Test in Toulouse, and their coach Jacques

Fouroux was not a man to take it lightly. His passion for the game and for his country burned like a flame. By kick-off time, when the French players emerged from the tunnel, Fouroux had ignited every one of his charges. The intensity of his men at Nantes that day superseded almost anything I have ever seen on a Test ground. All Blacks forward Wayne Shelford finished the match on the treatment table, having his torn scrotum stitched up.

Chris Laidlaw calls Meads 'the most complete player, in almost every sense'. He said, 'He was an all-round athlete, enormously strong, with a particular sense of timing and the ability to do anything, including intimidating the opposition. There just wasn't a better rugby player on the planet at that time.'

But did Meads overdo the intimidation?

'Of course he did. People knew if they got in his way or niggled him they would pay a very heavy price. That was one of the factors that kept us ahead, that sense of intimidation. He wasn't the only one. Others like Bruce McLeod [an All Blacks hooker of the era], Ken Gray and Kel Tremain – there was a variety of others who would use force when they needed to do it.'

Was it dirty play? Did they target key opponents?

Laidlaw says he is in Graham Mourie's camp on this one. 'There was never any conscious identification of a player to take him out. Yes, we identified a player who represented a threat. Yes, there have been moments, bad moments. But I don't think any of them have been planned.'

Was O'Driscoll not targeted? 'You wouldn't have thought so, but you never know. But South Africans have done a lot more of that than New Zealanders and the French did it all the time. The irony is, that the one time Meads was sent off, it was completely innocent. I was within feet of the incident. He was kicking at the ball. That scar stayed with Meads – he always resented the fact that he had been sent off. But maybe it was rough justice given the stuff he had got away with in the past.'

Those who have watched and played the All Blacks the most tend to be Australians. But no one has ever accused Andrew Slack, Wallaby captain between 1984 and 1987, of bearing grudges or having hidden agendas. The man is one of the greatest gentlemen the sport has ever known.

Yet Slack is frank on the topic. 'Are the New Zealanders ruthless?

Well, it is pretty similar, a ruthless determination to win and brutality. They are definitely ruthless. They were always individually willing to do things. Kicking, eye gouging . . . but then, those things happened in that era. Look at the French.

'New Zealanders always were ruthless, a bit brutal. Mark "Cowboy" Shaw was brutal . . . white-line fever hit him a few times. Richard Loe, too; no question. Yes, there were incidents. But I wouldn't label a people or a team on the back of individual incidents. There were some brutal people, it is true, but it didn't mean the whole team behaved in that way.'

Slack remembers being trapped at the bottom of a ruck against Wales at the Sydney Cricket Ground in 1978 and seeing a Welsh forward standing above him. 'He looked up to see if the referee was close by and when he saw he wasn't, he looked down at me and just whacked me. It's true there were elements in the New Zealand team willing to do that, too.'

Slack's self-deprecating sense of humour quickly surfaces. 'It's true when you play New Zealand, you play a nation not a team. It is one of the advantages of being a nation with only 4.8 million people. I have a lot of time for New Zealand and New Zealanders. If I hadn't been born an Australian, I would like to have been born a New Zealander. But the only thing wrong with that was that when it came to rugby, I would only have made about fourth grade,' said the thirty-nine-times-capped Wallaby.

If a certain place defines a nation and a people, then in New Zealand's case it is the wrong side of a ruck. For most of the game's history, this was definitely not the place to be on any rugby field occupied by New Zealand players. Irish legend Willie John McBride cheerfully traded blows with Meads, even as a callow youth back in 1963, early in his international career when Ireland met New Zealand in Dublin. Twice, Meads impeded the young Ulsterman as he attempted to jump for the line-out ball, and twice Meads blocked him. McBride said nothing. At the next Irish line-out, Meads moved across again in a blocking motion. McBride didn't move a muscle until a huge fist smashed into the New Zealander's midriff. Meads went down like a felled tree. 'Christ,' said one of McBride's teammates, 'you just hit Meads.' Most knew the sword of Damocles would fall. And all knew on whose head it would descend. The great Willie John, staunch

Northern Ireland Protestant and defender of right from wrong, replied, 'I don't care. I'm not accepting that behaviour all match.'

The only trouble was, a short while later and completely out of the blue, McBride too dropped to the ground, like a lone soldier hit by a sniper. Meads' captain Wilson Whineray had taken his team's revenge on behalf of Meads. 'I wasn't well for a while,' McBride cheerfully conceded. 'But then we got on with the game.'

These were the educations of a rugby life for young men like McBride. He had more to digest on the 1966 Lions tour of New Zealand. In the first match of that tour, the Lions lost 14–8 to Southland in Invercargill. McBride remembered, 'I think it was the first match I ever played in New Zealand. It was in the muck at Invercargill. The weather was terrible and physically it was very tough. I remember catching the ball and, as I did so, I must have been hit by six of the opposition forwards. They kicked and punched me for fifty yards, dragging me with the ball, but I still hung onto it. When it eventually stopped and the whistle blew, I got up but I was all over the place.

'Three or four of our guys said, "Why didn't you give them the ball?" I was absolutely furious with them. It was clear that a few of our players felt intimidated by the physical side of the game out there. They were rucking some guys out of it throughout the tour, and some of the Lions players didn't want to play in the matches. Physically, they couldn't handle it. The reality was, we were playing a team largely of New Zealand farmers who were physically and mentally as tough as nails.'

One of those farmers, Colin Meads, remembered an incident from that 1966 Lions tour. The Lions were captained by a second row forward from the Army, by the name of Michael Campbell-Lamerton. He played for Scotland and was just the type of chap the Lions selectors looked for to lead the team in those days. The right background from a good upstanding military man who would go down well in the Colonies. Or so the thinking went. The fact that he was completely ill-equipped as a rugby player for a tough tour in New Zealand's backyard, never occurred to the selectors.

Meads recalled, 'I pushed him and shoved him the whole day. I hit him and eventually he went back to number six in the line-out, which represented a victory for me. But Willie John McBride wasn't like that. When he hit me with that punch and I went down, Wilson

Whineray our captain hissed at me, "Get up, get up. Don't let the bastard know he has hurt you." I said, "It's alright for you." I had no breath.

'Willie John and I always had a tussle. We respected one another. McBride was one of the toughest I ever played against. Johan Claassen of South Africa, too. But McBride and I got on socially and we became great friends after that.'

As for McBride, it isn't just the physicality that he respects in New Zealand rugby:

'When something is on for the All Blacks, they don't miss the chance and they punish mistakes. That is inbred right through their years. It is a key reason for their continued success. They win so many games in the last fifteen minutes, and they always did that. It's that sort of attitude, a never-say-die approach that makes them such formidable opponents.'

The former Australian coach John 'Knuckles' Connolly concurs with the view that New Zealanders possess a special ruthlessness. But, as he says, 'All great teams in sport are ruthless in pursuing victory. You'll find it in any successful team in any sport. You need that obsessive personality and the Kiwis have got that.'

None had it more than Andy Haden, second row forward of the 1970s and 1980s with 117 matches for the All Blacks, including forty-one Tests. Haden would do anything to see his team win, including the incident at Cardiff in 1978 in a Test match against Wales. With New Zealand trailing 12–10 in the final minutes, Haden made a theatrical dive out of a line-out in a bid to win a potentially crucial penalty. The referee, Roger Quittenton, blew his whistle (he said later not for an alleged push on Haden, but by Geoff Wheel on Frank Oliver, who also went down), gave New Zealand a penalty and the goal was kicked. The All Blacks won 13–12 and the whole of Wales seethed. The London *Daily Telegraph* later included the incident in a story entitled 'Ten Instances of Notorious Unsporting Behaviour'.

Haden's philosophy had been simple. He just did what he could to try to win the match for New Zealand. It wasn't physical violence; indeed, it contained an element of Whitehall farce about it. A key to New Zealand's depth of preparation for any eventuality came when Graham Mourie admitted that the New Zealanders had discussed it the previous evening.

Years later, Willie John McBride found himself in Haden's company at the Bermuda Sevens. 'Did you ever regret that incident?'

McBride asked him. 'No, never,' replied Haden. 'In New Zealand, you are taught to do whatever it takes to win.'

Here is another critical piece in the jigsaw that reveals why New Zealand dominate this sport worldwide. If ever you doubted their ruthlessness in pursuit of ultimate victory, the demand to win at all costs – and we're not just talking about players – then listen to former All Blacks coach John Hart. The man who coached New Zealand at the 1999 Rugby World Cup, when France destroyed them 43–31 in a stunning semi-final upset at Twickenham, was made to endure an experience no one in any sport, professional or amateur, should ever have to go through. With hindsight, this was probably a watershed moment for New Zealand rugby and perhaps for New Zealand society as a whole.

Hart knew and loved the game. He had played his first match when he was just four years old, for Mount Roskill. He remembered going along in a little pom-pom hat. 'I didn't know what I was doing. But I scored a try,' he said proudly, more than half a century later. When he was eleven, he and his brother slept outside Eden Park in Auckland, joining the queue for tickets for the South Africa Test. The year was 1956.

So he knew from way back the importance in New Zealand of winning rugby matches. Not long after his appointment as All Blacks coach and as he prepared his team for a Test match, he was surprised to be told one day there was a call waiting for him on the line.

'Who is it?' enquired Hart.

'It's Jim, the prime minister,' was the reply.

Jim Bolger, National Party leader and New Zealand Prime Minister from 1990 to 1997, began the conversation with a simple question. 'John, how do you think the All Blacks will go in the Test on Saturday?'

Hart was bemused. 'Well, Jim, we'll do our best, that's for sure,' was his cheery reply. The response was less lighthearted and jocular.

'We might need a bit more than that,' said Bolger. 'The election is next week and it could make a big difference if you win.' This was a precursor to John Key's own fears about the consequences for him as prime minister and his government if the All Blacks had lost the 2011 Rugby World Cup Final to France. If ever Hart doubted the importance of every New Zealand Test match, he was under no illusions after that conversation.

One other time came in 1998, when the All Blacks lost so many key men through injuries or retirement: Zinzan Brooke, Sean Fitzpatrick, Frank Bunce, Michael Jones and Olo Brown. And they lost *five* Test matches in a year. 'Can you imagine that?' Hart asks, rhetorically. 'It was,' he intoned with the deepest of breaths, 'pretty painful.'

But not as bad as what happened twelve months later at the World Cup. 'If you want to know about pressure, that was pressure,' says Hart.

'There had been an expectation that we would win, and it was awful. Probably because of what I got subjected to by a certain group of people, it probably helped future All Black teams when they got beaten. I was very disappointed in certain people and I didn't handle it at all well. I withdrew, I didn't want to go out, probably for as long as eighteen months. It was almost life-changing. Stress like that was probably dangerous to my health. My family had been at the World Cup and they arrived back a day before me. My son met me at the airport. I was supposed to go to Hawaii for a family holiday, but I thought that wasn't appropriate. I felt I had to come back and face the music.'

Even as soon as that after the defeat, Hart had announced his resignation. But it cut little ice with certain elements of the New Zealand public. Hart's son reminded him their horse was running the next day in the New Zealand Trotting Cup and suggested they all go and watch. It was, Hart said, the worst decision of his life.

'I got booed and spat on, it was horrific what happened. The horse had beer thrown at it before it went on the track. It was one of the worst days of my life, and a bad day for New Zealand.'

But it wasn't just the coach who struggled to accept such behaviour. The captain was copping it, too. Years later, Reuben Thorne explained his own experiences:

'The aftermath of the 1999 Rugby World Cup was the worst I ever experienced. I still don't know what it was about that time that made it so bad. The reaction in 2003 wasn't as bad. I don't know what had changed between those times, but 1999 was particularly bad. I remember going into a bar in Christchurch with friends and a guy walked up and asked me to buy him a drink because I had disappointed him so much at the Rugby World Cup. I didn't know him so I said, "Just walk away." The stuff in the media was awful and, of course, whatever players will tell you, you do read the papers. It was pretty unpleasant.'

Thorne was, and is, a man big enough to look after himself. But he is a taciturn figure, not unfriendly at all but reserved and quiet. He was never a guy you would find shouting his merits from a rooftop. He found it tough to accept the events of that time. 'It was difficult because of the pressure. You are living a life in which everything you do is heavily scrutinized. That was not what I signed up for as a rugby player and a few times I thought it crossed the line.'

Hart is quick to point out that not everyone behaved in such a way. But the fact that even a small percentage of his fellow New Zealanders could treat him in such a manner, shook Hart. He'd been a successful businessman and thought he could handle the knockbacks, adversities and disappointments. He quickly came to understand that nothing could have prepared him for this. It was, he said later, 'unbelievable.'

Yet perhaps most clouds have silver linings. He considers an important lesson that came out of his experience. 'That was a learning curve for a society that got captured by the game and by what the team did. I believe a lot of people saw that and said, "That's not New Zealand, we don't want that." '

Hart suspects much of the vitriol was driven by critics who had seen his attempts to make changes to the All Blacks ranks in the new era of professionalism. 'They thought I was trying to change the All Blacks culture and I was, because I had to. It was called professionalism. I had seen the very worst of All Blacks culture; the back seat of the team bus, the drinking etc. All those things. You just couldn't do them any longer because of professionalism, but some people resented change.'

Five years later, the new All Blacks coach Graham Henry would face an almost identical scenario after a wild, drink-sodden night in Johannesburg. Clearly, change was harder to enforce than Hart had hoped.

Hart was probably correct in one sense. This was not simply a burning desire to win a World Cup. It bordered on viciousness, and it spoke ill of a society that could behave in such a manner towards one of its own. That New Zealanders could treat a fellow Kiwi like that revealed a deeply unpleasant side of a society which some, especially outsiders, thought couldn't exist.

The catalyst for such behaviour was the game. Just as it was the reason for the awful assaults and terrible injuries inflicted upon the likes of Ken Catchpole and Brian O'Driscoll. It was shocking to know that a game could invoke such roaring demons within some of its participants and followers to the degree of physical damage that could have been life-changing.

It may well be that the John Hart affair shocked even New Zealand itself. So that, when one of Hart's successors, Graham Henry, came to make his own major changes to All Blacks' culture, he was able to do so without a similarly dire reaction.

But what of the changes in extreme physicality between those days and contemporary times? We have some idea of what a rugby Test match was like in those days from the testimonies of men like Meads and McBride. What of today, though? How do the toughest New Zealanders approach the intimidating physical hurdle they know they must scale for a place in the coveted All Blacks ranks?

Jerome Kaino enjoys a reputation as perhaps the toughest of the All Blacks. He can dish it out. But what is it like to take it? Do players this strong and this physically prepared feel the blows when they're on the receiving end?

Kaino makes no attempt to hide his delight at a physical encounter. 'I always love that physical side of the game. The more you play professional rugby, the more you see your role in a team. The more I can do on the physical side the better I get. I don't consciously go out thinking, "I am going to intimidate you." All I am thinking is, "I need to get into the game and this is how I am going to do it." For me to get into a game, I need to make a big carry or a big tackle. Something physical.

'Does the pain bother me? Yes. Sometimes you run into a big guy and get the odd stinger. Or they will get a good shot on you. But you can't show the pain, so you get up and hobble over to the next breakdown or scrum. But inside, you are half-dying.

'It's more like a bluffing game, a game of poker where you can't show whatever you have got. If you are delivering the pain, it doesn't feel that bad. But sometimes you are on the receiving end of some big shots. You try your best to bite your mouthguard and hide it. But if you dish out the hits, you have got to be ready to take them.'

Kaino rates the late All Blacks back row man Jerry Collins as the hardest guy he has played against. Collins, smouldering, silent and laden with physical intent, was fearless on the field. At times, he destroyed opponents' bodies as well as his own in a single game.

But, in terms of a guy who was more of a nuisance, Kaino opts for

Richie McCaw. 'No matter how many shots or how hard you hit him, he would come back just as hard the next time. He was always there, always a problem. He was relentless. Some people come hard at you for the first fifty minutes but then the intensity withers away. But Richie was constantly at you. He also had great intelligence to go with his physical attributes.'

The man who prepares the modern-day All Blacks for battle, in a psychological sense, is the team's mental-skills coach Gilbert Enoka. He casts a knowledgeable eye on both past and present requirements in this particular field. 'There have been some brutal incidents involving New Zealanders. There is an absolute will to win but at times there has been too much violence,' he concedes.

'In the early days before television, it was horrific. Some of the things people did on a rugby field was a licence to be lawless. That, to me, wasn't right. But since the introduction of TV and a greater deal of scrutiny, I think the game has got better.

'Before, there was a tradition that this was how you became a great man if you could actually express your prowess in that context on the rugby field. But in a lot of ways, it was just thuggery. Where brutality was used in the past, it was biting people's ears, gouging people's eyes. Nowadays, we are using skill sets to get the same awe. The game is now so much better.'

What Enoka means by that is that sheer pace and physicality are now the instruments of torture for opponents. Watch the first forty seconds of the 2015 Rugby World Cup Final between New Zealand and Australia, he says. You see the impact of precise timing and accurate execution done legally, as in Jerome Kaino's hit on Israel Folau. There is now, he says, a different form of brutality. The precision that comes from perfect execution has become the sword used in battle. The fist or boot are now redundant. And this requirement, this demand for precision of execution, transcends all sports.

As an expert in his field, Enoka understands the fast-flowing rivers of motivation within young sportsmen unleashed for sporting warfare. 'The testosterone that pervades the veins at various stages can turn people uncontrollable at times. That can have a really severe impact on people.'

This reputation is carried into battle by the All Blacks like a badge of honour. As the towering South African lock Victor Matfield put it, 'The biggest challenge about facing the New Zealanders was that every time you played them, you knew you were in for the hardest game. You always knew you were in a Test match against them. It was very tough, even for the toughest members of a Springbok team.'

Brutality? Everyone has their own mental image of some shocking incident. It is not an element of which rugby union should be proud. Sky TV commentator Tony Johnson cites the South African Johannes 'Moaner' van Heerden raking All Blacks lock Peter Whiting's ear as the worst he ever saw.

'There were terrible acts of brutality by some All Blacks,' he concedes. 'But they have been victims of a few themselves.'

But Johnson, for one, is encouraged by the reality that players can no longer get away with acts of violence on the rugby field and pretend it falls under the banner of 'sport'. 'In this day and age, you won't get away with it,' he says. 'Andrew Hore whacked Bradley Davies and it was the beginning of the end of him as an All Black. That sense of brutality has morphed now into how hard you hit [tackle] somebody. But you cannot do it illegally.' Twelve years after the O'Driscoll incident, Johnson admits he still doesn't know what to make of that. 'But something happened there. It looked like they were trying to hurt the guy.'

The views of present-day players are instructive on this topic. Isn't the modern game tough enough, without all that off-the-ball violence, I asked Wyatt Crockett, long-time loose-head prop for the Crusaders and the All Blacks. By June 2018, Crockett had played a remarkable 200 times for his franchise team, the most by any player in Super Rugby history, and had won seventy-one Test caps for the All Blacks. He knows his trade.

In a career of such longevity at the coal face, Crockett has learned the price to be paid for such prolonged physical involvement. His words reveal the huge physical demands required of a player in his role. 'The load you feel after the scrum hit is pretty immense. You see a lot of teams keeping the ball in the scrum for longer now, trying to sap the energy of opponents or show dominance-winning fitness. It's like a good 200 kilos on the squat rack; you take it halfway down and then hold it. Believe me, scrums have definitely not been de-powered, although they have obviously changed. After a major game, I am really sore all over. It is a feeling like you have been in a car crash. Sometimes it can be pretty tough to get up from the couch on a

Sunday morning. There are always a few old scars from game after game through a season.'

Crockett, we should remember, is no lightweight. He weighs in at an imposing 116 kg (18st. 4lbs) and stands at 1.93m (6ft 4ins) tall.

Considerably bigger, at 123 kg (19st. 5lbs) and 2.04m (6ft 8ins) tall, is the Chiefs' outstanding lock forward Brodie Retallick. Together with Sam Whitelock, the pair represent the best international second row combination in world rugby. Whitelock, at 116 kg (18st. 4lbs) and 2.02m (6ft 7ins) tall, is slightly smaller than Retallick. That is the bad news for anyone lining up against them. The good news is that Retallick does not see himself as a modern-day version of Colin Meads, the snarling, sinister forward laying waste to just about everything in his path.

On a crisp, early-autumn morning outside Hamilton, where the Chiefs training camp is based, we watch then-coach Dave Rennie put the squad through their paces. Already there is a chill in the air, nature's reminder of impending winter. Retallick finishes the session and approaches out of the mist, physically imposing. Is he an enforcer? He looks horrified by my question.

'I don't want to be the enforcer. I just try to have a good all-round game, have the ability to throw a good pass, and to clean out and go forwards. All that is vital to the game of rugby and it always has been. I think you need a complete all-round game rather than just one strong point.'

For a big man, Retallick's ball skills are phenomenal. Yet he insists he has never focused on them.

'Growing up in New Zealand, you are lucky you get the chance to play a lot of sports if you want to. When I was younger, I played cricket, volleyball, touch rugby, tennis and basketball. Maybe all that stuff increased my hand–eye coordination.

'I would have had a ball of some kind in my hands pretty much all the time when I was young. It was great growing up like that, especially with two older brothers. Looking back now, those skills probably helped massively to where I have got as a rugby player. It's the things you do as a kid that pay off as an adult. I like nothing more than using a bit of skill and beating someone. Especially when someone scores from it.'

Once upon a time in New Zealand rugby, the phrase 'beating someone' meant primarily one thing. We should all be glad that today it has a very different connotation for hard men like Brodie Retallick. It is irrefutable proof that the game has moved on.

RESURRECTION

Contributions from, among others,
Steve Hansen, Sir Graham Henry, Sir John Key,
Kees Meeuws, Gilbert Enoka, Doug Howlett,
Richie McCaw, Graham Mourie, Andy Haden,
Alan Jones, Dick Best, Victor Matfield, Brendan Venter,
Wayne Smith, Sir Brian Lochore.

'This was the time we began to understand that character is king. Everything that is special about this team must emanate from character. We had some flawed characters. We learned in the end that if you are the only person in the world with the skill set you have, if you are not a team player you will not make it.'

Gilbert Enoka, All Blacks mental-skills coach

Johannesburg was always a graveyard for the All Blacks. They hated the place. Six thousand feet up, no breath in your lungs and constant fatigue. Adapting to both made it tortuous. Then, you had rugby balls flying huge distances through the thin air. As for the city, think grim. Tough, deprived. Dingy and dirty. Here, the destitute sleep on street corners and often don't wake. A telltale trickle of seeping blood the next morning across the cracked, uneven pavement tells of a violent night. People inject and die. Those who survive are happy to have descended into oblivion for a few hours. Whatever the drug, whatever the cost. Anything to escape the nightmare of a living hell.

Here, certain house rules apply. The dead don't talk and the living walk. Away and fast. They saw nothing, know nothing.

The grinding poverty of Alexandra Township, just a short drive from wealthy Sandton, is a cruel, taunting reminder of apartheid's legacy. As for the driving, it's enough to scare even those with the steeliest nerves. You're told never to stop at red lights at night. Every colour of the traffic light means go . . . Everywhere, the senses are assailed. But then, these are the contrasts of Africa.

At Ellis Park, there were those enormous towering stands; ugly, cold, old-fashioned monuments of poured concrete. A relic from an equally ugly society named apartheid. They loomed threateningly above the men in black whenever they ran into the cauldron. It was like that from 1949, when the touring All Blacks lost the second Test 12–6 there, en route to a 4–0 series whitewash. That humiliation lasted seven long, painful years, before New Zealand had a chance of redemption. It was no better in 1960, 1970 or 1976. More anguish at Ellis Park for the All Blacks. Their dream of a first series victory in South Africa remained only that. Just under twenty years later, in

1995, another dream was shattered in Johannesburg. South Africa squeezed home 15–12, a Joel Stransky drop goal snatching the coveted Rugby World Cup trophy from New Zealand's grasp.

A year later, the All Blacks at last laid the bogey of never having won a Test series in South Africa. Yet, even then, they still lost at Johannesburg. New Zealand didn't win a Test in Johannesburg between 1928 and 1992.

*

Then, in 2004, an extraordinary incident seemed to compound New Zealand's angst in the place. In the small hours of a Sunday morning on 15 August that year, something happened that would change forever the face of New Zealand rugby.

'It was,' said Kees Meeuws, one of the All Blacks' forwards that day, winning his forty-second cap of a six-year international career, 'a turning point for the whole of New Zealand rugby.'

The All Blacks had been through a turbulent period since the advent of professionalism in 1995. There had been successes and failures, changes of coaches and new styles of play. Different philosophies, too. Defeat at the 1995 Rugby World Cup had seen off coach Laurie Mains. He was replaced by John Hart, who lasted only until defeat at the 1999 World Cup. In came Wayne Smith for a brief tenure in 2000 and 2001 – he was followed by John Mitchell, who exited after defeat at the 2003 World Cup. Coaching the All Blacks had become a carousel. People were jumping on or being pushed off at regular intervals. Long-term consistency, in terms of preparation, playing style and selection, had long since been compromised. Coaches, players – no one really knew where they were or where they were likely to be when the next regime arrived. Or departed. Even at the start of the twenty-first century, losing still felt like a capital punishment in New Zealand.

*

So 2004 was the first Tri-Nations campaign for the new All Blacks management trio of Graham Henry, Steve Hansen and Wayne Smith. But, as the trio quickly discovered to their horror, times of professionalism in the sport had not seen off some dire rugby habits from the old amateur era. It was bad enough that the All Blacks had lost to the Wallabies in Sydney the previous weekend. That alone ought to have focused minds in this new professional era that had begun in 1995, almost a decade earlier. But what happened in Johannesburg appalled Henry. It wasn't even so much that the All Blacks were hammered 40–26 by their greatest foe, five tries to two. Centre Marius Joubert, the personi-fication of the new professional rugby player with his speed, strength and muscular authority, scored a hat-trick. On the day, Joubert's epit-ome of flair and physicality was a combination that shocked the New Zealanders. All that was bad enough. The defeat guaranteed New Zealand bottom place in the 2004 Tri-Nations Series table, whoever won the following week's encounter between South Africa and Aus-tralia, a match that the Springboks would win 23–19 to take the title.

But as it turned out, the All Blacks management had far worse to face by the end of that night.

It was a quirk of amateur rugby that grown men sometimes felt the need to behave like idiots. Not helped, of course, by copious amounts of alcohol. Sane men, who had eminently serious professional jobs in their working lives, became fools, judgement lost in jugs of drink.

Johannesburg marked the end of that season's Tri-Nations for the All Blacks. All that lay ahead was the tedious twenty-five-hour flight home to Auckland the following day. The plan was simple. Have a big night, drown the sorrows of defeat and somehow stumble onto the plane to sleep it off on the way home. Yet it wasn't as straightforward as that.

By now, Graham Henry had taken up the reins. Things began to change, said Meeuws. And fast. 'Under the new regime, there was a lot of work done. It needed to be done, but it was rugby overkill. We were being worked from seven in the morning to nine at night some days. Sometimes, we could hardly even crawl into bed we were so tired. It was a turning point for professionalism within the game in New Zealand. Suddenly, teams you were playing were smarter and fitter. You had to work harder to stay ahead.

'Losing in Johannesburg that year, after the amount of work eve-ryone had put in . . . was tough. The players let it all hang out and got carried away. The [players] court session after the match got out of hand probably, because a couple of senior players running it had a few agendas. But we all felt we needed a blowout; it had been such a long year, and a tough one.'

So, a blowout they had. Drinking at the court session, drinking at the post-match meal, drinking long into the evening and into the small hours of the following morning. By early the next morning, some players were lying incoherent on the lawns of the team's five-star hotel in Johannesburg. It was some advertisement for New Zealand rugby in the professional era.

The height of ignominy, as far as the All Blacks' coaches were concerned as they viewed the distasteful scene, was seeing some of the South African players, most of them sober and still in their smart green Springbok blazers with yellow piping and immaculately knotted ties, helping place some of the All Blacks players in the recovery position. They were so far gone that they were actually in danger.

Among the onlookers, Henry, Hansen and Smith were appalled spectators. After all, it was barely fifteen years since the French front row forward Dominique Bouet had got so drunk on the 1990 French tour of Australia, that he choked to death on his own vomit in a hotel room in New Caledonia, Polynesia. They took him home in a coffin.

Meeuws said, 'There were a lot of drunk people in the foyer of the hotel. And a lot of mischief was going on between the rooms, with water fights, etc. It was uncharacteristic behaviour. Followed by a giant hangover in the morning.'

But was it uncharacteristic? Back in 1991 at the Rugby World Cup in the British Isles and Ireland, I'd flown to Dublin for the semi-final between New Zealand and Australia. By chance, I had been booked into the same hotel as the All Blacks and was given a room on the same floor. Never a good idea.

When I approached the hotel, a group of All Blacks seemed to be trying to drop some furniture out of a bedroom window. It wasn't the most promising scenario you could encounter. Certainly, the noise coming from their rooms along the corridor utterly defeated someone trying to work. I called up reception and asked for a room on another floor. But this was in the era of amateur rugby; the change to the professional era had been supposed to put all that kind of behaviour to bed.

Yet it revealed something else. This state of affairs had come about due to a sense of arrogance, of an imagined superiority to others, which had existed in New Zealand rugby for too long. Defeats were rare, headlines invariably complimentary. Too many of the latter had been digested and influenced the players' egos, and not for the better. Some seemed to feel that they did not walk on the same planet as mere mortals. What followed was a mistaken belief that rules which applied to ordinary people didn't necessarily apply to them. There was no consideration. It was an unsavoury part of New Zealand rugby and one that needed to die out. Little wonder, perhaps, that those 1991 All Blacks got their comeuppance a few days later when a David Campese-inspired Australia beat them 16–6 in the semi-final. No one looked more shocked at the outcome than the All Blacks themselves.

By 2004, such shenanigans ought to have been a distant memory. But they weren't. Graham Henry, a former schoolmaster well used to placing discipline at or near the top of his working priorities, told me in 2017 in Auckland, 'It astounded me the way they behaved.' But how serious was the mess he had inherited? 'It was what the All Blacks were. They thought it was the way it was. But it was time to move on. Professionalism was eight or nine years old by then and it was time to become a bit more professional.'

It was odd, because New Zealand had seemed to embrace professionalism within the game long before most countries, especially those in the northern hemisphere. Even prior to the 1987 Rugby World Cup, still eight years before professionalism was officially introduced, All Blacks players were featuring in television advertisements for assorted products. Northern-hemisphere players attending the first Rugby World Cup in New Zealand and Australia in 1987 were open-mouthed at the defiance of rugby's sacred amateur rules.

New Zealand players of that time already understood the growing commercial possibilities, but not the behavioural requirements of the new rugby world.

As Doug Howlett, who began his Test career in 2000 and would play until 2007, remembered, 'The All Blacks environment is bred on success. That applies to both players and coaches. You lived and died by the sword, or how the results went. But there were still parts of the amateur-rugby ethos infiltrating the team. We were enjoying our successes. Enjoying success with your mates was a big part of the reason I played rugby.

'We knew we had to curb some of our enthusiasm. It was becoming harder under professionalism to enjoy that side of the game because other teams were becoming more physical. We had lost our edge, others had caught up. The skill sets they were developing had been our point of difference for a long time. We had to look at ourselves and see what we could change. We knew we had to change.'

And yet even in 2004, in Johannesburg, Henry's thoughts were confirmed by the extraordinary sight of players drinking more on the long flight home the next day. It was so bad that, as assistant coach Wayne Smith vowed, 'If this is what the All Blacks environment has come to, I want no part of it.'

Smith was pure gold as far as New Zealand rugby was concerned. No finer man with better values has ever embraced the All Blacks' creed. As either player or coach. John Hart called him, 'Probably the world's best technical coach, an outstanding analyser of the game.' If he was seriously concerned, New Zealanders ought to have known there was a severe problem. But resurrection was nigh. Certain members of that raucous squad in Johannesburg found in time they would never play for their country again.

What Henry and his colleagues did laid the foundations for the hugely successful era New Zealand would enjoy. Aside from jettisoning some players, Henry had identified that this group of young men was lacking something else. Collective responsibility and a shared leadership. His wisdom was to understand that if you possessed half a dozen people with leadership attributes, you were potentially so much more effective a unit than if one man alone bore sole responsibility.

A single player, the captain, had always been the prime focus of attention in All Blacks rugby. In the previous fifty years or so, men like Wilson Whineray, Brian Lochore, Graham Mourie, Andy Dalton and Sean Fitzpatrick were regarded as talismanic. That didn't change when Henry appointed McCaw as skipper at the age of just twenty-three, in November 2004. But what the next eleven years would produce was stunning. McCaw was captain in 110 Tests, winning ninety-seven, drawing two and losing eleven. His win ratio was above 89 per cent. By the time Henry had finished coaching the All Blacks his win percentage was 85.4 per cent, a phenomenal return. He coached them in 103 Tests, winning eighty-eight and losing fifteen.

But there was a critical difference this time in the appointment of a new All Blacks captain. Henry didn't want just one leader, as good as McCaw undoubtedly was. He wanted several others to fulfil the equivalent of the cricketing role of 'vice-captain'. Henry himself had been a keen cricketer in his youth and he understood the value the 'vice-captain' and other senior players could bring to the team collective.

Henry concedes that what he calls the 'team-driven environment' was in the coaches' minds well before that infamous night. But

Johannesburg was the catalyst to do it quickly. It was, he said, a turning point. 'I am proud of the culture we developed and it is still developing. This current group knows what they need to do to keep on getting better. We didn't get it right initially. I wanted it to work tomorrow. But Gilbert Enoka [their mental-skills coach] said to me, "It's not like that." He was dead right. He was superb and very involved in the process. Players were elected but some didn't want that responsibility. So we had some reluctant leaders. Eventually we selected a couple and then in time it got up to seven. Now it's about nine. It became a much more potent group of people. It has constantly evolved.'

Enoka says that they simply had to correct the culture of 2004. 'We are a team (now) that is built very much on "we", not "me". But it was the other way around then. All the focus had been on "me". It was about ego. One of our core principles is that the team towers above the individual. It is alright to say that, but another thing to deliver. Professionalism had moved us to a particular way of thinking. But the individuals asked, "What can I get, what are the opportunities for me?", which created fractures. That defeat and its aftermath was one of the worst losses I have been involved in with the team. South Africa absolutely thumped us. I remember coming home, and when we sat down and discussed it, we said, "Right. We have got to pull this thing to bits." '

It was the start of what became known infamously as the 'No dickheads policy'. There wasn't much at stake. Only the future of New Zealand rugby. No one should underestimate the importance of the crossroads they had reached. It was a time when New Zealand could easily have slipped back into the pack of world rugby as just another team. Better than most, for sure, but roughly similar to two or three others. After all, Australia had already won two World Cups to New Zealand's one. In 2003, England had done the unthinkable, by beating the All Blacks in Wellington, a precursor to their World Cup triumph under captain Martin Johnson later that year. When the Englishman lifted the trophy in Sydney on that famous night, many would have bet on England, not New Zealand, going on to develop a golden era of dominance in world rugby. After all, they had everything: the money, playing numbers and quality, and the vast support of sponsors and fans. Twickenham was beginning to flood with money, something the much smaller New Zealand Rugby could never envisage.

If ever there was a moment when New Zealand might have stumbled, this was surely it. That it did not happen, although it would prove to be another seven long years before they won a second Rugby World Cup, was due almost entirely to Graham Henry and the men he assembled around him as his assistants.

Enoka went on, 'There was a core group that said, "This team is going to be great." We went into shared leadership models. We looked at our people and said, "We have got to develop them," because a lot of them weren't developed well. We had to put time and energy into them. Develop them as people. I think this was really about the time we began to understand that character is king. Everything that is special about this team must emanate from character. We had some flawed characters. We learned in the end that even if you are the only person in the world with the skill set you have, if you are not a team player you will not make it.'

The search for team men, for more leaders, unearthed plenty. Tana Umaga was initially the official captain but others stood up – Richie McCaw, Dan Carter, Keven Mealamu, Aaron Mauger. Others would follow. Mostly, they were the sort of men you'd want beside you in the trenches.

It became a major change, *the* change of their lives, thought Doug Howlett. Everything was studied with a microscopic intensity: preparation, recovery, game planning, building a team, coaching, how to play, and even how to handle the media.

Almost everything you see in the All Blacks today, on and off the pitch, can be traced back to the aftermath of that match in Johannesburg. As Howlett says, 'They were all aspects we had not paid a lot of attention to before. We had just played the matches without thinking about those things very much.'

Henry was always a taciturn figure, a man of few words. He had a sense of humour some might term 'an acquired taste'. He did not suffer fools gladly and could demonstrate a caustic wit. Some mistook that for arrogance, which was far from the reality. He possessed values, and cared for people, especially those around him. His judgement in that respect was impeccable.

Who brought Steve Hansen into the All Blacks fold as assistant coach? And who eventually persuaded Wayne Smith, against the latter's original rejection of the offer, to join his new-look coaching squad as assistant coach just two years after Smith had been unceremoniously dumped as coach because those in authority mistook his intrinsically reserved nature for a 'lack of passion'?

Who weighed up the runners and riders for the All Blacks captaincy when Umaga stepped down? Who chose McCaw as his captain, his right-hand man? Henry did, of course. But he did more than all this – he identified players with the character to support McCaw. One was Conrad Smith, destined to go right through to 2015 and become one of the soundest, most trusted lieutenants. Smith was the defensive 'brains', the rock upon which the All Blacks back line was forged. His selection was another triumph for Henry and those he had gathered around him. There were many others, too, who would step up to the plate, accept and take on responsibility. So although McCaw was clearly the front man, he was never without the moral support of key colleagues.

Howlett is in no doubt where the credit for what ensued should lie. After December 2003, he said, it was the same coaching team, right through to 2011. 'They have to take a lot of credit for identifying where we were, what had worked in the past but would not work in the future. It was never about one individual. We found a peer leadership group and my admiration for the coaches grew from that. They relinquished some of their power and handed over to the playing group. It went well.'

In essence, the players had to take on responsibility. They didn't have a lot of choice. If they didn't want to, if they still preferred the party image of the past, others were brought in to replace them. Under the Henry–Hansen–Smith regime, life in the All Blacks camp was about to get much more serious.

As John Hart said, 'Professionalism had to happen and it was the best thing to happen. It wasn't the best thing for rugby, but it was the best thing for the top end of the game.'

McCaw epitomized the culture, the type of person for whom Henry and his colleagues were searching. His mantra is the quintessential element, the absolute nuts and bolts of what became vital qualifications for a place in the hallowed unit. Hansen calls McCaw 'the greatest All Black ever'. But was he the most talented, I asked McCaw?

'No. Of course, you have got to have some talent. But the example I say to people is that when I left school I wasn't the best player at schoolboy level. But there is a choice at that point whether you really want to progress. There is a bunch of kids all with similar ability around the country who could all have made it. But it's the decision you make at that point which dictates whether you get there or not.

'Then, the perseverance and setbacks you get and how you fight your way through that. I think a lot comes down to that desire. There is timing involved, and being in the right teams as well. But you have really got to want to be the best. I think some people have the talent and get so far, but then they get sick of it or don't work out a way of going to the next level. No matter what you do, if you feel you have reached where you want to reach, you are either going to decline because you haven't got that drive or you look at something else to do. You look for a way out.

'The middle part [of his career] was the toughest challenge for me. There were periods there where it was hard work, mentally and physically. I never gave it away, but you think, "How am I going to keep progressing, how am I going to continue doing this for however long it was going to be?" That was the challenge, the bit that got me going each time, thinking, "How do I get better at this?"'

Contained within these words is a philosophy for a working life. One which goes far beyond the All Blacks or any sporting team. You might also be discussing your aims as an ambitious designer, a writer, an artist or a teacher. 'How do I get better at this?' is the perfect psychological spur to improve and enhance.

Young men with these ambitions were exactly what Graham Henry was looking for. People who would wear the All Blacks blazer with pride, knowing they represented their nation. Whether it was three o'clock on a Wednesday afternoon or two o'clock on a Sunday morning, the night after a match. People who would be constantly thinking of their responsibilities and commitment. Who would dress smartly, look and act the part and put team bonding and togetherness high among their list of priorities. Henry sought serious operators for what was a serious job in a professional sport. He was able to smile and share a joke. But very quickly he would switch back into professional mode. He saw his behaviour, and that of his coaching colleagues, as setting an example to the players.

The idea was to set high standards off the field, be judicious in finding good people to accept responsibility within the team and to encourage and inspire others. By doing so, you are laying crucial foundations for future success. Of course, it helps immensely if you have players like Richie McCaw, Dan Carter, Conrad Smith or Ma'a

Nonu in your team. But this philosophy goes deep – it applies to every level and every facet of society. People coming together with a common purpose, working for each other, supporting one another and showing a maturity in behaviour towards those goals. These qualities would benefit and enhance any club side or national team anywhere in the world.

Graham Mourie understood the process well. Mourie led the All Blacks in nineteen Tests. He was, and is, revered in his day as arguably one of the deepest thinkers about the game. The philosophy Graham Henry sought to put in place from 2004 was similar to something Mourie had embraced when he was captain from 1977 to 1982. 'When I was captain, you had to understand that you don't run the team. The senior players do. If you have got them onside, you are able to focus on the outcome. That is critically important. No coach or captain can control the total performance by himself. In a team, you have several layers of performance . . . it's very hard to line all those up. The more people you have who understand what needs to be done then you are getting control of the performance. It is a chain of responsibility.'

As he grew into the captain's role, Mourie would sit people down and ask them, 'What is your job?' He saw the role of captaincy as co-ordinating all the differing elements; the people in charge of forwards, backs, scrums, line-outs. He understood implicitly the values that were important.

'A good culture is so important, and that means knowing what being in the team is all about, knowing the standards of behaviour required. Personally, I would have been absolutely embarrassed to be an All Black in 1972–3, and even in 1970, because of the behaviour, the drinking.'

Mourie's mind went back to the night he was first made captain of New Zealand. Ian Eliason, who played nineteen matches for the All Blacks in 1972–3, was in Mourie's Taranaki team and told him bluntly, 'Just make sure it was not like it was when I was there.' Mourie knew what he was talking about. 'I certainly knew the behaviour had been pretty rubbishy. But I said to him, "What do you mean exactly?" He said, "It should have been the greatest thing in my life, touring Britain. But there were a lot of times I really hated it." ' Every time he used to go into a dining room, he alleged, Alex Wyllie used to throw knives at him.

Mourie said, 'It was that senior group of players that were totally dominant with no degree of responsibility. So when I was made All Blacks captain, I saw my role as definitely rebuilding the All Blacks culture and reputation.' Now, almost thirty years later, Graham Henry was setting out on a similar mission. The extent to which he succeeded is clear from the outcome of Tri-Nations series in the first decade of the twenty-first century. Before Henry took over, Australia were Tri-Nations winners in 2000 and 2001, South Africa in 2004. New Zealand won it in 2002 and again in 2003, but you couldn't say they were dominant every year in the southern hemisphere.

In the northern hemisphere, it was a different story. Scotland and Ireland had never beaten them, and Wales hadn't since 1953. England had been more successful, beating the All Blacks in 1973, 1983, 1993, 2002 and 2003. Even so, in all the matches played between England and New Zealand between 1905 and 2008, the All Blacks had won twenty-four of the thirty-one and England had won just six, with one drawn. It was a similar story against France.

We can examine Henry's impact by contrasting New Zealand's Tri-Nations results before he took over with what followed afterwards. Once the Johannesburg debacle had been cleared out of the way, New Zealand won the Tri-Nations in 2005. They won it again in 2006, this time in its expanded version with each team playing one another three times. New Zealand won it again in 2007, and also in 2008, so four years on the trot. In that time, they played twenty Test matches and won fifteen, losing only five. This, remember, with a gruelling travel schedule throughout the southern hemisphere. South Africa won it again in 2009 but New Zealand promptly regained the title in 2010 with six wins out of six before finishing second to Australia in the 2011 tournament. Even so, the All Blacks had won it five times out of seven in the Henry era. During his period as All Blacks coach, from December 2003 to November 2011, Henry was voted IRB Coach of the Year in 2005, 2006, 2008, 2010 and 2011.

But it wasn't all plain sailing. From 2005 to 2007, says Kees Meeuws, there was an arrogance within the All Blacks. Shades of times past? 'They were winning everything, but they became an arrogant team. What changed them was defeat at the 2007 World Cup. They became humbler after that. They started giving back to the communities and to the New Zealand people.

'A philosophy emerged of, "Put a smile on your face, be the best bloke you can be. On and off the field." This happened from 2008 onwards,' said Meeuws.

Another factor kept New Zealand rugby at the top of the perch, both during Henry's revolution and subsequently. As the British & Irish Lions captain Sam Warburton said after his men had drawn the 2017 Test series with New Zealand, 'the All Blacks remain the best team in the world.'

One reason for this is what former All Blacks lock Andy Haden calls 'the inherent knowledge of the sport not only by New Zealand males, but from plenty of knowledge by females. And they have their say.' In that regard, he suspects, it is hard to see New Zealand falling back for long. 'There will be leaner times. But with the expertise, they won't last for long.'

Former Australia coach Alan Jones echoed these sentiments. What makes New Zealand so good? Jones is in little doubt. 'There is a prevailing culture about New Zealand rugby, isn't there? The thing that always used to fascinate me about them was the women knew as much as the men.' This deep well of knowledge, from which anyone in New Zealand rugby can draw, underpins the entire sport in the nation. Somewhere, in a town, city or out on a farm, there is someone able to offer a clue or to provide an answer to a worrying question. Someone able to define a strategy, to offer an inspiration or idea. So often, the All Blacks are the beneficiaries. This was something Graham Henry knew and understood implicitly. Whenever he felt the need, he would use it.

Yet South African Victor Matfield highlighted yet another element as key to New Zealand's resurrection. 'I think it's their mindset which marks them out as so different. In their minds, they are not supposed to lose but to win every game they play. That is different to the players of any other country in the world. Expecting to win, which they do, is completely different. It gives them a lot of confidence. It is about how they are brought up and because of their performances in the last twenty years. They are there as players before they play for the All Blacks. The way their structures are, the All Blacks coaches just have to work to direct them. They already know the structures and expectations before they actually become All Blacks.'

If they keep those structures, Matfield believes, they will always be the best team. They may lose the odd game yet they will still be, as Sam Warburton asserts, the best team in the world, and their expectations will never change. New Zealand only ever open the tiniest of windows of opportunity to opponents. Even then, they are soon slammed shut again. In 2009, with the Henry regime in its fifth year, South Africa went past them. The Springboks had the temerity to beat their foes three times in that single year: 28–19 in Bloemfontein, 31–19 in Durban and 32–29 in the reverse Tri-Nations fixture in Hamilton. Matfield, not a man given to excessive self-congratulation or public expressions of emotion, called it, 'The highlight of my career. It was a fantastic feeling.'

Speaking in 2017, the Springbok had been part of the South African team that had won the Rugby World Cup ten years earlier. Yet beating New Zealand three times in a year remained the zenith of his career. Revealing.

'Playing them was definitely the greatest challenge of my career. You want to test yourself against the best and you knew you had to be on top of your game whenever you played them. They are the ultimate professionals. They identify any weakness they may have, address the failings and move on.'

2009 was a rare example of a New Zealand wobble. But the following year they were back on track, punishing the Springboks for those three successive defeats by beating their tormentors three times out of three. Revenge is a dish best served cold, and New Zealand rugby teams know how to administer the punishment. What they did in 2010 was a run-up, a starter course to the main dish of 2011: the Rugby World Cup, which they won for the first time since 1987. Long before then, though, another shrewd South African rugby brain, Brendan Venter, had seen the changes in the New Zealand mentality under Graham Henry.

'In 2004, South Africa were dominant in the Tri-Nations. But then New Zealand seemed to overhaul all of their rugby. Now, they are completely dominant, the best in everything. When you analyse them from a technical and tactical point of view, they are far better than anyone else. What did they do after that Test series [in 2004]? The way I think they did it was, they had a very good coach in Graham Henry. He had been a headmaster and, remember, headmasters are value-driven people.'

The biggest difference between New Zealand and other countries, says Venter, came in the modern era. But he says it is not one single thing they do that makes them so much better. 'This current All Blacks culture has changed. They definitely weren't the same twenty years ago. Their rugby twenty years ago was solid, but now it is amazing. They also improved their conditioning so much that they now have the best work ethic in the world. Then there's the legacy from the past. I believe they got their work ethic from that, and that's why they are superior. They contest the line-outs better than anyone else, they hit the breakdowns better than anyone else . . . they are better at everything they do. My question would be, who triggered that process?'

In Venter's case, the question is rhetorical. He knows Graham Henry was the guy. Yet Henry himself denies the popular theory that great sporting teams are scions of their coaches. 'The current All Blacks team is not Steve Hansen's team, just as it wasn't Graham Henry's team. It's the players' team and you have world-class people looking after these athletes and giving them the right resources to take ownership of this team. That is getting stronger and stronger. When it's their team, they give more. They take ownership, take responsibility and that process has been evolving for fourteen years.'

Yet it could all have been so different. There are still millions of New Zealanders alive today who will go to their graves cursing English referee Wayne Barnes, for allowing a try by France amid the hurlyburly of the 2007 Rugby World Cup quarter-final, after a forward pass. It was before the time of cameras and TMOs.

The result? New Zealand 18, France 20. It was one of the most spectacular failures in modern rugby history. But here is an equally stunning statement. 'I believe that one of the best things that happened to New Zealand rugby was 2007.' The thoughts of a disingenuous foreign coach, happy to see the All Blacks taken down a peg or two? No. The words of Steve Hansen in 2017, ten years after the event. Even so long after, however, Hansen freely conceded, 'God, it hurt.'

Wayne Smith remembers having to face scores of All Blacks fans at Tokyo Airport, en route for London. 'Some of the tour parties from New Zealand were on their way to the Rugby World Cup to watch us in the semi-final and final. Instead, we were on the way home. That was bloody difficult. We got home to a reception that was chillier and chillier. They were tough times. We had a great team, we had everything New Zealand Rugby could have done for us and we failed. That was really difficult.'

Gilbert Enoka is very clear on why the All Blacks failed that day. 'We had become arrogant, got ahead of ourselves. We had gone over to France waiting to win it. The pool rounds were so easy. We beat Portugal by 108–13, Italy by 76–14 and Romania 85–8. We beat Scotland 40–0, too. When we actually met opponents who had been preparing for this moment, to the point where they chose a jersey that would make us wear our alternative strip, we had learned that when you get into that knock-out phase, everything that has happened in history has gone and you had better know that. Because people will just put in superhuman performances to get the job done. We got found wanting in that forum.'

Even so, Enoka blamed himself for what transpired. He said that the All Blacks have learned that being great and staying great, you have to work on your abilities. But you must also look at your vulnerabilities. The All Blacks at the 2007 World Cup 'looked in the mirror', he thought. Honesty and brutal self-assessment go hand in hand in this All Blacks culture. It is another lesson of New Zealand rugby, and one all countries and teams should embrace. 'As regards my position,' Enoka said, 'I admitted they failed mentally because in the end we just didn't adapt to what was required. Yes, the referee was having a challenging day, but if that happened now, we would adapt and adjust in a far better way than we did then. It taught us some very, very good lessons.'

Hansen, never a man to use a dozen words when three will do, called it 'a monumental stuff-up'. Going by all previous habits and policy appraisals of New Zealand rugby, that should have been it. Henry, Hansen and Smith should have been toast. So why weren't they? Principally, because of one man, Sir Brian Lochore, revered and regarded as the great doyen of All Blacks rugby. Before a backdrop of the scaffold being erected, New Zealand Rugby met to review what had gone wrong. Many in New Zealand just wanted Henry to face the axe, and the man himself well understood the pressures. They are inherent in New Zealand rugby.

'I had to write a report on the World Cup for New Zealand Rugby, a pretty important report in which I had to analyse the game. The pressure of doing that made me physically ill. Unless you have got your body and soul involved in this, I don't think anybody else understands just what you go through.'

Henry was forced to reapply for his job, but left that meeting convinced he was history. 'I went to dinner with my wife and said, "It's all over, I'm out." I thought it had gone badly, and did not expect to be rehired.' He believes it was the fact that Richie McCaw and a group of senior players wanted him and his colleagues to stay that was decisive. The truth is rather more specific. The New Zealand Rugby board always held Lochore in the highest regard. Rightly so, for he is a colossus not just of the game in New Zealand but of the nation itself.

Upright, intelligent, industrious, of commendable values, Lochore epitomizes those early pioneers who somehow forged a path through adversity and came to prosper by their own immense deeds. He is also thoroughly down-to-earth, able to communicate as comfortably with Her Majesty the Queen as with some joker with a drop of grog inside him on a club rugby touchline. What's more, Lochore had worked with the All Blacks as a selector in the four years leading up to 2007. He'd seen close-up the coaches at work; he understood their ambitions and motivations.

With the issue in the balance, the New Zealand Rugby board summoned Lochore and asked him his views on the triumvirate. Should they stay or be fired? Lochore was unequivocal. 'I told them the easiest thing to do was fire them. But the best decision would be to keep them. We didn't play that well [in the 2007 quarter-final], but it was just a bad day at the office.

'It's true, before that time there was a four-year cycle for an All Blacks coach. But in 2007 they had a good thing going. They trusted one another. It wasn't a lack of preparation that cost us that game, it was a lack of understanding. They could have taken that game a little bit lightly. I was interviewed because I wasn't going to carry on and I gave my view. And I think the decision was dead right. They had a very settled and stable group of coaches, mentors and overall management. Why would you ditch it?'

Lochore applies his own unique criteria in assessing the requirements for a coach: 'The best coach in my view is the best bush psychologist. Somebody who can look at a fellow and work out what makes him tick, what makes him feel good. That is very important in coaching.'

Henry, as shown with the example of Ma'a Nonu, certainly had that. And Hansen? 'He has done a fantastic job, a wonderful job,' says Lochore. 'Now, he *is* a bush psychologist. He understands people.'

So Robbie Deans, an eminently viable alternative as potential All Blacks coach when New Zealand Rugby interviewed candidates in Wellington, missed the job. Henry, Hansen and Smith, together with their worthy accomplices such as Enoka, scrum coach Mike Cron, conditioning expert Nic Gill, manager Darren Shand and a coterie of others, stayed in place.

Post-2007, the mood in the nation had been so bereft that some began to think the All Blacks would never again win rugby's Holy Grail. New Zealander Gregor Paul wrote in *Black Obsession*, a book published in 2009, 'Could it be that the All Blacks are simply destined to bomb at World Cups? Is that the cruel fate afforded them by the rugby gods – a malign karma earned by their dominance at all other times?' He wasn't alone in expressing such a thought.

It has never been documented, but it's just possible that New Zealand Rugby made their decision in 2007 with one other thought in their minds. In 1999, England had been literally kicked out of the Rugby World Cup by South African fly-half Jannie de Beer, who had landed an extraordinary five dropped goals to dispatch the English from the tournament at the quarter-final stage. Everyone assumed coach Clive Woodward would be axed when he got back to Twickenham. But, in the event, the English Rugby Football Union renewed his contract and Woodward went on to lead England to the title four years later. Perhaps the English had set a precedent for retaining coaches, even if they had underperformed at one World Cup.

One thing was clear in the minds of Henry, Hansen and Smith when they met up following their reappointment. In Hansen's words, 'We didn't start again by saying, "Well, that wasn't our fault." A new coach would have come in and said that.

'We actually admitted we were responsible for it. We sorted out what we had done that was really good and what we did that was stupid and in hindsight we wouldn't do again. We did things for the right reasons but they were wrong.'

One of their mistakes was sanctioning a break for the players in the middle of the tournament, which they thought would refresh them. 'But it didn't work,' said Hansen. 'We also kept changing the side. It's about the team first so you cannot pick the best because it might upset the rest? The team is more important than individuals and what they think. Life is tough. You work together as a team. Other guys' time will come. If people don't like it and think "I am out of here", is that the right kind of character you want or the right work ethic? You are better off without them.'

They learned all these lessons and more. Much of the information was used to help forge the successful World Cup campaign of 2011. Henry and his colleagues might not have had any fingernails left by the time the last whistle blew at the 2011 Rugby World Cup Final. But they'd laid the ghost to rest, the one that jeered and sneered about the All Blacks being chokers when it came to World Cups.

It is the element of continuity that Henry believes holds the key to the future success of the All Blacks. When he took over in 2004, there was no one left from 2003. Yet when he retired in 2011, of the fifteen management guys, twelve were still there. 'That continuity of people,' reflects Henry, 'is essential and it will continue in New Zealand rugby.'

There isn't another country in the world that has achieved the continuity in personnel of New Zealand. 'Continuity of sporting staff is critically important, and hopefully they won't all finish together,' adds Henry. 'That is important and it should be part of New Zealand Rugby policy. They will bring in some new people but the people who are there are getting better all the time. That is part of the strategy and culture. They are learning from that environment and we learned so much from each other. You constantly learn from your colleagues and other people.'

It is for this reason that, at this juncture, it would seem incomprehensible for New Zealand not to choose Ian Foster as All Blacks coach post-2019, if Steve Hansen decides to step down. By then, Foster will have been involved with the All Blacks for seven years, a valuable period of experience. If New Zealand Rugby decide not to give him a chance as All Blacks coach, they risk returning to what Lochore called 'the four-year cycle' with all its attendant disruptions and uncertainties.

My view is that they should appoint Foster as head coach but move Hansen, if he wants it, to a new, consultative role. One where he would not need to endure for another four years the intense daily scrutiny demanded of an All Black coach but might instead fulfil a new type of role where his knowledge could be used across all levels of the game. Foster would handle the major responsibility, presumably with defence coach Scott McLeod still in situ and a new appointee. But Foster could use Hansen's experience as much or as little as he wanted.

However, if Hansen wants to finish, New Zealand will not be short of other candidates. The likes of Joe Schmidt, Vern Cotter, Warren Gatland or Dave Rennie would surely step seamlessly into a role within the All Blacks' set-up. Schmidt, highly respected both as a coach and a person by senior rugby people in New Zealand, is the obvious chief contender. His work with Ireland has been exemplary.

One of the hard lessons of 2004 is that establishing a group of quality coaches, knitting them together and grooming one or two for future responsibility as the head man, makes far more sense than endlessly chopping and changing, assuming you have personnel available of sufficient calibre.

As New Zealand Rugby found out in 2004 and was reminded of in 2011, one thing that is not lacking in the land of the long white cloud is good coaches. So how important was the 2011 World Cup win and resurrection? I crossed Auckland to a smart cafe in fashionable Parnell Village to ask a man who should know. He didn't pretend to know rugby as well as Graham Henry. But he certainly had the pulse of the nation. 'Had we lost to France in that final, had it gone the other way, I reckon there would have been a national state of mourning, given that we had not won a World Cup since 1987,' said former New Zealand Prime Minister Sir John Key.

'It's possible I could have lost my job on the back of that.'

'You're not serious?' I asked. But he was. Very serious.

'It is all about sentiment and the feel-good factor. Put it like this. Winning certainly didn't hurt our chances at the next election. That is the reality that helps the political mood. Losing a Rugby World Cup at home wouldn't have been that cheery. Hanging around the All Blacks doesn't do you any damage when you are PM, as long as they are winning. But equally, their having a line into the Government is not unhelpful either. So there was a relationship that worked on both sides.'

'As long as they are winning . . .' – the words that reveal the intimidating, sky-high pressure under which every All Blacks coach must operate. Does any outsider really understand the searing pressures incumbent upon any man holding that job?

Steve Hansen, for one, certainly doesn't think so. 'Not in the remotest sense. Nobody would have a clue about the real pressures,' he said.

For Steve Hansen, read Graham Henry, too. And every other All Blacks coach.

10

THE STYLE OF NEW ZEALAND RUGBY

Contributions from, among others,
Ryan Crotty, Digby Ioane, Alan Jones,
Steve Tew, Bob Dwyer, Nick Mallett, Wayne Smith,
Sir Tony O'Reilly, Nick Farr-Jones, Tony Ward.

'Rugby exactly suited our climate and our soil. It matched the temperament of the New Zealander and in large measure has moulded our national character. It's the team element which provides a spur to the weaker spirit, a curb for the selfish and discipline for all. It treats every man as an equal from whatever background he comes. There's no yielding to status in a rugby tackle, there's no privilege in a scrum.'

Chief Justice Wild's speech at the seventy-fifth anniversary of New Zealand Rugby in 1967

Those who climb the long, difficult ladder to the All Blacks coaching ranks know one thing implicitly. Their own minds. It goes with the territory. Even so, there is no doubt that these men are acutely aware of the requirements of a demanding New Zealand public. Just to play and win a Test match in this land is not enough. Success must be achieved with style. The idea of the All Blacks squeezing home to a shoddy victory by kicking penalty goals is anathema to most New Zealanders.

It happened most infamously in the first Test against the 1959 British Lions, when six Don Clarke penalties earned victory over the enterprising Lions' four tries.

That 18–17 'victory' for New Zealand was greeted with utter dismay. All Blacks captain Wilson Whineray said, 'When the final whistle went, I thought, "Oh hell, this next week or so is going to be awful. And it was with all the media and public criticism."'

One headline in the *New Zealand Herald* after that match called it 'New Zealand rugby's saddest victory'. What this does is dump a container load of unspoken pressure on the doorstep of those who coach the national team, with one crucial difference for today's coaches. Universal access to video coverage, social media and the traditional arms of the communications business mean that an entire nation now sits in judgement of men like Steve Hansen. There is no hiding place for anyone, coach or player.

If Hansen's team cannot show craft and invention in a Test match and score tries, a general outcry is raised. 'What is happening to the All Blacks?' is the question. All of society, from the village schoolteacher to the housewife, police inspector or hotel receptionist, is an instant expert. The matter is discussed and debated everywhere. Be in no doubt that this is another factor in the question of how this nation conquered an entire world sport. Other nations do not exist under this pressure. They don't need to.

At times, some argue, the pressure has been counterproductive. As the South African and former Italy defence coach Brendan Venter says, 'The New Zealand people are an obstacle to the All Blacks. The expectations of the people are too high. I think there have been times in the past when certain All Blacks have frozen under that pressure of expectation. It's almost like they are succeeding now despite the fans. I understand this syndrome – South African fans are the same.'

In such circumstances, the man in most people's line of fire is the All Blacks coach. For, it goes without saying, the more successful you are, the more the pressure is ramped up. Former Australian coach Alan Jones would understand that. Before his 1984 Wallabies set off for their tour of the British Isles and Ireland, Australia had never won a Grand Slam on such a tour.

*

Alan Jones is not your average Aussie. He's described by many as the nation's greatest orator and motivational speaker. At seventy-six, his ability to cut to the quick, to go straight to the most relevant point remains legendary. He showed it repeatedly during his time as Australia's rugby coach back in the 1980s.

His literary eloquence was renowned. A player who lost form suddenly? 'One day, King Rooster; the next, a feather duster,' said Jones. A succinct summary. He reminds us of his great intellectual capacity every day on his Australian nationwide radio show. And as for that tongue, it's sharp enough to slice cubes of meat from a steak. I fly to Sydney to catch up with him again. As ever, he's dapper, wearing an expensively cut suit, and perfectly knotted tie on a creaseless shirt. The shoes don't look like they were picked up in Coogee Market, either.

Jones once excoriated his own team for a defeat to New Zealand. 'I just don't get it why we go to pieces against these people.' So what is his verdict on this present-day New Zealand team? For a start, he buys my theory 100 per cent that of all the rugby Test-playing nations, New Zealand has stayed truest to the traditions of the sport: 'By and large, the All Blacks are playing the way they played in the 1950s. It is true that they have stayed truest to the skills of the game. Without them, people wouldn't be able to identify the sport. They are true to what we perceive. Running with the football. Which is what it was all about at Rugby School all those years ago. They still run with the football.

'Even in tight situations, they still believe that attack will get them out of trouble. They have a go, that's the mentality. Attack will be OK. They have been in a lot of trouble in many games. Not just the All Blacks, but their very strong provincial sides. But they will attack to find their way out of trouble.'

Jones emphasizes the need for a balance between forwards and backs. There are plenty of times New Zealand teams restrict the width of their attacks. They drive it up the middle, or just off the fringes, to expose a tiring opposition forward pack. To keep the fringe defenders honest. But intrinsically, they know when to unload it, to go wide. Importantly, they possess fast, precise half-backs able to play both types of game, because they can read a match. And that is the way they have played for decades.

While the difference today is that their fitness is on another planet, simplicity remains the watchword. 'There is no complicated chemistry about any of this,' says Jones. 'But no one wants to learn. If you had half a brain, you would imitate it, wouldn't you? In New Zealand, they imitate great players of the past, and why wouldn't you if you wanted to be that good? They are not trying to be something that has never happened before. That is why they have got depth. Every single team plays like the All Blacks and they all want to be there. There have been certain minor variations but generally they have been consistent to their history and to the tradition of the game.

'They ought to be the object of the sport's gratitude and admiration for what they have done for the game. But there are a whole heap of people who think they know it all and most probably think they have got nothing to learn from the All Blacks.'

Alan Jones is firmly of the view that simplicity lies at the heart of New Zealand rugby's success because they understand that at its fundamental level, rugby is a simple game. They have never tried to reinvent the wheel in pursuit of perfection.

But basics first. 'They [New Zealand] adopted a very simple premise. They belted you up in the forwards, and then came the natural instinct of using the ball. They have preserved all of that today and they are still doing it. They play with the football; no one else does to the same degree, although the northern hemisphere are having a bit of a go at doing that. In Australia, we have lost sight of all that. In most matches, we get the football and kick it away. New Zealand get it and run with it. They have got support, support, support all the time because they all want the football in their hands. I think you have got to give a lot of credit to New Zealand.'

Professionalism changed the face of rugby union forever. Everyone, from players to coaches to clubs and countries, became obsessed with one word. Money. How would administrators make enough to pay players? How could they lure big business in far greater numbers to sponsor their teams and organizations? And how could they meet the big salaries demanded by international coaches?

By contrast to England, New Zealand Rugby contracted its top players from the start. CEO Steve Tew and coach Steve Hansen both believe that has been a critical issue in the nation's success, at both provincial and international level. 'There is no doubt a significant competitive advantage for us has been a central contracting relationship with our players and the top coaches,' says Tew. It may seem to some that this has nothing to do with style or the principle of simplicity. But they are wrong. By holding control of all the best players, one broadly similar playing structure can be put in place throughout the New Zealand Super Rugby teams. Overall control means playing styles can be amalgamated. This works heavily in favour of New Zealand teams, and especially of the All Blacks. Uniformity of approach is invaluable.

Grant Fox admits, 'I thought it would be harder for us to be dominant when the game turned professional. It wasn't, in part because New Zealand still own the game.' Or, as Steve Hansen puts it, 'As soon as you get multiple owners, you get multiple egos. Don't let anyone tell you they don't have one. We all have them. Centralized contracts in New Zealand rugby have been a blessing. You have one boss and we can go in one direction. That is the key. By contrast, what fourteen club owners want could be fourteen different things. It certainly may not be what England or France want or need.'

Tew goes on, 'Even though we don't necessarily exert direct control on all of those people, day in, day out, we have got a much bigger influence over how they are, their employment conditions, how they are looked after, their workloads, their injury care. It has given us a huge advantage over what you see in France and England.'

Is New Zealand concerned about the French and English clubs? 'I think they are a threat to world rugby,' Tew admits. 'Particularly the French clubs because they seem to have no regard at all for the great institutions of the game, like Test rugby.' But then, if you were the owner of Montpellier, Toulon or Bath, you could turn that argument on its head and say the likes of New Zealand Rugby, the RFU, FFR and others are a threat to club rugby, given the way they're always trying to stuff more Test matches into the schedule.

The value of this universal playing approach, which is the hall-mark of New Zealand rugby, has been proven to be too much for overseas challengers from the northern hemisphere whenever they have crossed the equator. There was a simple reason for this. For years, while New Zealand teams chose attack as their playing mantra, the opposite was happening in the northern hemisphere.

Clubs and countries in the north went through a spell when coaches from rugby league were all the rage in the newly profession-alized union code. The trouble was, just about all of them came armed with a one-word tactic: defence.

Their *pièce de résistance* was the rush defence. It simply choked the great traditions of a running, ball-handling game that tradition-ally rugby union had been, even if it lapsed at times with too much kicking.

In the northern hemisphere, this was not a policy without short-term success. While ex-rugby league defensive coach Phil Larder was involved, Leicester Tigers enjoyed a four-year Premiership winning run, plus two Heineken (European) Cup triumphs in 2001 and 2002. Larder was also heavily involved in England's 2003 World Cup suc-cess. In Wales, another ex-rugby league man Shaun Edwards became highly influential and effective. A rock-solid Welsh defence provided the basis for Grand Slam successes in the Six Nations Championships of 2008 and 2012.

But alas, the policy was flawed. When these northern-hemisphere nations went to the southern hemisphere, and especially to New Zea-land, they found a game based hugely on defence simply didn't work. To beat New Zealand you had to attack and score tries against them.

In June 2016, James Neville, a graduate at the University of Limerick in Ireland, compiled some interesting statistics. As Wales,

Ireland and England all prepared for that summer's tours, Neville collated those countries' results in the southern hemisphere since the dawn of professionalism in 1995. The stats demonstrated once again the supremacy of the southern-hemisphere nations. And within those countries, New Zealand stands out beyond all others.

England's record was by far the best of the three northern-hemisphere countries. Of twenty-seven Tests played against Australia, New Zealand and South Africa south of the equator to that point, England had won five, drawn one and lost twenty-one. This rather put the records of Ireland and Wales into stark perspective. Wales had played sixteen Tests and suffered sixteen defeats. Ireland's record was worse; they had played nineteen Tests and had also lost every one.

Combine these three countries' Test fortunes when they leave their own comfortable backyard and you arrive at this horror statistic: played sixty-two, won five, drawn one, lost fifty-six. A win ratio of 8.1 per cent.

One tiny mitigation would be that England went on to win their 2016 Test series in Australia by three Tests to nil. Ireland then beat New Zealand for the first time in history, in Chicago, later that year. But if you're looking for consistent failure as opposed to New Zealand's consistent success, this would surely be it. Every northern-hemisphere nation has known that defeat is the likeliest outcome every time they confront New Zealand.

You always had to be creative and score tries to beat teams like the All Blacks. There was a reason for this. New Zealand understood the value of defence in the modern game and they practised it assiduously, just as they do *all* parts of the game. Both the Wellington Hurricanes (in 2016) and the Canterbury Crusaders (in 2017) won the Super Rugby title, the latter under coach Scott Robertson, with a strategy based on rock-solid defence. The Hurricanes didn't concede a try in three straight home play-off matches. Both sides denied so many opponents tries by the relentlessness of their defensive pressure, the so-called 'press'. Yet, when attacking chances came, both could score tries good enough to make the rugby gods smile.

New Zealand's attacking focus, based on speed and high levels of ball skills, could handle this defensive approach. In other words, New Zealand teams also work equally hard on attack, the part of the game the northern hemisphere forgot. Indeed, against better-organized modern defences, they knew they had to be a whole lot smarter and creative in an offensive sense, so outstanding ball skills were a pre-requisite.

Just hoping to outpace opponents and beat them with outside breaks, one of the classic images of the old amateur game, was no longer enough. Variety was essential. Being slick and shrewd with the ball in hand was crucial. So, too, were qualities like playing in the right parts of the field. Plus off-loading, as vital to an attack as the oxygen cylinder is to the deep-sea diver. New Zealander Sonny Bill Williams epitomizes this skill.

The much-respected former South Africa and Italy coach Nick Mallett concurs. 'New Zealand always strive to manipulate and iden-tify defensive weaknesses and attack where there is space, through passing, kicking or direct play.'

Steve Hansen confronts the issue of the rush defence with typical sangfroid. It is what it is, he shrugs. What is needed to confront it, he argues, are two elements. Firstly, good refereeing to make sure opponents are not offside. Secondly, everybody doing it, so that attacking players are forced to get better.

'That has been the cycle over the years. When the attack has been good, defence has had to improve to cope with it. That is why the game has improved its quality over the years. Right now, we are in a cycle where everybody is trying to put on a lot of pressure. Defen-sively, it has been happening in the northern hemisphere for a while. Not so much in the southern hemisphere, but it's starting to come in here, too. I know we are putting a lot of emphasis on line speed.'

Essentially, Hansen is positive about it. 'You do challenge people's skill levels. If they want to play running rugby, they are going to have to have higher skill levels. Plus better delivery and execution under pressure. I don't think that's a bad thing.'

Hansen isn't known as the canniest coach in the game for noth-ing. It has long been the case that the players with the highest skill levels in rugby are New Zealanders. They have more chance of hand-ling the rush defence and finding solutions than any other players on the planet because they have superior visionary skills and they prac-tise them almost from birth. They do so under pressure, too.

Hansen is right in another respect. If match officials were diligent in officiating the offside line, then it would free up space incre-mentally. Yet defenders are infringing the whole time, and all teams are guilty of it. Usually, they are level with somewhere in the middle of the ruck, which means only one thing. When the attacking team clears the ball, the receiver catches a physical hammering the moment he catches the ball, unless he stands deep in the pocket. But that renders an attacking philosophy largely redundant. It is why so many teams end up playing twenty metres behind the gain line, just to find some space. Thus, there is no time to act and no space in which to operate. In almost all instances, it is blatantly illegal. Yet the authorities turn a blind eye to a negative tactic which is strangling the life out of creativity and skill in the game, and turning it into a fifteen-man version of rugby league. Bewildering

This kind of negativity that has dogged the northern-hemisphere game for too long has been fostered to a degree by the frequent changes in personnel among coaches in countries like France and England. Tony Brown, the Highlanders coach of 2017, underlines the point. 'The continuity is huge in terms of coaching at the moment relating to the franchises and New Zealand rugby overall. There is a lot of continuity, and to me that is crucial. It helps explain why the style of the game we play is the same as the All Blacks and with that continuity we can only keep improving.

'By contrast, there have been so many changes in rugby in countries like France, Australia and South Africa. Under those circumstances, it is very hard to make progress. It makes it really tough for those guys to compete. It is the opposite in New Zealand.'

I offered Brown a few revealing statistics about rugby in France. In their 2016–17 northern-hemisphere season, Toulon played Clermont Auvergne in the quarter-final of the European Champions Cup. In that match, which Clermont won 29–9, Toulon made *one* line break, and *two* off-loads in the entire eighty minutes. If ever a few simple statistics reveal the poverty of ambition and the paucity of innovation and trust in players, these were surely the definitive examples. They are pathetic. They speak of a frightened outfit, of coaches terrified of a philosophy encompassing ambition and risk. They are anathema to New Zealanders.

Brown's response was calm but penetrating. 'There is no courage in those sort of stats. It is a safe way to play rugby and sometimes you can be successful. But that is failing in terms of a successful game if you employ that style. If you are not willing to risk anything, it is hard to achieve what you want. You have got to be prepared to come last to get first. That is my philosophy.

'All New Zealand teams have a similar mindset about wanting to play. It's about pulling out a secret move, creating attacking space, scoring tries . . . that's how everyone wants to play in New Zealand. You would struggle to fill a stadium and you'd lose supporters if you played another way. The supporters would get really frustrated.

'It is a mindset but I think what those negative tactics do is take responsibility away from the players, which allows them to back themselves on the rugby field. You have got to be brave as a coach to let that happen. Players will challenge themselves so much more playing in the New Zealand style. For a coach, it can be tough to watch if you are playing that risk game. But it is worse if you are not creating anything. If teams shut you down that is more frustrating than seeing mistakes.'

What the petrified coaches who scorn risk and adventure ignore is the fact that rugby has changed. Now a professional sport, it must offer one element in this new world – entertainment. If it doesn't, it will bomb like a bad show in the theatre – people won't go to watch, and then the sums won't add up. The vast swathes of empty seats at several Super Rugby games early in the 2018 season, especially in Australia and South Africa, were a vivid reminder of this. Yet coaches who are more concerned about saving their own necks ignore these basic facts.

It explains why the late Sir Colin Meads told me, 'I don't think any of us are happy with the game now. We don't understand it. If you can tell me anyone who understands the rules now I would be surprised. They are such a lottery. The game has changed so much, and money is a big part of it. I worry that the game right down to club level has become elitist. Unless you are good at it nobody wants you. In the old days in a place like Te Kuiti everyone played rugby, there was nothing else to do. Fat, thin, slow, fast . . . all sizes played. Now, you have got to be a good rugby player from school to be wanted. So many fewer numbers are playing the game and there are so many other things for kids to do nowadays.'

But at least in New Zealand, just as much time has been spent on attack as defence. It underpinned all their rugby traditions. Former All Blacks wing Doug Howlett managed forty-nine tries in sixty-two Tests. Wings Stu Wilson (1976–83) and Bernie Fraser (1979–84) scored ninety-six between them in All Blacks jerseys. Many came from attacks sweeping the length of the field. Compare that to South African Bryan

Habana, who in the 2007 World Cup Final against England touched the ball once in the entire game.

This atrophy of the game in the northern hemisphere played into the hands of a country like New Zealand. As long as their own defence was efficient, they knew that their opponents had little else to offer. Countries should play to their traditional strengths, but not to the exclusion of most other parts of their game. The trouble was, this focus which quickly became an obsession with defence, led to lopsided teams north of the equator. Yes, players were steely, committed and organized without the ball. Physically brave, too. The trouble was that most became like rabbits caught in the headlights; pre-programmed players, stuffed full of orders by coaches, lost the ability to make decisions on the pitch. They couldn't adapt and play what was in front of them, no matter how propitious the opportunity. Decision-making, in an attacking sense, had withered like the dying branch of a tree.

It is still the same in many countries. Take England's witless display in the Six Nations Championship against France in Paris in March 2018. Six points behind in the last moments, with a five-on-two overlap beckoning out wide; the English ball carrier sticks his head down, charges forward into contact, knocks-on and invites the final whistle. Rugby's traditional adage about finding space and running into it has been turned on its head. As the great Irish and record-breaking Lions try-scoring wing Tony O'Reilly joked, 'In our day, we used to try and run away from opponents, especially the biggest ones. But now, players get the ball and look to see who they can run into.'

Those who have advocated and perfected this awful strategy have damaged much of rugby's greatest tradition and attraction. Aspects of play like slick, flat passing, fast, clever footwork, vision, intelligence, skill, and an ability to make the ball do the work. You can see these skills in New Zealand but in too few other countries, and certainly not on a consistent basis.

For intensity, physicality, speed, skills and power, the first quarter of the Super Rugby match between the Hurricanes and the Crusaders in March 2018 was a lesson in supreme standards. I don't believe that two teams below international level could play the game in that way anywhere else in the world. You could have called it Test match rugby, except there are not two Test teams in the world able to perform in such a manner, with so high a standard of execution. Just one: New Zealand.

It would be naive to suggest the trend of overt physicality can be removed. Besides, whoever said even New Zealand don't drive the ball up, smashing into opponents around the fringes and hammering into any human body in sight? Ardie Savea and Jerome Kaino, to mention just two, have made careers out of it. Nor should anyone run away with the idea that New Zealand teams only run with the ball in hand and never kick it. They do. They sometimes kick a great deal, for it is an integral part of their game. After all, rugby teams always kicked the ball in some capacity; to goal, to touch, in the 'dribble', as it was then called, or as in 'the Garryowen' or 'the bomb', to use modern-day parlance.

The 1960s All Blacks wing Ian 'Spooky' Smith remembers: 'Compared to what they're doing today, the rugby in my time was boring. We kicked it up and down the side line most of the time and the forwards hardly gave the ball to the backs. We played one match in the UK one year and were desperate because we were losing. So the forwards gave us the ball. But that didn't happen much.'

There are two principal aspects to the modern-day New Zealand kicking game. The first is a desire to play the game in an advanced part of opposition territory. New Zealand under Sir Graham Henry and then Steve Hansen have been particularly adept at this tactic.

No one has better perfected the art of kicking as a weapon in an offensive sense than first five-eighths like Dan Carter and Beauden Barrett. Their ability to time the kick, keep the ball in the air for long enough to enable one of their wings or their full-back to be in position to make the catch (preferably at pace going forward) is the personification of pinpoint accuracy. The technique employed is a world away from a 'hit and hope' ploy. Each kick is directed either in front of the defending player or behind him, depending on their colleagues' ability to reach the ball first. Or to test the defender's defensive attributes in the air. The kick pass to a colleague out wide is another tactic increasingly employed to unlock structured modern-day defences.

Precision of execution is the key in all these tactics. The kicker must be roughly aware of the offside margins, as well as the position of the defender. His ability to 'hang' the ball in the air is often critical. All this, it goes without saying, requires endless practice to perfect.

These are the type of skills the top rugby players work endlessly to achieve.

New Zealand players, however, have another vital attribute. Their visionary skills are second to none. And their timing is so often superior to their opponents. Their teams often counter-attack from deep in their own half. This tactic can work spectacularly for anyone, as the Lions demonstrated in 2017, when they scored a length-of-the-field try at Wellington in the second Test, a sweeping counter-attack triggered by full-back Liam Williams and finished by Irish flanker Sean O'Brien. It was a stunning reminder that northern-hemisphere teams can still play this way.

New Zealand teams at all levels do this regularly. Damian McKenzie, drafted in as All Blacks full-back in the 2017 Rugby Championship Tests, is a good example of the New Zealand players' willingness to take risks. Yet they have a deep streak of pragmatism in their veins, too. Their structured kicking game reminds us of that. They'll roll the dice and see where they get. They'll have assessed the options and know the chances. They'll back themselves to take on anyone, but few will sign up to rash adventures likely to end in total disaster. Structure is an important word in New Zealand rugby.

What is more, the best coaches still seem able to produce players with vision and decision-making skills. Or at least, those who can look further than the end of their nose to see a game of movement, fluidity and innovation, as well as the need for physicality.

The decline in attacking quality among the opposition allowed New Zealand to open a sizeable gap between themselves and other nations. They played a faster, smarter and wider game. The All Blacks still had to be efficient, clever and clinical going forward. But if they achieved those fundamental requirements even just three or four times in a game it would likely be enough to beat northern-hemisphere countries, as well as others teams like South Africa and Australia, who seemed chiefly obsessed with applying defensive pressure and hoping to extract penalties from which they could kick goals.

New Zealand coaching pioneers such as Wayne Smith, Graham Henry, Steve Hansen, Joe Schmidt, Vern Cotter and others went to the northern hemisphere and preached the gospel of a faster and more skillful all-round game. But it still took years for the northern hemisphere to consider change.

The gap between New Zealand and everyone else was most brutally exposed when Wales toured New Zealand in 2016. Then, the New Zealand provincial side Waikato, despite being greatly weakened by All Blacks Test calls, humiliated them 40–7. It was the clearest example of how far they had fallen behind New Zealand rugby.

But then, the northern hemisphere does self-satisfaction like Carlsberg does lager. Probably the best in the world. Through these years, most critics in the northern hemisphere remained myopic about the rugby played in New Zealand. 'Candyfloss rubbish', they called Super Rugby, without stopping to consider the fact that a game played at greater speed required superior ball skills from its participants. Futhermore, those adherents would be practising those skills throughout an entire match, week in, week out, that they could then use in Test match rugby . . .

According to popular myth, when it came to the Six Nations Championship early in the New Year, this was proper rugby. Didn't you feel the frisson of excitement at that 9–6 Scotland win or Ireland's 15–12 success in Cardiff? Every point in each game a penalty goal.

Frankly, no. This type of attitude goes to the heart of why England, despite their riches and vast resources, the latter the envy of the entire sport, have only won a single Rugby World Cup in thirty years.

However, Ireland and England have made some headway in addressing the gap with the southern hemisphere, Scotland have had their moments and Wales are like the tide. On the turn. Alas, France have gone in the other direction. They threw away all their glorious traditions of attacking mentality, a once-exciting combination of fast, mobile forwards and fleet-footed backs able to challenge any defence in the world. Size became the criteria by which they played the game. Players of the quality and invention of former stars like Andre Boniface, Jean Gachassin, Jo Maso, Denis Charvet, Jean Trillo, Thomas Castaignede and a host of others became redundant. Now, physical brutes wore every jersey. France became as exciting to watch as paint drying.

Yet countries of the northern hemisphere have always produced rugby players of quality and skill, and continue to. But in too many cases, what they have lacked has been a coaching regime willing to take risks and embrace attack as a philosophy. Taking calculated risks has epitomized the All Blacks under Steve Hansen. Those of his kind have both the courage of their conviction and the backing of their paymasters to keep advancing the game, even if it means losing the odd match along the way.

As South African coaching maestro Brendan Venter says, 'I admire the All Blacks. They are the most remarkable team. Their execution is the best, their consistency has been the best. They always have a remarkably concise plan. And they have done better than anyone else. Steve Hansen's biggest asset is he has got time in the saddle. He lost nineteen of twenty-nine matches when he was Welsh coach, but he took the New Zealand assistant coach job under Graham Henry and he just learned and learned. This system is vital to success, in my view.

'There are not enough old coaches out there. Old coaches coach not just rugby but life. That is essential. They have a better work ethic and a proven environment in which they play. You can't be that skilful if you just turn up at All Black camps. These players must be working on their own. Which means they have bought into the culture. And a strong part of that culture is, they don't let young people get ahead of themselves. That is possible because the coaches have been around the block a good few times. The All Blacks have the most experienced coaching staff imaginable.

'There is something about this coaching group that has got the best out of the All Blacks. They [New Zealand] have one big edge on everyone else, one outstanding thing they still have better than others. They have more ball carriers with the ability to beat defenders than others. It is a genetic advantage that island players in particular have got. If you look at the explosive ability of their players, it is remarkable. This is a key factor in their ability to cut the line so often.

'They usually take the right option, too. If they break the line six times, they score three times whereas countries in the rest of the world score once. Or not at all. It is because their decision-making on attack is much better. They do the right thing naturally and the quality of their passing is so good. But it is the decision-making that marks them out from other players in the world. They also possess an ability to transfer their weight quicker than others. But that pure out-and-out explosive ability is the Holy Grail of rugby.'

Without risk, any attack is compromized. Too many fine players in the northern hemisphere in recent years have been sold down the river by ordinary coaches crippled by fear. Firstly, of taking a risk and losing a game, and secondly, of expanding their philosophy, losing too many games and ultimately losing their jobs. It isn't the main factor. But it is another reason for New Zealand's supremacy at the top of the world game.

The 1980s Irish and Lions outside-half Tony Ward agrees. 'Too often, it's an ugly game these days,' he says. 'When Ireland play France, invariably it's a slog-fest. I was brought up to believe that the great French teams had style. You knew you dare not kick them the ball because you knew what would happen if you turned over possession. It's sad to watch these slog-fests in the Six Nations, but I've never thought that about the All Blacks.'

There is another reason why the northern hemisphere fell significantly behind. Law changes to the game, and there have been many in recent years, have been aimed primarily at speeding up the sport. The advent of professionalism influenced some in authority who sought a game of greater ambition and expansion, with entertainment key. The desire to target those who were intent on killing the loose ball at the breakdown, thereby denying attacking opportunities to the side going forward, has been evident in a series of law changes.

These changes have, generally, expedited quicker second-phase balls from the breakdown and given attackers the opportunity to rupture tightly structured defences.

The irony is that, even if you give players more opportunities to attack and run with the ball, it doesn't necessarily follow they will exploit them. Firstly, they need the vision to unlock defences, even off second-or third-phase balls. Secondly, they will need the ball skills to get through, over or around defences. Even splintered ones. That requires timing, vision, handling and precise, highly accurate kicking skills, all performed at pace and under pressure. What is clear is that the officials can motivate the players to play more attractive rugby, but without the basic skills others will not be able to compete consistently.

It is ironic therefore, that law changes that were meant, in part, to level the playing field for other teams chasing the All Blacks, have instead served to extend New Zealand's supremacy. Until players all over the world can do the basics consistently accurately and execute them with precision, the All Blacks' dominance of the sport will continue.

What are these basics? Giving and taking a pass properly, throwing it in front of a support runner twenty times out of twenty rather than behind his ear or down at his feet half a dozen times. Making the ball do the work in timing of passes, running straight, taking out opponents with a clever pass, operating in a tight space under heavy pressure, being accurate and inventive when it comes to putting the ball behind an aggressive defence and playing what they see rather than slavishly following a coach's dogma. Then there is the issue of players' body positions in attack – low, compact, legs pumping – so often assisted by a colleague. And constant support for the ball carrier and the thinking that goes with running intelligent lines of support. That will do for starters.

It is from their players' mastery of these basics of the game, that coaches in New Zealand are given the time and space to calculate where the game of the future may go. They're moving on already. Their vision and in-depth knowledge of rugby puts them comfortably ahead of all opponents. As Wayne Smith says, 'It's a challenge, but a really positive challenge. What is the game going to be like in 2020 after the next Rugby World Cup? It is going to be totally different, so once you get an idea of that how do you take the present forward so that you get a jump on the rest of the world?'

Smith tells a story from 2009 when rugby had largely become a game of kick tennis. The ball was kicked backwards and forwards down the field, sometimes into touch but most often not. Cricked necks were common among spectators. Yet three New Zealanders – Henry, Hansen and Smith – refused to buy into this kicking philosophy. Initially, it was costly. South Africa beat the All Blacks three times in that single year, and France did once. New Zealand caught the downfield kicks, counter-attacked with ball in hand, made errors – especially at the breakdown – and were penalized. Opponents scored, usually from penalty kicks.

'We came under a lot of pressure, especially from the media,' remembered Smith. But wise, cool heads prevailed. Henry insisted the game would not stay like that. He told his colleagues there was no way the IRB would allow the game to be played in such a manner with the attacking team getting no protection. So the All Blacks kept quietly working on their own plans.

In December, the IRB acted, changing the laws to give more protection for the advancing team and greater opportunity to attack without being penalized at the breakdown. When the law change came, New Zealand were at least twelve months ahead of every Test-playing nation. The following year, 2010, in Smith's words, 'the All

Blacks exploded'. They won thirteen of their fourteen Test matches, lost the other by just two points, and scored tries at will. 'It was an example of sticking to your vision and looking into the future. Making a decision and making changes before they happened,' said Smith. This is just one example of where New Zealanders lead the pack.

Australia's 1991 World Cup winning coach Bob Dwyer believes the last fifteen years have been critical in New Zealand's rise – in other words, since Henry was appointed coach. 'It is in that time they have really started to escalate in their rate of development and improvement,' he says. 'They are definitely getting better year after year. They also understand very well the need for absolute excellence in the fundamentals that underpin performances. They have added enormously to the foundation they had.'

At the end of March 2017, I was given a vivid reminder of this New Zealand demand for what Dwyer calls 'absolute excellence in the fundamentals'. All Blacks coach Steve Hansen was in Dunedin to watch the Super Rugby match between the Highlanders and the Melbourne Rebels at Forsyth Barr Stadium. He wanted to watch certain players and I went to the match with him and his son. Hansen is a man who generally keeps his cards close to his chest. But as the Highlanders torched their opponents 51–12, even he couldn't contain all his thoughts. As the Australian side made another costly error to gift the Highlanders yet another score, Hansen exclaimed, 'These guys can't even do the basics.' That was unforgiveable as far as the All Blacks coach was concerned.

Listen to Dwyer again on the subject. 'New Zealand have been a great rugby nation for longer than I can remember. They will leave no stone unturned to ensure that anyone that comes through has a clear understanding of those basics. Then, when those players reach the highest level, they will just brush off some rough edges.

'The excellence of the players around them demands high performance. One thing feeds off another. It is a big mistake to try to educate young kids with too much detail. If you want to be a good rugby coach, you should watch a toddler develop. No one teaches them, they teach themselves. They start to speak, they try to walk . . . 95 per cent of it they do themselves. The way to learn best is to let them play and emulate the things they see in others. It should be natural.

'They develop with no pressure and it's like that in New Zealand when they are younger. They just play and enjoy it. The pressure comes much later but by then they have developed the fundamentals. But another advantage they enjoy is that it is a very distributed population. They have lots of open spaces and a desire to play. Just taking a ball and improving fitness and hand–eye coordination skills . . . New Zealanders do a lot of that. And they have some great, simple ideas. They play barefoot when they're young, which is a fantastic idea.'

This chimes with Hansen's desires that we have already learned about to see boys and girls in New Zealand playing all kinds of different sports for as long as they possibly can. Enhancing hand–eye coordination and improving fitness and ball skills will be of lasting benefit, whichever game they finally decide to concentrate on.

Simplicity. That is the word that stands out in the minds of men like Dwyer, Hansen, Smith and Alan Jones. 'It is a simple game,' says Dwyer. 'Any try scored is usually the sum total of some very simple things. Firstly, it is the proper execution of skills under mental and physical pressure. New Zealand understands these fundamentals. They are the key struts on which you build your play and your game. I certainly admire New Zealand's excellence. The gap is huge at the moment between them and us. Not just us. It is the same with South Africa.'

The date is 16 September 2017. The location is Albany, Auckland, and a Rugby Championship Test. New Zealand 57 South Africa 0. New Zealand scored eight tries for their biggest ever victory margin over the humbled South Africans. The individual decision-making of the New Zealand players was exemplary. Dwyer's point proven, as it also had been in New Zealand's remarkable 40–6 first-half demolition of Australia in Sydney the previous month. Two statistics from the Sydney game are particularly revealing: New Zealand made eighteen offloads and a remarkable twenty-seven clean line breaks.

The worry is that, in the light of New Zealand's excellence, other teams are getting left behind, at both Super Rugby and international level. Former Springbok wing Ashwin Willemse said, 'Rugby in my country has become just a tool in the hands of politicians. 57–0 when New Zealand meet South Africa? I'd say something like that could happen seven times out of ten. A 70 per cent chance. 24–25, the scoreline in Cape Town later in 2017? A match as close as that would probably happen only twice in ten times. In other words, a 20 per cent chance.'

Willemse's words underline the importance of New Zealand helping other nations as much as they can. Some, like Ireland, Wales and England, probably won't need much. Many others will, like South Africa. Then there are those at a lower tier, the likes of Canada, the USA, Samoa, Fiji, Tonga, Romania and Georgia.

Bob Dwyer says, laconically, 'These days, New Zealand play like Australia used to play, with their alignment and keeping the ball moving. Meanwhile, the Australians play like the New Zealanders used to back in the late 1960s . . . just drive it up based on dumb forward play. We are not good at it either.'

There is another important element here, another key reason for New Zealand's rugby ascendancy. The shrewdest of rugby eyes influence the careers of these wannabe All Blacks young men. Dwyer remembers two examples, the first concerning Ardie Savea, the second Aaron Smith. He watched Savea play a Super Rugby game sometime around 2014-5, before the player broke into the All Blacks Test squad. Dwyer talked with Graham Mourie and mentioned the younger Savea. 'I told Graham I couldn't understand why Ardie wasn't in the All Blacks extended squad. He showed such tremendous promise. He would have been in the top group if he were involved with the Wallabies.'

Mourie had a simple response. 'He plays too high above the ground. He plays vertically so he won't get picked. You have got to have your nose half a metre from the ground.'

Dwyer also highlighted the example of half-back Aaron Smith. 'There was a time very early in his Test career when he was replaced at halftime in one game. I thought at the time I knew why. He lifted the ball up, took a step sideways before passing it. The next match he was on the bench and only went on in the second half. I have *never* seen Aaron pass the ball like that since. Now, no New Zealand half-back ever takes a step sideways.'

This precise attention to detail, forged in the toughest rugby proving ground in the world, is a key element in keeping New Zealand at the top of the sport. It has nothing to do with luck; just hard work and inherent knowledge. So often, what we see with New Zealand rugby teams, whatever the level, is the finished product. What most don't see is the arduous work put into preparation for it.

Take the example of the late Jerry Collins, when he first broke onto the scene. Everyone could see his potential. The trouble was, every-one could also see he couldn't pass. Well, not from left to right, anyway. The remedy? They stood him between two walls and made him do up to a thousand passes a day, for two months. He could pass after that, alright.

No rugby nation on earth can match New Zealand for the relentlessness of their approach, their diligence in preparing for as many eventualities as possible. As Dwyer says, 'They are technically better than the rest of the world in a large number of aspects of the game. Not all, but a large number.'

There is something else, according to Dwyer. He cites the New Zealanders' 'amazing capacity' to do all the easy things in the game really well. Vivid evidence of this deep-seated confidence in the ball skills of their colleagues and themselves came in November 2013, when Ireland played New Zealand in Dublin. The start to the match was explosive and dramatic. Ireland seized an early 19–0 lead and Lansdowne Road crackled. Even the All Blacks briefly resembled lost sheep wandering on unfamiliar hills. Gradually though, they gathered their senses and reasserted themselves until the final moments, when Ireland still led, 22–17. Then they conceded a penalty with seventeen seconds of the eighty minutes remaining.

Aaron Smith tapped the penalty and started the movement. One more error, a dropped pass or any other infringement, would be the end of the match. It would also be Ireland's first win in history over New Zealand, going back to 1905.

This was surely Ireland's moment, even if New Zealand had hold of the ball. Yet up in the coach's box, Steve Hansen muttered to a colleague, 'If we keep the ball we should score.' No panic, no gesticulating or screaming instructions. Hansen and his colleagues simply put their trust in the ball skills and decision-making of their players. They sat back and waited, expecting to score. That is the difference.

The All Blacks moved the attack left, and then they went right. Then they tried down the middle, before another switch out left. Then to the right and back again. All the while intently focusing on their job, recycling possession, working their way ever deeper into Irish territory.

Eventually, after a movement of twenty-four passes spanning ninety-eight seconds, with exemplary ball retention, they found the crucial gap in an exhausted, mentally shattered Irish defence. Ryan Crotty took the pass and scored out wide.

At 22–22, defeat was avoided. Television analyst Brian Moore, always a shrewd eye in the sky, called it 'a phenomenal passage of play'. But New Zealanders don't do draws, certainly not with joy as an attachment. At his second attempt (after Ireland had charged too early), Aaron Cruden slammed over the conversion from out wide, and New Zealand had won 24–22. More tears than Guinness flowed that night in Dublin.

Four years later, I sit in a bare room at the Crusaders' training complex in the Christchurch suburbs. Formica bench tops, bare walls, bog-standard chairs. A bland meeting room. Ryan Crotty comes in – he is friendly, personable and cheerful.

First, he surprises me by revealing he's had a good offer to go overseas this year, and even admits he's seriously considering it.

'Be careful,' I counsel. 'No matter where you go, you'll never find as professional and high a standard as here. The Crusaders and the All Blacks? It doesn't get any better than that.'

Sure, but there's the money and his future, he suggests. But you'll have time for that after 2019 and the World Cup in Japan, I tell him. 'Just make 100 per cent certain you have really had enough of playing at this level before you sign anywhere else. Because it'll never be the same elsewhere, playing-wise.' A month or two later, I'm intrigued to read that Crotty has decided to stay in New Zealand and has signed up to the 2019 World Cup in Japan.

Crotty smiles at the memory of that try against Ireland, as he explains why New Zealand rugby players' ball skills and decision-making are superior.

'In some ways, that try has made it one of the most famous All Blacks Test matches, and it was great to play a part. That score was all about belief and confidence in yourself and your mates. There is a massive belief and confidence in the guy standing next to you, who-ever it is. He wouldn't be there if he wasn't special. That philosophy has been sustained over a long period of time. I remember at one point in that last-minute try standing there looking at Richie McCaw and thinking, "We have got this" even though we were still in our own half. It wasn't arrogance, it was the belief I had in my teammates. If we do what we train and execute what we plan, we think we can get any job done.'

The allure of this style of rugby is obvious to most people. Digby Ioane played thirty-five times for Australia between 2007 and 2013.

Yet when the chance came to join the Crusaders for their 2017 Super Rugby campaign, he grabbed it.

'For a start, I'd been playing for Stade Francais in Paris and also in Japan. I felt it was just a job at the latter, especially. Wake up, go to training, come back . . . I was just going through the motions. But coming to play at the Crusaders made me love rugby again. The rugby here is exciting. For me, it is the little things you work on, like skills, that makes New Zealand different and better. They work on basic stuff so much – catching and passing. Another thing is, everyone may be fighting for a spot but the team always comes first here. When you have players that actually care for the team and they want you to do better, it is one reason why New Zealand teams are so successful. I never saw that in Australia.'

Ioane is in his early thirties now, and at the end of the 2017 season he moved on, to the Panasonic Wild Knights in Japan. But he said he was re-energized by his experiences at the Crusaders. 'These guys here, no matter who you are, they are trying to improve your game. It's not the same in Australia. They don't want to help you, they don't tell you things to work on. As for the style, New Zealand has gone to another level of the game and I love the running rugby they use.'

Learning the basics. It is a recurring theme throughout New Zealand rugby, a point with which Dan Carter concurs. 'I agree completely. It's not the fancy moves. When you go to coach kids, they're expecting drills that they've never heard of before. But the key to success is just doing the basics well. Over and over again. Better than any other team.

'We put hours and hours just into the fundamentals of the game; each pass, running square, just the absolute basics. How to catch the ball early, how to follow through with the pass . . . stuff that five-year-olds are learning. But continuing to persist with that.

'A lot of the tries are scored just from doing the basics well . . . great pass, great running lines, putting the man into space. I think that's been a huge key to the success of the All Blacks. It's a simple game and sometimes you can overcomplicate things. A big part of the way the All Blacks play is to keep things simple.'

In May 2017, shortly before they began their three-match Test series against the British & Irish Lions, I was invited to attend an All Blacks training session. Under the watchful eye of head coach Steve Hansen, assistant coaches Ian Foster and Wayne Smith took the session. Hansen said of Foster, 'He's been an integral member of the All

Blacks coaching and management group over the last five years and he brings a lot of composure, rugby nous and intellect to the team.'

It is not like going to watch training at the great soccer clubs of the world, Real Madrid, Manchester City or Bayern Munich, where the club car parks are filled with Bentleys, Lamborghinis and Ferraris. No New Zealand rugby player earns that kind of money. But they still earn enough to buy flash cars and yet there is hardly one in sight here. They travel to All Blacks training together on a basic team coach.

The reason that it's unlikely you will see the latest Ferrari or Lambo behind the gates of an All Black's home is the tall-poppy syndrome. There may be the odd one who is different, but most New Zealand rugby players have long since been made aware that such ostentatiousness strays into the world of arrogance. And if they didn't understand it, every watching inhabitant of this nation would cut them down to size in a trice if they demonstrated such traits.

At an All Blacks training session, anyone expecting the creation of tries from ninety metres and flowing, intricate movements would have been disappointed. Someone searching for tactics never before seen in public would have felt equally let down. The All Blacks keep it so much simpler than that. Instead, the players and coaches worked assiduously in tandem to perform and perfect the basics. It rained heavily in the Auckland suburbs that morning, but there were no excuses for dropping the wet ball.

Half-backs Aaron Smith, T.J. Perenara and Tawera Kerr-Barlow were engaged in an exercise that required the instant release of the ball. As the trio took it in turns to fire out passes to Beauden Barrett, a coach placed another ball on the ground, ten or fifteen metres away. The next half-back due to pass had to be there within split seconds. And so it went on.

No stops for breath, no slowing down to check positions, no taking a step or two sideways before releasing the pass. In one movement, one instant, the ball on the ground had to go, delivered fast, flat and accurately, with Barrett running onto it. If Barrett was forced to check to take it, even momentarily, the pass was considered a failure. Simple? Yes. But it summed up everything the All Blacks seek to achieve. Namely, a complete mastery of the basics, always under pressure.

On another section of the training ground, coach Steve Hansen was blasting the ball at flanker Sam Cane from two metres away. He wasn't expected just to charge it down, but to catch it. Every time. Up at the other end of the field, players worked on line-out drills and scrum practice, the latter under the knowledgeable eye of scrum guru Mike Cron. When the backs came together, skills and movements were practised under pressure.

This constant, never-ending search for technical perfection is at the heart of so much of what New Zealand teams are about and explains much of their skill supremacy over other rugby nations. Just about none of it was so complicated it bamboozled you. Unless you regard things like hands out in front of you with fingers pointing upwards, the non-negotiable position for players waiting to receive a pass, as rocket science. Likewise, the constant desire by Barrett and then-deputy first five-eighth Aaron Cruden to perfect the attacking cross-kick as a means of finding space on the flanks.

As Wayne Smith said, 'The game is as complicated as you want it to be. It is probably an enigma, but the All Blacks' session would be the least complicated programme I have seen. Led by Steve Hansen, we are essentialists. He is really keen for everyone in that programme to focus on the critical few things that are really important. We end up drilling down so that what we put to the players is absolutely essential and what is right for now. It is a very uncomplicated campaign. The difficulty of that is, if you are going to use simplicity as a by-word, you actually have to do more work to make sure that the simple things are the right things. But that's our job. You can be as complicated as you like and people can make the simple complicated. But we try to make rugby simple.'

11

CLUBS: A TIME FOR CHANGE

Contributions from, among others,
Frank Bunce, Brad Johnstone, Wayne Shelford,
Steve Hansen, Steve Tew, Dane Coles,
Sir Brian Lochore.

'Some might say New Zealand doesn't have to sell rugby to its kids. Believe me, it does these days.'

Ex-All Blacks prop Brad Johnstone

Frank Bunce has a problem. Down in the dressing rooms of the Manukau Rugby Club, out in the suburbs of South Auckland, forty-five extremely large and increasingly hungry young men are getting showered and changed after their afternoon exertions. The overwhelming majority of the boys are Tongans. Big lads with appetites to match.

Think triple cheeseburgers here, and then there's the fries. You can keep the fruit . . .

The trouble is, there's a calamity brewing upstairs. Club President Bunce has been let down by his normal food supplier. The pizza shop near the Manukau ground can't provide forty-five pizzas within the next half-hour.

It never used to be like this. Clubs such as Manukau had club members beavering away over hot stoves, providing a meal for the players. Not long ago, they would put out fourteen or fifteen teams each week. The drumming of studs on the dressing room's concrete floors told of impending conflict. It was as deafening as gunfire. That's changed, too. It's down to five or six teams a week these days.

Now, Manukau are like a lot of clubs. They've had to rely on rustling up takeaway meals from a local shop.

Of course, we know Bunce in another guise. Tough, solid and physically combative, with sharp eyes that read a game like a book. He was a member of that marvellous Western Samoa team that beat Wales in the 1991 Rugby World Cup in the UK. That gave rise to one of rugby's most often-told jokes.

'What did Dai say to Gareth when they heard Wales had been

beaten by Western Samoa that day?' 'Good thing we weren't playing the whole of Samoa then, boyo.'

Frank Bunce is still lean, physically impressive and mentally sharp. Which is just as well, because the president at a club like this is often the general dogsbody. He's involved in almost everything these days. Attending meetings to discuss an ever-decreasing supply of funds. Trying to ensure the referee is welcomed in the bar afterwards. Worrying about some of the showers not working. Trying to collate results from the lower teams.

The clock is ticking and the boys are in the showers. One pizza company reckons it could do twenty-five. That's no good. Frank consults his list of numbers and companies. He makes another call on his cell phone.

'Topping? What can you do? Yes, yes, that's fine. Here's my card number . . .'

He clicks the button on the phone to end the call. Cheeks blow, face grins. 'Close one, that,' he mutters.

Frank Bunce is a special man in terms of rugby. Born in Auckland in 1962, he is chiefly of Niuean descent, and played four times for Western Samoa at that 1991 World Cup. Once the tournament was over, All Blacks coach Laurie Mains selected Bunce to represent New Zealand, so he hopped nations.

He was already thirty years old when he made his debut. Even more astonishingly, he then won fifty-five caps for New Zealand, playing until he was thirty-five years old. Former Australia captain John Eales told me in Sydney, 'I think the 1996 and 1997 New Zealand teams were as good as the All Blacks side now. They were the best All Blacks teams I played against. And I always felt that, of all their fine players, a guy who was so important to them was Frank Bunce. He was the rock of that team.'

Even today, some twenty years later, he looks fit and wiry. But then, the club keeps him busy. Bunce's situation is typical of many. They're conservationists, trying to keep once-famous clubs from the edge of extinction. But it's a 'fingers in the dyke' exercise. You just don't know how much longer they'll be able to prevent the inevitable.

Yet the watching world has no doubts. All seems well within the firmament of New Zealand rugby. Alas, this is a widely held misconception. All may be well for the All Blacks and at Super Rugby and schools level. But dig a little deeper and a far less rosy picture can be found at club level throughout the country. Clubs are in trouble all over New Zealand.

*

In April 2017, a leading New Zealand daily newspaper emblazoned a headline across its sports back page. It read, 'Club Rugby "Alive and Well"'.

It was a well-constructed headline. Its author, an employee of the *The Press* in Christchurch, demonstrated considerable wisdom in dumping the onus and justification for the statement firmly upon the person who had uttered such words. The quote marks made it perfectly plain this was not necessarily the view of *The Press*. Rightly so, too.

The story said that All Blacks captain Kieran Read had declared club rugby 'alive and well' after he had played his first game for University in nine years, at Linfield Park.

He was recovering from a long-term wrist injury that had kept him out of the game since the previous November. Playing a club match was an ideal way of helping regain some match fitness before returning to the elite levels.

Read was quoted as saying, 'Club rugby is alive and well when you've got a crowd like this turning up. I really enjoyed the atmosphere down here.'

But the All Blacks captain turning up for a match like this was akin to David Beckham turning out for Leytonstone Football Club in east London. Especially when it's the first time he has appeared for them in nine years. You might expect a few more people to pop down to the club if he's appearing. But it's not like that every week. The problems outlined in this chapter are a stark reminder that club rugby requires some practical help.

*

Frank Bunce coached Manukau, his old club, for four years. He remembers it like it was all yesterday. 'Every day of the week I was travelling, living in my car. Doing everything. We don't have the people anymore. I had to get involved in admin, coaching, the lot . . .'

He sees the problem clearly. 'The only emphasis is on elite-level rugby now so the small clubs suffer. I used to enjoy that old-style rugby. Now the real focus is only on the All Blacks. But not everybody is keen on that focus because of what it does to rugby at community level. Buck Shelford said we are in danger of creating only All Blacks fans in this generation. They're not only just interested in the All Blacks but a lot of them are not rugby people. They're All Blacks people. It should not have gone that way in pro rugby. But professionalism has done it.'

Bunce isn't complaining at the All Blacks' successes. After all, he's a former player of immense standing, and was once voted the sixteenth greatest New Zealand player of all time. He's very interested in the fortunes of the national side, but doesn't think it should be at the expense of everything else:

'The top level is pretty good and the Super Rugby teams always perform. But a lot of club people are upset at the way they get treated. There doesn't seem to be any interest in the competitions below the All Blacks and Super Rugby.'

This is one enormous dichotomy. The top schools produce the finest players. You only have to watch games played by the best schools in New Zealand to realize that the standards at this level are superb. Ball skills, vision, fitness levels, understanding of the game, tactics, execution under pressure – many of these kids have the lot. They're frighteningly good for their ages. As Beauden Barrett points out, a clear path exists for young players. Excel at school, get into the 1st XV, work hard and play well. Recognition by New Zealand Secondary Schools usually precedes an invitation to one of the Super Rugby academies who will offer you a place. There, you can hone your physique and skills, ready for the more physical fray of Super Rugby. You're on the way.

After that, the Holy Grail beckons: All Blacks selection. As Sir Graham Henry said, 'As regards rugby, there might be a drop in numbers. But there is no drop in talent.' But the trouble is, one level of the game has been ignored. Side-stepped. The clubs. Consider another, rather less appealing, pathway to Barrett's description. You're a decent player, inspired and committed. You do your best. You've been there or thereabouts. The trouble is, there's another kid in your age group whose boots seem sprinkled with magic.

You make the 2nd XV regularly. You cling to the memory, like a tackler to a pair of legs, of the time you played for the Firsts – but only because your main rival was injured for a week or two. When he was fit, he went straight back into the 1st XV, and you were bumped back into the Seconds. Truth to tell, you're not that interested in always coming up short. Even so, you're in a better place than a lot of kids. Many schools only have three teams. It means a lot of youngsters, enthusiastic, ambitious but not super-talented, never get a look-in. They get disinterested, and rugby loses them. It is the price to be paid in a rugby nation obsessed with the best – the rush to the top means there are victims that get left behind.

Common sense ought to kick in here, but it doesn't. As Bunce says, 'You don't have any club grades for players from thirteen to eighteen. At college age, there is no focus in the clubs. New Zealand Rugby want them to focus on schools rugby but the limited number of school teams means many kids miss out entirely. If you are in that age group and you don't make it at school, that's it. Everything is focused just on that elite schools level. The top kids are contracted into academies. But if you are not in that system it is very difficult to be noticed now, and a lot of kids drift away from the game. This has led to a lot of grudges being held by some club people these days.'

Why? Schoolkids in New Zealand cannot play rugby for a club between the ages of thirteen and eighteen. A law, says former All Blacks prop forward Brad Johnstone, that has always been there, and certainly has since the 1960s. It was, he said, designed to promote the school rugby teams that went on to become all-powerful. You had to play for the school if you were going to make it.

Johnstone has the classic old prop's look; solid, with a shaven head, bulging neck muscles, big thighs and a powerful torso. He's a man who has given much of his life to the game that he continues to serve. But it's time to change the structure, he says. 'In those days, teachers coached rugby after school hours as part of their job. But most don't have the time for that nowadays. They have so many more non-sporting commitments at school. Now, it is quite a foreign thing to happen. The majority of schools in this country struggle to find adequate coaching staff for their sports.

'Takapuna Grammar School in Auckland is supported by my club, North Shore. But with the development of other cultures, the number of teams at the school has dwindled. They used to be our feeder school, but now we are lucky if we get four or five kids a year at eighteen years old coming through to the club. In 2017, we had no Under 19s whereas we have always had at least one team at that level.

'Frank Bunce is right in what he says. I am not slamming the schools, but the development of our game and these youngsters has got to be moved back to the clubs again. We have all got the facilities and ability to look after these kids.'

At Manukau, in the heart of South Auckland's strong Polynesian community, another worrying trend has emerged. Bunce explains that many of the kids who can't make it into their school 1st XVs turn up at the club asking for a game. 'But we have to tell them, you can't play. Come back in three or four years' time when you're eighteen.'

All because of a law that is outdated. But be careful what you wantonly cast away into the wilderness. 'The problem is, there is a Rugby League club almost next door to us. So they go there and ask to play and they're welcomed in because they don't have any such restrictions. They have teams at every level from thirteen to eighteen. It's mad. We are losing so many youngsters who would build up a relationship with our club for the years ahead,' says Bunce.

It goes without saying that the kids playing social rugby today for the 2nd, 3rd or 4th XVs are usually the ones representing the future of the entire club. They'll become their club's coaches of junior teams, the club secretaries, admin officers, bar assistants and such like, for decades to come. It's the way this quaint old world of rugby works. So losing potential players at a young age means jeopardizing your whole club's future.

This process of self-generation will be familiar to rugby men and women the world over. You couldn't begin to imagine the long hours of tireless sacrifice made by legions of people who happily serve their local clubs. Andy Hunter, coach of 2016 Otago Premier Club champions Kaikorai, confirms the problem.

'We find a lot of kids give it away and I know the high schools find it challenging as well. If you don't make the 1st XV in your school team, there are a lot of other sporting options for kids these days. Like riding mountain bikes, surfing or playing something else. So the numbers coming through are definitely dropping.

'We see it in our club. We have two Colts teams, Junior Colts and Premier Colts. But our Premier Two team, which is the team just under our first team, is struggling for numbers. Those are the guys who maybe played 2nd XV at school, so perhaps they were never going to play Premier rugby. That is the group that are not coming through anymore. The trouble is, they represent the good club men of the future, guys that maybe don't aspire to be top rugby players but just like playing. Those are the future officers of a club . . .

'Grassroots rugby will end up being just two teams, a Colts team and a Premier team, if this trend continues. Not much else. Then where do you find your club officials, who are crucial to how a club runs?'

Amateur rugby has been a part of New Zealand culture since the days of the founding fathers. It has underpinned the social life of people and communities, from Manawatu to Manukau, Napier to Nelson. Walk through the doors of a rugby club anywhere in New Zealand and you'll find a friendly atmosphere. In no time at all, you'll have started to make good friends. It might sound overly sentimental, but to lose this would be to squander a key feature of this country.

North Shore RFC, 145 years old in 2018, is among the best clubs for those qualities. Strangers become friends, and associates become mates. Brad Johnstone is passionate on the topic. 'Amateur rugby is still the soul of our rugby. If we just kill it through negligence and we end up with one-team clubs like it was in Italy when I was there, then we will be guilty of failing so many of the future rugby-playing kids of this country.

'I have a huge passion about my club. Dad played and coached there, I did the same. Now my granddaughters play there. Some of my greatest memories in rugby come from my North Shore days. I still love the passion of amateur rugby. Just going out there and trying your best with your mates and either winning or losing together . . . that is slowly getting lost.'

If ever a New Zealand family epitomized this image of long-term service to clubs it would be the Boticas, at North Shore. Exactly half a century ago, Nick Botica, a New Zealander with Croatian ancestry, was working on the motorway being built north of Auckland. He was out for a run one day and stopped for a chat with a stranger. The conversation soon got around to rugby. Odd thing that, it always seems to in New Zealand. 'Why don't you come down to the North Shore club,' said the stranger. That conversation began an association of fifty years with the Auckland club that has now encompassed eleven members of Botica's family, including Frano (who played twenty-seven matches, among them seven Tests, for the All Blacks).

'It is a club that, from the minute you walk into it, you are made welcome,' says Nick. 'It is a great family club. I played for them and, years later, my two sons played there. Now, two grandsons have represented the club. Plus, six of my younger brothers have played there [he is the eldest of ten brothers].'

When his playing days were over, Nick coached there, too. Nick's father was born on the Dalmatian coast, his mother was part Maori, part English. His mother's grandfather had arrived in New Zealand as a baby on one of the first ships back in the 1840s. He had been born in Falmouth, Cornwall. One of his sons married a Maori girl and Nick's mother was one of their children.

Nick himself was a good enough prop to play for Wanganui–King Country against the touring 1965 South Africans. Behind him at lock were the formidable Colin and Stan Meads. 'We only just lost to them, 24–19, I'll remember it all my life,' he said.

I assume he meant the memory of having Colin and Stan Meads hammering into his backside at every scrum put down over the eighty minutes. But what memories.

Brad Johnstone is another who makes no apologies for his lifelong love affair with the game. When I saw him, he'd had an operation on his elbow, a knee replacement op and another for decompression in the spine – the legacy of a rugby life. But, like most others, these old rugby men bear their wounds with the pride of servicemen wearing their medals. It is the passion that still drives him, and still sees him down at his local club on as many Saturdays as he can manage. His words are important and deserve careful consideration.

'The grassroots have been ignored. Playing-wise, we are shrinking in numbers annually from nineteen- to thirty-year-olds. We used to put out ten senior club teams but we're now down to four and struggling to keep those competitive. We lost eleven Premier One players over the summer in early 2017. Two went to other provinces in New Zealand, two to the Blues franchise, two to clubs in France, one to Japan, two to clubs in Australia and two just disappeared.'

North Shore managed to rebuild the team, albeit with young players, and they qualified for the top six play-offs in July 2017, a considerable feat. There, they lost their first match but ended up winning the Plate. Yet how much longer can clubs cover these types of losses? Johnstone says, 'We have also dropped from 400 junior boys to around 250 in the last four years. These are five- to twelve-year-olds. Do the sums yourself – at that rate of decline, how many will be left in five years' time?

'A lot of clubs are hanging in there by their fingernails. They're just trying to survive from one sponsor to the next. It's about the culture of the game and New Zealand Rugby have to sell that back to the people. Right now, they are constantly putting out fires about concussion and other things. But that is being reactive. They are not selling the game to the kids.

'Some might say New Zealand doesn't have to sell rugby to its kids. Believe me, it does these days. You only have to look at the decline in participation numbers to know that. Kids today in New Zealand have so many other sports to interest them when they're in their teens – they no longer have to make a commitment to just one sport. Sure, the best will always gravitate to rugby. But under the systems nowadays, the clubs don't see them much, anyway. The problem is, less and less kids want to commit themselves to three or four months of regular training and playing, especially in winter.'

Dane Coles echoes those thoughts. 'In New Zealand, there are many things other than rugby. It is everything: climbing mountains, trail-walking, fishing, whatever. New Zealand is the best country in the world for young people to grow up in a healthy environment. Life is, for me, the best here. You see great places around the world but there is nothing like being back here in New Zealand. For me as a person, rugby has been the way to express myself and enjoy life.'

Rugby union, says Johnstone, has to be advertised to fifteen- to eighteen-year-olds, without just relying on the All Blacks brand to promote it. For the fact is, he believes many kids don't realize what they can achieve out of the game. He cites the fun, camaraderie, discipline and value of working with others, learning the lessons of teamwork. These are core values of life. Rugby teaches them for free. It's true that some other sports would claim they offer as much, but rugby is endemic to this nation.

Frank Bunce shares such sentiments. 'Rugby would be mad to let all this die. Not only is rugby going to pay a hell of a price if it does. The country and especially the local communities, because of the social problems and issues that will follow if it all crumbles at this level. You will have lots of young guys, full of beans with nothing to do. What happens then?

'If they become part of a rugby club, kids get coached, they learn about a team and its demands. They are learning values when they really need them. This is where you learn respect, learn how to talk to people, older people, too. You are acquiring social skills which all age groups and social levels need. Some of the issues we have got now as a society come from this. If kids don't learn values at a young age, even if they're eventually successful as rugby players, it all goes to their head.'

Brad Johnstone is by no means North Shore's only famous ex-All Black. Wayne Shelford, who played forty-eight matches including twenty-two Tests for New Zealand between 1985 and 1990, is another distinguished member. We chew the cud in a fashionable North Shore cafe, overlooking the curved beach at chic Takapuna. Little boats chug in and out of the small landing point, dogs run on the beach and the energetic move slowly past on stand-up paddle boards. It is an idyllic scene on a sunny autumn morning.

Eyes sparkling, eyebrows arching, Shelford pinpoints three other critical reasons why so many rugby clubs are struggling. Firstly, New Zealand's drink-driving laws are now among the toughest in the world. Trying to beat them is a mug's game. 'But what they mean to a club like ours,' he says, 'is that people will only have perhaps one drink. Or maximum two.' North Shore RFC, near to Devonport, is landlocked. There is only one road in and out to Takapuna. So it's easy for the police to set up breathalyser testing on that road.

'We see that problem every year in our bar takings dropping by 15 to 17 per cent.' It is even worse at Frank Bunce's club Manukau. Because it is in the heart of South Auckland where so many Polynesians live, interest in the bar on a matchday is almost non-existent. It is fascinating to walk around the ground on a Saturday afternoon; anywhere in the UK or Ireland, Australia and South Africa too, spectators would be clutching pints of beer or lager. But here, there is not an alcoholic drink in sight – most Islanders don't drink. It's hard to make money from the bar under those circumstances.

The second problem identified by Shelford at North Shore is that it is in a highly popular, expensive area of Auckland. Real-estate prices have soared here in recent years. 'The kids playing rugby here are all local kids. But when they are eighteen or twenty they all move out because they can't afford to live here. Their only way of staying is to remain at home and many don't want to do that.

'So they move out of the area to a cheaper one but they don't come back to play for our club. Another reason for that is the terrible traffic all the time here, day and night. Traffic-volume figures have risen 20 per cent in the last eighteen months in this area. So they go somewhere nearer where they live or somewhere easier to get to.'

The third reason is the overseas factor. That is affecting clubs the length and breadth of both islands of New Zealand. In 2016, Kaikorai, captained by Blair Tweed and coached by Andy Hunter (the club's 1997 captain), won the Otago Premier Club Rugby Final for the fourteenth time, as well as the Speight's Championship Shield. They beat Dunedin 29–22 in the final at Forsyth Barr Stadium, home of the Super Rugby franchise, the Highlanders.

The club estimates it has produced more than 3,500 rugby players in its time, many of whom have gone on to win higher honours. It was Kaikorai's first Championship title since 1997. Yet within the space of a few weeks, Kaikorai began to see the price they would pay for their success. Hunter said, 'There is not a lot of money in New Zealand if you are not quite at the top level. That is the real problem. This is the next level of players who are disappearing abroad on good overseas contracts. We lost three players to clubs abroad from our 2016 Championship-winning team. Two went to Top 14 French clubs, one to an Aviva Premiership club in England. You would have to suspect they would be earning at least twice what they can get here as a semi-professional.

'They had around 200 first-class caps among them, and you take that out of a club team you feel the difference. We have essentially replaced them with nineteen-year-olds. Our future is based on these guys learning over the next couple of years. So you must have a cyclical view of how sustainable your selections can be, and build for the future. There are two ways of looking at that. It exposes the kids earlier and gives them opportunities. But the truth is, young guys learn best from playing alongside senior quality players. That is the real loss to the club, both on and off the field.

'This is happening all over New Zealand. France is attractive from a financial point of view, Japan likewise. Then there's the UK and Ireland. It is good money at any of them.'

The long-term consequences of all this, in Hunter's eyes, are serious. 'The talent is there and the structures are fine. But any pyramid is only as strong as its base. If you start eroding these club structures, then the boys who are at the top either don't have to work so hard to get there or even stay at the top . . . That would be the issue.'

Yet Steve Hansen is one who challenges this view. The All Blacks head coach believes it has been the case since the game went professional that New Zealand rugby was built from the top down and not from the bottom up. What is more, he argues, it is the case in every country.

'The money that is made for the clubs around England is from 83,000 people coming to Twickenham every time they play. If England stopped putting money into their clubs, they would all be broke.

'The rugby unions that are struggling financially I guarantee are struggling at the top and not bringing in enough money. For us to be able to do that with a population of just 4.8 million people is a hell of a credit to the brand and the people who work in our organization.'

New Zealand Rugby CEO Steve Tew is a tough-talking, no-nonsense operator who offers a brisk, businesslike persona to the outside world. Tall, angular and bustling in his demeanour, he is a guy who won't use two words if one suffices. Strongly built, he's the epitome of a solid New Zealand citizen, perfectly able to deflect the arrows frequently fired in his direction. It goes with the territory, he'll tell you. He's frank, too, on the problems confronting rugby in his country.

'The desire to achieve in this country creates an elite and those that won't reach the top fifteen now are giving the game away. They quit. How do we arrest that? It is definitely an accurate observation, but it could be applied to a range of sports. I have three young adult daughters who played netball to A-level at school. But that was the end of their netball careers.

'My eldest daughter, Ruby, is involved in the national rowing programme and she went to Rio for the 2016 Olympics [she came fourth in the women's eight]. But all the kids she rowed with left rowing at secondary school. Clearly, this is not just a rugby issue. It is an inevitability that people will do different things through different phases of their lives. The need to get young people engaged in our sport is still there, that's for sure. We have always had a drop-off between primary and secondary school, and another drop-off after secondary school. But the drop-off rate is high. We lose a lot of kids at that primary-school age.'

But there are other factors at play here, too. Nowadays, youngsters want disposable income. Tempted by the technologies of the modern world, myriad products take up their time. Along with the rise in technological distractions, there are more serious social issues to contend with, like an increasing number of single-parent families. Getting kids to and from training is a big factor. Commitment to a sport is becoming less attractive to young people.

Yet Tew remains optimistic. 'Somehow I hope people will come together and play the game. We have done a lot of research and have asked kids why they kept going or stopped. Most of the issues are things we can still have some control of . . . experience, coaching, attitude of parents, behaviour of people watching on the sideline. Those things we can have some influence on, making the game more interesting and encouraging to a broader, more diverse group of people of every ethnicity and socio-economic background. That is really important to us. We are working hard and looking closely at this area.'

It's not just rugby men the wrong side of fifty who hold these concerns about the future of club rugby. Some, like Dane Coles, stand firmly in the Bunce–Johnstone–Shelford camp. Which may surprise some.

'I have a great appreciation for grassroots rugby. I played three years at club level and absolutely loved the time with my club, Poneke, in the eastern suburbs of Wellington. I make sure I have still got a good connection with them. I go down there from time to time and do some simple basics.'

Poneke is doing better than most. They have nine teams: Premier, Premier reserve, two first grade, Under 21s, Under 85 kg, President's, Golden Oldies and a women's team. Their ground, Kilbirnie Park, is a hive of activity much of the time. Coles admires these unknown warriors, the simple foot soldiers of the game: 'Those guys turn up on Tuesday and Thursday evenings, because they love the game. But some kids now won't even play club rugby. They go straight from college into pro rugby. A lot of the academies now hold back those players, they don't let them play club football and that is sad because clubs love the All Blacks going back to them and having an affiliation with them. I was on the bench for first-team club rugby for the first two or three years. I was twenty-one or twenty-two.'

The meaning of this is simple: even future All Blacks have to serve their apprenticeship. He learned painful lessons during this time, too. A youngster like Coles, with his speed and ball skills, would inevitably be a target in club footy. Most grizzled members of the 'Front Row

Union' don't take kindly to a young pup of a hooker able to run almost as fast as some second five-eighths.

'I have definitely been intimidated on a rugby field, especially in my younger days,' he concedes. There is nothing personal or ungentlemanly in that; it is just the traditional rules of engagement. 'You learn how to handle others and you learn how to handle yourself in those situations. Sometimes you get put in high-pressure situations. But I know how to handle them now. It is experience, things I have learned along the way because of my time in club rugby. But there were periods in the early days of my career when it was more difficult.'

That is where club rugby is such an education to all young players. Whatever level they intend to reach. You learn how to survive, how to ride the blows and come back for more. It is, intrinsically, a tremendous proving ground, both in a technical and a mental sense, in which ball skills and survival skills are tested to the utmost.

Sir Brian Lochore underlined the value of young people growing up in country areas and playing local rugby. 'Dane Coles was brought up in a small country town, he wasn't a city boy. He joined his local club. But so many of these country clubs are now struggling. We have got to be careful we don't allow that to die. If we do, we will go for a while but then tip over. If the country people weren't playing rugby even now, the All Blacks would not have the strength they have.'

The first move that would offer the clubs immense hope would be a public rebuttal of the long-standing rule that youngsters can only represent their school between the ages of thirteen and eighteen. If New Zealand Rugby came out with a clear change in policy allowing kids to play for their clubs as well, much would change.

It would not necessarily alter the framework by which New Zealand rugby has become so strong at school level. The very best players, those with obviously superior talent to the majority, would still seek that prestigious 1st XV place in their school team. But those who will realistically never achieve such heights could still be playing and enjoying the game at club level, and a vibrancy would return to so many clubs.

How best to make this change as seamless as possible? One man has a perfectly credible answer. He won't have been heard of anywhere much outside his own rugby club and community. But Jeromy Knowler is a man with a plan . . .

*

Just over 150 years ago, the Prebble family from Mersham in Kent went on an adventure. The so-called 'Garden of England' wasn't for them any longer – they chose to make a new life in faraway New Zealand. They sailed on one of the first ships and arrived around 1855. What they found upon their arrival was a land called 'wild and uninviting' by one historian. Edward Prebble acquired fifty acres of this rough land and divided it into small sections. The owners promptly set about taming nature and making the land habitable. Approximately 14 km south-west of Christchurch, in Selwyn County, the town known today as Prebbleton was one of the earliest on the Canterbury Plains. It began with a small store and these individual sub-divisions. But like so many early New Zealand settlements, it soon grew into a reasonable-sized hamlet. A church was built, and then a general store. A school inevitably followed. Here were the seedlings of a prosperous future community. Rudimentary to begin with but founded on deeply held Christian principles by honest men and women who wished to carve out a new life for themselves and their offspring.

Farmers from Kent, a clerk born in Oxford and a baker from Linlithgow in Scotland; they clustered together, like leaves blown by an autumn wind, to lay the foundations for this new land. Today, Prebbleton is at the heart of one of the richest agricultural districts in the country. The original solitary church has now multiplied to three – Anglican, Presbyterian and Wesleyan. The first general store has been joined by three others. There is a hotel and bar. It is a most prosperous community in the increasingly fashionable southern suburbs of Christchurch, with a population now of more than 3,000.

Among them lives Jeromy Knowler, the President of Prebbleton Rugby Club. Prebbleton is a junior club and puts out twenty-six teams, making it the biggest country club in the Canterbury Union.

You don't do that without a great many people offering a whole lot of input. Former president Tony Grimwood sets a strong example, putting in close to thirty hours' service a week. All for free, of course. He is now retired, which means he can put in even more time – Grimwood is the 'heart and soul' of the club, according to Knowler. 'He does a fantastic job, anything from marking out the lines on the pitches, doing painting jobs around the club, fixing things, discussing ideas and suggestions, sitting in on meetings,' says Knowler.

In all his spare time, Grimwood is manager of the Division One team and is one of thousands across the country who give up their time for the love of the game, and love of their community.

Knowler and his wife Jolene roll up their own sleeves on a regular basis to help. You'll find him down at the club early on a Saturday morning, putting the giant joint of roast pork on to cook. Then there's a hundred or so potatoes to peel. These are the true servants of the game. One of the traditions they love and are determined to maintain is to offer players a good meal after their match. His role is sous chef, while Jolene is the club cook. Providing meals is another way to encourage the boys to stay, they reason. Like thousands of others at similar clubs, they take pride in playing their small part in the big picture of New Zealand rugby. 'It is never a chore, we enjoy what we do.'

But even in their successful club they see the problems outlined by Frank Bunce, Brad Johnstone and others. 'I understand Frank's view,' says Knowler. 'I have the same conversations with people at other clubs at our level. I talk to a lot of coaches, committee members and school rugby people. This problem is happening all over the country. Something has got to change.'

Knowler thinks he knows what. 'What needs to happen is on Wednesdays, schools should play rugby, and on Saturdays the youngsters should come back and play for their club. Everybody you talk to involved in a club set-up would agree. The school 1st XV is becoming a big business for finding these players that will go through. That puts a lot of pressure on boys to play school rugby. It's the kids from the 2nd XVs and Under-16A teams – they're the kids we want to be available to us in the clubs.'

What happens if the clubs continue to fail to get those youngsters? Knowler echoes Bunce's warning. 'A lot of clubs, even Division One clubs, are struggling. You are losing your better young players and they are not coming back. We are strong at junior grades but we're losing players at senior grades. New Zealand Rugby hasn't listened to these complaints. Now we have a new CEO of Canterbury Rugby Union, Nathan Godfrey. He came from Australia and worked in the AFL over there, although he's a Kiwi. He is listening. He is really interested in this predicament.'

It is not just a country problem, says Knowler. In fact, he thinks it's a bigger worry in the towns. 'You don't even try to have kids in those grades. The problem is, the schools don't want to see the big picture.

But some clubs a hundred years old or more are in real danger of folding. That would be a disaster.'

It's fair to say that even the most diehard club-rugby aficionados accept the reality of modern-day professional sport. As Colin Meads said before his death, 'There will never be another All Black from Te Kuiti.'

True as that might be, it shouldn't mean the end of club rugby. These clubs provide a core focus in their local community. Whether it's a small village in the middle of the country, a highly populated area of South Auckland, or somewhere else.

Besides, as Steve Hansen himself suggests, you never know where the next Richie McCaw or Beauden Barrett might be lurking. Even if you disregard that factor, there are two other great elements to club rugby in New Zealand. The first is the sheer aesthetic pleasure of watching or playing rugby in some fantastic locations. So many clubs enjoy enchanting vistas. You can stand on a touchline in this country, marvel at the views and just breathe the clean, fresh air, irrespective of the rugby.

The second is even simpler. The clubs, large or small, are meeting places. For people from all walks of life to come together and pursue their love of the sport. Bringing people together and getting them involved in activities that help other members of the community – these are hardly inconsequential aspects of a modern-day society.

Frank Bunce talks of people passing the Manukau club when a big rugby match is being televised. They'll ask, 'Can we come in and watch the game?' and are welcomed like lost brothers. They watch the match, have a pint or two, maybe order up a takeaway and then stay afterwards for a chat and another pint. Complete strangers yoked together by the game.

On a beautifully sunny, crisp autumn afternoon, I made my way out to Harbour Rugby Club at Port Chalmers. A few miles along the coast from Dunedin, right down at the bottom of the South Island – and, in fact, the world. All Blacks like Jeff Wilson, Tony Brown and Waisake Naholo plus Black Fern Fiona King have played here for the famous Harbour Hawks. In July 2017, they would reach the Premier One Grand Final, losing 24–15 to Southern.

It's a charming club in a gorgeous setting, with the hills behind the clubhouse and the waters of the harbour running close by one touchline. It isn't commonplace at most rugby clubs to find two large metal poles with nets on the top, rather like outsized fruit pickers. But here, they're essential pieces of equipment. The youngsters standing on the touchline closest to the water grab a pole, the moment a ball is about to be kicked into touch. If it is hit too strongly, the ball ends up in the harbour, whereupon the the youngsters' 'fishing' skills become vital. Snare the ball as it bobs up and down in the water and they can haul it in and save the club money. Miss it, and the ball just floats away forever down Dunedin Harbour. 'We might lose anything up to ten or twelve a season,' grins a rueful groundsman.

Club rugby was the bedrock of the old amateur game in New Zealand. It spawned mighty men and famous foes. That route to the great All Blacks no longer exists, but it doesn't mean that many of those clubs should now die. Arguably, their role as institutions where young men and women can come together and learn some of the core values of life is more important than ever.

Down the years, youngsters were inculcated at an early age in the values espoused by rugby clubs. Like friendship, working together, thinking of others and enjoying healthy physical activity. Few have looked back in later life and regretted their involvement. Some have gone on to put a similar amount back into the game through their own efforts. This sense of giving long since became generational.

Fixing the problems that undermine many of these New Zealand clubs may require patience and a vision. Give and take on all sides would ease the process, too. But it is hard to believe those problems are insurmountable.

12

WOMEN IN RUGBY

*Contributions from, among others,
Judy Clement, Darren Shand,
Melissa Ruscoe, John Hart, Steve Tew.*

'You can't grow up in this country not knowing who the All Blacks are. I think the All Blacks are an inspiration. But I would like to think the Black Ferns are getting to the same level. Certainly, in terms of New Zealanders supporting them and being proud of them.'

Melissa Ruscoe, Captain Black Ferns,
Women's Rugby World Cup Winners 2010

It is Christmas morning. Not the starry night, snow-clad fantasy of northern-hemisphere Christmas cards, and nor that dire Bing Crosby dirge about dreaming of a white Christmas. Give thanks for that. Just the first day of a peaceful New Zealand Christmas.

The weather is OK. There's a little sun, especially on the central and eastern beaches of the North Island. Down in Wellington, they're anticipating a late southerly wind. They're used to them. It'll be pleasantly mild, a gentle twenty degrees Celsius in most places.

For once, no one is thinking about rugby. Families are at the beach, their car boots loaded to the gills. The rugby fraternity has fragmented, ahead of the New Year training camps.

However, one renowned rugby man has not left town. The streets of Hamilton are quiet, as Chiefs and All Blacks forward Liam Messam waves goodbye to his family, and leaves for a women's refuge in the city. There, he will greet most of the residents, sit down with them, have a cup of coffee and a chat. Put an arm around some troubled souls while he does what helpers do best – give their time, and just listen . . .

When that is done, he will stay around to help serve Christmas lunch. His own family must wait for his company this Christmas Day. But then, Messam has always been a make-a-difference sort of guy. He is here because of a programme run by the Chiefs rugby franchise in Waikato. Its core philosophy is twofold. The empowerment of young rugby men into roles valuable for society. Plus an enhancement of their own career prospects when their playing days are over.

The scheme is headed by Judy Clement. But not even she knows how Messam is spending this special day. It is his own initiative. Clement has been Personal Development Manager at Chiefs Rugby

Club. She has spent more than eight years in the job, an occupation she calls 'amazing', and considers herself privileged to have filled this role. She is just one example of the women playing important roles in New Zealand rugby, an extension of the role they have played in the history of the country. In the earliest days, they helped clear the rough land with their hands; in wartime, they fulfilled myriad tasks to help the nation overcome the loss of so many men and in modern times, they have continued to contribute mightily to all aspects of Kiwi life. Furthermore, their knowledge of rugby union is more extensive than many men's in other countries of the world.

They might not enjoy the high profile of their male counterparts such as Steve Hansen and Graham Henry. But behind the scenes, assiduously working or supporting, encouraging, planning and advising, are many women in a huge variety of positions – some paid, but many not. They are mothers who sit on committees and wash the Under 7s' kit; others who make the teas, cook the sausages and chips at the local club and serve behind the bar in the clubhouse. Others still help coach the young Kiwi girls who dream of one day pulling on the jersey of the Black Ferns. None of this should be overlooked – for the role that women play in New Zealand rugby is another reason why this nation conquered a world sport.

Women's rugby is the biggest growth market in New Zealand sport. The Black Ferns produced the country's best-ever performance at the 2015 Olympics, winning the silver medal, and followed that by winning the Women's Rugby World Cup in Ireland, in 2017. Also in 2017, their Sevens' women won their fifth World Series tournament out of six.

All Blacks manager Darren Shand might be concerned chiefly with his role for the nation's premier male rugby outfit. But his comments reflect both the men's and women's game in the country: 'We are pretty hard on ourselves as New Zealanders in rugby. When you live in a goldfish bowl you take it more seriously. In fact, we are incredibly tough on how seriously we take the game.'

That includes the coaches who guide the Black Ferns. Plus their highly committed players, but also people like Judy Clement, who fulfil an equally vital task. The uninitiated might regard it as unimportant, but the reality could not be more different.

New Zealand Rugby and the New Zealand Rugby Players' Association employ full-time Personal Development Managers (PDMs) at

Colin Meads visits his statue at Te Kuiti, shortly before his death in 2017.

Australian halfback Ken Catchpole, whose international career was ended by a tackle from Meads in 1968. Catchpole, too, passed away in 2017. Before his passing, Meads admitted to the author that at times he had gone too far in terms of violence on the field.

Above. Bryan Williams: note the power and balance that made him so difficult an opponent to stop.

Opposite, top. Ian 'Spooky' Smith: 'The forwards never gave us the ball in our day'.

Opposite, bottom left. Frank Bunce, an exceptionally talented player who didn't make his All Blacks debut until he was thirty. He then won fifty-five caps, the last when he was thirty-five years old.

Opposite, bottom right. Conrad Smith, an outstanding member of the All Blacks' World Cup-winning teams of 2011 and 2015, and a qualified barrister and solicitor of the New Zealand High Court.

Clockwise, from above. Damian McKenzie, Waisake Naholo, Beauden Barrett and Julian Savea. Each has a different style yet all are hallmarked by their dynamic running and finishing.

A superb image of Doug Howlett and his unmistakable running style beside the sea. Howlett is still New Zealand's record try scorer with forty-nine from sixty-two Tests. Yet, alluding to the All Blacks' intimidatingly high standards, he said, 'I never once felt certain of my place in the team.'

The hugely talented Barrett brothers (from left): Scott, Jordi and Beauden. They follow a distinguished line of brothers down the years who have gone on to represent the All Blacks at Test level, including names such as Brownlie, Clarke, Meads, Brooke, Going and Franks.

Liam Messam, a man with a deep respect for his Maori heritage and Maori rugby.

Jerome Kaino, one of the hardest men ever to represent New Zealand. 'You wouldn't want to be hit by him,' admitted even legendary hard man Sir Colin Meads.

Sonny Bill Williams with fans. The All Blacks have always understood the importance of the relationship with their fans.

Left. Adieu to a star: the great Richie McCaw waves farewell after New Zealand's victory at the 2015 Rugby World Cup. McCaw played 148 times for his country, far and away an outstanding record. And when he finished Test rugby, he turned his back on a potential 5 million euro bonanza with a French club, a hallmark of the man and his values.

Below. Richie McCaw with the author at his Christchurch Helicopters base in 2017.

all the rugby franchises, and part-time PDMs in all the Provincial Unions within the country. The programme, in which many rugby men like Liam Messam get involved, has been running for twenty years in the New Zealand game. The model is set up with funding from the 'Player Payment Pool'. A percentage is put aside to fund it.

The programme is managed by the New Zealand Rugby Players' Association and New Zealand Rugby. Each PDM has a budget to deliver a quality programme.

In the Chiefs' region, Judy Clement supports four other part-time PDMs who are based at the region's Provincial Unions.

The key elements of the programme devised by the NZRPA and NZR are as follows:

1. Career development. Ensuring players have an active plan for a career after rugby – helping them to investigate options, manage their studies or partake in work experience.
2. Personal development. Encouraging self-awareness, self-reliance, self-understanding and helping them spend time giving back to others. Some, like Messam, are passionate about supporting those less fortunate than themselves.
3. Professional development: drug-free sport, integrity, media. All the things that help the players in the prof-essional game.
4. Advising players financially. Helping to set budget goals and sorting out their finances so that they do not give all their money away to their families. They are told that if they look after themselves first, they will be in a position to help their family.

Two examples illustrate the idea. All Blacks and Chiefs lock Brodie Retallick, the 2014 World Rugby Player of the Year, has an engineering degree, but he will almost certainly need more qualifications than that when he finishes rugby to enjoy a lifestyle comparable with his present one. He can tap into the knowledge available through this scheme, and a future life can be planned.

Some may fail to see the link between this programme and the basic question I have addressed in this book. What on earth do play-ers' controls of their finances have to do with how New Zealand conquered an entire world sport?

The truth is that the two are tightly interlinked, like hand and glove. Programmes such as this one empower young men, take them out of their comfort zone and force them to think through issues and make decisions accordingly. It induces qualities such as character and judgement. The same attributes demanded on the rugby pitch.

Young men and women for whom everything is done and decided for them off the field will make poor decision-makers on it. They have no experience, no yardstick and no experience of assessing situations and deciding for themselves the best action to take. It is no surprise when they replicate those qualities on the pitch.

John Hart is one of many who sees the point: 'Too many young rugby players in this country are pampered far too early these days. It's all given to them on a plate – most of them don't even have to think about ordinary, everyday life. They've got loads of clothes and training gear given to them, half of which they don't need. Everything is done for them. They go to training, they're fed, they're given cars; it's just crazy. No wonder some of them fail later in life. We have gone over the top.'

What Judy Clement has been involved in is an offshoot of this philosophy, that tries to prepare young men for life and encourage them to mature earlier. It is different with girls, who mature quicker than boys, anyway. Clement has a basic philosophy to apply these programmes and schemes. 'Above all,' she says, 'we need to care more about our players. They are not just rugby players. They are people. The need is for supporting players and educating them. We are not asking them to go out and sort out the nation's problems. But we are educating them and giving them some of the skills to go and talk to people, to have conversations with them.

'Too many western societies don't teach kids about relationships, financial management or how to be good parents. Or about how to communicate well. Very little of it is being taught in the schools. Society became obsessed with acquiring degrees and qualifications, rather than being good citizens.'

Clement's inflence grew exponentially with the job. When she first started, she felt she was a little surplus to requirements, a token to be endured or suffered. Maybe, she thinks, that was partly to do with the fact she is a woman. But now, it is different, and she is taken very seriously. Last year, New Zealand Rugby took on another five PDMs, so now there is a pool of about twenty. There is a PDM for Men's and

Women's Sevens, and a player-services manager who helps those players who are moving overseas or returning home. Another goes around the schools, educating young players about entering professional rugby.

A PDM might work three to four days a week during the Mitre 10 Cup programme from July to October. Out of season, they continue to work with the Academy. The programme is so extensive it tries to reach anyone who is an Emerging Professional Player in New Zealand.

It would be wrong to suggest this innovation belongs solely to New Zealand. Other countries operate a similar scheme, and Clement had a chance to assess their work at a conference in Paris in 2017. There were ninety delegates from twenty-seven countries, representing sports as diverse as rugby, baseball, Australian rules football, rugby league, ice hockey and handball.

What Clement saw and heard hugely encouraged her, enhancing her belief that here was yet another area in which New Zealand rugby was laying down a pathway for others. 'I came away with the firm belief that New Zealand is leading the way in this field. I told them about the work I was doing and it became clear we are ahead of the rest. The way our programme is set up, New Zealand Rugby and the Players' Association work together which is very special. A lot of other rugby-playing countries know they need this but they haven't set up such a programme. They don't have the time or expertise. The Japanese Rugby Union doesn't offer this. England, Ireland and Scotland are fairly advanced in the field, but not as much as we are. They might not get the time we get. France? Very limited. Maybe they have one PDM to cover fourteen teams. That is the sort of acceptance of it. It is a token gesture.'

In New Zealand it is different. An increasing amount of work and effort is being put into it. The Chiefs players spend four hours each week on the programme, usually from eight in the morning to twelve noon on a specified day. They also go out and do work experience, shadowing someone in a job in a field they may like to work in one day. They get contacts through sponsors and have to set it up themselves. Clement insists it is not her role to hold their hands through this process.

Of course, if you have a nineteen-year-old whose sole ambition is to be an All Black, his total focus is on that. It can be difficult to convince him to think long term. However, a serious injury, or perhaps loss of form that means the player loses his place in the 1st XV, broadens most thought processes.

Clement has learned not to push these young men. They must want to get involved and see the benefits for themselves. As she says, 'It is great to see players hold a conversation when they first enter the professional level, grow and develop and become leaders in the team. It is a privilege to watch. They are at their most powerful age – they are the people that can make a difference. They can really change the world; maybe help change people's lives.'

She always enjoyed the job. 'I am passionate about this kind of work, I love it. You are often the longest-serving person in the organization, which means you know how things work. You can see if things are not quite right. I can see the coach and say to him, "You haven't got the balance right or maybe the players need more time." If you put in place the right education . . . for the players . . . you hope the message will get home.'

Gradually, the players have bought into this concept. Senior players will turn up to do education with academy players. The stars of the present talking to and answering the questions of the stars of the future. They hold an academy camp every February, and about eighty young men from the region attend. Present players playing a big part in educating the newbies – it is good for their own development to give something back to the game. Offering advice on finances, especially to players with origins and commitments in Polynesia, is further valuable exercise.

Perhaps, says Clement, it is all down to professionalism in rugby. But she believes it is mostly about caring for people and thinks it's absolutely something business needs. 'If you care about the people you employ, demonstrate that you need to look after them and make sure you are not using them as a piece of meat, then you are showing them you're doing this so that they can be successful in life.'

Of course, such a process has potential for frustrations and failures. Certain incidents involving rugby in the Waikato have led to national exposure. In August 2016, a stripper booked to waitress and perform a strip routine for the team at the Chiefs' end-of-season 'Mad Monday' celebrations at a hot-springs pool near Matamata alleged that players touched her inappropriately and that she had to kick one of them to get him to stop.

Events quickly got out of hand, especially when the media got hold of the story. So much of the good work done behind the scenes by people like Judy Clement seemed to have gone down the plughole.

Clement admitted several months later, 'The boys were quite negative about some of the programme. They felt the blame for certain incidents involving the Chiefs were being laid at their door. They felt they were being targeted. But it is about being open-minded and honest. I talked to them about why it was important we carried on with it rather than spat the dummy.'

She had some frank thoughts on the issue herself. 'They are just young men. You bring them in saying, "You can be a normal young man." But then you say, "But you can't stuff up." Sometimes it feels to me like we set them up to fail. They will stuff up from time to time but that is not intentional. They are normal young men but sometimes they can't act like it. Everybody needs them and wants more time with them.'

Steve Tew does not attempt to mask the reality of such incidents. 'We have had a tough run with player behaviour, driven by headlines that haven't always helped. Nor have they always been accurate or completely balanced in their analysis.'

Maybe not, but we won't start blaming the media here. They didn't dream up such incidents, after all. Tew acknowledges the point and accepts the responsibility. 'They [the press] have been reporting bad behaviour, bad decision-making and bad attitudes that manifest themselves in our game. But rugby is just a part of this country. We are a reflection of all the other influences that come into a person's life. Our job is to give everyone who comes into our sport the best opportunity we can. There are some great wins for us as a sport but there have been some failures.'

Respect and responsibility are two key struts of the programme. It is hoped that, by expanding this programme throughout New Zealand, some major social issues can be challenged. Like the fact that domestic violence rates in New Zealand are higher than anywhere else in the western world. Or that suicide is the second most common reason young people die here. By mid-2015, the provisional suicide toll had risen to its highest figure since the coroner's office started releasing the statistics. Between June 2014 and May 2015, 569 people died by suicide or suspected suicide. The rate of suicide is highest among Maori and those with Polynesian heritage between the ages of eighteen and twenty-four. But the reason remains a mystery.

Clement has personal knowledge of two such cases. 'I knew a couple of young guys who ended their lives, although neither were rugby players. One was twenty-eight, the other nineteen. There were no drugs involved and the families just cannot tell you why they did it. Was it related to mental-health issues? Who knows?'

In 2017, the Chiefs put in place a programme of suicide-prevention education for the players. They hoped they might be able to help other sections of the community. 'We are trying to get them to be the best young men they can be. We're trying to enhance their life skills. Maybe this is lacking in some homes,' Clement suggested.

If a well-known rugby man could talk to an audience of young people, the results could be invaluable. It seems inevitable that kids would listen more to star players like Liam Messam, Brodie Retallick and Damian McKenzie than to people their own age or their parents.

Clement says no pressure is applied to young rugby men to take on the burden of tackling society's endemic problems. But some, like Messam in the women's refuge on that Christmas morning, simply want to do what they can to help. 'It's about saying, you have been successful to make it to this level of rugby but it's also about being successful in life,' says Clement. If the programme is kept relatively achievable, she says, most of the squad buy into it and see they are benefitting from it. 'But sometimes you have to do things that fit with their age and stage. It's about knowing the boys and what their needs are. Also, emphasizing what a great opportunity it is to have these conversations.'

In September 2017, Clement decided that, after almost a decade at the Chiefs, she wanted a fresh challenge. She moved on, into business, planning to start her own company. She was offering her skills in the field of career, well-being and personal development to companies in order to help support their staff. The news was well received by her many business contacts. 'Not an easy decision when you still love what you do, but I am being true to myself as it is time for a new challenge and I really want to make a bigger difference. I guess I'm also practising what I preach to players and moving on while the love is still there for what you do. Exciting times ahead,' she said.

Before she left her role, Wayne Smith paid a handsome tribute to Clement. 'We have some of the best Player Development Managers in the world working with our professional players. Judy Clement is absolutely outstanding at ensuring that the players do their studying or get work experience or prepare for work when they are going to schools to learn how to speak to kids. It is an incredible programme . . . It's such a big part of a professional player's work now that some coaches probably think they spend as much time on player development as rugby. But I don't know a coach that doesn't see it as a good thing. It's a real positive in the game now.'

Other women who work as PDMs include Fiona Brading (North Harbour), Jo Moore (Auckland), Victoria Hood (Blues), Kylie Sousa (Counties Manukau), Rachel Stephenson (Waikato), Lisa Holland (Taranaki), Nikki Gunning (Manawatu), Virginia Le Bas (Crusaders), Maree Bowden (Canterbury) and Emily Downes (Sevens). In addition, Gemma Brown is Commercial and Operations Manager in the NZRPA Management team.

Smith adds, 'These are fantastic people in charge of that area of the game. They're all around the country and it's not just at Super Rugby level, it's at Mitre 10 Cup level as well.'

The role all these women, and others, play proves that it is not just on the rugby field that women are having an increasingly important influence in New Zealand sporting circles. Some might even argue that roles such as those filled by Clement and her colleagues to support the infrastructure of the sport are just as important as the roles of the players in the Black Ferns team. As she surveyed the rugby scene in New Zealand, Judy Clement was cheered by what she saw regarding the role of women. Of the six full-time and fourteen part-time PDMs in New Zealand, eight were men and twelve were women. The balance had tipped; it had been very much the other way when she first started. There were, too, a number of women in other important positions in rugby; at the time, three teams had female team managers, and there were a number of female physios. In addition, there were several female team nutritionists and sports psychologists.

The New Zealand Rugby Board now includes Dr Farah Palmer, the ex-Black Ferns player who grew up in the small country town of Piopio, where Clement also came from. 'I hope that we bring some balance and a different perspective and perhaps talk about subjects other than the game,' said Clement.

Women like Clement offer many key attributes to their important roles, such as tolerance, patience, diligence and understanding. It is a similar story among the women at other professional franchises in New Zealand rugby. Meanwhile, down in Canterbury, another woman deeply involved in the sport believes that rugby could hold one of the keys to improving women's health throughout New Zealand. It might be a bold claim, but Melissa Ruscoe's pedigree as a sportswoman is strong enough to support it. Ruscoe, who is half-Dutch, has represented New Zealand at soccer and rugby, the latter at both Sevens and fifteen-a-side. She played in twenty-three Test matches for the New Zealand soccer ladies, many as captain, and also represented Taranaki, Waikato and Canterbury. In 1997, she was voted New Zealand Player of the Year and in 2000, the New Zealand International Female Footballer of the Year.

Then, after switching to rugby in 2003, she was voted New Zealand Women's Rugby Player of the Year in 2005, helped the Black Ferns win the 2006 World Championship and captained them to the Women's Rugby World Cup title in 2010. Somewhere along the way, in all her spare time, she also played touch rugby, basketball and squash. In the 2011 New Year's Honours, she was awarded the Member of New Zealand Order of Merit for services to sport.

Ruscoe teaches PE and Health in a secondary school. It is the latter that concerns her most, even in a nation in which the outdoors is so important. 'Playing sport, and especially rugby, is important. Obesity is definitely a problem in New Zealand, like the rest of the world. Rugby alone is not necessarily the answer, but it can contribute. I can see from my school experiences that organized sport has to be the big driver for getting kids active. Even a game of tag rugby is ideal. There has to be a culture of learning the values of physical activity. All sport comes into that.'

Just getting kids into sport and encouraging them to play will not be the only thing, she says. 'There is a huge range of other interests for kids these days. It is becoming a big worry in New Zealand, this issue. There is now a massive outlay of health funding money for activities in this country.'

In her early forties, Ruscoe is in the physical condition of someone closer to half her age. If anyone can inspire young girls to take up whatever sport and stick with it, she can. The role she is playing is critical to the long-term health of so many young people. It is also something of a labour of love. She couldn't put in all the hours she manages if it were otherwise. She spies a serious opportunity in this field, with headline-making achievements such as that of the New Zealand women's rugby squad winning their world Cup in 2017. 'Numbers of women playing rugby are definitely on the increase. The Canterbury Union [she is coach of the Canterbury Women] has recognized this. They employ a Women's Development Officer, one of two women's positions they now have. It is about getting people into key roles for women's Sevens and fifteen-a-side.'

As part of her brief, she attends training sessions at many different clubs and she is looking at key things the Canterbury Union would like them to employ.

Generally, what she sees encourages her at most age levels. For example, at a recent country game outside Christchurch, three Under-6 girls' teams were involved. That represents a clear, unambiguous sign of serious progress in the girls' game. Secondary school numbers, too, have increased on the back of New Zealand Women's Sevens successes. But Ruscoe disputes any thought that the focus should be on Sevens. 'We don't have the population just to have that. We still need the bigger version of the game.'

Yet she identifies a specific problem in the youth game. The pathway for girls to play the game is not always that clear. 'There is a law that girls can't play women's rugby until they are sixteen. But they have to stop playing in mixed teams when they are fourteen, so there is this two-year window between fourteen and sixteen. There is no structure, no female teams in that time. In other sports like netball, there is a structure so girls can play all the way through. But that doesn't exist in rugby and it needs to change.'

It is an oddity of this rugby-mad nation that two glaring hitches exist in the game offered to young boys and girls. The ban on boys playing for club teams from thirteen through to eighteen, as highlighted by Frank Bunce, Brad Johnstone and others, remains a gaping hole in the boys' programme, a void that has an echo in the girls' game.

Ruscoe continues: 'For girls, you play until you are fourteen but then you can't play anymore until you are sixteen, apart from in the schools. But with your school, there is no direct pathway. If you want to win a Black Fern cap or a Canterbury jersey, there is no stepping stone and it is a big jump suddenly to play women's rugby. There is no Under-16 Canterbury women's team, and no Under 18s either. You have got to go right into the seniors. You might get one or two that could do that but most of the girls would not be able to do it.'

Ruscoe says her logical solution would be for girls to play for their club as an Under-16 on Saturday mornings, and make a school team to play Saturday afternoons if required. Wednesday afternoons would be used for training sessions. This, she insists, would bring schools and clubs together.

Another difficulty is the fact that she believes there is too much for secondary schools in general to be involved in. 'They have that trophy 1st XV as hoped-for winners. But the long-term benefits to the game are outweighed by these schools' focus just on the top XV. They fear they might lose that trophy they have if they cater for so many more than the obvious 1st XV candidates.'

Fundamentally, the problem is that if a school can become champions of a competition, they will always prioritize that above the long-term benefits to the game. This is endemic in almost all schools across all nations.

However, if a nation urgently requires a fitness programme to be spread out across all its regions, and at all age levels, then inevitably some focus will be lost on the tip of the pyramid. Many schools are unwilling to allow this. Their reputation as trophy winners takes precedent over every other consideration.

As Ruscoe puts it, 'At that secondary level, you are fighting with your neighbouring schools for numbers and it becomes a battle of prowess among schools. It's like four different wheels trying to do the same job. We are all trying to drive the same bus. But we all have different wheels.'

Women's rugby surprises some people, but it shouldn't. Many of the skills of the game can be seen far better without the distracting extreme physicality of the men's game. For rugby purists, the skills of the women's game can be a delight.

'You often don't have out-and-out physical domination in women's rugby. So you rely more on your skills,' says Ruscoe. 'Women's rugby is a very skilful game by and large. Maybe that is because skills are looked at at a younger age, before the physical side of it. As knowledge and people's understanding gets better and the strength and conditioning side of the game improves, they can get that strength and power.'

Intriguingly, too, it has emerged that, while women rugby players clearly want to learn, they want to understand the nuts and bolts of what they are being asked to do. 'I know from male coaches coming into the female game, it's that questioning that females do a lot more,' says Ruscoe. 'They will ask, "Why would I do that?" I think this is true in all female sports – perhaps a boys' team wouldn't question it as much.' To the neutral observer, it seems that women rugby players actually seek out space on the field and use the ball and a pass to beat an opponent. Which, when you think about it, harks back to the original ideals of the game.

Rugby is a great leveller in almost all corners of Kiwi society. It's a game you can discuss with anyone, from the sales assistant in an Invercargill clothes store, to a former prime minister in a coffee shop in Parnell Village, Auckland. Or to truckies in a roadside cafe en route from Auckland to Hamilton. From Te Kuiti to Te Anau, and from Southland to Northland, the game has the nation by the throat when the All Blacks are playing. Melissa Ruscoe remembers one of the great highlights of her life: getting up in the middle of the night as a little girl, and sleepily settling down in front of the television to watch an overseas All Blacks Test match with her dad.

Men or women, boys or girls – all sign up to the cause, and all share the delight at victory, the despair at defeat. And the women and girls in this equation bring wonderful qualities, perhaps chief among them a sense of perspective. 'You can't grow up in this country not knowing who the All Blacks are,' says Ruscoe. 'You automatically support any New Zealand team. I think the All Blacks are an inspiration. But I would like to think the Black Ferns are getting to the same level. Certainly, in terms of New Zealanders supporting them and being proud of them.

'When I was at senior school in the late 1980s and early 1990s, I didn't know there was a Black Ferns team. Today, I would hope all six-year-olds know there is a New Zealand Women's rugby team. There are so many opportunities in this game for women now. Knowledge of the game is growing, too. You see Women's Sevens and fifteen-a-side on TV. That has heightened people's awareness.'

She believes this process can lure many more girls and women to the game. Yet one thing above all else will be needed if that is to happen: more coaches. You can make do with volunteer coaches for a certain time. But you need experienced coaches to prepare girls for the higher levels. What did rugby give Melissa Ruscoe above all else, I asked her? She thought carefully, before answering: 'The greatest benefit is self-confidence and the belief in yourself to compete physically. Whole body contact is different. Physically, females are not used to that and society doesn't see rugby as an option for women. But it is changing hugely. That grit and determination when you get knocked over, to get up again and carry on – these are lessons for life.' Mental toughness and resilience are definitely things rugby brings, says Ruscoe. 'If we can bottle that and give it to kids, we will be magicians.'

Those on the ground do report encouraging numbers of girls taking up the game. Richard Kinley, General Manager of Otago Rugby, says his province now has competitions for the first time for girls only in juniors. They have Thursday-night rugby for Colts (Under 20s) and they're looking at exploring ten-a-side competitions. Sevens, too, is now a lot more popular with girls. In Otago alone, they have 7,800 registered players and 1,250 of them are girls. Most are aged thirteen to twenty, and it is their biggest growth area. They created a junior secondary schools Sevens tournament for girls. The idea was that it was a perfect forum for girls to learn the basic skills. It was successful, and numbers grew rapidly.

Kinley doubts we're talking of a potential explosion in the women's game. But that is not to minimize the healthy numbers already enjoying the sport. 'I would love to have a full-time officer handling women's rugby. But we are doing it through the existing roles. We have to be careful about resources. Women's numbers won't match the number of men playing rugby, partly because netball is a massive winter sport in New Zealand. But we're finding that a lot of female athletes from other sports are being drawn to Sevens.'

So how important is women's rugby in New Zealand? 'Very,' says Crusaders CEO Hamish Riach, 'and it is growing. It is increasingly a big part of the game here. At a business level, it is a far more competitive sport than the male version. It is a really good news story in this country. Canterbury had a women's team from long back. More recently, women's Sevens has been successful. But it demands adequate resources.'

There was more good news for women's rugby in New Zealand in March 2018. New Zealand's top female rugby players heard that thirty top players are to be given contracts by New Zealand Rugby on a Black Ferns contract. The top seven will have a retainer of $20,000, with a further seven receiving $17,500. Another seven will get $15,000 and the remaining nine players $12,500 each. In terms of professionalizing their approach, members of the Black Ferns squad will assemble for fifty days each year for training camps and fixtures. They are to be paid $2,000 per week, adding another $14–15,000 to their potential earnings. In addition, $100,000 will be made available from a new 'Black Ferns Legacy Fund' and allocated across the thirty-person squad. Finally, members of the 2017 World Cup winning Black Ferns squad will also receive a one-off payment of $10,000 to become a Rugby World Cup legacy ambassador. They will participate in an agreed amount of promotional activity to help promote and grow rugby. Each player will be expected to spend ten to fourteen hours each week on rugby, leaving them free to pursue study or career opportunities outside the game.

In addition to the thirty contracted players, twenty more will be included in a wider training squad. All Blacks coach Steve Hansen called the move to professionalism in the women's game 'exciting'. He recalled that men's rugby had to go a hundred years before it was professionalized.

By complete contrast, the Rugby Football Union in England announced in mid-2017 that the England Women fifteen-a-side players would no longer be paid full-time. Not for the first time, New Zealand and England seem to have gone down divergent paths. It is easy to overlook the role women are playing at every level of New Zealand rugby. But do so and you miss an important clue as to how this nation has established a global supremacy in the game coveted by the entire world.

13

THE BUSINESS OF RUGBY

*Contributions from, among others,
Steve Hansen, Steve Tew, Sir Graham Henry,
Andrew Slack, Sir John Key, Brent Impey,
Hamish Riach.*

'The All Blacks are now beyond just rugby. They're like certain other freakish sports teams. If the New York Yankees came to town, people would flock to see them even though no one gives a toss about baseball. Likewise, the All Blacks are known even in non-rugby countries. They have become an enormous sporting entity.'

Andrew Slack, captain, 1984–6 Wallabies

Rugby used to be such a simple game. Run around with the ball for eighty minutes, kick it when you got a bit tired. Then adjourn to the bar. There, the serious part of the day began. The treasurer would count his pennies or cents from a modest gate. But no one ever got terribly concerned about very much.

Contrast all that with the modern day. Sir Graham Henry spells out a danger to New Zealand rugby that could have unimagined consequences for the future of the sport in his country. It might appear unrelated to the business of professional sport, but the truth is that it strikes at the heart of New Zealand Rugby's financial well-being.

'South Africa has major issues. It's not likely they are going to be a serious presence on the world stage again. A huge number of players have moved away from South Africa and are playing for other nations or in other countries. Too many South African taxpayers are leaving and this is dissipating the strength of sport there, especially rugby,' Henry told me.

In late 2016, Sir Tony O'Reilly echoed such fears. 'South Africa are really appalling now. Watching them struggle against an average Irish side [in South Africa in June 2016] was just awful. They've lost it. There wasn't a single penetrating player in their whole back line.' By mid-2018, South Africa had performed a dramatic U-turn and relaxed their rules on not picking players based abroad. But, even then, they were probably still well short of the quality required to beat the All Blacks on even an occasional basis.

What of Australia, traditionally the All Blacks' closest rivals? 'Australia have gone backwards, and that's frightening,' says Henry. 'I hope they can resurrect that because these weaknesses in our two southern-hemisphere rivals won't help New Zealand. The disappointing part is that South Africa don't suggest that they're going to resurrect themselves into a major force again. It is a huge problem and it has happened so quickly. They have just fallen away, especially in Australia. It has taken everybody by surprise. There were indications of it for three or four years but it has imploded very quickly. If Super Rugby in Australia is any indication, it is a real concern.'

Henry was talking in the early months of 2017. Later that year, his words looked horribly insightful when New Zealand annihilated Australia in just forty minutes of the Sydney Test match, scoring forty points in the first half alone. Then, in late November 2017, Australia were hammered 53–24 by Scotland at Murrayfield. This wasn't so much defeat as capitulation. The fact was, Australia had not got their hands on the Bledisloe cup since 2003. And by May 2018, they had not won a Test match in New Zealand since 2001.

The Wallabies finally beat New Zealand 23–18 in the third Bledisloe Cup match of the year in October 2017, in Brisbane. However, there were numerous mitigating circumstances. Firstly, New Zealand had already retained the Bledisloe Cup for 2017 by winning the first two Tests. They only agreed to a third match to raise some badly needed funds for the financially impoverished Australian Rugby Union. Furthermore, the All Blacks had just returned from a long, exhausting Rugby Championship trip to Buenos Aires and Cape Town.

For a variety of reasons, they left many of their key players at home – the likes of Beauden Barrett, Brodie Retallick, Owen Franks, Joe Moody, Ben Smith and Israel Dagg were all missing. New Zealand were, in effect, using a Test match against Australia to see what some of their youngsters were made of. If that doesn't tell you about the decline of Australian rugby, nothing will. The subsequent massacre by Scotland underlined just how far the Wallabies had fallen away.

It was much the same against the South Africans in Cape Town in late 2017, a match in which the All Blacks were without several key first-choice players. Most of those who had missed the aforementioned match against Australia were missing, though they had others like Jerome Kaino, Ardie Savea, Luke Romano, Anton Lienert-Brown, Waisake Naholo, Ngani Laumape and the exciting Vaea Fifita all waiting on the sidelines, ready to step in. South Africa can only dream of possessing that type of quality, never mind as back-up, as can the Australians and the Argentinians.

These are serious problems with which New Zealand Rugby CEO

Steve Tew grapples almost every day. It is a supreme irony that a nation with the best rugby team in the world may be confronting difficult financial times in the future. Due in large measure to its own excellence. Through their own endless quest for improvement, coupled with the collapse of their nearest geographical competitors, New Zealand has eviscerated all opposition in the southern hemisphere. The one-sided results indicate a serious malaise in Test rugby south of the equator. The question to be addressed is, 'Who is going to deal with it and what responsibility, if any, does New Zealand Rugby have to help the game at large?'

The Rugby Championship in the southern hemisphere has become entirely predictable. As the English media analyst and former British & Irish Lions player Stuart Barnes wrote in 2017, 'The Rugby Championship, or the Tri-Nations as it was originally, used to be exciting, back at the turn of the century, when Australia won back-to-back titles in 2000 and 2001. Since then New Zealand haven't gone two consecutive years without winning the title. Twenty-two tournaments and fifteen championships. What you call dominance. This season the All Blacks won the tournament before a ball was slipped out of the tackle in Argentina. Done and dusted, a third of the competition remaining.

'These are the standards to which England must aspire if they are to become the world's number-one nation. I don't think the RFU's new chief executive officer, Steve Brown, realizes how far New Zealand have been ahead of the rest of the world or for how long. England are ranked number two [they would slip to number three, behind Ireland, in March 2018] but there is a chasm between them. England have the financial resources but New Zealand the cultural excellence.'

The reality of this may have explained New Zealand Rugby's decision to stage the 2017 fixture against South Africa at Albany, on Auckland's North Shore. In a stadium of little more than 25,000. Better to see that ground full on television than for there to be vast swathes of empty seats at Eden Park, where the capacity is just under 50,000.

Yet if New Zealand, the best team in the world, is struggling to fill a 50,000-seater stadium, what does that mean for its finances? What, too, if South Africa and Australia continue to fall away as serious opposition? Who then fills the void, and who will fill the coffers? You can be sure that interest will tail off if southern-hemisphere rugby really means just one nation. Even euphoric Kiwis may then see the reality. Remember, too, that New Zealand couldn't sell out the 30,000-capacity Forsyth Barr Stadium at Dunedin for a Test against Australia, also in 2017. Yet the venue has the reputation of being the best spectator facility for rugby in New Zealand with its closed roof.

Steve Hansen insisted in mid-2017 that South Africa would be strong enough opposition for the All-Blacks, if they picked their best team. 'It's whether the country wants to fix the problem,' he said. 'They are the only team in sport I know that doesn't pick its best team. I understand what they are trying to do but ... Nelson Mandela understood it better than anyone else. He knew that the Springboks was a team that could unite the nation. I still believe it is. If they got things right and allowed it to develop naturally, it would. And you would get the right people in the team. In the end it would be a multicultural team.

'Rugby wasn't a black man's sport, but it was the sport that would unify the country in a way that no other sport or business could. Now I think that unity isn't there so much. As a nation, it has got such a lively history and it has created a whole lot of things we will never understand, because we were never part of it.

'There is a lot of ill feeling. But the thing they don't want to fall into is actually reversing that. That is a pretty political statement but when you look at the rugby, one of my great mates, Heyneke Meyer, found out that having to select a team based on what colour a man's skin is, goes against all the principles and spirit of sport. What it does is create a situation where 1) you are not picking the best team and 2) the guys that get picked are thinking, "Am I here because of the reasons of quota or because I am good enough?" '

He offers New Zealand as an inspiration to the South Africans. 'Look at the All Blacks and see how we have come together as a multicultural race of people to unite behind one thing. They could do the same. It is not for me to tell South Africa how to run its country. But at the moment, it is at the crossroads. It would be terribly unfortunate if we were to lose such a traditional foe and one of the great countries of rugby.'

Does South Africa really have twenty-three players of Test match quality to choose? Hansen retorts, 'They have heaps more than twenty-three. But people are securing their futures by going overseas and economically, at around 16–18 Rand to the UK pound, there is big money available. But South Africa haven't wanted to pick players who are offshore. Because then everyone goes and that makes it difficult.' He should know. That is the clearly stated policy of New Zealand Rugby, too.

What it does is underline the reality of professional rugby. New Zealand are out on their own at the top, with Ireland and England battling to close the sizeable gap. But the rest, at the start of 2018, were largely nowhere. It is an alarming concept for New Zealand rugby, never mind the world game. Especially in the southern hemisphere. This is one direct consequence of World Rugby's failure to grow the game to any meaningful extent. There has been window dressing, but little more. And, as Tew says, 'Any decline in rugby in those countries [South Africa and Australia] is a concern for us.'

Geographical isolation might help New Zealand in some respects. However, when it comes to travel, it's a hugely expensive exercise. 'Trying to run any competition we are in is difficult. You have to get on a plane and travel a very long way. If you are doing that on a week-by-week basis it is very expensive and it takes its toll. It makes it difficult to run competitions that people understand,' admits Tew.

It's clear that no one understood the Super Rugby competition of 2017. Besides New Zealand, there were teams from Australia, South Africa, Argentina and Japan. But the only real opposition the New Zealand teams ever got was when they played their own domestic rivals. So why spend hundreds of thousands, or even millions, of dollars flying New Zealand teams around the globe when there was no opposition worthy of the name when they got there?

The tournament was let down by poor leadership, as well as an obsession with the idea that 'bigger is better'. Rugby around the world has been plagued by ineffectual leadership for years now. It became so obvious that SANZAAR forcibly axed three teams from its bloated Super Rugby group. A Super 15 played the 2018 season. Yet in truth, this was a cop-out. It should have been cut to twelve: five New Zealand teams, three each from Australia and South Africa and one from Argentina. No more.

As John Hart said, frankly, 'We've made some terrible mistakes in that [Super Rugby] competition. Expanding it to eighteen teams was just a joke. Because the competition has become inequitable, they have ended up with structures that are foreign to rugby that don't work. We have New Zealand teams dominating everything.'

Finding ways out of a financial impasse is something at which

New Zealand Rugby officials have become quite adept. Tew lays it firmly on the line. 'You can only do so much in this economy. That is our reality. That is why we have a global deal with key sponsors. That was why we made a very considered decision to put another brand on the jersey. It's not a New Zealand company, because we can't find one to make that level of investment we required.'

So they went to New York. AIG, a multi-national insurance corporation, wanted more global exposure for their business. The All Blacks jersey, recognized globally as a symbol of excellence and success, was a neat fit. The two sides did a deal. 'It was a big step,' said Tew. 'But the reality is, we were running out of money, we weren't generating enough funds.'

The demands on New Zealand Rugby for cash come from many corners. The community game requires significant funds country-wide, likewise the provincial unions. Rugby in New Zealand is a sport that funds down rather than up, as we have seen. There are advantages and disadvantages to that, as Tew concedes. 'It is a significant, constant drain to increase our revenue,' he says.

Then there is the financial challenge of keeping top-line players like Israel Dagg, Ben Smith, Beauden Barrett, Brodie Retallick and a host of others out of the clutches of the wealthy English and French clubs. English clubs will pay the market rate, plus more, to get New Zealand All Blacks squad players. Some, like the ambitious and wealthy Bristol, will pay almost anything. Then there are the French clubs. They pay Monopoly money.

But to be recognized as the best in the world at international level, and thereby to attract lucrative contract business deals with companies like AIG and Adidas, the All Blacks must keep winning. Therefore, they must hang on to most of their best players. Which means paying them salaries that entice them to stay in the country. A very expensive process.

The concerns in this drama reach all stages. Right up to prime ministerial level. Former PM Sir John Key said, 'New Zealand Rugby's problem is that international salaries for international players are going up. Look at the example of South Africa. They have a real problem going forward. So many of their really good players are leaving [or have left] to go overseas. We in New Zealand are increasingly seeing that pressure, and the All Blacks are feeling the pressure on their players. So they have to make some big calls about how much money they turn down to stay here on the basis they might be on the bench. I know that Steve Hansen is genuinely worried we might get priced out of the game.'

Innovation is a watchword in this saga. Which is why, when England and New Zealand were discussing arranging a Test match at Twickenham in November 2017, New Zealand Rugby suggested an enlarged appearance fee of £2 million. After all, they reasoned, the All Blacks, as the world champions, are the biggest draw in world rugby. Traditionally, the home side pays its visitors an agreed lump sum. But the home nation essentially cleans up. New Zealand, for example, made over NZ$30 million (£15.36 million) from the 2017 Lions tour.

The RFU scoffed at the demand and turned them down. But, as former Auckland CEO Andy Dalton says, 'It was the RFU's prerogative to turn it down. The game is not over exposed over there. You only see France at Twickenham once every two years. Also, you have the population clamouring to see those games. By contrast, Australia plays New Zealand three times a year. England doesn't need us to the extent we need them.'

At the time, former RFU Chief Executive Ian Ritchie sneered, 'Build your own 80,000-seater stadium.' He touched a raw nerve with that statement. Long before the 2011 Rugby World Cup, the then Labour Government of New Zealand offered to fund the costs of a swanky new stadium on the waterfront at Auckland. Eden Park would have been sold for housing to part-finance it, with the taxpayer picking up the remainder of the bill. It would have been a major statement regarding New Zealand's growing status in the world. Several futuristic designs were advanced, including one that was based on the shape of a Maori canoe. It was a stunning image.

But in the end, it all came to nothing. The Auckland City Council was in favour, but the Regional Council voted it down unanimously. As someone said, 'History will say that Mike Lee [Chairman of Auckland Regional Council at the time] looked a gift horse in the mouth.'

Sir John Key told me, 'It was the wrong decision. Having a stadium like the one proposed would have said a lot about us as a country. It would have been a massive part of what needs to be a future development down on the waterfront. Everyone would have got the benefit from it. Whether people like it or not, Eden Park is in the wrong place. And it's never going to improve. It's not well connected from a transport or entertainment point of view.'

Tew, adopting a more diplomatic stance than evident in Twickenham's brusque retort, says, 'Hats off to the RFU. They have put their balance sheet on the line. They have built what is probably the best rugby stadium in the world. It's a fantastic place, an amazing place to be in. But they have the numbers.'

Would a new stadium have changed New Zealand Rugby's policy of taking the All Blacks' Tests around the country? Tew doubts it. 'We don't sit in one city and even if we built a significant stadium – and I don't think we have got the balance sheet to do it ourselves – there would be big question marks about how many games you could play there.'

New Zealand play seven or eight Tests at home each year. Tew says he cannot imagine a situation where New Zealand would play every match in Auckland. But never say never. 'Other people might make a different decision,' he warns. The trouble is, how great would be the disconnect with the wider New Zealand population in cities especially in the South Island, not to mention Wellington? Tew almost winces when he says it would be a big call not to play any Tests in the South Island anymore. 'Although,' he admits, 'not a hard one given the infrastructure currently available to us. But tough all the same.'

Earthquake-ravaged Christchurch is not likely to have a major new stadium for ten years. Forsyth Barr Stadium in Dunedin cost NZ$198 million and, though it is impressive, with its closed roof, it has a capacity of little more than 30,000. It's hard to make large sums work with such small numbers, and Tew does not overlook the problems: 'It's all very well for rugby to say, "Build us a rugby stadium in Auckland". But it might only be full three or four times a year. Possibly less. Yet you are investing NZ$500 million to NZ$1 billion for that kind of return. But other stadia are not perfect. At the Westpac in Wellington, you are a very long way away from the play.'

Unless a future New Zealand government offered to match the previous Labour administration's largesse, New Zealand Rugby would have to plunge deep into debt to meet the costs of a signature stadium. What about attracting the finance from big business? Tew knocks that one firmly on the head. 'We have got a scale commercially and our commercial partners are maxed out.'

Besides, there are other concerns. Hamish Riach, Chief Executive of the Canterbury Crusaders in Christchurch, admits it is a fear that in time a new stadium could be built in Auckland and all New Zealand's major Test matches staged there. That, he says, could sound a death knell for rugby in Christchurch, and indeed the South Island. So the need to get on with building a new 40–50,000 capacity stadium in Christchurch is paramount.

'If that [a new Auckland waterfront stadium] did happen, I think rugby would become less relevant in our city, without the All Blacks. Maybe it would become less relevant in the country overall. The All Blacks are a big part of New Zealand life. They are truly our only consistent world-best team. If you are going to feel proud of your country, then the All Blacks create a huge amount of that pride. Rugby and the All Blacks are consistently the best representatives for this country. It is all linked.'

New Zealand Rugby Chairman Brent Impey believes NZR will grow its future business principally in three regions: the Pacific Rim, north and south east Asia and North America. For Chicago 2016, the venue for the New Zealand v Ireland Test match, perhaps read Boston 2020 and Beijing or Shanghai 2021. Tradition in rugby is starting to get the kind of kicking once reserved for opponents on the wrong side of a New Zealand ruck.

'The All Blacks brand is probably the biggest brand in New Zealand. It is an attractive brand internationally, too,' says Impey. 'We are looking more and more at the growth areas of the world for future economic support. Rugby is a fast-growing game. There will be opportunities in these markets if we do it right. We need to, to fund the beast. We can afford a third major sponsor on the All Blacks jersey. The digital technology these days makes that possible. Again, we will look for international partnerships.'

Impey says New Zealand Rugby is investing 'a great deal' in technology. He regards being up-to-date with consumer behaviour as vital. Role models proliferate worldwide. Impey himself was in San Francisco in 2017 and attended a 49ers game, calling it 'an amazing experience in a world-class stadium.' So we can expect plans to be revealed soon for a new 70,000-seater state-of-the-art stadium in New Zealand? He smiles. 'Not everyone can afford that. But what is clear is people now demand an entertainment experience. They won't go to a cold stadium, have a warm beer and pay top dollar for a seat.'

It is against this backdrop that offers arrive on a regular basis for talented New Zealand players. The insidious tentacles of agents grasp ever closer at the body of New Zealand rugby. The size of the sums alone make one thing certain: the New Zealand Rugby Union is not going to be able to keep every talented player in the country. Dan Carter, Ma'a Nonu, Charles Piutau, James Lowe, Steven Luatua and Malakai Fekitoa are among those who have gone already. Lima Sopoaga, Jerome Kaino and Liam Messam were due to leave in the second half of 2018. There will be plenty of other players departing – in many cases due to dependent families and their needs. It is the Achilles' heel of New Zealand rugby.

Thus the reality, given New Zealand Rugby's limited means and in light of their other commitments, is that they have a critical question to answer. At what point do they stop trying to match the sky-high financial offers from European clubs or northern-hemisphere provinces?

Beauden Barrett, obviously, and probably Ryan Crotty, Brodie Retallick, Sam Whitelock, Sam Cane, Rieko Ioane, Aaron Smith, Ben Smith and Damian McKenzie are some of the star All Blacks who could command annual salaries in the UK or Europe of anything between 800,000 and one to two million a year, in either pounds or euros. They'd likely be offered a two-year deal with a one-year clause. Or a straight three-year contract, like Carter at Racing 92 in Paris, so potentially, around three to four million UK pounds or euros. In August 2017, Aaron Cruden left New Zealand to take up a three-year deal with French club Montpellier for 800,000 euros a year. It was reported early in 2018 that Barrett had rejected an offer of 3.4 million euros a season from a top French club.

Can New Zealand Rugby raise such sums to keep them all in the country? Unlikely. But the Kiwis have a card to play, and it is a diamond. They possess something every one of those players covets. The All Blacks jersey. It would be impossible to put a precise value on its worth, which is far more than just financial. The kudos and sense of pride felt by every single player who has ever worn it has never diminished. It is a powerful factor in any equation.

Some will leave because they no longer measure up to the exacting standards. But those wishing to stay who invite New Zealand Rugby to match the sums on offer from French or English clubs have to be told, 'Sorry, we can't.'

At some point, New Zealand Rugby is going to have to call the bluff of a first-choice player. There are two reasons why they should do that. Firstly, you can't accuse French clubs of paying crazy money that threatens the game and then set about trying to match them. And secondly, the All Blacks selectors have to trust in the system that is the best in the world. If a top player goes, who is to say someone won't emerge and become perhaps even better in time? The emergence of Beauden Barrett proves that. Dan Carter was a genius, but not irreplaceable. In New Zealand, there will always be another player ready to come through the ranks. And it is a reminder that, as important as the individuals are, it is the team and the legacy that transcends all other priorities.

Dan Carter, Richie McCaw, Conrad Smith, Ma'a Nonu and Tony Woodcock all retired after the 2015 Rugby World Cup. Many felt New Zealand would stumble, if only for a short while. It was inevitable, they said, given the collective loss of such quality. Yet New Zealand played fourteen Test matches in 2016, won thirteen and suffered a single defeat, to Ireland, in Chicago. Some called them 'the greatest New Zealand side in history'.

Beauden Barrett was just one of those to seize the mantle. If Barrett left, who would bet against Damian McKenzie emerging in time as an equally talented player? In other words, New Zealand Rugby should not throw all its hard-acquired cash at a bunch of top stars. Some of it, yes. But not all. There is a wider game being played across New Zealand and it, too, needs support – grassroots rugby. Let that die and history won't be kind to those who presided over its demise.

Brent Impey says, 'You can say the production line is there . . . and someone else will always emerge. But we must have the best players in the world to keep the All Blacks the best team. People have to understand that the only thing that makes money for New Zealand rugby is the All Blacks. Choices have to be made to keep the All Blacks successful. You have to pay more for top All Blacks.'

He says New Zealand Rugby is a house built on rocks because it is anchored to the community game. The fact that New Zealand Rugby is owned by twenty-six provincial unions proves it, he claims. NZR could make a huge profit by paying less money to the provincial unions. 'Our revenue in 2017 was about NZ$160 million and the loss was about $7 million, but we gave an extra $9 million funding to the provincial unions.'

And there are always other issues to consider, like the question of injuries. In 2016, 62,337 New Zealanders claimed injuries on the rugby field, which cost the Accident Compensation Commission NZ$78.2 million. As for concussion, a major study produced over thirty-six years and published in *The Lancet Psychiatry* in the UK in April 2018 revealed that a single case of concussion raises a person's risk of developing dementia by 17 per cent. People who had sustained a traumatic brain injury were 24 per cent more likely than their peers to be diagnosed with dementia. Might this have alarming consequences for rugby in the years to come?

These results came on the back of another report which advised that rugby should limit, or ban entirely, contact training sessions during a season to reduce the risk of brain injury. Dr Willie Stewart, a consultant neuropathologist, said that the rates of concussion in professional rugby were 'unacceptably high'. The latest injury audit for English rugby showed that concussion was the most reported injury for the sixth successive season in 2016–17, while more than one-third of all injuries were sustained during training. The rate of concussion rose for the seventh year running, reaching a level of nearly twenty-one concussions per thousand hours of match play. It is a higher figure than similar reported rates in boxing.

World Rugby issued a statement in response to Dr Stewart's comments, saying that, 'World Rugby and its unions are committed to an evidence-based approach to injury reduction at all levels of our sport, including the priority area of head injuries. We have implemented a number of education, management and prevention initiatives that are proven to be successful in further protecting players. These include the HIA, Graduated Return to Play and Tournament Player Welfare Standards at the elite level as well as lowering the acceptable height of the tackle, global education and the Activate warm-up programme across all levels of the game. Research highlights the importance of individual player load management in reducing injury risk in training and playing environments and we have previously outlined our view that everyone in the game should pay close consideration to this area.'

In light of the injury audit for English rugby, World Rugby was urged to lower the legal height of the tackle. Dr Simon Kemp, RFU Head of Medicine, called not only for the height of the tackle to be lowered, but also for the better enforcement of World Rugby's directive for more stringent punishments for head-high tackles. Kemp said, 'We would like World Rugby to give consideration to thinking about reducing the legal height of the tackle from below the line of the shoulders, because as it is currently configured, the margin for error is very small. What we need is a clearer, more consistently and easily understood message around what constitutes safe and unsafe tackles. If you increase the sanction for the high tackle, which is what World Rugby did, it needs to be consistently applied by referees. From the data we've got in 2016–17, that sanction hasn't resulted in our game in a reduction in concussion risk.'

To be exact, it was said that 36 per cent of all injuries occurred in training and the most common recorded injury was concussion. What has been unknown until the publication of this book is that one of the world's most senior rugby men attended an IRB discussion, at its Dublin headquarters, about players' concussion back in 2004–5.

Speaking in 2017, Sir Brian Lochore told me at his Wairarapa home that he had gone to Ireland at that time to instigate discussions with the then IRB about players' concussion. 'I made the point then that they needed to have a cut-off point below the shoulders to make it safer and eliminate most of this problem. Under the armpit would make it very much easier for the referees.'

Lochore alleged that, 'The representatives of England, Scotland and Ireland said no, we can't do that. I said, "I think you are wrong." It has taken them twelve years to work that out. People were starting to go high and that is very dangerous.'

But Eddie O'Sullivan, the Irish coach at the time, had a different interpretation of Lochore's idea: 'From what I remember of that conference, I think there were suggestions about preventing tackling above the waist because of players slipping above the head. That was why it [the idea] didn't get any traction. It would have been a different sport, because it would have made it impossible to defend, because you couldn't stop a player off-loading. If my memory serves me, that was the conundrum.'

I requested a comment from World Rugby with regard to this statement on 5 April 2018; an automated response confirmed receipt of my request. On 16 April, I again requested a response. The same day, a personal response acknowledged my request and thanked me for my patience, promising to come back 'as soon as feasible.' On 29 April, I sent a further updated request, my third approach, for a comment. On 3 May, four weeks after my original request and following another request in which the schedule of publication for this book was outlined, there was a response that said, 'Thanks for the update.' At the time of going to press, there had been no further comment. Whatever the reason for that delay, the story underlined how New Zealand rugby's thinking is ahead of all others.

Lochore recalled, too, an incident of that nature from his own playing days. 'I got barrelled a few times. The classic time was when the 1965 Springboks played Wairarapa Bush at Masterton, on the Tuesday before a Test match. I played the game but didn't remember a thing. I "woke up" with five minutes to go and looked at the scoreboard – 3–0 had become 36–0. I was playing the game but just wandering around, doing it by instinct. But I still played in the Test match four days later. It was OK, but I wasn't 100 per cent.'

Governing bodies of sports and individual unions the world over may need substantial financial reserves in the future to help care for victims if this trend is not halted and then reversed. Further urgent solutions are clearly needed.

But can New Zealand Rugby forever balance on their financial tightrope? Can it continue to hold this burden of central funding for provincial unions? Impey says yes, it's a challenge they're up for. Another money-making idea being discussed by New Zealand Rugby is to have a SANZAAR Lions team meet the British & Irish Lions in a three-Test series. But, in the boardrooms of English clubs like Saracens, Northampton and Gloucester, it will likely crash. The rapacious English clubs already want to trim the four-yearly Lions tour from ten matches to eight and will oppose the proposal of a Lions tour every two years rather than four.

Sevens is a game that has made huge strides, and it's likely to make even more now that it has been recognized as an Olympic sport. But Impey carefully outlines his serious reservations about Sevens and its vulnerability to the bête noir of any sport, match fixing.

'The fifteen-a-side game is an unlikely target for match fixing. Countries that play at the top level of fifteen-a-side don't have a match-fixing culture. But Sevens is different and it would be easy to do. A bunch of new countries are coming into this new form of the game, and it would be pretty simple to make a couple of deliberate mistakes to give it away. Why wouldn't it happen in Sevens? There are countries where there are many poor kids in the street. I have no examples of this but I do believe we need to stay on the front foot and be aware of it. I am saying we should be vigilant, especially after the examples in cricket.'

Impey's professional background is in broadcasting. It is in this arena where he expects the biggest changes to come in the years ahead. Encouragingly, he believes New Zealand Rugby has the ability to exploit this market.

Current models of spreading coverage are likely to alter radically, he suspects. Buying a TV package from Sky has been the usual mode but increasingly, people will get access through other means, he says: 'The model will change. The current model is exclusively around being a TV subscription model. That will change to an OTT [advertising] model. How far we go along that line is not known at this point. It will differ in each market, compared to New Zealand and Australia. There is potential for growth of the game in Asia and Polynesia, which will mean partnerships with broadcasters. A key will be content provider with teams getting direct access to the fan base. You want to know who is buying this coverage and watching which games. In my view, the market for payment for sports rights is underdeveloped. It could net significantly more in the future. We have to think entertainment. What other things do people get excited about from the personal world they are in? Competitive sport is pretty much right at the top of that list.'

Tew echoes those thoughts. 'In the last contract negotiations, there was the threat another party could be in the mix. That drove the market forward. This was three years ago but this world will continue to change. We are all going to have to adapt to that, as will Sky. The critical issue is, whatever tool you use to receive what you want to watch, you will still need content. The one thing sport has managed to be is rich in content which people are prepared to pay for.'

I don't want to rain on New Zealand Rugby's sunshine parade. But I will. Everything Impey says is true. But he omits one factor that might be the most important of all. People will not pay money to watch a series of one-sided routs. Perversely, it doesn't even matter whether their team is winning or losing all the time. If all they see when they buy tickets is a series of boring, predictable thrashings, they'll drift away. People want a real contest. If sport isn't that, what is it? That is why England against New Zealand in November 2018 is estimated to earn in excess of £20 million. The two countries had not met for four years and the expectation of a stirring contest was elevated. Likewise, the Ireland v New Zealand match a week later.

Unless New Zealand, or indeed World Rugby, addresses the greater issue about the lack of quality opposition at provincial or national level to New Zealand teams, financial concerns will proliferate within New Zealand rugby. What a bittersweet irony it will be if New Zealand rugby's healthy future is threatened most by their own excellence and the complete subjugation of all others.

As Australia's 1984 Grand Slam-winning captain Andrew Slack said, 'I used to think everyone in Australia took nothing but joy from Steve Waugh's cricket team winning and winning. But it bored me stiff by the end. So will New Zealand [rugby] create that kind of supremacy . . . if they haven't done so already?'

Slack calls himself an optimist. He sees good progress being made by Ireland and England. So he doubts that New Zealand will have a five-year run where no one gets within twenty points of them. But he buys into Graham Henry's theory about the South Africans: 'I agree, it may be difficult for South Africa ever to regain the power and supremacy they once enjoyed. As for Australia, rugby will never be a national sport. There isn't the interest in Western Australia and Victoria.'

As for the All Blacks, Slack suspects they have soared beyond their previous parameters. 'I believe the All Blacks are now beyond just rugby. They're like certain other freakish sports teams. If the New York Yankees came to town, people would flock to see them, even though no one gives a toss about baseball. Likewise, the All Blacks are known even in non-rugby countries. They have become an enormous sporting entity.'

If you accept that the All Blacks have moved beyond their traditional sporting boundaries, then you have to ask the question; do they really have the skill base to win over an uneducated crowd through their entertainment value alone, like the New York Yankees or Harlem Globetrotters?

In May 2017, Slack told me in Brisbane, 'What I admire most about them at the moment are their skill levels and depth. When you talk about a bloke like Beauden Barrett, there is a temptation to be too fulsome in your praise. But I am not sure I have ever seen a better footballer than the way he has played in the last eighteen months. Every single aspect of his play is absolutely phenomenal. If you want a bloke who can play in any circumstances, any situation, he's surely the guy. If you want someone who can handle the ball whether it's bone dry or soaking wet, he can do it.

'I played alongside some pretty special number tens like Mark Ella and Michael Lynagh. But to me, Barrett is better than them.

Mark Ella was a genius but he wasn't the worker Barrett is. When Dan Carter retired, people thought no one would ever be better than him. But this kid is. His speed is phenomenal, you could select him on the wing and he wouldn't be out of place. He kicks perfectly in open play, tackles hard and reads it like a book. He is astonishing. He makes watching rugby so good.'

The current All Blacks team? Slack adds, 'This is probably the best of all time. The depth they have is incredible. What Australian rugby would give for Aaron Cruden.' And he doesn't even play for New Zealand anymore. Then there's Damian McKenzie, coming up fast on the heels of Barrett, with speed as explosive as cordite.

But the second factor in the equation is perhaps more complicated. Would interest at home wane because it has become boring watching a constantly supreme All Blacks side blast the Boks by fifty, annihilate the Aussies by forty and render Argentina's challenge pusillanimous? Or will the brand's international reputation allow it to negotiate deals of a sufficient magnitude to withstand the loss of some bums on seats at Test matches in its own backyard? The head of any international company likes the idea of being associated with winners. But if big business eventually agrees with fans that one team handing out a public flogging every time it goes on the field just isn't entertainment, clouds will loom above New Zealand Rugby headquarters in Wellington.

It isn't just at Test match level where this superiority threatens to become counterproductive. I went back to Christchurch, past the scaffolding-clad houses and buildings of the wrecked centre and east side of the city, to upmarket Merivale. Here, the smart coffee shops do a roaring trade, and BMWs fill the car parks. It is almost like Twickenham on the day of a Test match.

Hamish Riach is the longest-serving CEO of the New Zealand Provincial Unions. He's been in the job seventeen years and has known dire days and tumultuous times, mostly all mixed up together. In late 2010, the Crusaders' rugby world seemed assured. Improvements had been made to AMI Stadium, the old Lancaster Park, in readiness for the 2011 Rugby World Cup matches that would be staged at the ground. After the tournament, the Crusaders would have a stadium for the future. Their business model seemed set for twenty years or more.

Those dreams were shattered at 12.51pm on Tuesday 22 February 2011, when an earthquake registering 6.3 on the Richter scale hit

Christchurch. 185 people were killed. Not only was AMI Stadium damaged beyond repair. it eventually emerged. But communities had been savaged and people were forced to leave the city. The Crusaders were left without a home. Magnanimously, the Canterbury Rugby League club buried their past differences and offered the Crusaders the use of their Christchurch Stadium ground. But back in the club offices, Riach pored over some disturbing balance sheets and figures.

'We had lost a 36,000-seat stadium and found ourselves playing in a 17,000-capacity replacement out in the suburbs at Addington. It was run-down when we took it over, with one stand under repair even before the earthquake. It wasn't a modern playing surface, either.

'Canterbury Rugby League were wonderful, they agreed to vacate their lease for the good of the city to attract events. There have been league games played there as well as Crusaders matches, soccer games and concerts like Bruce Springsteen. But it's obvious we need a new ground. It's not an international-class stadium, it has a lot of scaffolding for seating and it's clearly temporary. But the repair bills are mounting up.'

Before the earthquake, the Crusaders averaged 22,000. Now, the average is 12–13,000. The greatest frustration is, they can't drag their average up for the big matches against fellow New Zealand Super Rugby teams the Hurricanes, Highlanders, Chiefs and Blues because they can't cram in more than 17,000 people. When they had AMI Stadium, they could withstand smaller attendances for Super Rugby games against the less attractive Australian or South African teams by virtually selling out the 36,000 stadium for the big paydays against New Zealand opposition. Then there was the bonus of staging a Test match. In 2010, when Australia were in town, 39,000 people crammed in.

But Riach says it will be ten years before Christchurch has a proper replacement stadium for Lancaster Park. He likes the site earmarked, right in the centre of the city, rather like Melbourne or Cardiff, but is frustrated by the slow progress towards it. 'Sure, it wasn't a priority to begin with. Essential things like water and sewage had to be repaired. But that's been done now. Yet we're still looking at another decade before we have a stadium big enough. Where we are at the moment, the community doesn't love the stadium. It has obvious limitations and that's why we don't get sell-out crowds now. It's hard to get to, it's not a spectacular venue when you get there. After five years, people are weary of that.

'We have managed to survive because of the increased support from our sponsors. That has compensated for the loss in gates. We went to them, said we are in trouble and they listened. We managed to break even the first year after the earthquake. But not since 2012. There has been a loss each year.'

Riach highlights another difficulty confronting professional sporting organizations like the Crusaders that is starting to affect the All Blacks, too: 'There is a risk of bursting the balloon in Super Rugby. Tastes are changing and society is picking one-offs much more. One reason is, people are spending their money on other things. When so many musicians lost a lot of money through their music being taken from the Internet, they started touring again. They were getting royalties from their music but that started drying up in the digital revolution. So they went back to touring for additional revenue.'

From Nice to Napier, Vegas to Vanuatu, you can't escape the continued warbling of an elderly Elton John, Rod Stewart's throaty impersonation of a young tyro or Bruce Springsteen's eye-wateringly tight jeans. It has had a big effect on other fields of entertainment. The money spent in this field has been taken from sport's pocket.

'It has spilled into sport. The best events are still highly appealing. But people don't go to a Super Rugby Round 17 match against a team like the Melbourne Rebels. It's not a lack of interest in rugby, because we will usually sell out the stadium for the matches against the Highlanders and Hurricanes. But it's different for the other games,' says Riach.

As the Crusaders began their preparations for the 2018 Super Rugby season, they focused heavily on this syndrome. 'People are being more discerning. That will change our business. What we have to do is maximize the big events, the major matches people do want to see. We need four big games against New Zealand teams every year. That makes a big difference to our business. We are looking at different pricing levels for those games. Certain opponents will have a different value.'

As Ryan Crotty said revealingly, 'The New Zealand derbies are as close to Test matches as you get.'

Riach is honest. 'It's a shitty way to run a business. But that's our lot, what we have got. You can't rail against it, that won't do any good. We need to do the best we can around revenue and allocate resources very carefully.'

It is worth making the point that even under the severest of financial pressures and restrictions, men like Hamish Riach still put the interests of New Zealand rugby first. It is yet another of the key reasons for New Zealand's eminent position in this sport. Regional franchises like the Crusaders are allowed to have a couple of overseas players. But no more than that if they're not eligible for New Zealand. Compare this with the lunacy of French rugby. At one stage a season or two back, out of the fourteen clubs in the top French league, twelve had foreign players at outside-half (first five-eighth), players in a key position, none of whom were eligible for France. Is it any wonder France have struggled to find a world-class number ten for their Test team in recent years?

When French Top 14 club Montpellier announced its thirty-four-man squad for the 2017–18 season, less than half were eligible for France. Sixteen Frenchmen, and eighteen foreigners. But that is what happens when multi-millionaires run clubs. They have their own agenda and it does not concern the national team.

Riach says, 'I am a businessman, but I wouldn't compromise the success of New Zealand rugby just to have a thriving business. We would never get to the situation in the UK or France where a wealthy owner can bring in fifteen players of his own choice from anywhere. Our Super Rugby teams don't employ the players, they are employed by New Zealand Rugby and they watch very carefully to make sure that couldn't happen. They are very mindful of the positional impact. All five Super Rugby franchises can't have a number ten from overseas.'

In reality, they wouldn't have any. Which was why, in the 2018 Super Rugby season, four of the five franchise teams had number tens of international standard.

'I want something successful that serves New Zealand rugby. That is the construct we have here,' says Riach. But if he's honest, isn't there friction at times? Yes.

'It is immensely frustrating at times and we have differences of opinion regularly, us and New Zealand Rugby. We certainly have a lot of vigorous discussions with them. I would say they partially understand our problems. But they are a complex business themselves. I don't think they fully appreciate our position, their world is not ours. And ours is not theirs. They are not sitting here fifty hours a week wondering how to be successful.'

Proof that it isn't all glory, beauty and light in the world of New

Zealand rugby. However, that is not to undermine the central tenet; essentially, it is all about the All Blacks. In terms of a winner's podium, they come first, second and third. Incredibly, just about the whole nation signs up to this mantra. Is it any wonder that New Zealand rugby sits like kings at the top of the world game? The whole rugby structure of the country is geared almost totally to that end.

The key point is this. Rugby union and New Zealand are inter-linked. They go as deep as the roots of a mighty kauri tree. Steve Tew admits, 'The game here is still based on the fact that rugby is a really important part of the fabric of our communities. You have seen how rugby teams, like the Crusaders in Christchurch after the earthquake, became a rallying cry for the people during a very tough time. You can't have the level of engagement rugby has got at community level and at a fan level and generate not only the spirit but also the funds we need to have a professional sport in a very small country, without intense focus from outside. If you have all that going on, you have to expect that the flip side is people are watching what you do. We are analysed day in day out and it does bemuse me sometimes how we become the lead story when other things are going on in the world. But that is the way it is.'

Former England coach Dick Best tells a tale on that topic. Best toured New Zealand in 1993 as assistant coach to the British & Irish Lions. 'We were sitting in a hotel or motel somewhere one evening and the evening news began. The first item was the All Blacks team chosen for a Test. This covered several minutes of analysis and quotes. Then the announcer went on to other news. 'Six people died today in a vehicle accident,' Best remembers. 'I couldn't believe what I was hearing. The All Blacks were far bigger news than six people dying in a major road accident. You would never get that in a country like England.'

14

THE WITCH DOCTOR

*Contributions from, among others,
Sir John Key, Steve Hansen, Sir Graham Henry,
Gilbert Enoka, Darren Shand, Conrad Smith,
David Galbraith, Ceri Evans, John Eales.*

'We were far behind in the field of mental skills at one time and had to develop a programme rapidly. But now it's an integral part of what they do. There is a strong mental-skills segment now, which they use through the week. That has been a massive advancement in the last ten years and it has helped players handle and execute under pressure.'

Sir Graham Henry, former All Blacks coach

He's the man they call 'the mind behind the All Blacks.' The shadow, the ghost. He's there, but in the background. Most of the rugby-playing world wouldn't have a clue who he is. Or what he does. He smiles, a touch shyly, at that. He likes it that way.

But never overlook Gilbert Enoka's role in the All Blacks' triumphs during most of these past fifteen years since the Graham Henry and Steve Hansen era began. It has been immense.

Sir Graham Henry calls him 'the backbone of the whole thing'. Officially, his title is 'Manager – Leadership'. However, his crucial role with the All Blacks has been in the field of sports psychology as mental-skills coach.

When New Zealand won the 2015 Rugby World Cup, Prime Minister John Key went into their dressing room after the match at Twickenham. Politicians like those kind of photo ops. As Key himself said, it never does any harm for a politician to rub shoulders with winners. This time, he was given a piece of advice by Steve Hansen: 'If you're giving out honours for this, make sure you acknowledge Gilbert Enoka, because he's a massive part of the team.'

Even the Prime Minister listens to the All Blacks coach in New Zealand. In 2016, Enoka was made a member of the New Zealand Order of Merit. Yet once there was a time when Enoka probably thought he'd never be a part of anything in his life. His father came to New Zealand from Rarotonga, in the Cook Islands. He met a Pakeha woman in Palmerston North. They had six sons in nine years, Gilbert being the youngest.

But his father didn't stay. He returned to the island, leaving his disabled wife to care for their children. Sadly, she couldn't cope. All six boys had to be put into children's homes. Gilbert Enoka was eighteen months old when it happened. His brothers were at different places. Their time together as a family was next to non-existent. He spent the following ten and a half years in different homes. No family, no mentor. His dreams of a normal family life evaporated, like a street puddle in the sunshine.

Until one day, his mother visited him with good news. She was marrying again and he could come home to live with them. He imagined a simple but beautiful home where he could find, for the first time in his life, family contentment. He could live an ordinary life. But a happy one.

The dream began to die the moment he walked into the house. His stepfather had plastered the walls with pin-up models from *Penthouse* magazine. Then there was the drinking. His stepfather's life revolved around alcohol.

He knew he had to leave. Finally, at sixteen, he did so. His escape was to university in Canterbury and a course in physical education. Kids grow up fast in that type of environment. The boy had soon become a man.

But you'll glean a fair picture of the type of man Enoka is from this statement:

'I bear no grudge against my mother or father. When I met my dad later, he was a simpler man. My mother, with all good intentions, tried to do the right thing. In hindsight, I had many helping hands at the orphanage. And a lot of things assisted me as I moved on through my journey.'

With that kind of background, Gilbert Enoka has probably forgotten more than anyone else could ever learn about mental skills in their whole lifetime. What he has achieved has been through his own graft. Dedication. Belief. For there was a time when even professional rugby players scoffed at the phrase 'mental skills'. He has always believed it's the final frontier. But convincing others wasn't easy, especially in the early days. 'When I first started, people pooh-poohed the idea and I was called 'the witch doctor'. Some players had pretty obvious problems with the programmes until they got into the thing and actually got some help in terms of what they did.

'I have had people come up to me afterwards and say, "When you first joined, I thought it was a load of crap." A lot of it is to do with the way you work. The therapist is more important than the therapy. So it is what I do, and the way I do it that becomes more important than the area.'

New Zealand needed him. They couldn't understand why they dominated the rugby-playing world between World Cups, only then to collapse when it came to the sport's top tournament. It happened in 1991, 1995, 1999, 2003 and 2007. Serial winners, but then serial losers. Why couldn't they get over the line?

Enoka knew. They'd become arrogant, believing they were the best. Which they were, on most days. A part of their mind told them all they had to do to win the next World Cup was turn up. When they didn't, few made the connection between that arrogant expectation and failure. It wasn't necessarily a matter of changing players. Most were good enough. They'd proved it time and again in the four-year cycle between World Cups. It was only on the big stage they stumbled. It took a mental-skills coach to unravel the problem. Step forward Gilbert Enoka. There are people still in the 'witch doctor' camp of disbelievers. But they ignore the critical part Enoka's skills have brought to New Zealand rugby; its importance has surprised even him:

'I used to think this was just a spoke on the wheel. Now, I think it is the hub of the whole wheel. In the end, you don't access any of your physical skills and your talent unless you have got your brain absolutely working in sync with everything else. Now, people are starting to understand that. Everything has a component to it. I don't think it's 70/30 in importance, or 80/20, or even 90/10. It's 100/100. That is, 100 physical, 100 mental. The greatest gains come from exploring this. We have been doing it for some time and others are now doing it. There isn't a stigma attached to it anymore. This is an area that offers so much more potential, much more exploration.'

But is it simply a case of sitting down with a player and telling him things? If so, what sort of things? 'It's not as simple as that,' says Enoka. 'This whole area is not a menu-driven thing. This is where a lot of people get it wrong. It is a balance between knowing where an individual is at, knowing what he or she needs and then determining an "execution plan". Just as you would in the physical-skill domain.

'Often these change for individuals, circumstances and situations. I guess the "critical ingredient" is the bridge between the application being an art or a science. The people that really make progress in this space are the ones that can nail exactly this. I know I don't get it right every time, but I'd like to think I do more often than not.'

He first got involved with the All Blacks in 2000. By then, remember, they had already failed at Rugby World Cups in 1991, 1995 and 1999. Wayne Smith, who already knew him, was fascinated by his thoughts about the mental side of a player's preparation. Smith didn't know a lot about the subject but, always an innovator, he asked Enoka to work with the All Blacks. But in this field, things do not turn around overnight, a point even Graham Henry had to accept. In some cases, it can take years for the messages truly to sink in. After all, even with Enoka on board, New Zealand took a further eleven years to win another World Cup.

He likes to work one-on-one with players rather than in a group. I surmise that's because not everyone makes the same progress in this field as others, nor at the same speed. 'Sometimes, yes, but other times you may need to leverage off the group or others to create the awareness for change. This is the "critical space" – nailing the context and method to create awareness in the player. Without this nothing will move. With it, anything is possible. This is where the magic happens!' he says.

Ask him what sort of things he would tell players, and he says he doesn't really like to 'tell them'. That would create a sort of hierarchical structure, in his view. 'It's about getting alongside them and together unfolding layers that generally identify things that can be improved. Sometimes I lead, but if done well, they will lead without them really knowing it. Getting an understanding of it and in particular what happens when you get into the moments that are decisive, is huge. There is a big group of people attempting to understand it. Lots more can be achieved mainly in terms of accessing your best when it matters most. This is what people are after.'

Gilbert Enoka is now the longest-serving continuous member of the current All Blacks coaching and management group. It's fair to say he had to battle, especially in the early days, to 'sell' the concept. Where he benefitted was from having 'The Three Wise Men' working alongside him: Graham Henry, Steve Hansen and Wayne Smith. Men with the vision, patience and willingness to rattle the cage, to take a risk and see what could happen.

Coaches of a blinkered disposition would have strangled Enoka's concept at birth. That did not happen precisely because of the acumen of Smith, Henry and Hansen.

This insatiable search for improvement, the desire to get as close as possible to perfection, has been a hallmark of New Zealand rugby in the last fifteen years. In Cape Town, forty-eight hours before New Zealand met South Africa in the return fixture of the 2017 Rugby Championship, I sat down with Steve Hansen and asked him to rate his men's performance in the 57–0 victory against the Springboks in Albany the previous month. Scoring fifty-seven points in a Test match is not exactly common in any world sport, whatever the opposition. Not conceding any in rugby is rare. So what was Hansen's take on that astonishing achievement? What he said reveals so much more about the man. 'When you get a game like that, you are 98 per cent happy with the performance. But you are always looking for something else because you always want to get better.'

In other words, that extra 2 per cent. Against the best, such tiny margins can be crucial, which explains why the All Blacks coaches have embraced Enoka's beliefs. Even when, it's probably fair to say, they haven't quite understood all the meanings and implications at the time. Henry says, 'We were far behind in the field of mental skills at one time and had to develop a programme rapidly. But now it's an integral part of what the All Blacks do. There is a strong mental-skills segment now, which they use through the week. That has been a massive advancement in the last ten years and it has helped players handle and execute under pressure.'

Hansen didn't take over from Henry until after the 2011 Rugby World Cup. But he had witnessed at first hand the value of Enoka's work long before that. 'We train physically, we train our rugby skills,' he said. 'But our brain is the biggest computer we have got in the world. It either fries us or makes us cope with what we have got to cope with. So it's a tool we have got to be able to use. I know from my own playing days, if I had known a lot of the stuff I know now, I would have been a better player. So I always thought, "OK, let's go with it. As long as we keep it simple." You can't make it too complicated. If it is, everyone switches off.'

The rogue element in Hansen surfaces in his dry sense of humour. 'So your mad professor has to have the ability to simplify it. Or you have to help him simplify it. Gilbert was brought in for the very first time when I was still playing for Canterbury B. Then he was with us when I joined the Crusaders, with Smithy [Wayne Smith]. It's like everything else, you have got to keep challenging yourself. What was working back then is different now. We know more about it. But I think it is a massive tool that allows players to become free and express themselves to do the things that they are capable of doing.'

How much more capacity is there to develop in this field, in Hansen's view? 'It's like everything. There is a never-ending potential to it. You never reach your full potential in anything. All you do is keep striving to grow it. Sometimes we don't know where the hell we are going but we know we are going somewhere with it. So we just ride the tiger and see where we end up.'

Implicit within Hansen's words is that the ever-burning desire of New Zealand rugby men to go on improving, never to accept even what you think could be your best, not even a 57–0 win. It might be unimaginable to those from other nations, but New Zealanders go quietly back to work. Somewhere, on a rugby field at home or on a foreign field, they park whatever their most recent result has been. Then they move on to the next challenge, intending to do even better. It is this relentless pursuit not just of victory but perfection in performance that puts them at the zenith of world sport.

Yet at sixty, Gilbert Enoka is no spring chicken. How does he relate to young men who could be his sons, or even at a pinch, his grandsons? He grins, a touch painfully. 'I was on a tour recently and sat down with Rieko Ioane. I said, "Do you know, when you were three years old, I had my first year with the All Blacks?" It aged me big time. He looked at me and said, "What!" He was nineteen at the time.

'I am a great believer in connecting with people on an individual level. I think if you give people attention and value them for who they are, then they will have a positive relationship with you. Teamwork and team value is making sure that everyone is valued as individuals. It is important to break through the hierarchies that exist within structures so that you connect.'

What kind of suggestions would he make to players to enhance their understanding of this? 'Understanding is king! Without it, the power within the mental domain will remain untapped. I often make players aware that several components impact how they perform on any given day or in any given game – physical fitness (PF), game specific skill sets (GSSS), experience (E) and mental management (MM). Now, if you were to play in a game or competition you often find that three of these factors stay reasonably constant – PF, GSSS, E. The one that fluctuates the most within a game, and often when everything is on the line, is your MM. So you would be a very dumb player not to strengthen this component. Once this understanding is grasped, traction usually follows.'

But is it solely linked to decision-making under pressure or are there other component parts of it? He likens decision-making under pressure to the water coming out of the hose – this is what you see in the big moments. 'But there is a plethora of what I call "other componentry" that impacts this. The skilled practitioners are the ones that can identify these factors, work on strengthening them and then we have greater reliability in the players when they have to make decisions in the big moments.'

But what is it actually like to sit down and work with Enoka? Are you caught up in a world of gobbledegook? Is his message so technical only geeks can understand it? Conrad Smith had many sessions with Enoka during his long period with the All Blacks between 2004 and 2015. He knows him as well as any recent All Black and understands his messages, his ways of working. And he offers a valuable insight into a man who has been critical to New Zealand rugby's golden era these last fifteen years.

Smith told me, 'Bert always makes things very simple to understand, that is undoubtedly his strength. He takes a topic such as mental skills and breaks it down to very simple terms as to how it affects rugby players, how it is like any other skill that can be improved with a little bit of work and why it can have massive benefits for players.

'As an example, Bert would simplify "sports psychology" into how a rugby player can perform under pressure. He would always explain that we all feel pressure, that it is entirely normal. Even the greatest athletes feel pressure. But it's how we react to this that is important. And this reaction can be improved – it's not as if some people are born with an ability to deal with pressure and some people can't. It's simply a matter of recognizing your own reactions when you are under pressure; going quiet, trying to do everything at once or doing nothing at all. And then finding something that works to counter this – simple things like deep breaths, positive affirmations or talking to someone.

'These simple messages always have a massive impact on players, because we often spend hours in a gym trying to achieve that extra 1 per cent, whereas we overlook the value of how our thought process can easily be altered by the pressure of a big game. And yet we can still help that area of our performance by spending thirty minutes thinking about game situations, how you have reacted in the past and something you could do differently.

'Aside from the mental skills, the other major role that Bert plays is monitoring the "team culture". He works a lot with the leadership group, but also with social groups, making sure the All Blacks environment is healthy, so that we have the balance right with a drive to be the best as well as having a bit of fun and enjoying each other's company.

'For me, this is a massive part that the All Blacks have done very well over recent times, but it's not always easy. Bert leads the group, spending a lot of time, particularly early in the season, identifying who we are, what things unite us, make us want to win every game. This ties in with the history of the team, our culture, the haka, and it is an important thing that I think a lot of other countries and teams overlook. Bert isn't the one necessarily giving the messages, it is usually the players and coaches. But he will always remind us if he thinks we are ignoring it or haven't spent enough time on it.' Wayne Smith is another who feels that these elements are things some countries and teams overlook. Whereas the All Blacks consider them so important they cannot be ignored.

Enoka is a visionary; he can see the difficulties. With the All Blacks' management so stable for over a decade, it has been inevitable that a divide has opened between the youngsters joining the squad and an ageing management group. Typically, the management confronted the issue. Head-on.

'We talk about it and we have conversations around what we need to do to make sure we don't lose that genuine connection. So we don't develop a culture of secrecy where you are missing a beat with these men and they are heading off and doing their own thing,' he says. This is anticipating problems before they even arrive. But then, the attention to detail of this New Zealand rugby group is the best in the world. They drill down as far as they think they can go. Then they drill some more.

Enoka says, 'We have to make sure we stay connected to these youngsters. Everybody contributes to leadership and there is an expectation that you give more than you take. For us, it is about hand up, not hand out. That is the philosophy.'

Someone who has seen the value of work in the discipline of mental skills is Darren Shand, manager of logistics. Shand had a highly successful career with the Crusaders before joining the All Blacks as manager in 2004. Continuity? 'We have only been here fourteen years but we've had a good start,' he grins.

If you are looking for an impeccable testimony as to Shand's worth within the All Blacks structure, it's worth listening to former coach John Hart. 'There are a lot of people, unsung heroes . . . within the [All Blacks] management. But none would be more important than Darren Shand. To me, he is the hero because you never hear of him or see him. But he's done a brilliant job in bringing and directing this team together. Steve Hansen has got the public role, but this guy has got the job of pulling all the pieces together. If ever a guy should be knighted for services to rugby, I say it should be the manager.'

Shand is like a lot of people employed within the All Blacks inner circle. He has rich life experience, which is an undoubted advantage in his current, high-pressure role.

He cheerfully admits he doesn't have a rugby pedigree, and that he wasn't even a particular fan. Whisper it in the players' team room, but he says he's more passionate about skiing and surfing. He defends it like this: 'It's an advantage to me in my role not to be passionate, because the emotion doesn't get to me as much. I am not affected by the result. My role is to get things right off the field. A big feature of this team is that they're ruthless on the field, but humble off it, as we see ourselves in general. Winning off the field is important.'

One trait is invaluable. He reckons he reacts well under pressure. As you would if your previous job had been in the world of outdoor tourism which sometimes involved life-or-death decisions. 'When you have eight Japanese tourists in the water with their life raft upside down, that's life-or-death stuff.'

He did that for ten years, based in Queenstown. It also gives him an objectivity in seeing and assessing situations and the value of mental skills. 'It is the coaching of it which is one of the biggest differences now. In 2007 when we failed in Cardiff, we didn't convert our chances. We felt the pressure of the moment. But I think now, we can do the right thing at the right time. That is one big difference from then.

'That's what the field of rugby is. Yes, there is a physical element, but it's about making decisions under pressure. That has become more apparent to us. You have to learn that, in your life and on the training pitch too. Of course, the more you practise, the more chances of getting it right. Players have to manage themselves on the field under pressure and the environment has to reflect that.'

Helping players know how to understand, handle and come to terms with those pressures so that they become natural and players embrace rather than fear them, are fundamental to Enoka's role. In other words, one element of an All Black's preparation is never more important than another. Everything comes together, each component part, to complete the whole. Rather like working on attack *and* defence.

Shand reveals the crisp, businesslike approach to this field that has helped mark out New Zealand teams as supreme. 'Things are moving forward all the time, and it is how well you keep progressing that decides how successful you will be.

'When Graham Henry left and Steve Hansen took over it was a seamless transition. And that was the expectation, that it would be seamless. Even in 2016, after the "Big Eight" left, the expectation was that the replacements would step up. They were told, "You have sat beside these guys for five years, now it's your turn. Go and produce it." And they did.

'We don't rebuild, we just re-establish. There is a difference. Great companies don't rebuild; that means they have failed. We have a more holistic view of the game now, a greater understanding that it's not just playing and training. It's about being good with commercial partners, good with the community, good in media work. That is truly professional.' It is a mentality on a completely different level to that of many other rugby-playing nations.

At the heart of this lies another simple philosophy: tomorrow starts today. New Zealand had known since 2011 that five or more of their senior players would retire after the 2015 World Cup. So they began the process of grooming successors then. When it eventually happened, they had players with four years of experience, not just of Test rugby, but of the All Blacks environment and their way of operating. It was no wonder the transition became seamless.

All manner of factors come together to service this All Blacks juggernaut, says Shand. 'It is not one ingredient that is the secret, it is the mix that makes the difference. The All Blacks are a squad that lives on the road. We don't have one gymnasium, one hotel or one training base. So we have to adapt to everything. That helps the decision-making process because people are not in just one comfort zone.

Now, we are better at sifting through stats, data and stuff like that. We get more info now than ever but the art is sorting the crucial info. We don't have the resources to buy any flash system. There's not a cryo-therapy chamber in sight. We don't have the money of the [England] RFU, which probably means we ask ourselves tougher questions. "Is this the right thing? Will this make the biggest difference?" '

The All Blacks' fifth consecutive failure at a Rugby World Cup in 2007 steered New Zealand rugby increasingly down this path according to David Galbraith, a performance psychologist in Sports Psychiatry who has worked with the Chiefs franchise for the last nine years. It was a critical juncture: 'New Zealand's loss at that tournament pushed us into this area nationally. Also, New Zealand Rugby keeping the national coaches in place for the 2011 tournament broke the shackles. The 2011 Rugby World Cup win was such a success, allowing both Pasifika and New Zealanders to celebrate and express themselves. It probably revolutionized rugby as an expression rather than just performance.

'2011 was about breaking the chains, having to win. But in 2015 it was like they played rugby for the fun of the sport. It was like backyard rugby sometimes. The goal was to be ourselves and love rugby. There are so many levels in this country that just love the game. Guys are playing with their mates but the struggle is to keep the personal dramas at bay. Western philosophies of sport compromise that. They end up making it way too serious. Traditionally, white New Zealanders took the game too seriously. It became about ego and status rather than love of the game. Winning became everything.'

Galbraith believes there is a direct link between what he calls investing in people, being concerned for their well-being as people off the field as much as on it, and performance. This is an area of mental approach that not everyone has yet grasped in the modern game. 'You need absolute trust that your belonging will maintain itself irrespective of performance. Then . . . subconsciously . . . you let go of fear of failure. It becomes about playing to win, not playing not to lose. They are different universes. You can see it in line speed. It is all instinctive. It is faster than thought.

'It is when you get to a situation where you feel it is not a team of fifteen, but a team of one. Then you know you have arrived. It's like soldiers. They don't fight for good, or even for their families. They fight for the man beside them. So many people fighting in war have said that. They feel connected to each other. If players are mentally invested in the spirit of the team and each other, then they have a feeling of belonging. Which is crucial.'

He says there have been 'massive changes' in less than ten years in this field. 'There was a lot of apprehension to begin with. But it has developed so much. Not many people understand this stuff. In most people's world, it's only about performance. The narrative is only about winning and losing. That is where our culture is different. Our definition of integrity is linked wholly to how we play.'

The presence of people like Galbraith means that, for the players, exploring this idea is not restricted solely to their time spent with the All Blacks. As one of New Zealand's leading franchises and Super Rugby champions in 2012 and 2013, the Chiefs regularly contribute several players to the All Blacks squad. They arrive at a national camp fully aware of developments and guidance in this area of preparation.

Ceri Evans is a New Zealand-born psychologist who has worked with the All Blacks since 2010. More recently, he was hired by English Premiership soccer club Arsenal. But he works closely with Gilbert Enoka, and his experiences of involvement with the All Blacks players are revealing. 'Gilbert and I are in frequent contact working together in that space. It is a strong focus. I am working with him continuously.'

How do the All Blacks players handle this stuff, I asked him? 'Very respectfully and welcoming. I like to work with them. They are engaged and very supportive. That is not going to go astray, it is part of the story. As a group, I have been working with them for a while now. They have been extremely respectful about the things I might bring to them. That might indicate the seriousness of how they project their work. That is part of the picture.'

What about the area of why some people don't perform to their potential? 'If you study the reasons for that, then you have to look at people's vulnerabilities. I guess for some people that is an unusual way of looking at things. They might be concerned that makes them worse. But there is a lot of belief around positive thinking. So they are wary because there will be some people very interested to see the gains. But a lot are ambivalent.

'It varies what people say publicly to what they say privately. You have very good people that feel sure sometimes. It's not the complete explanation. If people are consistently at the high end physically and technically, they arrive at this area. That is understandable. See how people step up in this part of the story.'

Richie McCaw is one of the players who has praised Evans' work with the All Blacks. His in-depth knowledge of the New Zealand sporting scene – he played soccer for New Zealand, winning fifty-six caps between 1980 and 1993 – is an obvious advantage.

In the field of decision-making, Evans says, 'The focus is not the decision itself but the information that leads to good decisions. Decision-making is a skill as well and all skills have an internal structure. Once you can structure the processing for them to get the right information, they tend to make better decisions.'

Specific to the All Blacks, he says that character is an important component of what being an All Black means. 'The identity is an important driver. It's not the only thing but it's one of them. Some of them I have seen grow in that environment but that is not true for all of them. It is a beautiful environment that often brings out the best in people. It's easy in New Zealand for them to take on a status – there is something very beautiful about that. It's a great strength, but also a great weakness. If people treat them like that, they become something they are not. If you idolize them they won't remember things they need to in different environments.'

Multitasking across a variety of sports can be valuable for anyone, Evans believes. He has introduced things into the All Blacks environment that he has worked on elsewhere, outside rugby.

What this demonstrates are the lengths to which New Zealand rugby coaches will go to examine every potential area that might give them a slight edge. We may be talking only small percentages, so much so that some might wonder at time spent in this field gleaning such meagre advantages. But, as men like Steve Hansen well know, it is those small percentages that can make the difference.

As John Eales says, he is not sure precisely how he would catalogue it. But the fact remains: 'The All Blacks players and coaches seem to have a wonderful understanding of the game. They educate players to manage the game, or just to sneak a win perhaps. Or consolidate a lead. The All Blacks have always been ruthless in how they manage a game. That is one of the hardest things to develop. Other teams don't have that same in-bred nous.'

Or, for that matter, the same nous when it comes to off-field aspects. Like handling that ever-growing army of supporters, every one of them desperate for a selfie or a signature.

*

On a Sunday morning in Cape Town, in early October 2017, I drive across the city to see the All Blacks before they leave for home after the Rugby Championship Test match against South Africa. From where I live on the other side of the mountain, it's an easy journey. Far below the Kloof Nek Road that climbs up the mountain above Camps Bay lies one of the world's most spectacular panoramas. The beaches and South Atlantic Ocean are laid out below. The colours of the ocean are exquisite: a deep blue with soft hues of green and white surf crashing onto the beaches.

I drive up to the entrance of the All Blacks' hotel. Majestic mountains of the Western Cape tower above the property at the back, peering down on lush lawns. At the front, a single blue rope, discreetly drawn across the entrance, separates the haves inside from the have-nots outside. The fans must wait at the gate. It is the story not just of this hotel, but of all South Africa. The object of these South African fans' attention are the All Blacks players. They pull back the rope for me and I drive in. Desperate eyes scan the car in case one of their favourites is on board. Alas, no. Just a writer.

But amidst the group of fans, one player is agreeing to any requests. Anton Lienert-Brown is only twenty-two. He wasn't in the Test team that played the Springboks yesterday, and wasn't even on the bench. But he's listened to others and watched his peers enough to know that sometimes you have to put yourself out for others. It's his time to do that. So he's busy signing autographs, posing for selfies and shaking hands.

Others filter into the reception area of the hotel. I see Ryan Crotty, the brains and the eyes behind the New Zealand back division structure. We haven't seen each other since Christchurch in March. He looks slim, fit, the epitome of health. Even the morning after a game, wearing a crisp white T-shirt and grey shorts with trainers.

'How is the book going?' he asks.

I roll my eyes. 'So much to do.'

He smiles. 'Keep going, it'll be worth it.'

'Can I have that in writing?'

He smiles again.

Across the entrance hall, Beauden Barrett is surrounded by strangers. They want pictures with their mum, dad, son, daughter, cousin. But then, like every other All Black, he's used to this.

Barrett has grown up with this adulation. It's just the same at the Hurricanes, back in Wellington. Didn't it overwhelm him at first?

'Yes it did. You are surprised when you are asked for a signature and you almost need to practise it because you have never done that before. But the more time you spend in a professional environment, the more well known you are. It comes and it's great. As you go through your career, you do learn to deal with it better and engage with people much more comfortably.'

Darren Shand calls it the '4–11 ratio'.

He explains, 'We talk to the players quite a lot about it. It is all part of this field of being mentally prepared, mentally able to handle everything. Do something good and someone else tells four people. Do something bad and they will tell eleven. It's about understanding that it's very easy to do something small but good. Do something wrong and the impact is massive.

'We ask players, now you are in this club what does that mean? What do people expect of you, what do we expect of you? We want to be as great off the field as on it. We knew we had a big supporter base here [in Cape Town] and we acknowledge it. It's about making people's day, it's not hard.

'Since Graham [Henry] took charge, when we re-established what it meant to be an All Black, this has become part of the landscape. We don't coach it, but from time to time we will talk about things like that and what we expect of each other. When the leaders do it all the time, the young guys think, "Oh well, that's what I have to do here." '

Sonny Bill Williams is the best at it; outstanding, says Shand. 'He attracts such attention he has got to have a way of dealing with it. Every time he walks outside, he is public property. It's a burden as well, but he is very good at dealing with it. These people are fans but they are quite pushy and a bit manic at times. So you have got to be patient with them.'

Williams is. He poses for selfies in reception, politely thanks those taking photos and then makes his way outside to the gate. Squeals of excitement come wafting into the reception area through the open doors . . .

But within the hour, they're gone. A two-hour wait at Cape Town

International Airport, and then a two-hour flight to Johannesburg. A three-hour transit, then a fourteen-hour flight to Sydney, followed by another three-hour transit and a three-hour hop over the Tasman back to New Zealand. Near enough thirty hours travelling, door-to-door, even though the bulk of it is in business class. Only on flights of less than four hours are they in economy.

There was a poignancy about this particular journey, however. Just thirteen years earlier, the All Blacks had made this same flight in disarray and disgrace, after that 40–26 thumping by the Springboks and their own poor behaviour after the game. It had become a watershed moment in the All Blacks' story – so much had changed in the New Zealand rugby environment since that time. From where they were then to where they stand today, is the width of an ocean.

They clambered onto the plane at Cape Town, fresh from a massage and a morning swim, standard procedure after a tough, bruising Test match. Despite that, some guys won't be in great shape physically for several days after a game. They're bruised and battered. Some rugby-playing nations swear by their cryotherapy chambers and whatever. It's interesting that the world champions, a nation at the very forefront of technological aids and trends, rely on more old-fashioned methods to care for their athletes.

'A massage, nutrition, sleep and stretching. These are the key ingredients,' says Shand. 'Nothing is better to aid recovery than sleep. All our research shows that hot and cold compression, cryotherapy . . . all those things are not as effective as eating well and getting good sleep.'

The trouble with sleep though, is that you're not receiving any medical care or attention. Well, you can be, say the All Blacks. Several of the players have their own personal recovery pants. Manufactured in America, they contain a mini-compressor that pumps cold water around your limbs. If you have a knee injury, you can wear them to bed and set up a timer to turn on and off silently every two hours, for a two-minute period, during the night.

Shand says the first twenty-four hours after a match is critical in a recovery process. Eating is an important part of any recovery. A tough Test match takes a lot out of the players and they need to put it back, which means eating every three or four hours.

Learning to handle the difficult demands of air travel has taken time. For example, when your players have been crammed up in airline seats for twenty-four or thirty hours, you can't expect them to get off and get straight into training – it just doesn't work like that.

'Everything has got to be opened up again in your body and that takes time,' says Shand. 'We had three days in Argentina before we did anything much more than 40 to 50 per cent of running. The same with lifting weights. You don't lift heavy until you've had two or three days to adapt. The body couldn't take it.

'It seemed like a long time, that week in Argentina, because we didn't do anything in those days. The coaches were getting bored. But we have learned lessons about this. Two or three years ago when we went to Argentina, at the first line-out practice sessions, the boys couldn't catch a ball. All their timing was out, their reaction times were still slow. The next year we went a day earlier and we all said how much better it felt. Everyone was sharper, ready when we started training.'

In Argentina and Cape Town 2017, we saw yet another innovation being tried by the All Blacks. The standard routine would be for a squad to be chosen for the trip and everyone to go to both venues, even if they don't play each game. This time, they left several key players at home. Some, like Brodie Retallick, didn't go to either venue. A group missed Argentina and flew direct into Cape Town. Some went only to Buenos Aires.

What they are trying to do is unearth, from within this constant logjam of Test rugby fixtures, a pattern, a method of protecting their best players from burnout. Give your best players a schedule like that every year, with fourteen Test matches a season plus all their Super Rugby games (and the associated travelling), and they'll end up broken, maybe even years before they should be.

But they're shrewd, too. As Shand says, 'We are lucky. With the depth of talent we have, we can do that. 2017 was the year when we wanted to expose new players to Test match rugby. So you have the knowledge that people have played at this level, been in the environment and toured. Because you know you'll get injuries in World Cup year. Along the way, you have got to take a few risks, too.'

Mental skills or mind games? The two merge seamlessly under the guidance of the shrewdest coaching unit in world rugby.

15

COACHES: THE WISE MEN

Contributions from, among others,
Ian Foster, Steve Hansen, Nick Mallett, Pat Lam,
Grant Fox, Graham Mourie, Beauden Barrett,
Tony Brown, Darren Shand, Wayne Smith, Richie McCaw,
Conrad Smith, John Hart, Alan Jones, Ashwin Willemse.

'There is a lot of credit given sometimes when maybe it should not be. Maybe because we have been successful it creates the perception that all these people are greater than they really are. All of us are just Kiwis, people who enjoy rugby. We are fortunate that we seem to be reasonably good at rugby in this country.'

All Blacks coach Steve Hansen

This is the inner circle, the cabal. At its heart sits one man. The All Blacks coach. He heads an executive-leadership team of five. But one man is the hub, one man drives it. The engine. The dynamo. The man. Steve Hansen.

He's a tough cookie, too, and diligent in his work. When he had to change from being backs to forwards coach, he went to see All Blacks scrum guru Mike Cron to learn the intricacies of the scrumma-ger's art.

'I didn't want people to say, "You don't know what it's like or how it feels." ' He insisted the pair put down a lot of one-on-one scrums at his home. 'He twisted positions, twisted a lot of things,' was Hansen's report. They spent hours and hours talking about it. His attention to detail is extraordinary. But then, Steve Hansen is someone who covers all bases.

You think you know the man? Few do. They might know a part of him, but little more. If he keeps his cards close to his chest on All Blacks duty, then his private life remains almost completely hidden from outsiders.

The All Blacks coach's job, says one former holder of the role, is high stakes. There are immense consequences and there is huge public scrutiny. Every decision you make is judged and commented upon. You need huge resilience to keep working under such pressure over the years. Hansen can be a hard marker. But you have to be, in his job. No comfortable team has ever won consistently. You must keep an edge within the squad. Hansen understands the value of having people around him who will debate and challenge. People with experience. You need that, too.

He would far rather discuss others than himself. But across the world, as we talked in venues as diverse as Rome, Christchurch, Auckland and Cape Town, the All Blacks coach pulled back the curtain a little. It revealed some intriguing aspects about the man. I doubt there is another sports coach in rugby who would answer this question the way Hansen did.

'What is your greatest achievement?', I asked him, as we sat in the study of his stunning, architecturally dynamic modern home at Prebbleton, 14 km outside Christchurch. Framed All Blacks rugby jerseys hung on the wall, his desk was a clutter of papers and books. It was a deliberately simple question. You think you know the answer even before you're told it. 'Winning the so-and-so Cup in whichever year'.

Yet Hansen surprised me. What he said revealed more about the man than the rugby coach. 'I think probably the greatest thing I have done is understand my own identity, so I can become a better person. And therefore be a better father, a better husband and a better friend. Those things are enormously important. I would say those things took me longer than they should have done.'

Even if my question had been rugby-related, which was not my intention, Hansen would probably have flouted expectation. 'In my rugby life, I certainly don't think winning World Cups is my greatest achievement. The greatest achievement and the reason I coach, whether it is my club, province, the Crusaders, Wales or the All Blacks, whether as head or assistant coach, is to be able to help a player achieve something he wanted to achieve. Sometimes he didn't necessarily know how he could achieve it and therefore become a better player and a better person.'

Invariably, if not inevitably, from the father comes the son. Hansen acknowledges the role of both his parents. 'They were very hard-working. My dad, Des, was the provider, and at one stage he was doing three jobs in a week. He was trying to save up enough money. He came from a poor family financially and in his generation the work ethic was everything. We ended up going farming and he taught me and my siblings a real work ethic.'

The deaths of parents are usually a seminal moment in most people's lives. Hansen and his parents were especially close, which explains his heartfelt words at their passing:

'Mum had a major heart attack because of a tumour in her lung during the 2007 Rugby World Cup. She managed to survive the heart attack, but passed away in January 2008. She had sent me away to bring back the Rugby World Cup, and we didn't. So when we won in 2011, it was partly a sense of relief of actually being able to do it for the country and ourselves. But there was a small part of me that felt, "There you are, Mum; that's that job you asked to be done, finally done."

'She didn't see that side of it. But she saw me become part of the All Blacks, saw me do a lot of things and I think she was proud of what we have done. Dad was a bit more fortunate, he was around a bit longer and saw a bit more. But he had a stroke just before I went to Argentina in 2012.'

Hansen is unarguably a tough man. Some of the hard decisions he has to make are all but laced with cyanide. Yet there is a sensitivity, too, that he is not shy in sharing. 'He and Mum taught us the values of respect and honesty and those sorts of things, too. You try to live up to them most of the time. Probably I have more so in the latter part of my life. There have been times when I have done some things I have regretted, but that is part of growing up. I would say I have had two failed marriages and those are reasonably big mistakes. Those are painful for your children and for everybody involved. But I have worked my way to a point where I am very happy, and I think I am a better person now than I was when I was twenty.'

This is no confession. But it is one man's frank assessment of his own life and times. 'I think the man I am today is because of all the things that have happened to me along the way. So not necessarily are you going to change a lot of those things, but you may have done some of them differently. It's not a bag of coal you have to carry round with you. It is what it is. I think one of the greatest gifts we can give our youth, our children in New Zealand is getting them to understand who they really are, rather than who they think they should be. Understanding their own identity allows people to get on with life, cope with some of the things that haven't been great in their life. So they don't have to carry round the baggage of their parents or of their siblings. I am what I am, and this is what I want to be.

'Whether I come from a rich or poor background is irrelevant. This is what I want to be and I understand that if I do these things, I can be those things, that person. I think that is immensely important because it will make us a better society and a better place in the world to live in.'

He doffs his cap to fortune, that ethereal element that transforms some people, and taunts others. 'I have been very lucky in my life, especially to find a wife like Tash. She is a challenging soul who cares about people and has brought a better side out of me. I was also very lucky with the parents I had. Not only were they great parents and supportive but they were also, in the case of Dad, a great rugby brain. That allowed me to get a bit of a head start in coaching. Because I was sitting at the same table as he was and hearing his wisdom.

'My dad always wanted to know when, why, how and what whenever we were talking about rugby. "When would you use that? Why would you use that? How would you use it?" That makes you understand that sometimes that particular skill won't work against that defence. And that defensive skill won't work against that type of attack. That is one thing that really helps us develop the players we do.'

Wayne Smith, who retired in late 2017, remembers Des Hansen well. 'He was ahead of his time as a coach. His strategic thinking around the game was out of the ordinary. Steve is like his dad. He doesn't follow the herd. He does it his own way. He understands people and the group probably better than he understands himself.'

Merve Aoake, who used to play against Hansen, said there was always something else about the future All Blacks coach. It was clear, he said, that the younger Hansen was learning good things from Des. 'His dad loved the game. He coached Steve when he played senior rugby and he was a great communicator. After a match, he would talk to just about everyone in the room before he went home. He was well known and highly respected throughout Canterbury. He was a great one for thinking about the game. Yet he didn't push his own ideas that hard. He would have a conversation with others, examine their ideas and then he might suggest something he had thought of. I think Steve reflects a lot of his dad, of those qualities. He is, like his dad, a very good communicator. That was his dad through and through.'

Hansen Junior, thought Aoake, was always aware of what was going on on a rugby field. He could always see the big picture and he never shirked the tough duties. Today, it's the same. As All Blacks coach, he tells people good and bad news. When he drops a player, he calls him, doesn't leave it to the manager. He is honest and players like that. They feel they can talk to him. His father, too, was a straight shooter, he said.

Beauden Barrett agrees. 'Steve Hansen is outstanding, but very tough. Yet you can challenge him. OK, you have got to have a pretty good case if you want to. But that's good. He does accept challenges, he will listen.'

Challenges like the one posed by Keven Mealamu during a Rugby World Cup campaign. Hansen is a stickler for timing. On and off the field. If a meeting is scheduled to start at 1pm, it starts then. Not at 1.05 or 1.10. A slight inconvenience, then, for the All Blacks coach to be delayed by a call on his cellphone as he was making his way to the team room for a meeting one day. When he got to the room, only two or three minutes late, Mealamu stood up. The hooker looked at his watch, tapped his wrist and simply said, 'Coach. One o'clock.' Hansen put up his hands, copped it. That's the guy he is.

Barrett calls him a very knowledgeable man. He knows how to get the team going and what it needs, he says. However, Hansen has not been without his critics. Former All Black Andy Haden is one of them. 'What the All Blacks and their coaches have done has been a very good achievement. But it hasn't been extraordinary, because of the strength of the opposition. They haven't improved all the time and got better and better, but just stayed ahead of the others by resourceful means, such as using the raw material they have from a very good feeder system.'

Sometime before the 2011 Rugby World Cup, Andy Haden was asked by a journalist how he felt the All Blacks forwards were going. He didn't think they were going very well at all and, in his usual frank way, he explained why. He said they were young and they needed a coach. He went on, 'Steve Hansen's only qualification for coaching the forwards are the numbers on his bathroom scales.' He admitted that he thought the only thing a former midfield back could bring to the job of coaching the forwards was the tactic of kicking to the corner and barging around from there until they won a penalty. It wasn't the most complimentary remark, but then Haden doesn't do complimentary. He won't soft-soap anyone. Just tells it how he sees it. You either handle that, or you don't.

Hansen wasn't pleased, and asked to see Haden. They met, exchanged some frank views and agreed to disagree. Nothing wrong with that; straight men straightening out some difficulties and exchanging robust opinions. But Haden then said something else. He told Hansen there was a move he should always remember because it was a nailed-down certainty to produce a try. But he warned him it should only be used in extreme situations, when backs were against the wall. Even then, never in a match where it wasn't that important whether the All Blacks just squeezed home or fell by a point or two. It should be kept for a critical moment, such as a World Cup semi-final or final. When the wolves were at your throat.

He also insisted the move should never be practised. It was too simple and word would leak out, he said.

Fast forward then to the 2011 Rugby World Cup Final. France, written off by just about everyone including their own media and supporters after enduring a difficult tournament from their perspective, had suddenly turned up. As they tend to do. New Zealand nerves were as taut as piano wire.

In the fifteenth minute, New Zealand had a throw to a line-out near the opposition line. Unusually, the forwards were split into two groups, with the main group of players, lifters and jumpers at the back. Just a couple of guys were at the front, and then there was a small space, with one guy, a prop, alone in the middle and the five other forwards at the back. The French knew for all money where the throw was going. To the back. It was blindingly obvious.

Every eye was on the back group – until the throw went straight to the guy standing alone in the middle, prop Tony Woodcock. No one put a hand on him as he caught the ball, burst through the line-out and rumbled over the line for the try. It won the final in the end, as New Zealand scraped home 8–7.

Where had the move come from? 'I retrieved it from the memory banks,' said Haden. 'We had used it somewhere during my playing days, on some All Blacks tour, I think to the UK and Ireland. I can't remember when. But you can only use it once nowadays, whereas in those times there wasn't access to all these video clips through which you study every aspect of your opponent's game.'

In this typically pugnacious way, Haden offers an opposing view to the general acclaim of the All Blacks coaches. Another dissenting voice comes from a former All Blacks captain, who cheerfully describes Steve Hansen as 'a dictator'. Is he, I asked him?

'Definitely not. My job is to facilitate an environment that allows our athletes to perform, an environment where we can be proud of them on and off the park. You can't do that by yourself so you have got to empower other people. You can't say, "Do it my way or the highway," and then expect longevity. Dictators don't last. They have short-term success of two or three years. No more.'

All the same, he can be forthright with those around him. He will say what he thinks. He can appear highly inscrutable in front of the media. Brusque too, if he wishes. And self-effacing, a quality that has enabled him to drive forward this ever-demanding All Blacks legend, the success of which is now expected by the people of his country. But he insists that there is a democratic process thriving within.

'A lot of what we do has been robustly discussed. It might be my idea, it might be Fossie's [Ian Foster's]. It doesn't matter whose idea it is. What is important is the idea gets smashed around, so you can work out its failings and its strengths. You can't do that as a dictator.'

Nor can you do it without a tight, caring environment. I ask him if he's aware of something called the 'Liverpool Boot Room'. It was a forum that allowed a succession of outstanding Liverpool soccer coaches – Bill Shankly, Bob Paisley, Joe Fagan and Ronnie Moran – to get together to discuss and analyse back in the 1970s and 1980s. This present All Blacks coaching unit reminds me strongly of that.

'I have heard about it. But I can't claim we deliberately went down the same road. All I know is that, of the teams I have been involved in, I have always felt it was natural to create a family-type environment that is genuine. One where we care about each other and we value the people involved. An environment where we are prepared to have robust discussions and not be offended and take it personally if some- thing one of us thinks is a good idea gets pulled to bits. If you do that you always end up getting close.

'There is a vulnerability and that creates a trust that drives you tighter and tighter together. There are moments that are sad and moments that are really liberating. In that moment in time in your life, these people around you become like your brothers and sisters.'

He believes allowing some to disagree creates a better environ- ment. Quite often, he says, a player will come forward with an idea. He's pleased to see that. 'That is why we have a leadership group and the more that leadership grows, the better.'

The values he seeks to inculcate among the young men in his charge are the same values that he used to underpin his own life. Effort, dedication, a work ethic. The latter is a phrase he uses con- stantly. But there is a problem. 'As the generations have gone on, we have tried to give our children a better life than the one we had. The things we couldn't have, we've tried to provide for them.

'But we have given them too much without getting too much

back. We have created a sense of entitlement. It's a very different generation now and it's not their fault, it's ours.'

Of all the values that underpin the All Blacks, he cites integrity within the group as one of the most vital ingredients. It's an honesty, the same that every team and business has, he thinks. But the key is living them daily. 'It's about living them from the top down rather than expecting the young guy to do it and the guy at the top not having to. That is the difference between a good culture and a bad one.'

These are the core qualities that men like Henry, Hansen, Smith, Enoka, Cron, Shand and others have brought to the All Blacks domain. Theirs is a relentless task, forever attempting to keep ahead and to stimulate mentally some of the best young rugby players in the world. You need concentration, commitment and consistency. There are few real 'down' times, high summer and Christmas excepted. Yet he insists he can compartmentalize. 'I have always been able to switch off. I think that's because I understand it is not life and death.' Famously, former Liverpool manager Bill Shankly once said that about football. Trouble was, he added a caveat – that 'it's far more important than that'!

But Hansen isn't joking. 'I understand now that my identity wasn't built just about rugby. Yes, one of my identities is Steve Hansen, All Blacks coach. But I am also Steve Hansen the husband, Steve Hansen the father, Steve Hansen the brother, Steve Hansen the uncle and Steve Hansen the friend. We have all got different identities and it is not healthy to zero in on just one. If you understand those identities, you have to be able to be versatile and say, "right, I am a father now, forget about the rugby".

'When you are in the project it is OK to be obsessed with it. We often talk about when we are away from the family. Use it as a driving force rather than a handicap. Try to be the best you can be while you are away from those around you. That is a beautiful way to put it because it is your family that makes the sacrifice.'

Which prompted the next question. Does anyone understand the pressure of being involved with the All Blacks? Those broad shoulders heaved. 'No one has a clue. It's not just being the All Blacks coach. It's the All Blacks baggage man, the All Blacks assistant coach, the All Blacks manager . . . everybody in the All Blacks is under pressure. Because once you become a player or coach, whatever your role is within the team, it's there with you for life. You are not Steve Hansen any longer. You are Steve Hansen, the All Blacks coach. Or Steve Hansen, the ex-All Blacks coach. That is with you all the time.

'The pressure that comes from the constant scrutiny is immense. Because we have been successful, people want to know what we are doing. That is what this book is about. People are fascinated by the story, by the myth. So they are looking. What is he like, what is she like? How does he behave, how do they operate? There is a lot of credit given sometimes when maybe it should not be.

'But maybe because we have been successful it creates the perception that all these people are greater than they really are. All of us are just Kiwis, people who enjoy rugby. We are fortunate that we seem to be reasonably good at rugby in this country.'

Early in the New Year in 2012, a highly important meeting was held among senior All Blacks management, coaches and players that basically asked this question, 'Where do we go from here?'

New Zealand Rugby Chief Executive Steve Tew said much of the reason was that a lot of teams peak for a big event. Nothing had been bigger than the 2011 Rugby World Cup, which New Zealand had just hosted and won, but what would follow? 'There was a meeting of guys like Steve Hansen, Wayne Smith, Darren Shand, Mike Cron and a lot of senior players,' said Tew. 'They made a big commitment to go through to 2015. They wanted to build something quite special and become known as the most dominant team in sporting history. They immediately set about doing that. It required resetting goals and a whole lot more hard work. How do we get fitter? How do we get better skills? How do we take the game to another level? We said the same thing in 2016, which was as remarkable a year as 2012 had been, given the number of Test caps that retired. But we had been building from experience in depth.'

But are the expectations ridiculous at times? Hansen shrugs. 'When you first come in, those expectations can overwhelm you. If you don't support those people who are coming in, whether it is management or players, then you can lose them. But we wouldn't change the expectations, because it is what has made us so strong. The external expectations have to be met internally. So if the external expectations are really high then the internal ones have to be even higher. So that you can not only match them but go beyond them.'

He believes that, subconsciously, he has taken things from his experience in the police force to use in rugby. The police have so many different spokes in their wheel, he says. You are dealing with a lot of things and at times you are under great pressure. Being able to cope with that and stay calm is a big thing.

One element is non-negotiable: the support of the entire All Blacks coaching and management team. As former All Blacks coach John Hart said, 'As All Blacks coach, you hit the wall frequently. When that happens, you just have to hope you have good people around you. Hansen has. But he himself has done an outstanding job. He has taken the All Blacks to a different level. I think he was far more influential in the Henry era than people realize. But the All Blacks have just gone up from there.'

No one knows Steve Hansen better than Richie McCaw, captain and inspirational leader for the 2011 and 2015 Rugby World Cup successes. Together, they travelled widely, traversed many hills and valleys. His respect for Hansen is clear.

'An example of the relationship between Steve and myself that I really enjoyed is that he would always back my decisions as captain on the field. He left it up to myself and the leaders to make on-field calls we felt were right.

'For example on the odd occasion we would have a penalty which maybe required a decision between taking a shot at goal or going for a line-out. Mostly we were on the same page, but a couple of times I heard one of the trainers pass on a message from Steve suggesting one thing while I made a different decision. The first time this happened I spoke to Steve after the game, saying that he perhaps wanted me to do something different. But he said, "No, I'll back whatever call you make on the field. I was just giving you an idea."

'Steve also had a great way of making sure we addressed the facts as to how we were playing both as a team and as an individual, especially if things weren't going as well as they should have been. He has a unique way of pointing out the areas that weren't good enough but never made it personal, and you always went away knowing he believed in your ability but that there was a way to be better.

'He also had a great feel for when it was time to finish training. Some coaches, when things weren't going well, would keep going to try and fix it. But his theory sometimes was, it was better to just finish and come back tomorrow. He didn't make a big deal out of a day that was average. The thing I really loved about Steve was that he was prepared to try something different. I am quite conservative, but he would always want to figure out a different way of doing it and try it. That was one of his strengths.

'The other strength he had, especially in the latter years of the All Blacks, is that nothing went unsaid. He really made sure he was honest and that we didn't pussyfoot around. We had honest conversations in terms of feedback on your game. His unique ability was to be able to sit down and tell you when you had got everything wrong, but you still went away thinking, "He believes in me." Not many people can do that.

'Another thing about Steve is that he has a really good feel for what is needed, during a match and during the week leading up to a game. He has got a feeling of when you need to give the team a real rev-up or you just need to put your arm around everyone and say, "Just hang in there." He has great man-management skills. He does quite a bit on the fly, too, which is another strength. He grabs some tough situations pretty damn good and pretty quickly. He also is really good if you sit down and want a yarn about your game. You end up answering your own questions with him prompting.'

This, they always said, was a distinctive characteristic of the outstanding 1971 British & Irish Lions coach, the Welshman Carwyn James. He would sit his players down before a Test match and canvass opinions as to how the Lions should play. James invited views from as many players as possible. Cleverly, by the time the players had spoken, they had invariably outlined the tactics James would later admit he himself would have advocated. But the players had done it for him.

Hansen can have the common touch, says McCaw. Like sitting down and having a beer with a player. He's not too grand for that. Just like Brian Lochore used to do when he was All Blacks captain. But Hansen the pragmatist can quickly re-emerge. 'An hour later, he can be having that tough conversation as well,' said McCaw. 'That is a pretty good skill to have. He is absolutely a special guy.'

Another close observer of the All Blacks scene said, 'Steve is a country boy originally, so he has got that kind of laconic, farmer way of coming across. His messaging is clear. He is not an academic, but he has got a great mind. You don't have to be educated to be intelligent. I would say that's Steve. He hasn't got a great education but he's smart. And he has a capacity to understand even the sports psychology and strategic stuff. He can pick that up quickly. He has really good all-round abilities, he is trustworthy and he loves his players.'

Hansen says he couldn't do the job without the team he has around him. In his eyes, it is unfortunate that when a team is successful, the head coach gets all the credit. But then, at the same time, when you are not he gets all the blame, too!

'I can't emphasize enough how lucky I am to have the staff we have and the contribution they make. On a daily basis. All of them. There is not one that doesn't make a difference. To me, that's important because they are important. You allow them to grow and become the people they are capable of becoming. If that happens then our whole environment gets richer because of it. Whenever we win awards, it's not me that has won it, but the team. On the field and off it.'

But long before smart All Blacks blazers and ties are donned to receive awards at ceremonies around the world, the nuts and bolts of coaching are applied. The depth of detail explored is intense. Grant Fox is one of three All Blacks selectors, along with Hansen and Ian Foster. Hansen asked Fox to join because he sensed the need for someone independent.

I went to three Super Rugby fixtures with Fox. What exactly was he looking at in a player, I asked him? 'We look at one player. There may be a particular area we have identified a player needs to work on. When we go to games we see the work that a player does or doesn't do off the ball. We can look through a computer to assess his on-the-ball stuff. But what you don't see is what they do off the ball. It's not just the work rate but it's about making the positional play. You are marrying the two up to build a picture.'

He might attend a match to watch three players. He'll study every movement of each one of them for twenty or twenty-five minutes, then move onto the next.

He will also check up on established All Blacks players. Aaron Smith, for instance: 'Because he was so much smaller, he wasn't able to take on physically and beat up people in the way a half-back like T.J. Perenara could. Therefore, all he would do all the time was practise his passing. Faster, flatter.

'He can weight a pass beautifully for his forwards. You can't throw a pass to a forward in the same way you throw one to a first five-eighth.

'The All Blacks play a faster game than the provinces [i.e. the franchises] with greater accuracy. But in some ways, the All Black players keep it simpler than Super Rugby players. They concentrate totally on the basics and concentrate on doing them 100 per cent well all the time and sustain that.'

Fox's reputation precedes him. A World Cup winner with the All Blacks in 1987, he was the team's master goalkicker. But he quickly discovered coaching wasn't for him when he retired.

'Rugby coach is a very unfriendly job. I found two things when I coached. Graham Henry put it the best way when he said that players who play at a high level find coaching difficult because they lack the influence they had as a player. As a coach, you have done everything possible to make the team the best you know how. But you don't always get that on a Saturday. I found the emotional roller coaster tough. When I played somewhere it was to get rid of the adrenaline. But I really struggled as a coach. I had five years with Auckland, one year with the Blues. I stopped coaching in 1993.'

But he found a rugby vocation in the end. As national selector. Fox is invaluable. He gives me a perspective on many aspects of my quest; because he is not involved the whole time, he can look at situations afresh. He's a busy man, but generous with his time. He may be no artist. Yet he paints a revealing picture.

'I have often pondered why rugby has the profile it has in this country. I kept coming to the conclusion that, because we are small and isolated geographically, it's the one thing we can do better than the rest of the world most of the time. That gives the nation a sense of pride. I always thought rugby in South Africa was a religion. But here it's a way of life. There is a difference between the two.'

Fox became involved as an All Blacks selector in 2011. He was delighted to accept Hansen's offer to come on board.

'I love footy. I get the privilege of being involved with the All Black team. It's rare you get the chance to play for your country and then be involved after your playing time is finished. This gives me a chance to be involved with the team that is very close to my heart. But I don't have the time to do much more than this. The All Blacks coaches are away from home more than 200 nights a year. That is what it takes to get the job done.'

Fox is like a lot of New Zealanders. He possesses a rich knowledge of the game and is happy to pass it on. He says he always knew the All Blacks set-up was a very professional, slick operation, but he didn't realize just how good it was. 'Our environment is multilayered. There is not one secret to our performances; rather, there's a whole lot of little things that need to come together to achieve success.

'The key to it all is what happens from Sunday to Friday. In other words, that's the preparation. Everything we do is geared to what we do for every game's preparation. If you haven't nailed every little detail in that time, you won't get the performance and result you want. The little things that need to come together are not rocket science. I guess the key is to get them aligned and in sync during a game and also game after game. They are, basically:

- The structure of the week from a training perspective, to ensure quality management delivery.
- Coaching expertise as a key part of quality management delivery.
- Preparation – physical and mental (needs to be bone deep).
- Strategy/game plan – needs to suit the skill set and mindset of the team for each game as well as for an entire campaign/season, and to take into account what we expect our opponents to bring.
- Skill execution.
- Decision-making.

'But you don't have to be very far off your game to lose. Chicago [when New Zealand lost to Ireland in 2016] reminded us of that.'

The All Blacks learned an important lesson from that Chicago experience. When they sat down to analyse the loss, they quickly pinpointed some key reasons. The training ground they used was too far away from the team hotel, necessitating a difficult journey through busy city streets each day. And Chicago was in big party mood, the Chicago Cubs having recently ended a 108-year drought to win baseball's World Series. The whole city was *en fête*, and the All Blacks got caught up in it all. They never used those circumstances as an excuse for their defeat. But the match post-mortem focused heavily on such factors. Then there were some of the individual selections that raised more than a few eyebrows. Like choosing Jerome Kaino in the second row.

But when you have completed all the arduous preparation? 'Just go and have fun and play,' says Grant Fox. 'Because playing *is* the fun part. You do it because you love it. The players are not standing there before the match thinking, "I get paid for this." It's the pride and the pleasure. That's the key to all this, that's the fuel that sustains us.'

Fun, taking pleasure from the process doesn't figure too highly in the lexicon of many coaches. You might think that the really top ones, whatever their sport, would scorn any light-heartedness. But sometimes the opposite applies. Take the examples of Johan Cruyff and Pep Guardiola, during their time in charge at FC Barcelona. Enjoyment in a playing sense was high among their priorities. They sought talented players but especially those who could play with a smile on their face.

Guardiola has espoused the same philosophy at Manchester City. The pressures are inevitable, yet he doesn't look like a man with the cares of the world on his shoulders. Crucially, he encourages his teams to play with exuberance whenever possible. His philosophy is that player enjoyment is a key ingredient in a successful team. Manchester City have in 2018 been a mirror image of their coach in the football they play: bright, elegant, inventive and stylish. And, above all, entertaining and attractive to watch.

Relate these qualities to Steve Hansen as All Blacks coach and you might think they could not apply. Very often, Hansen offers the outside world a lugubrious expression. He can appear secretive and withdrawn. Coaches with such characteristics rarely produce inventive teams laced with style and entertainment. Functional, yes, but little more.

Yet New Zealand are currently, by some distance, the most enterprising, visually exciting rugby team to watch anywhere in the world. It suggests very strongly that, deep down, Hansen is a whole lot more than just a pragmatist, a dour operator intent only on results. His teams have played some of the most enterprising rugby of any All Black sides. It is proof that, in the case of this All Blacks coach, the whole is greater than the sum of the parts.

But what of the pressures on the All Blacks coaches? In late summer, I also went to the homes of Wayne Smith and Ian Foster. You can tell the moment you walk through their doors they're relishing their down time; they enjoy it, because they know it won't last long.

Fox explains it like this. The greater public, he says, don't understand what is involved. 'The professional side of the game has been egged up for over twenty years. But long before professionalism, there was always this huge expectation on the All Blacks to perform. Today, the fans believe that part of their hard-earned money is paying the players, so they are judged more harshly now. Does it give the public a greater right to have a say? No, I don't buy that. Relentless attention, unless you have a very thick skin, is not easy to deal with and it's the wives and parents particularly who suffer most when the criticism is negative.

'They find it tougher than the players do. People say, "Don't listen to the radio or read papers or look at the Internet." But that's not easy. It's human nature to read reports and comments.'

Yet, despite the intimidating pressures, plenty of people take up rugby coaching in New Zealand. A good percentage of them move overseas to ply their profession. But just why is it that New Zealand keeps producing these outstanding coaches? 'Coaching is part of our success,' says Fox. 'I don't think northern-hemisphere countries have that layer between. We have a layer in the middle between club and international rugby. For us, the provincial sides like Auckland, Wellington or Canterbury were vital, and that layered structure has helped us.

'I'm not talking just about players. It has helped to develop other experts, from physios to medical people to coaches. There is an all-round excellence associated with this. New Zealand coaches are in demand throughout the world because of the success we have had with the game in New Zealand. Is there more rugby knowledge here? Possibly. Perhaps it's because of the place rugby has in New Zealand society. This sport is front and centre of everyday life in this country.'

When you adapt to those pressures as a coach and understand how to handle them, your value as an operator rises exponentially. Little wonder then, that countries like Australia, Ireland, Scotland, Wales, Japan, Fiji, Italy and the USA have chosen New Zealanders as their head men or coaches. The knowledge they bring and impart is second to none. Then there are the clubs or provinces around the world who have appointed Kiwi coaches: the likes of Bath, Cardiff, Clermont Auvergne, Northampton, Montpellier, Leinster, Connacht, Ulster, Glasgow, Stade Francais, London Irish and several more in Ireland and Japan. When you hire a New Zealand coach, you don't just appoint an individual. You embrace an entire culture. One that has been tried and tested endlessly. This is the Rolex of watches. Only the best.

At its heart lies a single word that defines most New Zealand coaches compared to their counterparts around the world. Risk.

'New Zealand coaches have a slightly different vision of the game to the rest of the world,' says Wayne Smith. 'Consequently, more work tends to go into skill development and the use of those skills under pressure. There is more thought around ensuring that you shape the opposition more with your tactics. That doesn't always mean just with ball in hand. You need a kicking game that forces them to defend certain spaces. Then you can attack how you want to.

'This goes back to 1905, and Dave Gallaher's team. It's the way that New Zealand has [always] played. It suits our nature, suits our pioneering spirit to take chances and attack. Risk something to succeed. Therefore, we develop the skills. I don't think we are necessarily more skilled than other people. We just work harder at that area of the game. And having an adventurous attitude is also really important.'

Smith tells the story of a coaching course he ran in Argentina around 2012 and 2013 with then Chiefs coach Dave Rennie. They put up on the screen a video from a Chiefs scrum on their own twenty-two during a match. There were 220 coaches watching, and Smith asked them to raise their hands if they would tell their players to kick in that defensive position. 220 hands went up. Then they played the clip. The Chiefs secured scrum ball, attacked the wide space and ended up scoring under the posts at the other end. Rennie told them 'Put your hands up now if you would still kick that ball.'

220 hands went up. Smith said, 'They were Argentinian club coaches and it was their mentality. They were probably saying, "Yes, OK, it worked for you guys but we are not going to do that." In a lot of countries around the world you would get the same response. They wouldn't run it from there, inside their twenty-two.

'To us, this is where the opportunities are. But the simple basics are the most difficult to perform. It's always more difficult to catch and pass unless you are doing it day after day after day and put in those scenarios. But it's not just practising. You have to create game-like pressures when you are practising it. I don't mean just physical pressure, but mental pressure, too. Unless you can simulate that somehow you are not going to be able to do it in the game.'

To former Australia coach John Connolly, the logic is simple. In Australia, he says, young talent is not identified by coaches as it should be, and certainly not as well as by the Kiwis. 'Over there, the best ones have always arrived on the scene as nineteen- or twenty-year-olds. That hasn't changed. Look at the emergence of guys like Beauden Barrett and Damian McKenzie. That's because the quality of their coaching is massive. They have a vision and it's a successful one. By comparison, ours in Australia is poor.

'Plus, the modern game suits New Zealand's players. It used to be a game that required very strong structures. But now the game has evolved to multiple phases. Coaching multiple-phase attack and the skill set required for it is crucial. That is the key. They have such good skill sets because they keep working constantly to improve them. People in Australia don't bother with that to anything like the same degree. But essentially, New Zealand know how to develop their players better than anyone else.'

Connolly says the case of Quade Cooper is a perfect example of what he calls 'Australia's arrogance' compared to the New Zealanders' insistence on basic skills. 'In 2011, Quade Cooper had his best-ever season for Queensland. He was twenty-three. But six years later, he is no better now than he was then. That has got to be the system's fault. He still can't kick a ball; his skill set is poor. He still has a magic pass but he hasn't improved as a football player.'

The supreme irony is that Cooper is New Zealand-born. Had he stayed on that side of the Tasman, chances are he might have been developed by shrewd coaches into one of the All Blacks' most effective first five-eighths. As Connolly says, 'The system in Australia is not strong enough.'

The combination of consistently good results, enterprising play and the steady honing of exceptionally talented young players into All Blacks stars of the future, inclines me to one conclusion above all else. We are witnessing a unique era of New Zealand rugby in terms of its coaches. What is more, it seems clear that, as long as New Zealand continues to produce outstandingly talented youngsters plus world-class coaches, their future is assured. Only if either of those links breaks will the picture change.

As the 2019 Rugby World Cup approaches, Hansen leads a shrewd, diverse unit of coaches, including Scott McLeod as defence coach. McLeod played ten Tests for the All Blacks and was assistant coach of the Highlanders. The quality of coaching at almost every level in New Zealand is outstanding.

There are no shortage of suitors around the world for the top Kiwi coaches. Chris Boyd, who steered the Hurricanes to the Super Rugby title in 2016, was set to join English club Northampton, a club which Wayne Smith coached from 2001 to 2004, in the second half of 2018. Smith was asked by Northampton to comment on a list of candidates. His comments on Boyd were positive, as were his views on some others. Northampton then went through their own processes and settled on Boyd.

All around the world, Kiwi coaches are excelling. It is like a New Zealand export. And they are not afraid to lose top coaches overseas, because they know the production line remains strong in their own land. As for those who go – Henry, Hansen, Gatland, Schmidt, Cotter and the like – they acquire a wealth of knowledge about overseas countries and their rugby philosophies that would be valuable if they are one day involved in the All Blacks coaching unit.

Vern Cotter, Warren Gatland, Joe Schmidt, Chris Boyd, Jamie Joseph, Tony Brown – any of these men currently overseas could play a highly important part in any future coaching role associated with the All Blacks. Compare that with England's desperation when they hurriedly sought a replacement for Stuart Lancaster in late 2015. There wasn't an English coach in sight as the RFU appointed an Australian, Eddie Jones. And they only got him by the RFU CEO rushing down to Cape Town and offering Jones the job *after* he had signed for Super Rugby outfit the Stormers. Jones had already given a press conference as the new coach. The RFU had to agree to a compensation package for the South African franchise. The contrast between New Zealand rugby's long-term planning and England's short-termism was stark.

Graham Mourie's perspective on all this makes for absorbing listening. He agrees that New Zealand coaching is now a step ahead of most other countries. Even so, that can bring certain difficulties. 'Some of these players may be incredibly competent about playing the game but absolutely incompetent at running their own lives, managing money and understanding they should not drink. So you have got to manage different people in different ways in different spheres of their lives.'

Mourie says that former All Blacks coach Laurie Mains' teams were never going to be outstanding, because the players had to perform to a formula. But what he terms good All Blacks coaches are different. 'Graham Henry managed to drag himself from autocratic to democratic and the people around him managed that process. Steve Hansen is very good at player management – he has a pretty high emotional IQ. He manages people and gets them to take responsibility for what they are doing.

'The current All Blacks team is pretty well coached through their rugby. You have to give players enough responsibility off the field so when they are able to manage things and run them on the field, they succeed. American sport is totally autocratic. But you can't coach in that style and at the same time expect players to think. All they are used to saying is, 'Yes, coach; no, coach.' I think this system in New Zealand and the teaching of coaches helps them understand the relationship between style and stage.'

It is indisputable that those players, when given responsibility and asked to make decisions in training and in matches, to play what is in front of them, have far more chance of choosing the right options in the heat of the moment. An overpowering coach ends up limiting the decision-making of his own men simply because they are not used to having those decisions to make.

It ought to alarm England that they have fallen into the 'rabbits caught in the headlights' syndrome three times now in the last couple of years. It happened most notably against Italy at Twickenham in 2017, when they were bewildered by Italy's wily tactics that meant England could not work out the offside-line difference between a tackle and a ruck. Amazingly, they trailed Italy at halftime in that game. When they asked French referee Roman Poite to sort it out for them, his memorable answer was, 'I am the referee, not the coach.' England had to get back into the dressing room at halftime to hear from their coach how to solve the problem. Was that because the coach was too dominant in his planning which meant that no single player wished to take responsibility for a critical decision? Or was it just that his players did not possess the character to take control and change the game plan? New Zealand rugby men believe that players have to make decisions for themselves and solve their own problems during a game. If they can't do that, they're probably not good enough to be wearing the jersey.

Steve Hansen invariably sends out highly prepared teams into the Test arena. That's his job. But as Richie McCaw revealed, he believes in allowing his players to think, giving them licence to come up with their own solutions to problems that will inevitably arise during games.

Doug Howlett confirms Mourie's claim that recent All Blacks coaches have encouraged players to hone their own thinking process. 'I wouldn't pick out one coach ahead of any other,' says the former All Blacks wing. 'But the All Blacks coaches definitely challenged me to think in different ways. You are asked to challenge yourself. It's the same when it comes to the development of playing patterns or plans. You are thinking on another level to what you have known before. It's like chess. You must think and work three or four moves ahead. But you still have to execute moves one and two.'

Wayne Smith concedes that one of the crucial elements in the game that keeps New Zealand ahead is decision-making. 'If there is an edge that New Zealand has got in the game, I think it is probably that,' he says. 'You listen to coaches and players around the world now and they talk about playing "heads-up rugby". But I think, "What does that mean?" If you have your head up but don't know what to look at and you are trying to see everything, you will see nothing. Not only that, but it will make you sluggish because you are having to think too much.

'Teaching players simply what they need to look for and where they need to look is critical in the game. It is a big part of New Zealand rugby – really good decision-making based on simple cues. Rugby is a multilevel, decision-making game and you need everyone on the same page. When they see the cue, they need to react in the same way. That's what great decision-making is.'

South African Nick Mallett, a former coach of both the Springboks and the Italian national team, concedes that New Zealand coaches are a step ahead of anyone else in the world. Essentially, he thinks, what New Zealand have achieved on the playing field is all about coaching. 'By contrast, some of the coaching at even top clubs in countries like France and England is abysmal. There is a strong New Zealand intellectual capital they are sharing with the world, in terms of coaching and playing. Yet it is undeniable that they are not nearly as effective as players when they are on their own, away from the New Zealand rugby environment.'

From a technical point of view, Mallett is a master coach and admires what New Zealand players are taught. 'The players are coached to take the right option and coaching always mirrors what they will do in a game. They train with the ball in hand. There is always an opposition. Consequently, they get used to taking the right option.

These players have skills and decision-making drummed into them before every match. All the factors get coached during the week and they're also working all the time on their skills. Other countries don't do this, certainly not France, South Africa or England.'

It is New Zealand's mantra for success. As a member of their coaching staff put it to me, 'Simplicity = Clarity = Intensity.' This is how they operate.

The 2017 Highlanders coach Tony Brown says that, coaching-wise, New Zealand are always pushing the game forward. 'A guy like Wayne Smith has typified that. He wants to improve the game all through New Zealand. The experience he brings after so much time spent coaching is enormous. What is so good is that coaches at every level throughout the game are getting all this knowledge because guys like Wayne, plus Steve Hansen and Ian Foster, talk to coaches at all levels. They see it as an important part of their role. Even club teams get this coaching knowledge.

'In my view, it helps keep the New Zealand game ahead of every-one else in the world. It is the continuity and security of people all working together and the people at the top sending this information down to all levels. It is constantly evolving, too. The information you had last year is not relevant this year. People are trying to do some-thing better every year.'

Wayne Smith claims it's not true that New Zealand Rugby is a closed shop, a secretive organization jealously guarding all its secrets, as some people like Bob Dwyer believe. 'At the end of a season, we freely give our ideas and tactical plans from that season to coaches in other countries, if they ask. We want to help them improve. But what it also does is force us to come up with new plans, new tactics for the next season. That way we are always evolving, because we have to. It is the way we have forced ourselves to innovate and keep changing our game.'

In other words, you spend your whole time trying to run down the rabbit. Just when you think you're in touching distance, you find it has reinvented itself. It symbolizes the never-ending search for improve-ment within New Zealand rugby. The status quo might be acceptable in some countries, but not this one. Another piece in the jigsaw of how this nation has come to dominate a world sport.

Smith goes on: 'The world at the moment is always looking at what we are doing and trying to work out what it is. But if you are doing that, you are only going to where we have been. You won't go to where we are going to go next. We have huge pressure on us always to move forward, to try and change our game, to develop and see what the game is going to look like in the future.'

As for secrecy, Tony Brown says he has never come across a coach in New Zealand at professional level who said, 'I can't help you with that because it's my secret style.' 'Everyone is willing to help everyone out. They all know it is vital that to keep the game moving forward here, you have to share information. We all do that. We have coaching teams come into our environment [Super Rugby] to help them develop as coaches, help them get ideas for their team. If you are sharing ideas you get information back as well. It has helped me take my coaching forward. There is still room to find innovative ways to beat opponents and be better teams. If you are creative and brave enough and if you can install belief in players that you are doing the right thing, you can beat anyone.'

Like Brown, former All Black and Western Samoan international Pat Lam is another New Zealand coach who has taken his skills overseas. He enjoyed great success in Ireland with Connacht, before switching to ambitious Bristol, in the south-west of England. Lam is insistent that the roots of New Zealand rugby's success at all levels is in its coaching.

'Without a doubt, standards are extremely high. That is where youngsters acquire these skills. It goes across all classes. You don't have to go to a private school to acquire these skills from good coaches. Access to quality coaching and understanding of the game is available at all levels.

'So many people contribute to All Blacks coming through. The system has been proven over many years which means that kids will always come through. That's the advantage New Zealand has. There are many people that love the game. Most are not paid. You start off coaching at club level, giving something back to your community. That system will always produce talent.'

Lam believes there is this excellence of coaching for one standout reason. 'Because we know the game, we understand it. Once you *know* it, you start thinking about it as you grow up. It is about enjoyment of the game and understanding the principles and tactics of it. Being part of the team. A lot of us ended up leaders or drivers because we have a real love for the sport. Even if you are not coaching, you are talking about the game constantly.'

So much of this story comes back to coaching. It is in their depth of detail and knowledge that New Zealanders score so highly. All Blacks Assistant Coach Ian Foster picks out a small element that crept into Dan Carter's game when he was in the team.

'Dan Carter was an amazing decision-maker, his record is pretty clear. When I came in [to the All Blacks fold] I thought, "What can I teach him?" I had no idea. But I started to learn that there was one thing that, if Dan didn't do it, he didn't play well. You could see it clearly. It was where he caught the ball, where in relationship to his body. When he was bored, going through the motions and just being a link for everyone else, he would catch the ball on his outside arm and just wander across the park. He would be co-ordinating every-thing. But when he was really in the mood he would catch the ball earlier and go straighter.'

Foster understands the game deeply and has a streak of realism within him. Ask him why New Zealand players consistently execute with far greater precision than others around the world, and he looks a touch surprised. 'Because we expect them to. You only expect some-one to do something if you have prepared them to do it. Come matchday, we expect them to do it because they have been coached and prepared. It goes back to the basic tenets of the game – pass, run, catch, tackle, make decisions. But how are you going to do those things? That is the difference.

'Ireland are very good at executing their game. They have a set game plan and that's how they execute it. The challenge is, what hap-pens if their game plan is not actually working? Which is why you need more than one game plan to win a match. Pressure can close you down, dim your mind. Other emotions come in and you don't think clearly.'

This expectation to execute the basic skills to a consistently high level is at the core of rugby in New Zealand. It doesn't matter which level you're discussing; schools, provincial, Super Rugby, the All Blacks. Every coach demands it. The search for perfecting those skills continues. Darren Shand puts it like this: 'You need the character of good people around you with a thirst to get better all the time. Because you always feel the dogs snapping at your heels from the chasing pack. That's the pressure of being number one but it's good and you need it to stay up there.

'It blows me away how people constantly want to get better. After that late win over Ireland in Dublin in 2013, we sat down with the players early the next year. You would think people would be comfortable after a year like the one we'd just had. But then we got started on a run of eighteen consecutive Test wins by a Tier One nation. We just sat down and said, "How are we going to do that again?" That is the drive, particularly around the leadership. It's how hungry we are.'

Pressure and expectation. They walk side by side in New Zealand rugby. But are the pressures too much on these coaches? 'Not at all,' says Lam. 'That's another area of our culture. There is an expectation that you have got to win, whatever team you are playing for or coaching. By the time you get to the All Blacks level you know that well enough.'

You had better win. But you can't do it every time. Even so, Steve Hansen says he hates the phrase, 'You learn best when you lose.' 'It's inevitable you are going to lose occasionally,' he says. 'But it's a cop-out to say we will learn out of it. Well, why weren't you learning when you were winning? It's probably the hardest thing in sport, but it doesn't mean to say you should not be looking to do it. Difficult is not a reason to give up.'

New Zealand rugby men's desire to improve is relentless. It drives men like Steve Hansen in their every waking moment. And from him is transmitted a similar message right through the player ranks of the New Zealand game. Grant Fox agrees: 'We are constantly challenging ourselves and our players. We are restless to improve. There is no single secret. But what we do have is brutal honesty. If you're high profile as a player or coach in New Zealand, there is nowhere to hide and you need a thick skin.

'The relationship between Steve Hansen and Steve Tew reflects this honesty of approach. They have some brutally honest conversations between themselves, and why not because attention to detail is critical. Hansen's emotional intelligence is extremely high. But there is one thing that matters more to Steve Hansen, in a rugby sense, than the All Blacks. That is the game itself.'

Hansen readily admits it: 'It is true the game is more important than the All Blacks. How we play the game, how we treat it. If we don't do that right, the All Blacks can't be part of it. The game will go away.

For me, it is common sense. We are just one part of the puzzle of the game of rugby. Whilst we are good at it, that doesn't give us the right to mistreat the game that has been good to us.'

For a time while I was writing this book, I wasn't sure Steve Hansen or the New Zealand rugby hierarchy 'got it', in terms of my quest. It wasn't to hide a camera or microphone somewhere in the All Blacks dressing room, to get to see a team training session in the hope that a couple of players would end up in a fist fight. So what was it? What matters is the game itself and its growth right around the world. But if the All Blacks are so far ahead of the rest, then not just New Zealand but the whole sport will be in trouble. I consider it New Zealand Rugby's responsibility to help other nations improve, to drag them with them in the search for better, more highly skilled players and coaches. Isn't that the role of leaders in any field?

Some didn't get this. One New Zealand Rugby official told me bluntly, 'It's not for us to help our opponents. We've got to concentrate on keeping being successful.' But that's the point. If virtually all opposition falls away, it will affect New Zealand, too. People want a contest in sport. Remove that and you lose bums on seats at matches, never mind declining television audiences. As former Wallaby Andrew Slack recalls, it became boring watching Steve Waugh's Australian cricket team beat everyone in sight.

Understanding the relentless pursuit of excellence is one lesson New Zealanders can teach the world. Hansen puts it like this: 'Years ago, people said, "You can have an era, then you drop off, then you will come back." But I really hate that – it's a load of poppycock. The only reason you drop off is because you are comfortable and you allow yourself to drop off because all the things that made you good, you stopped doing. You think you have arrived. But if you keep striving to honour, respect and enhance the legacy that you are responsible for, then you won't drop off.'

These are intimidating standards. But they are the ones that the rest of the rugby-playing world must embrace, if other nations are to mount serious, sustained challenges to New Zealand's hegemony. Sounds tough? It will be. But aren't the greatest prizes the hardest to achieve?

These other countries need to dare. Dare to dream. Dare to attack. Dare to risk. Dare to have a go. It should be the only way. The problem is this. Is it really in the genes, the DNA of young rugby men in coun-

tries like Wales, Scotland, England and Australia to commit themselves as utterly and ruthlessly to the cause of their national team as
their counterparts in New Zealand do? Or do they have another
mindset? Yes, they want to play for their country. But does sorting out
a lucrative contract with their club or province and deciding whether
to buy the latest BMW or Porsche come equally high on their list of
priorities?

One thing Hansen said cheered me particularly. He does 'get' the
point about any country being so superior in the game that no one
else is close to them. Remember, in Japan at the 2019 Rugby World
Cup, New Zealand will try to make it a hat-trick of World Cup triumphs. If they do it, their supremacy will be cemented.

'This game will only be strong if we are all strong. If world rugby
is strong. So how do we help each other? I would say New Zealand is
helping by sending its players and coaches all over the world and we
share our ideas. We don't hold back too much.'

He suggests certain other nations might have a bit to learn here:
'A country like England could turn around and say, "OK, we will have
a bit of revenue sharing." But no, they don't want to do that because it
might give New Zealand, or someone else, an advantage. I don't see
it like that – you don't need an advantage. You just need to be helping
each other so that our game becomes stronger. Because if the game
goes, none of us have got a job.

'That is why it hurts to see Australia where they are. As much as
we love beating them and they love beating us, because it is that
brother ANZAC thing, we have got a massive respect for them and we
want them to be strong. I honestly believe in my heart of hearts that
New Zealand Rugby actually cares about the game. Cares about the
future of it in every aspect. We go to World Rugby conferences, but
we're not going there for our little patch, which I think is a common
thought process. Everyone is there for themselves.

'But we cannot afford to go there just for ourselves. We have got
to go there for the game of rugby. Then adapt and adjust to what
comes out of it. Who adapts the best will be on top. But don't go there
saying, "I want to do this because this is right for New Zealand, or
Australia, or England." That's not right for the game.'

Hansen's views are important in this context because it is the
leading coaches of the rugby nations who drive so much of the
agenda, steer the game in a way they see as propitious.

But hold on. Haven't New Zealand been as introverted as any other nation in past times? Isn't that a major reason why World Rugby has been unable to grow the game properly in the thirty years since the first Rugby World Cup? As Alan Jones says, the quarter-finalists at the next Rugby World Cup in Japan 2019 will be virtually the same as at the first tournament in 1987. It doesn't matter whether rugby started on the Gilbert Islands, Antarctica or in Eastern Mongolia – it hasn't made any serious progress beyond its traditional strength nations. What's more, those so-called 'strength' nations are all to blame, to a degree. When did they last vote for a bigger slice of the pie for the smaller nations?

Andy Haden, for one, is vocal on this subject: 'If you haven't had a terribly well-organized opposition, it's easy to be the best. Other countries have wanted to win but they haven't gone about it with the detail New Zealand has. The young players New Zealand bring through have all been in a good school system.

'It's true that some lesser-known countries like Kenya have found some impetus, in their case through Sevens. But in the fifteen-man game there has been very little sign of such progress. You can look at countries like Italy and Japan and yes, it is a step forward for the game. But very few are getting much better. You would like to measure improvement with something tangible, some success. But that doesn't happen much. Argentina are a bit better but . . .'

Haden blames World Rugby for this state of affairs. Very little has changed since the first World Cup in 1987, he says. 'Countries like Italy, Canada, the USA, Samoa and Japan are really there only to make the numbers realistic. Apart from the odd freak result, like Japan beating South Africa at the 2015 World Cup, there has been very little tangible progress in these nations. More than a hundred countries are playing rugby, but most are irrelevant.

'Therefore, New Zealand has not had the incentive to be much better. If you want the sport to be bigger and better, then countries like New Zealand have to do a lot more. It hasn't been very difficult to be terribly good in rugby because there's not much opposition.'

Haden suggests the situation will have no ending while the present distribution of finances remains as it is. 'What the game needs is to spend its money from the World Cup in a far more even-handed way.' At present, he alleges, the distribution among the countries is that the top eight get about 80 per cent of it. 'All that does is maintain the status quo, it doesn't stimulate the game worldwide. If they really want to grow the game, the globally generated money should be much more even-handedly distributed.'

Hansen doesn't duck the point. 'I think all the countries have been guilty of that in the past. I was lucky enough to have been involved in the Six Nations [with Wales] but the first thing I noticed was, it was "us against them". Then I come back here and I am seeing it, too. I am going, "Guys, it's about the game."'

He bemoans the fact that when he praised England for being successful in 2016, people thought he was being insincere. 'I really meant what I said. They are a big rugby nation and we need them to be good. Ireland beating us in Chicago hurt and we have got to take that responsibility. But it was good for the game.'

Far away from the small country at the bottom of the world, Conrad Smith has been playing in the south-west of France, at Pau, for the last three years. Smith played ninety-four times for the All Blacks in an eleven-year career. How important does he believe the element of coaching is in New Zealand rugby?

'The influence of good coaches is huge. When I came into the team, Wayne Smith was the backs coach and very quickly he became a mentor. He was the guy I'd go to and ask whatever I needed to know. Smithy is hard, very challenging. There were times when I swore at him. But he just wants the best out of you and he really cares about the All Blacks and the players. He is a singular man. You couldn't have three Wayne Smiths as All Blacks coaches at the same time – it would be too intense an environment and it wouldn't work.

'In New Zealand, it's not just a desire to win but play in a way we feel the game should be played. No doubt this adds to the pressure on the players. But especially on the coaches. In a country like France, they just want to win and it's a battle. But it's different in New Zealand. You might win a game but if you don't play the right way the crowd will be silent. It's not enough just to win all the time. If you win without scoring tries, no one is happy.

'That is the expectation and it will be incredibly tough always to be above any other country. I know the team is very aware of that. We have been facing that challenge for over a hundred years and that motivation for every All Black team to keep trying to do that is always there.

'You have to say the All Blacks have been successful through their hard work. It is not luck. There is a history of more than a hundred years of All Black passion. It is the flagship of the nation. The All Blacks are seen to represent everything that is good about the country. The team digs in to that a lot. Sometimes it's hard to see how that wins you rugby matches. But I think it gives you an advantage. But the pressure we are under when we wear the jersey is immense. That is such a big part of the challenge. That pressure to perform comes from the supporters, from a country that motivates a team.'

It is the pressure under which all New Zealand coaches must operate. Truly, a never-ending quest.

There is no doubt that the excellence of New Zealand's coaching and management comes high on the list of reasons for this country's dominance of the game. Since 2004, New Zealand has had an exceptional group of coaching and management personnel at various stages in these key roles.

The depth of rugby knowledge and organization these men have brought to their respective tasks has been world-class. No other rugby-playing nation on earth has had anything remotely like this amount of wisdom. Not just about the game either, but in the field of New Zealand culture and people. The players who have passed through under their tutelage will never know how fortunate they have been to live in this era.

New Zealand had great players before. Plenty of them. They had, too, frequent spells of ascendancy. But they rarely achieved such sustained success. Why? Before 2004, the approach was too hit and miss. There were still lingering elements of amateurism, which held back proper professionalism. And personnel, especially their coaching staff, changed too frequently. Inconsistency off the field was mirrored on it. That should have been no surprise.

The fact that sustained success has happened in this era is primarily due to the exhaustive efforts of the men and women who make up the All Blacks coaching and management group. They have proved themselves highly talented operators – by far the best in the world, and perhaps a once-in-a-lifetime combination. They couldn't have done it under the structures of the 1990s and early 2000s when New Zealand coaches were changed constantly. But New Zealand Rugby learned lessons from past failures. And they listened to men of sound judgement like Sir Brian Lochore.

Other countries have had their moments since professionalism, but they have often chopped and changed. New Zealand, on the other hand have, since 2004, laid a template for their whole future. Ensconced deep within the corridors of its master plan lies the fact that continuity and consistency of coaching personnel, allied to high-class players, are proven elements in their success. There would seem no reason whatever for them to tear up this template after the Rugby World Cup of 2019 and the inevitable departure of some members of this special group. Which is why Ian Foster should become the next All Blacks coach.

As for players and a production line that simply doesn't falter, we should never overlook the contribution of unknown people all over New Zealand. The junior school coach who stayed long into the evening to offer a young Dan Carter advice. The assistant provincial coach who saw at once Beauden Barrett's potential and worked assiduously to ensure it emerged. These examples and more outline how the people of a nation of 4.8 million contributed to the conquering of this sport. Just by their roles, however large or small, in the whole process.

Sports teams are like companies in big business. They have myriad talents available to them. But if the people at the top are not totally committed and planning and preparing for almost every eventuality while demonstrating wisdom and vision, then nothing is achieved. Inertia reigns. The company falters and declines.

National rugby teams are the same. Far too many nations have failed through flawed personnel making the wrong decisions, failing to set a proper template and then select the right people to implement it. Their choice of coaches has often been poor. In some instances, hopelessly ill-equipped people have been employed. With underwhelming results.

New Zealand are a very significant exception. They have worked assiduously in their search for the right people in the correct roles. This is not an elementary process; it requires acumen, faith and good judgement. But their reward has been New Zealand rugby's incredible run of success from 2004 to the present day, that could yet reach a crowning glory with a third successive Rugby World Cup in Japan in 2019.

16

THE JERSEY

*Contributions from, among others,
Gary Player, Ian Foster, Kieran Read, Nick Farr-Jones,
Beauden Barrett, Sir Colin Meads, John Hart,
Wayne Smith, Ryan Crotty, Dane Coles,
Liam Messam, Alan Jones, Doug Howlett,
Bob Dwyer, Jerome Kaino, Gilbert Enoka,
Craig Dowd, Joel Stransky, Dan Carter,
Wyatt Crockett, Ian Smith.*

'How to explain this All Black aura? It's got such a beautiful history and heritage. It's been gathered together through lots of hard work, planning and good coaching. There have been good players and there has been this marriage of the various elements. Add on to all that a very strong will to win and an equally strong sense of not letting that great jersey down. I think all that enables us to pull out that little bit extra to get across the line time and again.'

Sir Bryan Williams, ex-All Blacks wing (113 matches, 38 Tests)

Richie McCaw buried his head in it before every match. Another player cried tears of joy at receiving it. Then blew his nose on it to regain composure. 'I thought, "That's OK, it's going to get blood and mud all over it." It wasn't disrespectful,' said Wayne Smith.

Ryan Crotty made his All Blacks debut in Sydney and his parents flew over. Afterwards, he put it in the arms of his proud father. 'After my debut and giving my jersey to my dad, I held on to every one of the next ten. You are extremely grateful for any opportunity to wear that jersey. Every person wearing one is a quality player,' said Crotty.

As a youngster, Dane Coles lived in a small town on the Kapiti Coast. Christian Cullen, the great former All Blacks full-back, lived nearby. One day, the twelve-year-old Coles got the chance to visit Cullen's home and see his collection of jerseys. 'Going into that room was mind-blowing,' he says. 'I tried on an All Black jersey. I thought to myself, "I want one of these." ' Years of sacrifice and sweat ensued. All from that single fitting.

Wayne Smith gave every one of his away. He felt the *mana* would live on better with others, that he'd taken all he needed from it.

The 'it'? The jersey. The All Blacks jersey. If ever a single item of sporting clothing were revered, with an almost messianic zeal, this is it. How much has this simple rugby jersey actually mattered to this nation?

There is probably only one comparison in the entire sporting world. It is from another sport, and in another country. Top-level rugby, like cricket, is a team sport played against a limited number of countries. Whereas a leading golfer competes against the world's best individual players from every corner of the globe. But the famed Green Jacket at Augusta National is the only other garment to rival the aura of the All Blacks jersey. Although, of course, the Jacket is a reward for winning, whereas the Jersey gives the opportunity to play. But both offer a glittering, tantalizing enticement to those at the peak of their sporting powers.

Who would know best how they compare?

South African golfing legend Gary Player won at Augusta National in 1961, 1974 and 1978. Does Player understand the almost religious reverence New Zealanders have for the black jersey worn by the All Blacks players?

'Yes, I do. Absolutely. To be successful in business or sport, one has to have passion. As we all know, this is something New Zealanders don't lack, especially in rugby. Without passion, you don't have energy, and nothing great has ever been accomplished without passion. Even in a non-team sport like golf, without passion you will not achieve the highest echelons.

'Putting on the Green Jacket at Augusta definitely rates as one of the most memorable events in my life. I first dreamed of winning a Green Jacket the first time I picked up a golf club. As I am sure the first time a New Zealand player picks up a rugby ball, he dreams of pulling on his national jersey.'

It is true for all young New Zealanders. They fantasize, and all but salivate at the prospect. The dream of one day wearing the famous black jersey is never-ending. And those who eventually achieve it seem suffused with a pride most of us can hardly imagine.

Beauden Barrett tells of certain Hurricanes colleagues returning to Wellington ashen-faced at not getting their hands on the sacred garment. 'I have been lucky,' he says. 'I haven't missed a squad selection yet. But players who have missed one have come back saying it is the hardest thing they have ever faced, missing All Black selection and the chance to wear that jersey.

'Not being a part of it really hurt them. So you do everything you can to remain part of it. You maximize every opportunity. But the reality is, none of us really know if we are going to be selected the following week. It is all dependent on performances and how you are going at that particular time. It leaves no room for complacency.

'You are always on your toes, always having to improve, get better and challenge each other. You always feel the threat (of competition) in an All Black jersey. No matter who you are. Those guys in other teams can perhaps relax a little without all that pressure behind them.

But they are maybe missing opportunities to improve themselves. We are in a privileged position but it could end today. So we have to make the most of it, grab our opportunities and embrace the whole legacy. You want to give everything to that jersey.'

Nimbly stepping, free-running first five-eighths, or old prop forwards with ears like a couple of slices of calf's liver, it doesn't matter. They all feel the same pain, have the exact same fear of exclusion from the fold.

Crusaders prop Wyatt Crockett admits he's not too big a boy to cry. 'I have been in that situation myself. It is a pretty emotional thing. You might feel you will never get back into the All Blacks. I didn't think I would be an All Black after 2010 and then I was picked again.

'You work so hard to get back in there because you realize how much you loved it, how much it means to you. It is a great reminder never to take it for granted when you see other players coming back to their franchises after being dropped by the All Blacks. It is a huge privilege to wear the jersey, you have to remind yourself of that.'

Maybe Crockett is the best man on earth to explain the syndrome. After fearing his All Blacks days were over in 2010, he was still wearing the jersey in November 2017, for cap number seventy-one. At the age of thirty-four, too, although that was admittedly his last.

That is serious longevity. Or, more accurately, a lifelong love affair with the jersey. But then, others completely understand the emotion. Ian Stanley Talbot 'Spooky' Smith, an All Blacks wing in the 1960s, said being dropped from the All Blacks was the worst day of his life. 'I'd had a pretty good spin from 1963 through to 1966 [twenty-four matches, nine Tests]. But it sure as hell meant a lot of pain when it ended. It still does.'

Yes, but we're talking fifty-one years later. *Fifty-one years!* Isn't time supposed to heal a loss? Not in this case, it seems.

'To get an All Blacks jersey in New Zealand is special,' said Smith. 'My number was 644, and one of my neighbours still calls me that. I'm pretty chuffed I made it. To me, it has been a hell of a benefit in life to have played rugby for New Zealand. Money doesn't fall off trees just because you wore the All Black jersey. But people are prepared to give you a go.'

He always remembered Wilson Whineray's words of warning when he won his first cap: 'Just enjoy it, because it's never quite the same again,' the captain told him. He was right. Ian Smith said it was a moment that defined his life.

Old All Blacks stand, gnarled and wrinkly, like the branches of great kauri trees of the nation. They are long-time observers of the scene, custodians of values that underpin their society. Brad Johnstone, with forty-five appearances and thirteen Test caps, is just one of them. Ask him for the biggest difference between New Zealand and the rest of the world, and the eyebrows narrow.

'The All Black brand, the culture that the All Blacks have created over a hundred years. When you get an All Black jersey, you are taking on the world and you're shit-scared to let down the people that went before you.'

Men like Nick Mallett express bemusement at such statements. 'I don't believe that players in other countries have this same mindset. I don't think they feel those pressures, like All Black players do. That is another difference. But that is what they are good at, that is the key to their continued success.'

What of Australia? Now there's a proud sporting nation. Especially when the hated 'Poms' are in town. They pour national pride with their pints. But maybe the most telling thought on 'the jersey' comes from that side of the Tasman. In Sydney, Nick Farr-Jones made a frank confession that goes to the heart of the issue:

'Whether it can be said over the decades that we held the Aussie jersey in the same esteem as the All Blacks held their jersey, I very much doubt. It is that sense of the obligation driven by the honour of pulling on that jersey. How important it is in that small country, but massive country when it comes to history, culture and dominance of the game.'

Few men have ever worn the famous black jersey with as much pride as the late Sir Colin Meads. His was a lifelong devotion to New Zealand rugby. It defined him, like the bruises and blood on a warrior.

The grand old combatant paused when I asked him to put into words his respect and feelings for the jersey. There was a brief sigh, perhaps of admiration. Or did it denote that we were now on hallowed ground, and discussing an icon?

'The lure of the All Blacks jersey has gone on all these years. Even the modern players think about it. You hear stories of players sleeping in their jersey the night before their first cap. Some All Blacks would train in the jersey. But I didn't like that. I honoured the jersey. Always.

I felt you only put on that jersey when you played for your country. I never wore rugby jerseys socially or anything like that.

'I only ever wore an All Black jersey for a battle when I knew the body was going to get a hiding. When I first got it, I was scared I was going to break a leg before I played my first game. And if so, maybe I would never be able to say I was an All Black. That has happened to some people. They were never chosen again and could never call themselves an All Black.

'Being an All Black was by far the greatest achievement of my sporting life. You have your family and your sporting life, those are different things. You are proud of what you have got and your kids. But you are always proud of this jersey.'

What of its importance to young New Zealanders, compared with rugby men in the rest of the world? Meads again: 'I think it just matters more to the young men of New Zealand to wear this jersey than the young men of France or England to wear theirs. In England, rugby isn't even the number-one sport. France has many other sports, too.'

It is a view that Sir Brian Lochore shares. 'I started to think the power of the jersey wasn't as strong before I got back involved with the All Blacks again. But I found out nothing has changed in that respect. That All Black jersey is still just as important now as it ever was. It just means more to our young men than [to] other young men around the world.'

This is a core issue. Another critical piece in the jigsaw puzzle that comprises New Zealand rugby and its world supremacy. I doubt the rugby players of other nations could understand the barrelling emotions, the surging pride a young New Zealander feels when he or she pulls on their national jersey. Sure, everyone is proud to represent their country and you cannot doubt the emotions others feel.

It is just that in New Zealand it matters so much. John Hart agrees. 'I don't think anything else in the world compares in terms of sport and another country.

'In New Zealand, this is our culture, our identity. We still eat, sleep and drink the game. The passion for this jersey from a playing point of view is endless.'

The jersey supersedes any award of individual trophies or medals. Lock Brodie Retallick is just one great All Black to confess the latter get consigned to the dark corners of his home. 'Medals and awards don't make it into the living room at my house,' says the 2014 IRB

Player of the Year. 'I have just got a little shelf out in the garage with a few things like trophies and plaques.'

Gathering dust, presumably.

When Richie McCaw moved home, the new owner was astonished to find some personal mementoes, invitations to special dinners, prize-giving events and the like. All discarded, left behind. McCaw had no interest and had moved on, in every sense. But there weren't any All Blacks jerseys lying around.

McCaw explained his respect for the jersey like this. 'It's only a little thing but look at football. They have their own number, that's their [named] jersey. You don't have that with rugby or with the All Blacks. The number seven jersey is the All Blacks jersey. You are only there to look after it and make it better if you can. Then you move on, someone else takes it and does the job. I think that feeling was there when I arrived and it never changed. As soon as you start thinking it's your own, I think you have got a different attitude. I reckon the jersey is bigger than any individual.'

It is, but there's something else it elicits. A sense of comradeship, a shared cause or purpose. McCaw explains: 'It's that moment – you can't get this anywhere else, and the only people you actually share it with and understand are sitting in the changing room after the match. They know what each other has done and what you have had to do to get a result.

'That is the bit you can never replace. It is the bit you crave. You don't miss going out on the field and getting bashed around. But it's that feeling in the changing room that is special. It's hard to put into words exactly what it is. It's often just a look. That's the bit I miss. It was always the feeling afterwards that was so special.'

Or, as Ian Foster puts it, 'The allure of the jersey? That is the pressure that we all feel in terms of being guardians of the All Blacks legacy. We feel we have to create an environment and way of playing that they love and don't want to leave.

'We have to make sure we are the best we can possibly be in terms of environment and how we deal with the challenges. Some people ask me, how much longer can we keep these top players? I accept we are involved in a battle and it is not getting smaller.

'But we have still got the ability to offer the prospect of a black jersey. That is worth something. The desire for people to be an All Black is still pretty powerful.'

Age shall not weary them, nor their emotions, when it comes to the jersey. Wayne Smith played his final match for the All Blacks in 1985. But his acumen as a leading and highly influential coach has since all but surpassed his playing achievements. Sir Graham Henry calls him 'the best coach I've ever seen with the All Blacks'. Yet Smith brooks not even a serious discussion as to the differing highlights of his career.

'I have been involved in over 200 matches for the All Blacks. I had thirty-five games as a player, seventeen of them Tests. But nothing can beat that first All Blacks jersey as a player. Out of everything I have done in rugby, that is the pinnacle. I remember taking the jersey to bed with me that first night because we used to get them handed out the night before the game. That is the biggest highlight. It was in 1980. And thirty-eight years later, that moment is still the one.

'I always say to people, they are the best years of your life when you are playing. Coaching is great and I got into it because it is the closest I could get to the contest once I had finished playing. But for me, nothing beats playing, they were my best years.'

But Smith did more than make a personal confession regarding the differing merits of playing and coaching. He took me carefully through the entire psychological process of acquiring a jersey, and how certain people are affected by that experience.

'The thing about the jersey is, you take your *mana* from it however you like. If you are in the jersey it becomes part of you and you drag every bit of *mana* out of it. I have given all my jerseys away, because I felt I had already taken the *mana* I needed from them. My club has had some and the rest went to charity because to me they had served their purpose.

'An All Blacks jersey is not the sort of thing you keep in a cupboard. If you can give it to someone that's crook in hospital or someone else that can take their own *mana* out of it, it can keep doing good.'

He listened to Jerome Kaino speaking on the subject a while ago. 'He talked about when he hands his jersey on. He received it from Jerry Collins and he has been striving ever since to make the jersey better. But he doesn't think he has. So his whole life has been about trying to make that jersey like it was with Jerry, except better. When he hands it on, someone else can come and have the same challenge. Then, he can hold his head up. That is beautiful, I reckon.'

The first time you get together as an All Blacks squad, says Smith, the focus is not on scrums, line-outs or different plays. 'It's about knowing who you play for and what that means. That is the first thing you do with an All Blacks team. Other teams I have been involved with say, "We haven't got time to do that stuff, we need to get on and get the strategies of the game."

'Whereas our view would be, it is so important that we can't afford *not* to do it. Having huge personal meaning about what you do is a key ingredient of why All Blacks teams have been great. Because if you care so deeply about something that you are prepared to put your body on the line for it, then you are going to play better.

'It's a game that rewards attitude, bravery and courage. Therefore, you have got to create that and the jersey to us is part of that.

'If you are playing for the All Blacks, or coaching the All Blacks, there is a huge scrutiny around that. There are huge amounts of pressure. But the other side of that is, you are the only ones with the opportunity to win with the All Blacks because you are the only one in the jersey. You get your chance to be part of that history and that's a great thing. So there is a real feeling of being able to walk towards that pressure and enjoy the fact that you have your chance to be part of that pressure, and perform.

'I would say that is a massive part of any All Blacks team, more than any other team I have been involved in.'

Of course, the pressures and expectations inherent in this process are intimidating. Conrad Smith admits at times they're too much. His nerves used to be on edge on the Monday or Tuesday of Test week. Ultimately, he taught himself that you can only do so much. So by the Friday or Saturday he was calm, philosophical even. 'I got that way of thinking from the team. That's how you handle the pressure. We had fifteen guys like that, with that frame of mind, when we were at our best. You acknowledge the pressure but you have to do your best. That's all you can ever do, pressure or no pressure.

'But it's the pressure you are under when you wear that jersey. That is such a big part of the challenge. That pressure to perform comes from the supporters, from a country that motivates the team. The people care so much about the team and any All Black player is aware of that.'

This respect for the jersey is as solid as concrete throughout the nation. Ex-Australia coach Alan Jones says, 'New Zealanders are jealous, jealous of the jersey. Mind you, it has been diluted a little by changes in international law where you can get a jersey by going onto the field for two minutes at the end. I don't approve of all that. But at the same time, the players are jealous of the jersey and want to protect it and preserve it.'

Listen to Chiefs forward Liam Messam on the topic. Why is there this allure of the jersey, I asked him? 'It's the power of the black jersey. You wouldn't be playing Super Rugby if you didn't want to be an All Black. Everyone is striving to wear that black jersey and it comes with so much *mana*, so much prestige. So when you get there, you do anything you can to hold on to it. They say it's hard to get an All Black jersey, but it is even harder to stay in one. When you get into that environment you learn pretty quickly how hard you have to work to stay there.

'Every time I put on that black jersey I never knew whether it would be my last. So I always wanted to go out there and give everything to it.'

What Messam's words conceal, is that what we can call a 'fear of failure', hangs over this most exclusive of clubs. This fear, of being dropped and perhaps excluded forever, drives them constantly. It persuades them to murder every muscle, torture each tendon. It becomes close to paranoia. There is always a rival, a predator close by, searching for an opening, an opportunity to take the jersey.

Andy Haden readily concedes the point. 'The fear of failure has always been there. But it is as much a hunger for success in their blood, wanting to be successful All Blacks. Yet not even one in a thousand get there.'

Understanding the psychology and emotions that eat away at young men in these situations is Gilbert Enoka's business. But like so many other things in the All Blacks domain, this fear – seemingly, a negative – has been turned cleverly into a positive.

'You are so respectful of the jersey you want to extend your tenure in it. So you're always looking over your shoulder to see who is coming up to challenge you for the place. I think in the past, people have played injured so that they don't lose their jersey. Some people ask me, "What is the most common emotion the All Blacks experience?" It is actually relief . . . when we win. We have got better now because we understand fear is a good thing to have. It is not something that makes us scared of it going into places where great things can occur.

'I think it is the jersey itself they fear losing most. Fear has been a huge motivator and driver for a lot of players. You either move toward it or away from it.'

Perhaps Doug Howlett explained it best. 'I scored forty-nine tries in sixty-two Tests for the All Blacks [he is, to this day, the try-scoring Test record holder for New Zealand]. But there was not one time, one occasion when I felt completely sure of my place.'

You would not find that same fear from a champion player in any other rugby team on earth. It would, for example, be the hardest thing imaginable to instil that fear of being dropped, within a French, Australian or England squad. Does it matter as much to young players from those countries as it does to young New Zealanders to wear and then hold on to their national jersey?

Consider what certain England players themselves said, according to a report compiled by the Rugby Football Union relating to England's failure at the 2011 Rugby World Cup. The report gathered 'evidence' from 90 per cent of the England players. One alleged that in the aftermath of England's defeat by France in the quarter-final, a teammate said, 'There's £35,000 just gone down the toilet.'

As the player who revealed it said, 'It made me sick. Money shouldn't even come into a player's mind.'

But it does, and constantly. It also emerged that certain England players disputed the level of payment for the World Cup squad, prior to their departure for New Zealand in 2011. Then RFU Executive Rob Andrew was quoted as saying, 'I believe this led to a further unsettling of the squad just before departure, which included a threat by the squad not to attend the World Cup send-off dinner at Twickenham. It suggested that some of the senior players were more focused on money than getting the rugby right.'

We can well imagine Steve Tew and Steve Hansen's reaction to such malcontents in an All Blacks squad, even on the eve of a Rugby World Cup. They'd be sent home. And they'd never be chosen for New Zealand again. Even if the All Blacks had to lose a World Cup for it. It is what the RFU should have done. But didn't.

As former Australia coach Bob Dwyer said on this topic, 'Money is *not* the number-one motivation for New Zealand players, as it is in most of the world.'

Richie McCaw is the best example of that. Had his agent made approaches to the top French clubs in 2015 about joining them after the Rugby World Cup that year, McCaw could have commanded a salary of anything up to 1.5 or even 2 million euros a season. Perhaps even more. A minimum two-year deal, with a third year's option.

That's potentially 4.5 to 5 million euros. But what did McCaw do? Turn his back on it. 'I didn't have any desire to do it,' he said. 'If I had gone over there, I couldn't have just turned up, gone through the motions and picked up a big cheque. I thought, "Is that the right reason to play rugby?"

Yes, but for 4.5 or 5 million euros? There were plenty who would have done. McCaw is one of a kind, for sure. Again, it comes back to a difference in desire.

Might financial matters have been an important element in the thoughts of England-qualified back row player Steffon Armitage? The former London Irish player won three European Champions Cups with French club Toulon and, in 2013–14, was voted ERC European Player of the Year. You don't pick up that award if you can't play.

In the build-up to the 2015 Rugby World Cup, it seemed obvious that Armitage should play for England. They had no back row forward with the same ball skills, power and technique at the breakdown. Yet England stubbornly refused to pick him because he was playing his club rugby in France. If he wanted to play, they told him, he'd have to go home.

Armitage would not budge. He not only stayed with Toulon but when the time came to move on, he joined another French club, Pau.

Was the thought of wearing the England jersey again and adding to his meagre five England caps (won between 2009 and 2011) of little interest? Had money triumphed over any desires to wear the jersey again?

It's true that several All Blacks have gone overseas, including an increasing number of late. But you couldn't say most turned their back on the jersey. Fact was, it had become clear to players like Jerome Kaino, Liam Messam, Victor Vito, Ben Franks, Tawera Kerr-Barlow, Brad Shields, Aaron Cruden, Malakai Fekitoa, Lima Sopoaga and others that they were either no longer likely to be considered for All Blacks selection or that they'd only be backup to an established first-choice player. None were still strongly in the frame to be in the starting line-up to play Test match rugby for New Zealand.

If McCaw wasn't motivated by money, nor was Kieran Read when I asked for his thoughts on the subject. By the start of 2018, Read had earned 108 caps but there was no difference between the first and most recent, in his mind.

'Any time you go out and play for New Zealand, it is a great feeling. You seem to grow an arm and a leg when you put on that jersey. You've got to cherish it because it won't be there forever.'

Ex-All Blacks prop Craig Dowd had words of warning for those thinking of leaving. Especially soon after full-back Ben Smith had announced he'd turned down a lucrative contract with French club Pau to remain in New Zealand. Dowd, who himself played overseas with London Wasps for several years, said, 'At some point, those players who have left are going to watch an All Blacks game played on TV somewhere around the world. But if you're not ready to give up that jersey, then you don't go into that living room watching the TV, thinking, "I wish I was still playing for them."

'Ben Smith has still got that hunger. He has a lot of years left in him and I am sure he is on a very good wicket in New Zealand. He might have taken less money but stayed in a winning culture with a team that could possibly win three successive World Cups. You won't find that unique culture anywhere else in the world. It all comes from the jersey.'

Perhaps the salient question is this. Does rugby actually matter as much to the general population in other countries? The 1995 Springbok Rugby World Cup winner Joel Stransky has no doubts. 'The answer to that is no. In South Africa, our structures are poor and recently we have had a losing culture. But does it affect the country as a whole, in the way it would in New Zealand? I don't think so.

'It is not the be-all and end-all in other countries that it is and always has been in New Zealand. Rugby in New Zealand is a matter of national pride. In the UK, football will always be bigger and much more important. You can't say the same about the rest of the world as you say about New Zealand. It is the undisputed number-one sport there. But that is not as big a factor as it could be, because they still have fewer players than England or South Africa. But their production line is so strong. It is the people being brought through at young ages that marks them out as exceptional.'

With the jersey comes another element. The demand for humility. These days, it is ingrained in the young men who ascend to their nation's premium sporting stage. In the All Blacks, remembers Dan Carter, it is a key message for everyone that you must remain humble and grateful. Humility is a big part of their culture. Players are taught to understand not to get ahead of themselves or to think they're better than anyone else. The contrasts with the Australian cricket team of recent times could not be more illuminating.

'It's to do with the way we were brought up. But it's drummed into you even more at the highest level, which is probably the most important time you need it,' said Dan Carter. And the jersey? 'All Blacks teams represent New Zealand. But you've got Maori, Pakeha and Pasifika so they're all from different cultures. There is one thing that binds us together, and it is the All Black jersey,' says Carter.

The outsider might have thought that, given all living New Zealanders have seen 'the jersey' their entire lives, this aura might have started to wear off a bit by now. Nothing could be further from the truth. But why?

'Because for every ten guys that go overseas, the one that stays behind is the one that makes it,' says Wayne Shelford. 'He is the best. Those that go can't quite any longer cut the mustard.

'That jersey is the most successful brand in rugby in the world. Every young Kiwi dreams of being in the All Black jersey. It is unique. It drives standards of excellence, too.'

Intriguingly, Gilbert Enoka even links this passion for the jersey with some of the worst excesses of New Zealand rugby folk. By that, I mean demented parents shouting and screaming at youngsters, or hurling abuse at referees, in junior rugby.

A New Zealand friend told me, 'I recently watched an inter-region school 1st XV game and was appalled by the behaviour of the boys' families advocating on-field violence and abuse of the referee.'

Enoka concurs. 'I see more abuse on the sidelines watching five- and six-year-olds from mums and dads in this country because all the parents are thinking, "Is this person going to be an All Black?" It is every boy's dream to become an All Black, to wear that jersey. When they come into it, they put it on and feel superhuman.

'I agree with Colin Meads that it means more to young New Zealanders to wear it than it does to young men elsewhere in the world. I think that is because there is a deep connection to the soul of this land that comes with this identity. The brand of that jersey is special. I have been there seventeen years and people say, "Keep the jersey clean." ' They understand the jersey is nothing until there is the silver fern on it. Then it is special. We have been able to keep the allure of the jersey, because the mindset of the people coming into it is to want to add to the legacy. They understand that it is not theirs. They are caretakers of it for a period of time and want to add to it.

'The mystique, the specialness of it was never eroded. If "me" becomes more powerful than "we", then it erodes the power of the jersey.'

Part of Ben Smith's reasoning for turning down a lucrative contract in France was to continue in an All Black jersey, and Sir Bryan Williams readily understood his thinking.

'The allure of the jersey was what kept him at home. He still wants to keep wearing it. At the start, whoever it is, it is hard-earned. But then you come to value it more and more. That is how it is, no matter how big a star you may become eventually. Every young Kiwi wants to be an All Black. Even the many, many people in New Zealand who have achieved in other fields have said the same.'

Like ex-Prime Minister Sir John Key. 'We play lots of sports. But in our national psyche, rugby matters to us more than any other sport,' he told me.

It is unlikely you would hear a prime minister or president in any other country say such a thing. Key goes on: 'It is the psychological approach just as much as everything else that is the reason for their successes. There is a culture in pulling on that jersey. It's not just they pull it on because they get paid. They would pull on that jersey for nothing, it means that much to them.'

The culture surrounding these rugby men is powerful. Demanding, too. 'The New Zealand public wants them to win but there is an expectation they will win. They don't go anywhere thinking they might get second place. They go expecting to win,' Key adds.

In other words, there is always more pressure on these men in the jersey. They are expected to deliver. No arguments, still less excuses. The New Zealand public long since got used to them winning. Now, it is an obligation.

I asked the seventy-five-year-old man sitting next to me whether he still had his jersey. Instantly, it was as if someone had ignited fires behind his eyes. Dull and tired earlier, they now glowed, like beacons in the dark. Without a word, Ian 'Spooky' Smith rose up and walked firmly out of the room.

When he returned, the shoulders and back were sergeant-major-ramrod straight. He wore once more the silver fern on a black jersey.

The large numbers, fourteen, were on the back. He gleamed with quiet pride. Not least, for the jersey still fitted him comfortably after all these years.

A few months later, quite suddenly, Ian Smith passed away, joining others including Dave Gallaher, 'Bobby' Black, Sir Colin Meads, Sir Wilson Whineray, Jonah Lomu, Jerry Collins and so many more in the Elysian fields.

At the eleventh hour, of the eleventh day of the eleventh month in 1918, the guns had finally fallen silent to denote the end of the Great War, the terrible slaughter. In November 2018, exactly one hundred years later, around the time when the rain and mud once again scar this land, New Zealanders will once more honour the memory of their war dead. Men like Black and Gallaher, whose inspiration as captain of that first representative New Zealand national team to tour the British Isles back in 1905 was fundamental in the All Blacks legend.

Gallaher's resting place is a small plot of white chalk land in a lonely graveyard down a small track close to Passchendaele, in Belgium. Far, far away from his homeland.

Yet men like him and all those now departed shared one grand, glorious achievement. They had carried that All Blacks spirit right to the end. They had done what few men in history had ever achieved. They had worn the jersey.

Bibliography

Akers, C., Miller, G. & Hill, A. (eds.), *2017 Rugby Almanack* (2017)

Chester, R.H., McMillan, N.A.C. and Palenski, R., *Men in Black: 75 Years of New Zealand International Rugby* (2006)

'Hopeful', *Taken in: A Sketch of New Zealand Life* (1887)

King, Michael, *The Penguin History of New Zealand* (2003)

McBride, Willie John, *The Story of My Life* (with Peter Bills) (2004)

Mackenzie, Morrie, *Black, Black, Black!* (1969)

Manson, Cecil & Celia, *Curtain Raiser to a Colony* (1962)

Mourie, Graham, *Graham Mourie, Captain* (with Ron Palenski) (1982)

A History of Otago University Rugby Football Club 1886–1969 (published by *Otago Daily Times*) (1969)

Palenski, Ron, *The All Black-ography* (2007)

Paul, Gregor, *Black Obsession: The All Blacks Quest for World Cup Success* (2009)

Potter, Alex and Duthen, Georges, *The Rise of French Rugby* (1961)

Reed, A.H., *Heroes of Peace and War in Early New Zealand* (1959)

Tobin, Christopher, *The Original All Blacks 1905–06* (2005)

Waite, Major Fred, *The New Zealanders at Gallipoli* (1919)

Assorted, *All Blacks Media Guides*

Assorted, *Rothmans Rugby Union Yearbooks*

Index

Folau, Israel 167
Forsyth Barr Stadium (Dunedin) 211, 231, 266
Foster, Ian 139, 191, 216, 324, 326
Fouroux, Jacques 158–9
Fox, Grant 86, 198, 314–18, 327
France, French 22, 32, 46, 47, 61, 100, 134–5, 140, 142, 153–4, 157, 158–9, 159, 163, 187, 199, 202, 204, 207, 228, 231, 264, 278, 323
Franco-Prussian War (1870) 19
Franks, Ben 75, 347
Franks, Owen 75, 137, 260
Fraser, Bernie 203
French Championship 157
French Rugby Federation (FFR) 199

Gachassin, Jean 207
Galbraith, David 293
Gallaher, Charles 34
Gallaher, Dave 23, 26, 34–5, 45, 45–6, 47, 122, 319, 351
Gallaher, Douglas 34
Gallaher, Henry 34
Gatland, Warren 97, 102, 191, 321
Gatlin, Justin 129
George V 31
Georgia 81, 213
Geraldine (South Island) 78
Gilbert Islands 33
Glasgow 8
Glasgow Rugby 318
Gloucester Rugby 272
Godfrey, Nathan 236
Going, Ken 75
Going, Sid 75, 113
Golden Oldies teams 233
Goodfellow, Bruce 51
Goodfellow, Douglas 51–2
Goodfellow, Elspeth 50
Goodfellow, Hugh 50
Goodfellow, Peter 51
Goodfellow, William 50
Gosford 136
GPS *see* Great Public Schools Association of Queensland
Graduated Return to Play 270

Grand Slams 119, 139, 196, 199, 274
Gravesend (Kent) 9
Gray, Sir George 10
Gray, Jonny 137, 148
Gray, Ken 150, 159
Gray, Wynne 150
Great Public Schools Association of Queensland (GPS) 63
Great War 22–3, 31–41, 351
 Arras 23
 Chunuk Bair 22, 23, 32
 Gallipoli 22–3, 25, 32, 33
 Gravenstafel Spur 34
 Le Quesnoy 40–1
 Loos 32
 Messines Ridge 23, 32, 36–8
 Passchendaele 23, 32, 36, 38, 47
 Somme 32, 33–4
Green Jacket (Masters Tournament at Augusta National) 337–8
Greenock (Scotland) 50
Grewcock, Danny 157–8
Guardiola, Pep 317
Guilford, Zac 133
Gunning, Nikki 249

Habana, Bryan 203–4
Haden, Andy 85, 162–3, 185, 307–8, 330
Hagley Park (Christchurch) 57
haka 54, 91–103
 'Ka Mate' 91, 93, 96, 101
 'Kapa O Pango' 101
 mana 97–8
Hamilton 74, 169, 186, 241
Hamilton Boys' High School 55, 66
Hansen, Des 304, 306
Hansen, Grant
 on advantages of playing many different sports 86
 as deputy head of St Peter's College 58
 on difficulties of succeeding 87
 family and educational background 63
 on values learnt at school 65, 66
 and weight-restricted rugby 63–4

PICTURE ACKNOWLEDGEMENTS